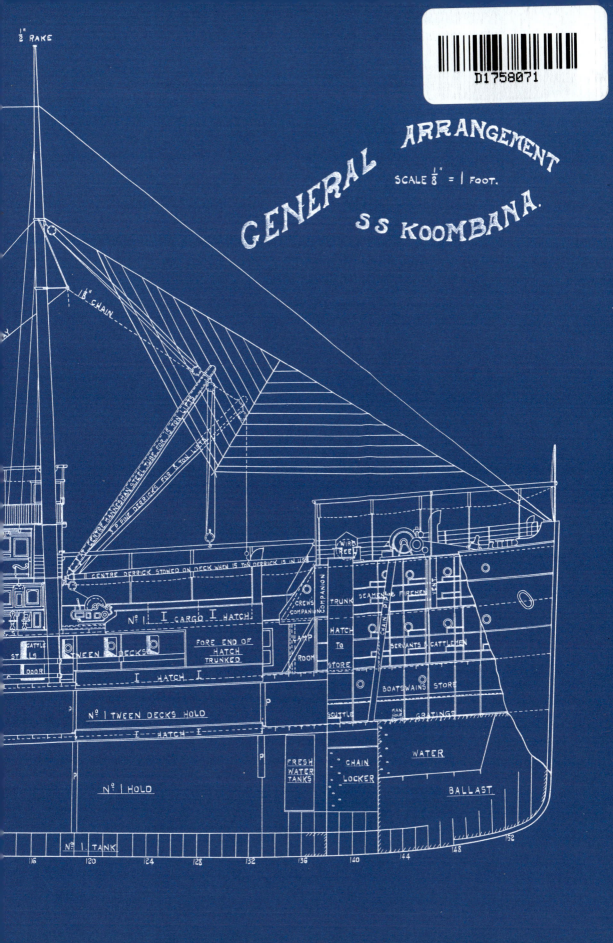

GENERAL ARRANGEMENT
SCALE $\frac{1}{8}$" = 1 FOOT.
SS KOOMBANA.

Koombana Days

Koombana Days

Annie Boyd

FREMANTLE PRESS
fremantlepress.com.au

First published in 2013 by
FREMANTLE PRESS
25 Quarry Street, Fremantle 6160
(PO Box 158, North Fremantle 6159)
Western Australia
www.fremantlepress.com.au

Consultant editor: Georgia Richter
Typeset in Stone Serif by Blue Ruin Design, Western Australia
Front cover photograph: *Koombana* crewmen, Broome, 1911. William Burkin
Back cover photograph: *Koombana* at Fremantle, 1909. Charles Walker
Endpapers: Ship plans, S.S. *Koombana*. Alexander Stephen & Sons, Glasgow.
Maps by Blue Ruin Design
Printed by Everbest Printing Company, China

National Library of Australia
Cataloguing-in-Publication entry:

Boyd, Annie, author.
Koombana days / Annie Boyd

Includes bibliographical references and index.

Koombana (Steamship).
Shipwrecks—Western Australia—Port Hedland Region.
Western Australia—Social conditions—20th century.
Western Australia—History.

ISBN: 9781921888885 (hardback)
Dewey Number: 994.13

 Government of **Western Australia**
Department of **Culture and the Arts**

Fremantle Press is supported by the State Government
through the Department of Culture and the Arts.

Publication of this title was assisted by the Commonwealth Government
through the Australia Council, its arts funding and advisory body.

To the memory of my grandfather
Everard Leslie Greig
who loved the language and whose
imagination was drawn to the sea.

LIST OF MAPS

Contents

Postcard illustration of S.S. Koombana by Alfred Dufty, Marine Artist, Sydney, c. 1909.

INTRODUCTION

KOOMBANA DAYS is a different kind of history; indeed, not so much a history as an *immersion*: a silent, splashless dive into a very different pool.

I have long been interested in the early days of what Western Australians call "the Nor'-West": that great, shimmering province to the north of the 26th parallel. In March 1909, the quality of Nor'-West life was improved suddenly by the arrival of an ultra-modern steamship named "Koombana". Built specifically for service on the challenging Nor'-West run, the vessel was a bold commercial experiment by the Adelaide Steamship Company. While gathering the facts of that enterprise, I was struck by the extent to which the ship became an emblem of progress for the remote communities she served. From *Koombana*'s first appearance, Nor'-Westers shaped their schedules to her arrivals and flocked to her saloon at every opportunity. At sea and in port, she was an island of ice and electric light: a cool relief from the present and a bright depiction of the future imagined.

Just three years later, this celebratory relationship came abruptly to an end when *Koombana*, with 156 passengers and crew, disappeared in a late-summer cyclone off Port Hedland. In the destination ports of Broome and Derby, the loss was intense and personal, but shock and disbelief reached farther. It is no exaggeration to declare that tragedy settled upon the Nor'-West like a change of season, and that *Koombana*'s disappearance cut deep into the optimism of those formative years.

Perhaps half of my research has focussed on the men, women and children lost with the ship. I have no familial link to *Koombana*, but the work has brought me into contact with many who have. The exchange of information with descendants has been enjoyable and rewarding, and I thank all those who have helped me to piece the human story together.

In the course of ten years, a mass of information has been gathered. I took an early decision to capture all material digitally, and to transcribe all written sources. My long-term objective was to create an online educational resource, offering items of interest to the descendants of those lost, and a wide selection of readings relating to an under-studied period of Western Australian history. Readers may be interested to explore extensive primary source material at www.koombanadays.com.

While my study of the ship and her complement proceeded well, I struggled to build a coherent picture of life in the ports in the early years of the twentieth century. Government reports were sterile, and local accounts often misleading. It was a time of fierce parochialism, when town-builders viewed their corrugated creations through rose-tinted glasses. In need of fresh eyes, I sought first-hand accounts by first-time visitors. Suddenly, I hit pay-dirt: I found not one but three sparkling commentaries, perfectly aligned to my interest. All three writers had recorded their impressions as they visited the Nor'-West for the first time. All had travelled by *Koombana*. Each had a distinct, well-defined reason for making the journey and each captured the experience evocatively. I could not have hoped for more.

Energetic young Irishman Jim Low was *Koombana*'s fourth engineer. He signed on in Glasgow for the delivery voyage to Fremantle, and remained aboard for a year of Nor'-West service. After *Koombana* had bumped and scraped through her first two Nor'-West voyages, Jim wrote a long, mischievous letter to his friend Peggy back home. It was intended for her amusement, never for publication, but his impressions of the Nor'-West make wonderful reading. Jim revealed a naive but keen eye, a surprising turn of phrase, and a wry humour that would serve him well in his adopted land. I am grateful that his letters were kept by his family, and that copies are now held by the State Library of Western Australia.

My most valuable informant—certainly the most eloquent—was a newspaper correspondent whom for several years I knew only as "Vindex". Some late detective work was required to establish beyond doubt that the *nom de plume* belonged to George Romans, a senior staff journalist of *The West Australian*.

The fit of Romans's writing with the evolving *Koombana Days* was perfect. In June 1910, as political roundsman, Romans accompanied Colonial Secretary James Connolly on a month-long tour of the Nor'-West. It is evident that the routine reporting of speeches and receptions did not fill George's days. In four weeks aboard *Koombana* he produced five essays on aspects of Nor'-West life. Any one of the five might have been made the feature of a weekend edition, but for reasons that may never be known, all were published in the space of seven days.

The final instalment—"Broome and its Pearls"—appeared on July 5th, 1910. This was the last occasion on which the tag "Vindex" would appear. Four months later, 29-year-old Romans resigned to join the staff of the Western Australian parliament. At a well-attended farewell, a newspaper colleague lamented the fact "that men gifted with a capacity for vivid and virile writing should desert the Press for the more prosaic work of parliamentary reporting."

George Romans never returned to journalism. On November 28th, 1946, in the Australian Federal Parliament, the Speaker informed the

House that Hansard chief Mr G. H. Romans would retire at the end of the week. A succession of speakers paid tribute to the former journalist's intellect and impartiality, and Prime Minister Ben Chifley went a little further. "Mr Romans," he said, "has made speeches for us in the Hansard far better than have been made in the House, and for that alone Members are deeply grateful."

My third pair of first-time eyes were those of Perth nurse Harriet Lenehan, who in 1908 became the first matron of the 'lock hospitals,' established on Bernier and Dorre Islands for the incarceration and treatment of Aborigines suffering from syphilis. Lenehan left the islands in the middle of 1910, but returned a few months later to act as chaperone when the first of the 'cured' were well enough to be returned to their home districts. Lenehan's account of the repatriation voyage—her first by *Koombana* to Broome and beyond—was published in *The West Australian* in April 1910. Her writing is effervescent and uncritical, but she earns her place by intimate association with an important issue of the time.

Any story may be brought to light; not all may be brought to life. The voices of Jim Low, "Vindex" and Harriet Lenehan greatly enlivened the first essays that I wrote. I realised that if other authentic voices could be found, the *Koombana* story might be told in a different, perhaps unique way. For three years, in libraries, archives and online, I read personal memoirs, court records, departmental correspondence and old newspapers, absorbing the issues of the period and casting for articulate voices. My spokesmen and spokeswomen, I decided, would not be the subject of any one essay; rather, their observations and opinions would be brought to bear on different topics at different times. They would be characters whom readers would come to know in a natural, unsequenced way. The success of this design will be judged by others, but it is safe to declare that this book is chock-full of forthright people. About a hundred have been directly quoted: once, twice, or often.

The events of *Koombana Days*, I must insist, are not embellished or dramatised. No gap in the historical record has been bridged from my imagination. There is some dialogue, but no invented dialogue; where my characters speak, their words are drawn from court transcripts or other sworn testimony. And where the spoken word has been lifted from a newspaper report or interview, the facts of the report have been cross-checked. I have made extensive use of personal letters, especially where the language is colourful and conversational. But where a letter is quoted, the source is acknowledged and the context made clear. Nowhere has the written word been recast as speech.

I have given a great deal of thought to the crafting of an 'immersive' history. Although a lively narrative is essential, it cannot be the measure of success. The greater challenge is to capture enough of the social and political milieu for voices to be heard and judged in the context of their time. The rendition must be rich in detail, and rich in *common* detail, of a kind often not recorded. The research effort, moreover, cannot consist only of a search for resonant voices. The issues of the time must be understood, and the range of contemporary opinion recognised. Only then can justice to the past be done.

Much of *Koombana Days* was written before I understood that my narrative could never be seamless. Rarely if ever are all historical facts within reach. A gap in knowledge may be de-emphasised by careful orchestration, but where uncertainty remains, the voice of the author must intrude to acknowledge it. The problem is inescapable, and my solution imperfect. To avoid breaking the immersive trance more often than necessary, I have endeavoured to limit my intrusions to three situations: where uncertainty demands acknowledgement, where old controversy pleads for new arbitration, and where misfortune is so poignant that detachment would read as disregard.

A second aspect of this problem should also be declared. The immersion of the reader demands that analysis be foregone, and judgment withheld, in favour of simple, unadorned portrayal. This becomes difficult where the opinions of the characters transgress modern sensitivities. Suddenly, the voice of the author is made conspicuous by its absence. This situation first arises in the essay "Gulliver's Travels." In a 1913 letter to the editor of *The West Australian*, a veteran of the Shark Bay pearling industry reflects with satisfaction upon the eviction of the Chinese from Egg Island Bay in 1886. What makes his letter striking is the absence of contrition. "Thus," he declares, "the coloured problem was dealt with successfully by a handful of white pearlers, assisted by a few police." In cases like this, the temptation to pass judgment is strong, but if the greater goal is to immerse the reader in a different paradigm, the temptation must be resisted. The beliefs are of another time; so must their rationale be.

Nowhere has the challenge of detachment been greater than in "The Great Divide," an essay on relations between white settlers and the indigenous population. Here, the challenge comes not from characters easily dismissed as evil or immoral; it comes from those who emerge as humane and conscientious, but whose views would now be deemed unacceptable. Here too, I have resisted the temptation to analyse. My characters are permitted to speak, and from their dissonant voices the dimensions of an intractable problem emerge. The result, inevitably, is a white colonial perspective characterised by profound pessimism for the future of the Aboriginal race.

When I began writing, I set the narrative voice, its tone and style, in the year 1923, when both *Koombana* and the Great War were of recent memory. I would have persevered with this, but for two strange post-scripts to the *Koombana* story. Both relate to Broome and its pearls, and both date from the 1930s. First was the belief, widely held in the town, that the graceful old bungalow known as "the Bishop's Palace" was haunted by the ghost of Abraham Davis, the prominent pearl buyer lost with *Koombana* in 1912. Closely related was a rumour that when Davis boarded the ship for the last time, he carried with him an exquisite but cursed pearl. These interwoven stories became widely known after the publication, in 1937, of Ion Idriess's *Forty Fathoms Deep*. Recognising that these stories could not reasonably be excluded, I changed my perspective and wrote from the standpoint of 1938. The last two essays deal with the mystery surrounding Abraham Davis and the Roseate Pearl.

Ultimately, however, my interest is not in folklore. My objective has been to bring an important untold story to light, and to immerse my readers in the matter and mindset of another time. More than once during the writing, the views and values of modern Australia have felt like an encumbrance. Increasingly, I have permitted the past to prevail over the present, but with growing conviction that wisdom is not the province of one or the other. As L. P. Hartley declared with wonderful, concise neutrality, "The past is a foreign country: they do things differently there."

Too often, the preoccupations of the present are permitted to colour the portrayal of the past. Caught between paradigms, history becomes ambivalent, even apologetic. It also becomes ephemeral, for while the present dates quickly the past does not. Here I should admit to a second, pragmatic reason for distancing myself from my own time. I have thrown in my lot with the bygone era in the hope that this book, the work of several years, will age gently.

This confession made, let the journey begin. May *Koombana*'s presence be felt, and may the voices of her time be heard and heeded.

Annie Boyd
December 2012

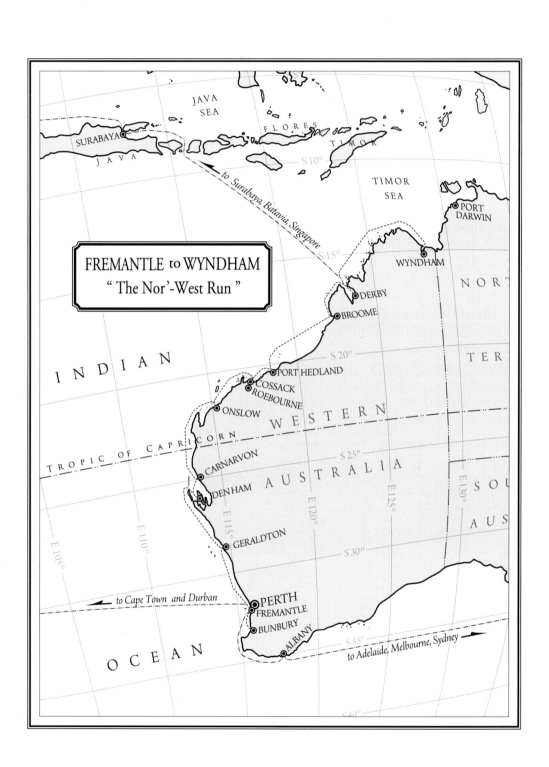

1

A Ticket to the Future

IT WAS ALL CAREFULLY ORCHESTRATED. As S.S. *Koombana* crossed the Indian Ocean, the Fremantle office of the Adelaide Steamship Company released a statement. State manager William Moxon told the press that although the vessel would arrive on February 11th, she would only remain in port until the following afternoon. There would be a brief opportunity for representatives of the press to come aboard, but any opening to the public would have to wait a few weeks, until the ship returned from necessary inspections in the east.

William Moxon admitted to a second reason for contacting the newspapers. There had been mischievous rumours, he said, that the new ship was too good for the Nor'-West and would not long remain on the run.[1] Yes, he conceded, she was larger and more luxurious than any vessel that had traded in these waters, but fears that she would be stolen away for other service were completely unfounded. The vessel had been designed and built for the Nor'-West run and no other thoughts were entertained.

Whether there were any rumours—or any mischief other than William Moxon's—may never be known. What is certain is that the promised press opportunity delivered precisely what the company sought: extensive coverage of the *Koombana*'s first arrival, and glowing reports that would reach the ports of the Nor'-West before the ship commenced her regular running.

The invited guests who came aboard on Friday, February 12th, 1909 were unanimous in their praise.[2] In its evening edition, Perth's *Daily News* declared:

> "The Last Word" in shipbuilding and general appointment is the most adequate phrase to be used in connection with the new Adelaide S.S. Co.'s Koombana, which put into Fremantle yesterday and sailed again for Melbourne and Adelaide at 2 o'clock to-day. At the invitation of the Adelaide S.S. Co. a number of shipping and mercantile identities,

S.S. Koombana, *1909*.

as well as representatives of the daily press, were invited on board the Koombana at 11 o'clock this morning, and were met by Mr. W. E. Moxon, the local manager, who introduced the visitors to Mr. G. P. Maxfield, the superintendant of stores for the Adelaide Company. The latter gentleman then devoted much time and energy towards showing the visitors over the new vessel, and when he had finished at 1 p.m., everyone felt that they had had a very interesting experience. Owing to the lack of space today, a full description of this fine modern craft will be held over till tomorrow, but it must be said that the Koombana is about the best-appointed boat that has ever been seen at Fremantle. Built especially for the Nor'-West trade, the comfort of passengers has been studied to the last degree, every invention and convenience known to the maritime world has been used in her building, in fact, in the language of one visitor, "she would do credit to any service in the world."[3]

ALTHOUGH THE TOP-DOWN TOUR began at the navigating bridge, it was along *Koombana*'s long promenade deck that the visitors began to realise that a new standard was being set. They were ushered inside, through wide double doors, past French-polished, bevelled-glass book cabinets and into an elegant lounge, identified by their guide as the First Class social hall. The pressmen were greatly taken by the charm and sophistication of this room, so distinct and somehow dissociated from the ship's industrial exterior. A correspondent for *The Hedland Advocate* reported:

> There is an air of repose about this room that at once strikes the visitor, and forces that person to make visual inquiry as to the cause. The first thought is that one has arrived in the salon of some grand dame, but a glance at the book case with its mullioned frames and bevelled glass rather modifies the idea. The couches, occasional chairs and tables are in polished walnut. The furnishing was done by Waring and Co., art furnishers, of Glasgow, and little more needs to be said. The scheme of colour is purple and green, the former being used in the upholstering, and latter for the carpets. The wood work is satin wood and panelled in sycamore stained art green. There are two Chippendale writing desks, and a Broadwood piano, the music stool being also the music cabinet. The light well and fanlight are artistically designed. Here, as in other rooms, the fanlights are controlled by a wheel and raised or lowered from inside. The ceiling is done in painted canvas with raised design picked out in gold.[4]

From the First Class entrance on the promenade deck, a broad staircase led down to the spar deck. The *Advocate*'s man continued:

First Class social hall, S.S. Koombana.

Koombana's *First Class dining room.*

> The dining saloons for both classes are on this deck, and both are done in green and oak. Ventilation has been particularly studied, and the pantry so arranged that orders can be served from both sides as soon as they arrive from the galley by the electric lift. The first saloon has seating accommodation for 75, and electric fans are provided here as throughout the ship. The lavatories, on this deck, are replete. The appointments of the dining saloon and the wealth of table silver are revelations.[5]

From the dining room, carpeted passageways led aft to First Class staterooms arranged in small 'islands'. It was clear to the visitors that even the corridors had received careful aesthetic treatment.

Perhaps some members of the visiting party were surprised by the keenness of their guide to take them down the galley stairs into *Koombana*'s kitchen. His intent was soon clear. For electrical wizardry the galley surpassed even the navigating bridge. A telephone switchboard and warning lights, it appears, were no match for an intelligent egg boiler and a mighty bread maker.

> The kitchen is also on this deck, and in it are all sorts of modern contrivances that should delight the heart of the chef, as well as provide delicacies for the passengers; steam egg-boiler, with electric

Looking aft along the port-side corridor on Koombana's *spar deck.*

adjustment, which may be set for soft, medium, and hard, swinging the egg off on the register being reached; an electric lift to the dining rooms; steam press with revolving hot plate rack; five stoves, bake oven and grill, and many other appliances. An electric dough mixer, turning out 300 loaves in eight hours, and the printing room are on this deck.[6]

Koombana's main and lower decks were fully enclosed, although with steel ventilation ports that could be opened or sealed according to sea conditions and the needs of livestock. Through this underworld the guided tour continued, past moveable cattle stalls, in and out of refrigerated storage, along the stanchioned sides of open hatchways one above the other, and ultimately to the engine room. Even to those untrained in engineering, the brand-new 4,000-horsepower triple-expansion steam engine was a commanding presence.

Koombana's *decks.*
Below the navigating bridge, shaded by a canvas awning, is the captain's cabin on the bridge deck.
The next level down is the promenade deck, where a girl in a white dress may be seen leaning over the rail and watching a boat being lowered. Behind her is the First Class entrance; through double doors and to the right is the First Class social hall. Directly below the social hall, on the spar deck, is the First Class dining room. And below the spar deck, behind portholes, are the galley and crew cabins of the main deck.
Lower still, fully enclosed, is the lower deck, sometimes called the orlop deck.

S.S. Bullarra, Koombana*'s immediate predecessor on the Nor'-West run.*

Through the two hours of the tour, the pressmen were kept so busy and so entertained that few probing questions were asked. All were impressed, but several wondered how so grand a ship, serving a string of isolated outposts, could possibly be run at a profit. It had been announced that when *Koombana* returned from Melbourne, she would take over the Nor'-West running from the old *Bullarra*. It was difficult to accept that two ships so different in scale and sophistication could reasonably be sent to the same work. This was no stepwise progression; it was a giant leap—and a leap of faith to boot. Company man William Moxon seemed unfazed by questions from *Koombana*'s nervous admirers. "This ship is ahead of the times," he told Fremantle's *Evening Mail*, "but with it we will build up trade and coax people to travel. Anyone who has looked over the vessel must be convinced that it will prove a powerful factor in developing trade with the Nor'-West."[7]

To understand the Adelaide Steamship Company's decision, it is necessary to trace its deliberation. By 1906, the company had recognised that the Nor'-West coast of Western Australia had a bright future. It was a self-defined province of pearlers and pastoralists, many of whom had grown wealthy on very simple principles. Indeed, almost all of those who had amassed small or large fortunes had done so in one of three ways: by growing wool, by fishing for pearls and pearl shell, or by raising beef cattle. A defiant optimism was now supported by three pillars of prosperity.

In 1905–6, the total wool production of Australia and New Zealand was almost 2,000,000 bales. The nascent Nor'-West wool industry accounted for only about one per cent of that gargantuan clip,[8] but the Nor'-West industry had some characteristics that made it attractive to the shipping companies. The state was huge, and wool-growing had proven profitable in almost every district. Because the small mixed farms of the south were fully twenty degrees of latitude from the million-acre expanses of the north, shearing seasons were greatly staggered; demand for wool shipment was spread across autumn, winter and spring. There was a broad consensus that an industry so dispersed was unlikely to fail. For more than a decade, wool production had grown steadily and stubbornly, despite bad years and an almost total lack of infrastructure. Promised improvements to roads, jetties and tramways could only enhance prospects, and some went so far as to predict that the industry would soon eclipse Broome and its pearls.

The rise of the Broome-based pearl-shell fishery had indeed been spectacular. Between 1902 and 1906, the pearling fleet had grown from 220 to 350 boats, and from 1700 to about 2500 men. Although the 'take' per boat had dropped a little, few doubted that the industry, already contributing £200,000 annually to export revenue, would continue to thrive. Like wool-growing, the industry had shown great resilience. During that four-year period, the price of shell had suffered a great concussive fall, from £205 per ton in 1903 to £105 per ton in 1904. Even at the lower price the industry remained profitable, and all indications were that exports to London would continue unabated.[9]

Not surprisingly, pearlers and wool growers reserved their greatest faith for their own industries, but to impartial observers it was the beef cattle industry that held the greatest untapped potential. It was a little over twenty years since the first herds had been driven westward across the top of Australia to the great savanna grasslands of the Kimberley. On unfenced land and with minimal husbandry, the cattle thrived and multiplied.[10] In the early days, dry-season droving was a problem, but the first artesian bores along the stock routes delivered sweet water in hallelujah quantities.[11] At the beginning of 1907, when the Adelaide Steamship Company began to consider seriously the construction of a dedicated Nor'-West steamer, the Kimberley and its cattle were very much in the news. On February 2nd, a correspondent for *The Western Mail* delivered a tidy summation of the state of the industry:

> On a map of Australia and with Wyndham as the centre, describe a circle having a radius of 400 miles. . . . The area within the circle will include all the Kimberleys and the best portions of the Northern Territory. According to stockmen who have recently been droving from the Western Australian boundary to Queensland, there are one

million head of cattle within this region. Official returns, admittedly defective, place the number at about 800,000. There can be no doubt, therefore, that by virtue of its geographical position Wyndham should become the Chicago of the North.[12]

The Adelaide Steamship Company understood that the transportation of livestock would be an important part of its Nor'-West business. Whatever else the new ship would carry, Kimberley cattle would come aboard as honoured guests.

Through the first years of the twentieth century, Nor'-Westers were keenly and self-righteously aware of their rising contribution to the state's coffers; they became ever more demanding of their distant government. Each official visit—by Premier or Colonial Secretary or Minister for Public Works—was seen as an opportunity to petition for civil improvements: roadworks, port facilities, flood mitigation, water supply and lighting. Inevitably, some action resulted; shipping agents reported a steady rise in northbound cargo, not only food and supplies for growing towns, but also the materials of progress: pumps, piles, fencing wire, sleepers, rails, timber, and the ubiquitous corrugated iron. Everywhere the inadequacy of cargo-handling facilities was lamented. By 1907, every Nor'-West port listed jetty and tramway improvements among its most pressing needs. For the Adelaide Steamship Company, with a new steamer on the drawing board, that demand crystallised as a specific design requirement. The new steamer would have capacity great enough, hatchways large enough, and winches powerful enough to lower a steam locomotive to the floor of her hold, and deliver it over her side to waiting rails.

As the company contemplated a new vessel, it looked for any avenue of expansion for its Nor'-West passenger service. Per head of remote population, demand for passage to and from the capital had always been high. For that, the harsh northern summer could be blamed or thanked according to one's viewpoint. Every year almost half of the white population[13] fled south at the beginning of the wet, returning only when the sky cleared and the temperature fell. In the quest for competitive advantage, luxury became the Adelaide Steamship Company's new focus. Two questions emerged: If a new level of comfort and convenience were offered, how much trade could be stolen from competitors? And how much would demand grow if the voyage ceased to be an ordeal and became an indulgence?

At a glance, the Nor'-West did not look like a luxury market. In fact, to first-time visitors, several of the ports seemed little more than shanty towns. The statistics, however, showed that the region should not be judged by its rusty facade. There was broad prosperity here: a few individuals of great wealth and a great many of comfortable means. The price of saloon passage did not seem to be an issue. There was no evidence that the pastoralists or pearlers had ever baulked at the cost of sending their wives and children south, for school or summer respite or even for wedding preparations. It seemed that well-heeled Nor'-Westers, deprived of luxury and entertainment in their winter working lives, would rush to enjoy whatever the company was adventurous enough to offer.

Through 1906, the Adelaide Steamship Company marked time and kept its own counsel, but two key developments during the year tipped the scales in favour of a bold move.

Nor'-Westers had long campaigned for the construction of a railway from the coast to the mining centres of Marble Bar and Nullagine. In March 1906, after a decade of disagreement and delay, important progress was made. A government-commissioned report delivered two unequivocal recommendations: that Port Hedland should be the starting point of the railway, and that work should commence immediately.[14] Although all of the shipping companies would benefit from the two-year, £250,000 project, the Adelaide Steamship Company stood to gain most. Almost all wool and pearl shell from the Nor'-West was bound for Britain and Europe, but the route taken varied from company to company. The Adelaide Steamship Company carried wool and shell south to Fremantle, for transfer to the Royal Mail steamers on the home run. Dalgety's, representing all of its competitors, shipped north via Singapore. Because the rails and sleepers would travel north from Fremantle, the work was a perfect fit for the company whose heavier loading was in the opposite direction.

For the board of directors in Adelaide, one prerequisite remained to be met. For several years the company had held the contract for the delivery of Nor'-West mail, but the current agreement was due to expire. Only upon renewal of the contract would the directors commit to the construction of a dedicated Nor'-West steamer. On December 7th, 1906, the company was advised that its tender had been accepted; a new contract, to begin on March 1st, 1907, would deliver £4,000 per year for three years.[15] The monetary consideration was not huge, but it was a reliable contribution to profitability, unaffected by drought or recession. It also carried a symbolism that could be turned to commercial advantage. Of all vessels regularly visiting a remote port, the mail boat was the most anticipated; indeed, the title almost guaranteed a positive engagement with each port of call.

In the combination of mail and rail, the Adelaide Steamship Company found the competitive advantage it had sought. Four weeks into the new mail contract, on March 25th, 1907, the directors authorised the preparation of detailed plans for a Nor'-West steamer, with every appliance and convenience available. In capacity and luxury, the company would go where no competitor could afford to follow.[16]

The broad requirements were quickly worked out. The ship would carry about ninety passengers in First Class staterooms and 130 in Second Class cabins. No lower standard would be offered. The ship would carry at least 4,000 tons of general cargo and a further 800 tons in cold storage. Moveable stalls on the main deck would accommodate about 200 cattle.

It soon became clear that the new ship would be similar in size to the company's interstate liner *Grantala*. A design challenge immediately emerged. *Grantala*, on her design draft of 24 feet, would struggle to gain admission to any Nor'-West port.[17] To negotiate the shoals of Shark Bay, the jetty at Carnarvon, or the sandbar at Port Hedland, the new ship would need to draw significantly less water. Precisely how much less would require a careful analysis of tides and port facilities, both existing and promised. It would also require an engineering assessment of the impact of reduced draft on the ship's stability.

Port Hedland quickly emerged as a limiting factor. Even on a draft of 19 feet, the ship would be unable to cross the bar and reach the jetty on a neap tide. She would be locked out—or worse still, locked in—for about three days in every fourteen. The problem was greatly exacerbated by the fact that the round-trip travel time from Port Hedland to the usual terminus port of Derby was seven days: exactly one quarter of the lunar cycle. If the ship northbound were to enter Port Hedland on a spring tide, with a few feet of water beneath her keel, she would inevitably be locked out on her return. The only possibility, it seemed, was to negotiate Port Hedland on the shoulders of the spring tides, arriving a few days before the full moon or new moon, and returning a few days after. One thing was certain: managing the new ship's schedule would not be easy. Finally, the company's engineers arrived at the design draft of 20 feet 11 inches, fully three feet less than that of *Grantala*. The shipbuilders, yet to be chosen, could advise on whether that stringent condition could safely be met.

In September 1907, at the company headquarters in Adelaide, plans and specification were presented to the board.[18] A few weeks later, tenders were called for the construction of a steamship to be named "Koombana".[19,20] And in the minutes of the director's meeting held on December 4th, 1907, the engagement of a well-regarded Glasgow shipbuilder was recorded:

> s.s. "Koombana".
> Cable to London Agents of the 29th November to accept the tender of Messrs. A. Stephen & Sons, Linthouse, for a 13 knot steamer, dead-weight capacity 3100 tons on 20 feet 11 inches draft, classed British Corporation, Babcock's boilers.
> Cable from London of the 3rd instant advising having closed with Messrs. Stephen & Sons for £92,500, delivery 20th November next.[21]

That "Koombana" required a leap of faith cannot be doubted. The greatest single risk for the Adelaide Steamship Company was its unavoidable reliance upon government assurances, especially with regard to port improvements and the construction of the railway. When the contract with Alexander Stephen & Sons was signed, the *Pilbarra Railway Bill* had passed through parliament, but no date had been set for the commencement of work.[22] Similarly, the government had committed to the construction of four new Nor'-West lighthouses, but it was difficult to predict when even the first would be commissioned.[23] At almost every Nor'-West port the viability of the venture depended on civil works yet to be completed, and recent history suggested that good intentions did not convert readily into tramways and jetties.

If the slow progress of port improvements cost the directors some sleep, their choice of shipbuilder did not. Alexander Stephen & Sons had built a reputation for high-quality workmanship, and had delivered several large luxury ships. Their work on "Koombana" did not disappoint. In the course of construction, there were several changes to the specification, all positive in effect. The builders had contracted to deliver 3,000 horsepower and a speed of 13 knots; by negotiation, the final result was 4,000 horsepower and 14½ knots. Even the design draft of 20 feet 11 inches was revised downward a little, the final measured value being 20 feet 8 inches.[24] The Adelaide Steamship Company's representative on site reported very favourably on the quality of equipment and fittings supplied. Significantly, Alexander Stephen & Sons understood the importance of luxury to the project. In *Koombana*'s cabins, dining rooms and social hall, they not only obeyed the letter of the specification;[25] they entered into its spirit and executed the work with great verve and finesse.

KOOMBANA RETURNED FROM THE EAST on Monday, March 8th, 1909. It was almost ten months since Captain John Rees had sailed for England by the Royal Mail Steamer *Orontes*. It had been a fascinating odyssey, through the last stages of *Koombana*'s construction, her launch and sea trials, and the voyage from Glasgow during which something new was learned every day.[26] Now he was keen to depart for the Nor'-West, taking *Koombana* to the work for which she had been built.

The first trip would be no gentle orientation. It was summer's end, the busiest time of the year, and manager Moxon had managed well. A great splash of positive publicity four weeks before departure had ensured that *Koombana* would begin her working life heavily laden and with a large complement of enthusiastic passengers. Moxon had made much of the fact that the ship had been specially built for the run, and Nor'-Westers were predisposed to accept his assurances. Somehow, the ship seemed like an acknowledgment: a reward for years of perseverance in the north.

On the morning of Friday, March 12th, a large crowd gathered at Victoria Quay, Fremantle. Although the usual banter passed between ship and shore, *Koombana*'s first Nor'-West passengers brought more than common cheerfulness to the rail. The mood was ebullient and celebratory. And when the last line was dropped and the ship slid into the stream, it was difficult to know whose success was being celebrated.

2

NARROW SEAS

ON TUESDAY, MARCH 16TH, 1909 the *Geraldton Guardian* reported:

> S.S. KOOMBANA.
> AGROUND AT SHARKS BAY.[1]
> VESSEL SAFE.
> Considerable surprise and regret was expressed in Geraldton to-day,
> when the news got about that the fine new steamer Koombana, which
> was so much admired on the occasion of her first visit to Geraldton
> on Saturday, was aground at Sharks Bay. The news was contained in
> an official message from Sharks Bay to the Geraldton Postmaster,
> received to-day, and read as follows:—
>
> "Koombana grounded 14 miles out 7 a.m. on Monday. Mails
> landed at 2.30 p.m. Weather hazy. Unable to see steamer yesterday.
> Haze cleared this morning; vessel now in sight through glasses; still
> aground. Local seamen are of opinion that Koombana will probably
> remain aground four days at least . . . No danger need be entertained,
> as the bottom is soft sand and seaweed . . . There is some fine fishing in
> this channel, and the passengers should have no difficulty in amusing
> themselves for four or five days."[2]

CAPTAIN REES HAD VISITED SHARK BAY many times; he knew it well. After
rounding Cape Levillain he steered the usual south-easterly course for
the Heirisson Flat Buoy, which marked the southern edge of a narrow
channel leading to Denham. Finding that sewing-needle opening would
be his first navigational challenge as master of *Koombana*; with a generous
helping of bad luck it would become his first major blunder.

In clear air the passage was perfectly manageable. A black buoy, the
port mark for the channel, was usually sighted first. If proper course had
been maintained, the red Heirisson Flat Buoy would appear dead ahead
a few minutes later and a gentle turn to port would bring the ship into
line. For *Koombana*'s first arrival, however, visibility was poor. Cloaking

everything was a thick haze that limited visibility to a few hundred yards. The early morning light was strange indeed: the sun, rising through the mist over *Koombana*'s port bow, appeared dull and red, and the foredeck was bathed in a warm orange light that seemed at odds with the darkness of the sea.

Koombana proceeded slowly, with Rees and his chief officer Henry Clarke together on the bridge. They agreed that with the sun low over the port bow the first mark could easily be missed. When a bright buoy appeared dead ahead, their shared assessment was that the port mark had slipped by unseen. The two men looked closely at the buoy ahead. They agreed that it was the red starboard mark. Captain Rees swung the ship to port and ordered Full Speed Ahead. Moments later, *Koombana* ran onto an isolated mound of sand and ground to a halt. She was stuck fast with her head east-south-east and a list to starboard, with the navigation channel and the incessant south-westerly wind on her starboard side.[3]

Sun and sea-mist had played a trick on two experienced men. Hidden in the brilliant white of sunshine are all the colours of the rainbow, but sea-mist does not treat all colours equally. Blue and violet are more easily caught and scattered away, while red and orange may pass unhindered. Stripped of its blue hues, the sun that rose over *Koombana*'s bow appeared as a rusty red ball. And it was the red remnant of a once-white beam that bathed the foredeck and gave a faded black buoy its rose tint.[4]

THE SHARK BAY LIGHTER *Success*, in anticipation of *Koombana*'s first arrival, had started out early and dropped anchor at the usual rendezvous point. When *Koombana*'s tall yellow funnel was spotted, all on board watched what appeared to be an extremely cautious approach. Some time passed before the observers realised that it was not slow progress that *Koombana* was making, but none at all. With more than an inkling of what had occurred, they weighed anchor and went to investigate.

When *Success* came alongside, good-natured banter passed between steamer and lighter. There was no indication whatever that the passengers perceived a serious problem or anticipated a long delay. And when two pearling cutters joined the lighter at *Koombana*'s side, the mood became positively festive.

The skipper of the lighter came aboard for a short conference with Captain Rees. The two men decided that nothing was served by delaying the discharge of Denham cargo. The work commenced immediately, with some passengers remaining on deck, chatting with the crews as slings of supplies were swung over the railings and lowered. Finally, after four or five disembarking passengers had made the crossing in a wicker basket, the job was done. *Success* and the two cutters departed in convoy.[5]

An arrangement had been made with the skipper of the lighter. On arrival in Denham he would send a telegram to Fremantle on Captain

Rees's behalf. During the night, an attempt would be made to free the ship; if that failed, Rees himself would come to town in the morning.

Until the next high tide, there was little for *Koombana*'s officers to do but to help the passengers pass the time. One passenger would recall:

> In the evening, in the exquisitely-fitted, tastefully-furnished music room a concert was held, and as is usual in the case of musical evenings organised in the dark, much pleasing talent was brought to light, some not quite so pleasing, but all doing their best to make the time pass merrily and pleasantly. The first officer's sympathetic baritone voice, the second officer's artistic handling of the mandolin, and the chief engineer's "auld Scotch sangs in the braid tongue" were received with special appreciation. The best part of the evening was when we gathered round the piano and heartily sang the old-fashioned choruses.[6]

As on most late-summer evenings in Shark Bay, the wind blew hard from the south-west. It was strangely reassuring to be aboard a ship so utterly unmoved by wind and white-capped sea. In rousing chorus around the piano, few found anything to be concerned about. The grounding was little more than a good story to tell friends and family in a few days.

While his officers attended to the serious business of keeping the passengers happy, Captain Rees retired to consider his position. The grounding had occurred at almost the worst possible time. If *Koombana* had struck at low tide, she would already be free, but he had run onto

S.S. Koombana aground in Shark Bay, March 1909.

the bank at the top of the tide. Worse still, the ship had struck the bank under full power and had ridden up. Precisely how much she had ridden up was difficult to gauge. He would order a full circuit of soundings in the morning, and then have the sea's rise and fall monitored hourly from the lee-side rail.[7]

Shark Bay tides were unusual: not for their range, which was only about five feet, but for their unusual lag behind the phases of the moon. At most ports the highest tides occurred a day or two after the new moon, but here in a shallow, windswept gulf that tapered away to marshland beyond the southern horizon, the highest tide could lag the moon by almost a week. The new moon was six days away. Even without local advice, Captain Rees figured that if *Koombana* were not refloated in the next two days, she could be stuck fast for ten. It is likely that he did not sleep well.

At daylight, after an unsuccessful attempt to pull the ship clear using stream anchors,[8] Rees declared his intention to visit the telegraph office. Three hours later the motor launch with nine men, a case of beer and a basket of sandwiches was ready to depart. To his friend Peggy back home, fourth engineer Jim Low wrote:

> The Chief went to drive her and I went to do the work. The Skipper and Purser went to send the telegram, three passengers went for excitement and two quarter masters were carried to bale her out.[9]

To passengers in need of diversion, the excursion seemed more like an expedition to a foreign land than a fourteen-mile dash to the nearest settlement. As the boat dipped into the swell, it became clear that none on board would arrive dry, if they arrived at all. For a few minutes the spectators watched as the bow of the launch cast sea-spray like fishing net. But when the propeller's milky trail suddenly darkened to sea green, all guessed that the motor had been swamped or had stalled. Up went a sail, and back came the boat.[10]

The second attempt was more successful, and when the source of amusement had shrunk to a speck, the crowd dispersed. One Broome-bound passenger, destined to be remembered only as "Chronicler", began recording his thoughts.

> The passengers, and even the officers, seemed in good spirits and confident of an early move, and so we set ourselves to make enjoyment. Some availed themselves of the fine library of fiction in the music-room, some of the ladies gave themselves to fancy needlework, the men were chiefly found in the smoking-room at cards or draughts. Many of the rest beguiled the hours at the exciting and noisy games of rope quoits and deck billiards, while a favoured few consoled themselves by the time-honoured and strangely fascinating pastime of flirtation.[11]

Deck billiards on Koombana's *promenade deck.*

It is said that the camera never lies, but this game of deck billiards was more challenging than the photograph suggests. This camera sat upon a tripod on *Koombana*'s promenade deck, but the deck was not horizontal. The ship had come to rest with a list of four degrees to starboard. Here now, at gravity's insistence, is the photograph realigned.[12]

Deck billiards, with a starboard list.

As the *Geraldton Guardian* had predicted, passengers soon discovered that there were fine fish to be caught from the rail. And "Chronicler", pleasantly surprised at the satisfaction to be had from this writing game, waxed lyrical.

> Fishing, too, was indulged in, and one fish-fancier hauled in a six-foot shark. He was a tiger, and vigorously objected to leaving his native

element. But when a Winchester sent five leaden ideas into his dull head, one per medium of his left eye, one through his nose, and the rest between his grinning jaws, he seemed more prepared to submit to fate. Then a noose was passed over his body, and he was hauled level with the lower deck, where a bright youth extracted half a dozen molars and another hewed off the tail for bait, after which the hook was cut free, the noose loosened, and the remains committed to the deep.[13]

ABOARD THE LAUNCH, the wind had strengthened soon after the second departure. The nine 'expeditioners' landed on the beach at Denham, soaked to the skin. After Captain Rees and Purser Reid had departed for the telegraph office, the others willingly accepted offers of dry clothes from locals keen to learn more of *Koombana* and her circumstances. A pearler's wife asked how the ship was getting on for provisions.

"Nearly run out," replied one of the passengers. "Fact is, ma'am, we're eating the poultry consigned to Cossack and other places."

The woman seemed taken aback. "Surely the captain has no right to kill other people's fowls?"

The invitation was too good to refuse. "What are we to do?" the passenger rejoined; "He can't see us starve. Anyway, we've nearly run out of chooks. But there's a donkey aboard, and there's talk of starting on him next."[14]

Jim Low was pleasantly surprised by the welcome that began on the beach in the morning and continued into the night. To Peggy he wrote:

When evening came the weather was too bad to go back so we had to stop in the tin hotel that night. The inhabitants thought it was up against them to entertain us so gave a ball and party in a tin shed. All the ladies turned up, the daughters and wives of the pearlers, the wife of the policeman etc etc. There is no class distinction in Shark's Bay except between White and Black. We had a most enjoyable evening and broke up about 3am.[15]

As the 'ball' wound down, Captain Rees informed Low and the quarter-masters that their services would be required at 5 a.m. for their first assignment of the day: to retrieve the launch, which had been left on a mooring a hundred yards offshore.

At first light, the boat was fetched and the late-night revellers roused and rallied. The party set off in good style, with the motor, as Jim was wont to say, "snoring along nicely." Unfortunately, snoring turned to apnoea as the launch ran out of fuel. To Captain Rees's annoyance and the young engineer's chagrin, sails were again hoisted. At midday on Wednesday, March 18th, after thirty hours away, the launch came alongside under wet canvas. It was, Jim conceded, "a most ignominious return."

Back on board, Rees was keen to review the soundings and tide measurements taken in his absence. The soundings had delivered useful information: *Koombana* was harder aground at the stern than at the bow. The tide results, taken by plumb line from the lee-side rail, were also interesting: the officers had discovered that the water level continued to rise for half an hour after the tide turned. Clearly, the currents here were not simple ebb and flow. It was as if the ship was on the rim of a great, slow eddy.[16]

The measurements also confirmed that the tides were lagging the phase of the moon by several days. The new moon was now only four days away, but the neap had only just been passed. Captain Rees drew some consolation from that. At the telegraph office in Denham, he had not known if *Koombana* was capable of freeing herself. He had erred on the side of caution and had requested that another steamer be sent to assist. Having now spoken with his officers, he was satisfied that his decision had been the right one. Early on Thursday morning, a boat from Denham brought news that another of the company's steamers, the collier *Winfield*, had left Geraldton in the early hours. She would be at *Koombana*'s side within 24 hours.[17]

The decision to discharge *Koombana*'s cargo cannot have been taken lightly. Crew morale was a prime concern. All had expected to be back in Fremantle at the beginning of April, but now the northward run might not begin until the last week of March. Certainly, the crew would be paid for the time they were away, but none would see their wives and girl-friends for another month at least. Upon the seamen in particular, the planned transshipment was a huge imposition. Work would continue around the clock, with the men working sixteen-hour days.[18] The firemen would be affected, too: some would be seconded from the stokehold to join the men on deck. Rees realised that morale would only remain high if the men's efforts were respected, and seen to be respected. They would be kept well informed of progress and, above all, be well fed. Fresh food posed a particular problem. *Koombana* had just delivered the only fresh fruit and vegetables in Denham; it would be impolitic to buy any of it back. But consignments for Broome and Derby were a different matter; indeed, most perishable consignments would not arrive fit for sale. Rees decided that, since cargo spoilage or loss would account for only a small fraction of the cost of the accident, he would place the interests of passengers and crew above those of the consignees. His men would work hard, but would receive grapes crisp and cold with their sandwiches at lunch, and be rewarded with beer and sardines at the end of each long day.[19]

It was not only the working men who discovered a new enthusiasm for food. "Chronicler" marvelled at his own dining-hall punctuality.

> As a relief in the programme of amusements, the sound of the bugle
> calling us to maxillary warfare was a thrice-welcome sound, for we

developed appetites of which our mothers might be proud—but anxious.[20]

Rees reminded his officers that to keep the passengers in good humour was an important part of their work. Here too there was evidence of creative thinking. In the evenings, the passengers had taken to gathering on the port side of the promenade deck, out of the wind. To create a bright, pleasant space in which passengers might mingle, the arc lights used for loading and unloading in port were switched on. The effect was sudden and surprising: into circles of clear, illuminated water swam sea snakes, turtles and fish in great numbers. Thereafter, evening conversations were often drawn to the rail and to the passing parade below.[21]

The suggestion was also made—by whom is not known—that passengers might be taken on a fishing trip in one of the ship's boats, with a member of the crew in command. It seems that Rees's reaction to the plan was a simple "Why not?" He could certainly spare a junior officer for a few hours. The first such diversion was a great success. With official sanction and company chaperone, the passengers sailed ten miles to a little island, returning at day end with sixty schnapper for the galley.

ENTRIES IN KOOMBANA'S LOG for Friday, March 19th, reflected new purpose and optimism.

> Fresh to strong SSW breeze.
> 6 a.m. Sounded West of ship and found 3½ to 5 fathoms.
> Hands employed lowering and hoisting boats, preparing gear and stripping hatches for the discharge of cargo.
> 2.15 p.m. S.S. "Winfield" arrived alongside and made fast.
> 3 p.m. Started to discharge cargo from No. 2 into "Winfield".
> Hands working cargo right through, one hour for tea, half hour for supper. Tanks sounded at frequent intervals.[22]

In principle, the plan was simple: sling by sling, hold by hold, *Koombana*'s cargo would be transferred to *Winfield*. At each high tide, a halt would be called. With the ships side by side, using both ships' engines, a new attempt would be made to break free. There was, however, one difficulty that no creative thinking could overcome. The ship had come to rest on a bank sloping down to starboard. Only on that side, to windward, was there water deep enough for *Winfield* to come alongside. For the duration of the transfer, at all hours, the two ships would bump and grind, scour each other's sides, and destroy every cork or wicker fender placed between them.[23]

Despite that ceaseless metal-on-metal antagonism, spirits remained high. With *Koombana* becoming lighter with each passing day, and the tidal range now increasing, the plan must ultimately succeed.

IN A FEW DAYS, *Koombana*'s unreliable motor launch had become a favourite among passengers craving entertainment. More than once it had departed under power only to return under sail. When the boat was lowered again on Saturday morning, passengers lined the rail in anticipation. Jim Low had been ordered to lead another excursion to Denham, to collect ten sheep tied up near the office of the shipping agent. This time, however, the engine gave no trouble and the launch disappeared from sight. The amusement of the gallery would come later—much later.

THERE IS SOMETHING ABOUT A SUNDAY, even upon a mound of sand in the middle of a windswept gulf. "Chronicler" wrote:

> On Sunday our rescuer stood off from our stern, almost at right angles, and, getting her anchors out, pulled on them, while the screws of both steamers spun round but, again, not an inch. That day we had church services conducted by a Congregational minister. We passed the day more quietly than other days, and some showed signs of being depressed. We commenced to lose faith in the ability of the "Winfield" to get us off unaided. And when the rumour went round that our rescuer was herself on a bank, our spirits went down below zero.[24]

The fear was well founded. *Winfield* had arrived with her cargo holds empty, but carrying enough coal and fresh water for two ships. Now she was heavy with *Koombana*'s cargo. The tides were now increasing, but with higher highs come lower lows. Twice each day now, *Winfield* was scuffing the seabed. The consequences were not dire, but the nerves of passengers were beginning to fray.[25]

Distraction, sorely needed, was delivered to *Koombana*'s side in the middle of Sunday afternoon. Word spread that the motor launch was returning. Four bedraggled boys were soon on board, looking and smelling a little sheepish. In his letter to Peggy, Jim Low repeated the confession that had amused his shipmates:

> I made an even worse fiasco with her. I was told off one morning at 7 o'clock to go in to Denham for ten sheep as we were running short of provisions. I had the 5th Engineer with me and two quarter masters. We got ashore, got the sheep and lugged them out on our shoulders through water up to the waist and dumped them into the launch. When we got out a couple of miles the weather got so bad we had to turn and run for it back to anchorage. We slept out on hard gratings with bits of canvas over us to keep the dew off, a most uncomfortable night, fine and clear but a heavy swell running kept us bobbing like a cork till we were bruised and bumped all over. The poor sheep were worse than we were as we had to hobble them to keep them aboard.

Next morning the weather was better but the boat had taken in water during the night and spoiled our starting battery and there we were 14 miles from the Koombana and not a move out of our engine. So we sailed back and got towed a bit by a lighter that was going out to the ship and when about a mile off, the battery recovered sufficiently to give us a start, then we were all right. We snored up alongside at full speed and the passengers lined up the rails and considered us as returned from the dead. We were nearly dead anyway, nothing to eat for about 30 hours. By good luck we had a little tank of water with us so we weren't thirsty anyway.[26]

Tuesday, March 23rd—Day 9—brought the first hint of success. To passengers emerging on deck in the early morning, the view seemed a little altered. Officers confirmed that they were not imagining things; during the night, *Koombana*'s bow had swung eighteen degrees to port. At breakfast, there was talk of imminent freedom, and at 9 a.m. a new attempt—the ninth—was made to free the ship. To dismay and disappointment it failed, as all previous attempts had failed.[27]

Over the next few hours, it became increasingly difficult for the passengers to forget their circumstances. After being rock-solid for nine days *Koombana* had begun to move, fitfully but perceptibly, in response to bumps from *Winfield* lying to windward. Spirits rose again, but what was heartening to the passengers was felt very differently by the officers. They recognised a new problem: *Koombana* was no longer firmly attached to the seabed, and with each sideways bump was being pushed a little higher on the bank. Unless the wind eased, there would be no alternative to anchor *Winfield* a little way off, and to call *Success* to lighter what remained of the cargo.[28]

The wind did not ease. In utter exasperation, John Rees accepted this most tedious of alternatives. For almost nine days the work had been difficult and dangerous. Now, at the very last, it became mind-numbingly slow. It took five hours to transfer fifty tons of Broome cargo to the lighter, with several slings smashed or damaged in the process. Another ten hours passed before *Success* returned for a second load.[29]

Late adversity notwithstanding, Rees now knew that this was a battle he would win. On Wednesday morning he ordered the motor launch, handed control to Henry Clarke, and set out for the telegraph station.

After the launch had disappeared from sight, Clarke and the other officers determined to give their captain something to smile about on his return. On the afternoon high tide, they tried a new approach. To lift the stern a little, the forepeak ballast tanks were filled. *Winfield* was then positioned at right angles off *Koombana*'s starboard bow. They sought to free the ship by pulling her bow into the deeper water of the channel. To universal disappointment, the power of two ships was not enough;

Koombana hung on the bank with her fore end afloat.[30] "Chronicler" honoured the effort but lamented the outcome.

> We had come round four points of the compass. But the stern had turned a little on a pivot of sand, and next tide must be waited for to complete the work. Meanwhile, the lighter took our anchor from the nose, and dropped it to starboard a few hundred yards from us to prevent any slipping back there. Then we waited the return of the captain. We were all sorry the attempt had not been fully successful, chiefly because we had been planning to greet the captain with three-times-three. For to a man the passengers are with Captain Rees, and freely express sympathy with him in this mishap.[31]

Koombana had been nine days stuck on a sandbank and yet no one turned against the man who had put her there. Captain Rees had willingly admitted fault and had done all in his power to make the ordeal bearable. Good-natured humility, it seems, spared him all recrimination.

AT DAYLIGHT ON THURSDAY, MARCH 25TH, *Koombana* was teetering on the edge of freedom. Surely, this would be the day. The preparations which had begun at midnight continued until midday. Anchors were repositioned, lines were run, and a heavy steel hawser was played out from *Koombana*'s stern. *Winfield* moved into position, took up the hawser, and waited. Urgency and excitement gripped all but the slowly rising tide.

S.S. Winfield *taking the hawser, March 25th, 1909.*

A few minutes after two o'clock, everything happened at once. Two ships shuddered as their great iron screws brought the sea to a rolling boil of silt and weed, and winches and chains joined the metal chorus as the steel hawser leapt from the sea and took the strain. In less than a minute, after ten days and seven hours, the gargantuan labour came to an end. *Koombana* slid free and straightened up.[32]

On the promenade deck there were whistles, cheers, and a spate of back-slapping. A few passengers, forgetting entirely the ship's rules, stormed the bridge to congratulate Captain Rees, who graciously permitted his hand to be wrung. "This has taken twenty years off my life," he told his smiling assailants. "If those buoys had not been altered, this would never have happened."[33]

Even in jubilation, all were aware that 500 tons of cargo would have to be reloaded. Few were keen to ask how long that might take. The answer was three days: three hard, unpleasant days with the two ships rolling and ranging on a rough sea. For the moment, however, nothing could spoil the day and its achievement.

AT 6 P.M. ON MONDAY, MARCH 29TH, after thirty hours spent bunkering coal, *Koombana* cast off and resumed the voyage north.[34] She was two weeks late, encrusted with salt and coal dust, and streaked with rust where *Winfield* and *Success* had scraped the paint from her sides.

This was not the debut the Adelaide Steamship Company had imagined, but the directors looked beyond their losses and remained philosophical. Yes, it was regrettable that Nor'-Westers would never see their new ship in new condition, but *Koombana* was neither designed nor destined to remain pristine. Hers was a different calling, of grace and grime in equal measure. She would enter her life of service not as an immaculate princess but as a duchess in overalls, willing and able to work.

And the Nor'-West stood ready to receive her.

3

GULLIVER'S TRAVELS

WHEN THE FRENCH CORVETTE *Uranie* dropped anchor in Shark Bay in
September 1818, expedition artist Jacques Etienne Victor Arago was unimpressed by what he saw. In his journal he wrote:

> The coast from the moment we saw it exhibited nothing but a picture
> of desolation; no rivulet consoled the eye, no tree attracted it; no
> mountain gave variety to the landscape, no dwelling enlivened it.
> Everywhere reigned sterility and death.[1]

But Shark Bay had something which Arago did not see, and which would
draw many boats to its shores. Vast quantities of the small pearl oyster
Pinctada albina littered a grassy seabed. Ninety years later, when journalist
George Romans came ashore from S.S. *Koombana*, he found a prosperous
pearling community untroubled by the absence of postcard scenery.
Under his *nom de plume* "Vindex", Romans wrote:

> The Nor'-West life is something distinct in itself. At Geraldton the
> southern civilisation ceases, and thence northward commences a
> gradual merging into tropical life and tropical conditions. Thirty
> hours afterwards the ship rounds the long Dirk Hartog Island . . .
> and glides through the sheltered waters of Denham Sound to an
> anchorage a few miles off the small town of the same name. Already
> the Nor'-West phase of life is opening up. The genial warmth of the
> sun, the white-roofed houses on the shore, the browned faces and
> white or khaki clothes of the settlers, the pearling luggers with their
> coloured crews, the sense of release from the small conventions of
> society, are the things that bespeak the North-West.[2]

In the early days of Shark Bay pearling, shell lay bare for the picking at
low tide. Later, when the beach lay bare, shells were collected by wading
in the shallows. Thereafter, to the limit of nature's resilience, the seabed
would be scraped by wire-mesh baskets dragged behind single-masted

sailing boats of shallow draft.[3] The technique of extracting pearls was also unique,[4] in a way that impressed itself on every first-time visitor. Fresh from the old country, *Koombana*'s young fourth engineer Jim Low took delight in explaining this in a letter to his friend Peggy back home.

> They bring the oysters ashore and rot them in the sun before opening them and the stink—well it beats anything you could imagine in your wildest flights of fancy, rotten eggs is perfume to it. Still they say it is not unhealthy. I don't know, anyway that beach is an offence. The shell in Shark's Bay is poor but the pearls are good. I sat down one day and watched the black gins (aboriginal women)[†] going through and opening the shells till I felt faint. They got a pearl every dozen shells or so mostly small ones. They scrape the putrid remnants of the oyster into what they call pogey pots and this after a further rotting process is boiled down and the pearls raked out at the bottom. These pogey pots are the climax. They cry out aloud to one another. In case we went away with false impressions of Shark's Bay one of the inhabitants took an oar and stirred one up, for the next few seconds nothing much mattered. We blindly fought our way to a sandhill well to windward and looked at that pot. Nobody said anything for some time but everybody felt queer. A black gin sitting near the pot threw her nose upwards sniffed approvingly and gently murmured "exbishin scent, bery goodt."[5]

Like Vindex, Jim Low was undaunted by Denham's appearance. The young Irishman had signed up for service on the other side of the world. Moreover, he had chosen a ship that would forsake even provincial ports to serve the little communities of a remote coastline. His employment may have commenced in Glasgow, but the adventure of his imagination began in Shark Bay.

The settlement had seen some wild days, but things were different now: a unique brand of law enforcement had reduced the population and restored the industry to profitability. In a letter to the editor of *The West Australian*, long-time pearler "J.S.D." reflected with satisfaction upon the action that he, with others of like mind, had taken.

> From 1886 to 1889 Sharks Bay pearling was in a flourishing condition. Shells and pearls were plentiful, and there was a good market for both. This fact attracted the attention of a number of Chinese traders, who, by that gradual process peculiar to the Asiatic, worked slowly into the business of small shop owners and boat owners. The position became intolerable, and forced European pearlers to combine, form a Sharks Bay Pearling Association, get legal advice about the framing of

---

† The brackets are Jim Low's and not the author's. The terminology and explanation are as they appear in the source.

rules, and make an offer to lease the whole of the Sharks Bay pearling grounds for Europeans only. For this privilege we agreed to pay to the Government £80 per annum, instead of paying a royalty per ton. Our offer was accepted, and the next problem was the colour question. After serious consideration and much legal advice, we petitioned the Government to make an offer to buy out the whole of the Chinese boats and plant for a fixed sum, and then give them notice to quit. To this the authorities agreed, but, as a precaution against rioting or bloodshed, a number of police and "specials" were sent up to join the local police, and to assist the white pearlers, as we were not sure in what spirit the China men would receive their notice to quit. As the Chinese camp was at Egg Island Bay, a notice was sent to that place warning them of our intentions, and shortly afterwards the Government Resident, police, and pearlers "rolled up" to assist in case a riot might occur. When all had assembled, the magistrate produced the official documents required in such cases, including the Riot Act, and the whole matter was explained to the Chinese through an interpreter. At first they would have none of it. They cursed the Queen, and they cursed the Governor, and all in authority under him. But in the end wiser counsels prevailed, induced probably by the military display made by law, police, and pearlers. So they accepted the terms offered, and within a fortnight had cleared out of the Bay. Thus the coloured problem was dealt with successfully by a handful of white pearlers, assisted by a few police headed by a Resident Magistrate. This event may give food for thought to those who are now studying the colour problem.[6]

When Jim Low arrived with *Koombana* in 1909, a community smaller and whiter was advertising its contentment. After accepting some local hospitality, he told Peggy:

The magnates of Shark's Bay take the cake. They live in corrugated iron shanties, making absurd additions as the family grows. They send out their pearling boats on Mondays and welcome them back on Friday nights sometimes clearing as much as £3000 in a year. The sons as soon as they are big enough go out with the boats. The daughters are sent round to the big schools in Melbourne and Sydney whence they return "finished" bringing with them the comforts of civilization in the shape of grand pianos, sewing machines and new fangled naptha stoves, and make pathetic attempts to disguise the baldness of the paternal mansion with pictures and muslin fripperies. Then try to import plants which gradually fade away and great spiders inches long make nests in the remnants and spin marvellous webs on them, great fat vicious spiders with scarlet bodies and long black legs, regular nightmares.[7]

Denham c. 1915: a corrugated-iron shanty town.

For the locals, it was a great frustration that *Koombana* could not be enjoyed here as at other places, where the ship's saloon became the focus of town life for the duration of each visit. At Denham there was neither water deep enough nor jetty long enough to meet *Koombana* halfway. The elegant newcomer could only drop anchor and remain aloof, delivering visitors in a wicker basket swung over her railings. In time, however, the Shark Bay pearlers would come to know her, as southbound saloon passengers seeking respite from pogey, flies and sand.

FOR KOOMBANA'S PASSENGERS, the passage north from Denham, in the lee of Dirk Hartog Island, was often enjoyed on deck. A few hours of downwind steaming would bring the ship to the head of a mile-long jetty, where a steam locomotive known affectionately as "The Coffee Pot" waited to bring passengers and cargo into Carnarvon. Like Denham, the town was prosperous, but it owed its wealth to merino wool rather than pearl shell. From the comfort of *Koombana*'s saloon, Vindex wrote:

> Wheresoever two or three squatters are gathered together there will the conversation be forever of sheep, and rain, and grass, and windmills. And the young Englishman sitting in the smokeroom looks up in the midst of an intricate bridge problem and says vehemently: "Damn these squatters and the incessant talk of sheep; the very rafters echo with sheep, sheep, sheep." Perhaps also, he makes bitter comment on the ease with which some people get their incomes, and then someone answers: "Yes, the squatter is envied and abused nowadays; it seems almost convenient to forget that he lived 20 strenuous years in this heat-blistered country before he was worth while being worried about by the tax collector."[8]

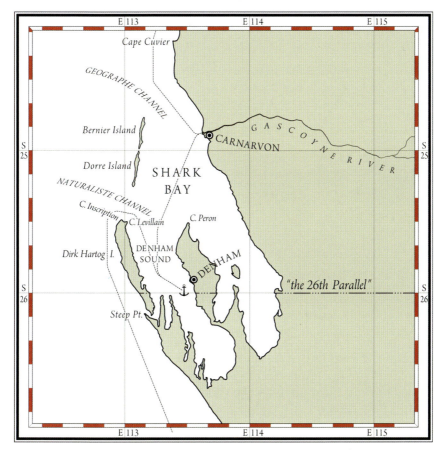

MAP 2 • *Denham – Carnarvon.*

From time to time, Carnarvon paid a high price for the privilege of a well-watered hinterland. When *Koombana* first arrived at the end of March 1909, the town was recovering from its worst-ever flood. A year later, the colonial secretary and chief harbourmaster came to town to discuss mitigation works and to demonstrate the government's commitment to the future of the Nor'-West. Vindex came too, to cover the tour for *The West Australian*. After the obligatory round of public meetings, he wrote:

> The trouble all comes from the fact that the founders of Carnarvon loved the Gascoyne River so well that they placed the town on its bank. They didn't know how much the river loved them, else they would not now be worrying year after year for a means of repelling the advances of the water. Each year the swollen river comes rushing down to the sea, and in the ardour of its affections attempts to creep all over the town. The consequence is that annually Olivia-terrace is reduced by about 50 per cent., and at times the river shows half a mind to take the whole town in its arms and hurry away to sea.[9]

February 1909: Carnarvon in the 'fond embrace' of the Gascoyne River.

Because the river was long and its catchment vast, the flooding of Carnarvon was not always accompanied, or even preceded, by inclement weather in the town. In 1909 the water came with a rush on a bright Saturday afternoon.[10] Mrs Atkinson, in a recently completed cottage by the river, was caught completely off guard. She was in buoyant spirit with a wild duck roasting in the oven when a neighbour burst in to declare, "The river's rising!" Her first reaction was annoyance, but when the house suddenly subsided and a wall opened up, his forthrightness was seen in new light. Mrs Atkinson grabbed her two children. "She literally threw us out, like a dog," her daughter recalled. Moments later, it was the mother's turn to be manhandled. Local bank manager Edwin Angelo saw that the house in its entirety must soon slump into the river. But for his prompt action, Mrs Atkinson may not have survived to rebuild, or to describe the feeling in the pit of her stomach as her oven, her duck, and the wreckage of a new home sailed away.[11]

CARNARVON WAS VULNERABLE TO ASSAULT FROM THE INTERIOR, but rarely from the sea. Below the town's horizon lay two long, low islands that shielded the mainland coast from the long swells of the Indian Ocean. Although the two were named "Dorre Eylanden" (Barren Islands) by seventeenth-century Dutch navigators, only the southern island kept its Dutch label; the northern island was renamed "Bernier" by the French more than a century later. In 1908 the islands, with prolific wildlife but no history of human habitation, were chosen as sites for the establishment of isolation hospitals for the incarceration and treatment of Aborigines suffering from syphilis. Inevitably the 'lock hospitals' (as they came to be known) were places of great dislocation and despair; many patients never recovered sufficiently to leave. But some did: by January 1910, the first of the cured were ready to return to their homelands. As if to defend its handling of a difficult situation, the state government decided that the repatriations would take place in public view. The natives would travel not by chartered schooner but as cabin passengers aboard the elegant *Koombana*, accompanied by their much-loved island nurse Harriet "Missie" Lenehan, who wrote:

> Passionate devotion to the bush is the principal characteristic of the natives, and when official intimation came to Bernier Island that the first batch of certified cured cases were to return to their different countries, there was joy unbounded. New overalls had to be made, hats to be trimmed, and hair to be cut. I organised a monster wash, and on the day preceding the departure repaired to the well a mile distant with abundance of soap and scrubbing brushes. One can imagine what a scene they presented, as covered from head to foot with soap they kept singing and dancing, wild indeed with joy. . . . I wish to pay a deep debt of gratitude to Mrs. Batty, the cook on the island, who helped me with unselfish enthusiasm to make their outfits, trim their hats, and altogether entered into their joy. We were also under a heavy obligation to Mr. Smith, manager for Charles Moore and Co., and Mr. Pitchford, of the Bon Marche, who provided the many coloured ribbons to deck the native lassies' hair, hats, and necks.[12]

On the islands, the grim reality of isolation and treatment continued but aboard *Koombana*, steaming northward, life was good. Lenehan watched with pleasure as her girls in particular were fussed over by the other passengers, who "loaded them with dainties and tobacco in abundance."

ABOUT THIRTY MILES NORTH-WEST OF CARNARVON, beyond the protection of Bernier Island, *Koombana* would feel the strength of the open ocean. Altering course to north-north-east, she would then run with the wind and the sea for 200 miles to the North West Cape, keeping well clear of the low land and its seductive coral embroidery. As the ship rounded the Muiron Islands and steamed eastward across the top of the Exmouth Gulf, the sea change was remarkable. Vindex wrote:

> The Cape is a sort of sartorial changing station. We are now in the tropics beyond all doubt, and the regular traveller as soon as he sees the North-West Cape on the horizon hurries off to his cabin and re-appears in white linen or khaki. We are in the calmest of calm oceans, the sun shows delightfully "the myriad ripples of the laughing sea,"

and turtles which have their nests on the neighbouring islands, inquisitively raise their heads above water and disappear again. Long yellowish snakes writhe along the surface of the water, and perhaps a whale spouting in the distance adds to the interest and enjoyment of travel. We are now in the land of incessant sunshine, of warmth and colour, and glorious sunsets. Dusk comes on and the sun has sunk below the level surface of the sea. On the horizon the blue ocean is wedded to a sky of saffron and pink. Night closes in, and in the gathering gloom the dark islands arise out of the calm bed of the sea, and after being silhouetted for a while against the sky, drift by into the darkness. The steamer's smoke hangs indolently in the air, and all creation seems placidly lazy and careless.[13]

AT EVERY NOR'-WEST PORT, *Koombana*'s first arrival was much heralded. Onslow was no exception, but as the new steamer dropped anchor in Ashburton Roads the fate of the little town, at least in its present location, was sealed. Few doubted that the district had great potential. Under the *nom de plume* "Progress", one resident wrote:

> I would like to point out that this has been an exceptionally good season, but good or bad seasons should make little or no difference in this district, in as much as the Ashburton River is some 600 miles in length flowing through some of the finest agricultural, pastoral, and mining country in the world (in which there is about one person to every 1,000 square miles, instead of thousands of people).[14]

Onslow, however, had a problem to match its potential. The new, larger steamers could not approach the existing jetty, and the jetty was poorly situated for extension into deeper water. A lack of foresight was not unique to Onslow, as Vindex observed:

> It now seems as if the early settlers' first consideration was to find a creek into which they could run their boats. Having found a landing they proceeded inland till they got over the tidal marshes and there they started a store and a hotel—the nucleus of every settlement. In course of time they wanted their landing place made into a port, and a paternal Government, greatly daring, came along and started to build a jetty. They built chain after chain of piles and planking till at the end of half a mile or so they had reached deep water. Of course the jetties could not remain isolated, and the building of tramways over the marshes at heavy cost was inevitable. This one imagines to have been the history of all of these ports. The consequence is that when a boat puts into that port, all that greets the passenger is a high gaunt structure of heavy timber projecting from the low uninhabited sandhills far into the sea.[15]

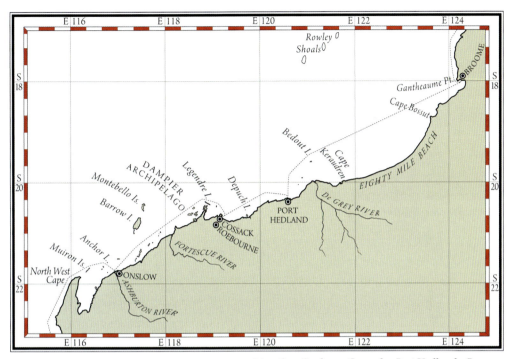

MAP 3 • *Onslow – Cossack – Port Hedland – Broome.*

While lauding the district and its potential, "Progress" lamented the situation at the port.

> On arrival at the anchorage a visitor has to pay four shillings to come ashore in the agent's cutter, another shilling for his tram fare, and 3d. for each package. Goods are brought to jetty by lighter, and frequently it takes hours to bring passengers from steamer to jetty—distance about one mile—owing to no wind.[16]

At ten shillings for a round trip into town, few among *Koombana*'s passengers ventured ashore. Vindex was an exception; he followed every tramline to its end. "It is the little retiring towns," he wrote, "that are worth pursuing to their hiding places behind the sandhills." Upon reaching Onslow he was surprised at how little he found: "It seems to comprise three stores and two hotels, and an altogether inadequate population to keep the five institutions going."[17] Along a wide, dusty divide were the complementary offerings of the Rob Roy Hotel and Peake's Temperance Hotel, a Mechanics' Institute hall that doubled as church and Sunday school, a post and telegraph office, the offices of the shipping agents, and a few houses.

On April 6th, 1909, a few days after *Koombana*'s first visit, a cyclone swept over Onslow from the sea, destroying the 'Institute' and stripping part of the roof from each of the hotels. From the pearling grounds came

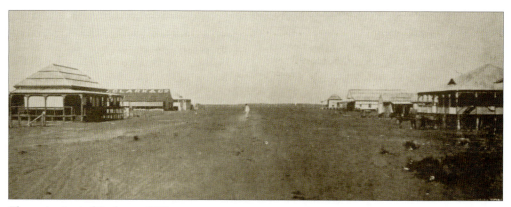

The main street of Onslow, c. 1910.

news far worse: four pearling boats, each with six Malay crewmen, had been lost. And at the port, the lighters upon which the town so depended were all ashore and damaged.[18] The storm was not the greatest, even of recent memory, but it was a harsh assault upon a town losing trade to its neighbours and whose future hung in the balance.

SOME BEGINNINGS ARE LOST IN TIME, others vaguely recalled, but the establishment of the first North-West Settlement may be pinpointed in time and place. In the journal of the barque *Tien Tsin*, on May 5th, 1863, Captain Jarman wrote:

> Coasting along under easy sail I saw from the royal yard a deep bay and tempting looking spot for landing, and the Mystery leading we rounded the north headland of the bay afterwards named the "Tien Tsin Harbor" by Mr. Hunt, and anchored in three fathoms at low water spring tide, about midway between Jarman Isle and Samson's Point . . . It is a fine little harbor and vessels drawing 13 feet can go in with safety and be perfectly sheltered from all winds except between N.E. and E.S.E.; small craft up to 7 feet by going into Butcher Inlet are completely land locked and can lie afloat at low water on that draught. At 2 p.m. Mr. Padbury and others landed, and I did so at 6 p.m. to meet him; there were several natives on the beach, and I do not remember having seen finer looking fellows in any part of the world. They bear much resemblance to the Maories about the north-west coast of New Zealand; I saw none among them under six feet in height, and they have fine muscular development with features not disfigured; they had no weapons, and carried Mr. Samson and myself out of the boat.[19]

Acting upon the glowing accounts of explorer F. T. Gregory, the enterprising Walter Padbury had gathered stock and equipment, chartered Captain Jarman's *Tien Tsin* and sailed north to establish a grazing settlement at Nickol Bay.[20] But just as Arthur Phillip of the First Fleet had found Sydney Cove preferable to the intended Botany Bay, Captain Jarman declared "Tien Tsin Harbor" greatly superior to the exposed mangrove forefront of Nickol Bay. And just as the first Australian penal colony would continue to be known as "Botany Bay," so would Tien Tsin be tagged "the Nickol Bay Settlement."

Relations between black and white would prove critical to the survival of the settlement. For a few years, pastoral operations teetered on the edge of failure, but the embattled graziers discovered that there was good money to be made by conscripting natives to dive for pearl shell. Indeed, grazing lived upon the proceeds of pearling until, under steady rain and management, it too became profitable.[21]

From the very first, the settlement was destined to be divided. At Tien Tsin no reliable source of fresh water was found. It was decided that the main settlement, later to be named Roebourne, would stand beside a deep permanent pool of the Harding River, some ten miles upstream.[22] The early success of pearling ensured that Tien Tsin remained as lively as the inland 'capital', but as its Asiatic population grew, some considered its name inappropriate. After Governor Weld visited aboard H.M.S. *Cossack* in 1871 the town was renamed "Cossack", in honour of Her Majesty and the visit of her colonial representative.

Cossack, 1898.

For the next ten years Cossack whistled and hummed. Glowing reports from the pearling grounds appeared regularly in *The West Australian*; some even found their way into the eastern dailies. But in March 1882, one such report unwittingly caught the turn of a great tide.

> NOTES FROM THE NOR'-WEST.
> 6th February, 1882.
> The *Ruby*, cutter, arrived at Cossack on the 28th ulto. Arrangements were at once made for her to return direct to Fremantle, as soon as she had discharged, touching en route at the Western pearling ground, somewhat to the Eastward of Exmouth Gulf. She accordingly took in a cargo of shells, and sailed for her destination on the night of the 31st ulto. The reason, why she was started so quickly was that favourable news had been received from the Eastern boats. Mr. M. Price came to Cossack in the *Water Lily* on the 24th ulto, with a cargo of shells from the Eastward, and reported that the five vessels in that direction, viz: the *Dawn*, *Amy*, *Harriet*, *Water Lily*, and the *Pearl* had all done well; the *Dawn* getting from 25 to 28 tons, the *Amy* 20 tons, the *Water Lily* 18 tons, the *Harriet* 13 tons, and the *Pearl* 5 tons. Another boat, the *Mystery*, came from the Eastward with only one ton, but she had not fallen in with the lucky craft. The exact spot is kept a secret, but it is generally believed to be in the neighbourhood of Roebuck Bay.[23]

This, it seems, was the first published reference to the pearling potential of Roebuck Bay. It marks the beginning of the gradual eastward migration of the industry, and the rise of Broome as its new headquarters.

For a time Cossack continued to grow. Post office, courthouse and customs house, all of stone, reflected the government's confidence in the settlement as the port for the mining and grazing province now called "West Pilbarra."[†] Visiting vessels continued to be well served. Luggers, schooners and even small steamers could tie up in the middle of the town at a stone wharf on the bank of a riverine inlet. By 1900, however, that convenience counted for little; the new, larger vessels of the coastal trade could not enter the inlet. Passengers and cargo, inbound or outbound, would have to be transferred by lighter. The government decided that a new jetty equipped for handling livestock should be built at Point Samson, a few miles to the west of Cossack, and that in time a new township there would replace both Cossack and Roebourne.

The first part of the plan was well executed; the second was not. When *Koombana* first arrived at Point Samson on April Fools' Day, 1909, she discharged to a jetty in the middle of nowhere. All passengers disembarking, whether for Roebourne or Cossack, faced a journey of several hours by horse-drawn tram.

---

† Spelling variations will be encountered. "Pilbarra" ultimately gave way to "Pilbara", and Point Samson was wrongly gazetted as "Point Sampson," the error being corrected years later.

The new jetty at Point Samson, c. 1907.

Most of the locals viewed the government's vision for Point Samson as nonsensical, but they saw value in the jetty. They argued successfully that the government should make sense of the money it had already spent by improving the tramway. Just a year later, *Koombana* arrived with special cargo. From her deck she delivered the first steam locomotive for the Roebourne-Samson tramway. She also brought Colonial Secretary Connolly and Chief Harbourmaster Irvine, to listen to the locals and to bathe, perchance, in the shining light of visible progress. Vindex came too; after a round of public meetings, he captured the mood of a town coming to terms with another far-reaching flourish of the premier's pen.

> As for the old capital, Roebourne is solid but not so actively prosperous as it used to be. It too has fine Government buildings and a model gaol, scrupulously kept, and it pins implicit faith to a resuscitation of mining. . . . Rightly or wrongly, Roebourne has never recovered from the fact of the Pilbarra railway being started from Port Hedland, and its people can scarcely possess themselves in patience until the failure of the Hedland route shall prove that Roebourne was the only possible starting point for the iron horse when it goes forth to conquer and transform the desert.[24]

From the government's perspective, the establishment of Point Samson was a rationalisation. The costly replication of government buildings and

Roebourne's first steam engine, June 1910.

services could not continue. But there was another agenda, selectively
discussed and privately pursued. The new town offered a fresh start: a
clean break from the cultural heritage of pearling. Point Samson, it was
hoped, would hasten the demise of Asian-dominated Cossack.

Having fulfilled a promise to the district, the government set about
encouraging the locals to relocate. But by bowing to local demands for
a better tram service it had undermined its own agenda. Thanks to the
cheeky little locomotive, the 'old capital' was now better connected to the
outside world than ever before. There was a further problem, not of the
government's making. Long-time residents had seen buildings torn apart
by storms of astonishing force. They refused to believe that the new jetty,
standing tall in open water, could withstand what nature would some day
hurl at it. Roebourne, they argued, had public buildings, services, hotels
and a sense of community, not to mention the best water in the district.
Samson was merely a jetty and a bold plan, and without that jetty it was
nothing. With tongue firmly in cheek, Vindex declared:

> For years people were equally divided as to the future of the jetty;
> some said it would be washed away in the first hurricane, others
> equally as stoutly maintained that the structure would last until the
> second hurricane smote it.[25]

When the first auction of Point Samson town lots took place in Roebourne,
scepticism ruled. Prices paid were low, and the lack of enthusiasm

delivered a supplementary slap in the face to the supporters of a White
Australia. In a letter to *The West Australian*, Cossack pearler James Ellery
noted wrily that one of the best lots had been "knocked down to a
Chinaman for £31."[26]

ON THE AFTERNOON OF SATURDAY, APRIL 3rd, 1909, *Koombana* arrived off Port
Hedland for the first time. A fine new jetty stood ready to receive her,
but entry was denied by the harbour's troublesome gatekeeper: an ever-
changing sandbar that could only be crossed safely on a high spring tide.
The future would have to wait until morning.

Koombana was grazed and bruised from her grounding in Shark Bay
but it would take more than a few scuff marks to dampen this town's
enthusiasm. Walter Barker, editor of *The Hedland Advocate*, wrote:

> Gratifying in the highest degree, to the pride of Nor'-Westers, was
> the announcement, on Sunday morning, that the s.s. Koombana was
> steaming up the entrance. Her supremacy (over other vessels visiting
> the port) in architectural model, equipment, and nautical appliances
> and conveniences had preceded her. A large number of Hedland
> residents forsook their usual Sunday diversions to witness the arrival
> of their hopes—a boat suitable for the Nor'-West passenger traffic and
> merchandise, and not one murmur of disappointment was heard; in
> fact, even those whose business interests would be expected to lead
> them to express an adverse opinion on the boat were heard to remark,
> "She will take some beating." In fact, the eulogies of the southern
> daily papers were thought to under-estimate the ship's worth from
> a Nor'-West point of view. The wildest dreams of residents in this
> climate, who contemplate a comfortable sea trip, are here realised:
> a luxuriously furnished bedroom, with every other conceivable
> comfort and convenience thrown in.[27]

Never was a newspaper more aptly named than *The Hedland Advocate*. Two
weeks earlier, as *Koombana* lay aground in Shark Bay, Barker had written:

> If the Koombana is to be expected to wriggle in and out among the
> numerous and ever shifting sand banks in Sharks Bay, the Govern-
> ment should do something to assist navigation at that place. The
> vessel is admirably designed to cater specifically for the needs of the
> Nor'-West, and it can hardly be fair that the populous centres should
> be penalised in order to serve the few at Sharks Bay. Much better for
> Sharks Bay to be cut off the list of calling places.[28]

In 1906, Port Hedland had been chosen as the starting point for the
principal railway to the goldfields of the interior. Three years later, as
construction began, visitors quickly came to suspect that this anointment
had gone to the young town's head. Vindex wrote:

S.S. Koombana *at Port Hedland, April 4th, 1909.*

Port Hedland, of course, thinks differently. Unlike the other northern ports, Port Hedland has pitched itself on the very edge of the water, and thus exposed seems to invite criticism of its bareness. Not a tree nor a shrub graces its streets, and deep though the harbour is at high tide, the receding of the waters discloses a most unimpressive stretch of sand and mangrove mud. The harbour may be good, but it is bare honesty to say that Port Hedland never reveals to the visitor those charms which the residents in their enthusiasm profess to see. Government expenditure however, is doing something to "make" the port, which is at present abnormally busy. The wharf accommodation has been doubled in recent years, and the cargoes of steamers calling there are swelled with rails and fastenings for the Marble Bar line. Hedland's expectations from that line are boundless, and it is to be hoped that they may prove to be well founded. In any case there is a hasty intolerance shown toward the doubter and the person who doesn't see Hedland through Hedland's spectacles.[29]

Port Hedland seemed eager to recommend itself as a proud outpost of White Australia, in sharp contrast to the oriental mish-mash of its northern neighbour Broome. A fortnight or so before *Koombana*'s first arrival, the *Advocate* had reported:

Port Hedland, c. 1908.

Two Afghans left Hedland for Singapore on Saturday by the Charon. By the same boat three Chinamen left for Broome, the latter forming part of a large contingent of loafing Celestials in Hedland who have been notified by the Hedland police that they must leave. It is pleasing to note that the local police are taking a commendable course, and the Broome "Chronicle" will have the pleasure, if it wishes, of chronicling a Broome welcome to many more Celestials of the same kidney as the two now enjoying the freedom given them in Broome.[30]

For three months the newspaper had been publishing searing editorials on what it termed "The Alien Influx." The first appeared on December 12th, 1908, as *Koombana* was completing her sea trials off Glasgow.

In many towns in the northern part of Australia the keen competition set going by the colored men (whose devious ways enable them to obtain goods without paying duty, and whose mode of living is far below the white man's standard,) has reached a point at which Australians whose patriotism means more to them than pelf, should stop and ponder—where is this going to end? . . . Not all the whites who have to live in places like Port Darwin, Wyndham, Broome or Hedland are color-serving, crawlsome creatures, who care nothing for the future of our young nation. There are many who would hail with delight Federal legislation which would put down this unfair competition and keep out all of the colored and inferior races.[31]

As far as can be told, Barker's weekly rants had little impact upon the newspaper's business clientele or readership. Hedland's Chinese shop-keepers continued to place their advertisements, and one enterprising Afghan soon called for expressions of a different interest:

> Challenge.
> I, Abdul Kader, will wrestle any man in the Nor'-West,
> Cumberland style, catch-as-catch-can, or Afghan style,
> for any sum of money from £10 up to £50.
> I want a fair go, and don't want any crook business.
> My reputation is good and I intend to keep it so.
> If you want me before Christmas, Nullargine is my address.
> ABDUL KADER.[32]

In the light of its anti-Asian virulence, the *Advocate*'s sympathy for the Australian Aborigine was striking.

> We have never been advocates of native labor, and do not agree with the excessive punishment meted out to natives who kill cattle, and yes, to others who are alleged to kill cattle. We are certain that if the Supreme Court were appealed to in 9 cases out of 10 where natives are convicted they would be acquitted.[33]

Social justice notwithstanding, the betterment of Port Hedland was never far from Walter Barker's mind. His editorial continued:

> On board the Bullarra, we saw 42 strong, able-bodied natives, chained with strong, trace-sized chains in gangs of 3 to 9 each, being taken to the already overcrowded gaol at Roebourne, and, we are informed, upwards of 100 more to follow. Even the most rabid socialist will agree that if natives are to be kept (some doing work and others exercise only) at Broome and Roebourne, Hedland is entitled to some of that labor.

The Pilbara railway was a boon not only for the ebullient town but also for the shipping companies. For two years, in all seasons, *Koombana* would carry sleepers, rails and equipment. The locomotives, too, would be delivered from her decks. While other cargo was seasonal, and mostly southbound, mail and rail would keep the run profitable. One English visitor wondered where all of this cargo could possibly be going. He approached a local leaning against a verandah post at the Esplanade Hotel. "Excuse me, sir," he asked, "can you tell me what's in the hinterland?" The local looked the tourist up and down, thought for a few seconds and replied: "Miles and miles of bugger all."[34]

THE HISTORY OF THE NOR'-WEST is a chronicle of changing fortune. Ten years before *Koombana*'s first arrival in Port Hedland, the town did not exist. Fifty miles to the north-east, the little port of Condon was the hub of a new cattle district and seemed assured of a bright future. Indeed, had Condon looked down upon a deep blue sea, her future might have been bright. But she did not; she stared across the vast, varicose tidal maze of the Amphinome Shoals. For the new steamers the shoals were not navigable; *Koombana* and her kind would take the "outside track" around Bedout Island and avoid the area altogether. And because the inside track was now off limits, the heavy instruments of Condon's demise would never venture near enough to witness it.

A long jetty had been planned but was never built. Here, as elsewhere, deep water was a long way off. And here, as elsewhere, locals knew from bitter experience that the wind respected neither edifice nor institution. Some also argued that Condon's twenty-foot tidal range and hard, flat seabed made a jetty unnecessary. Steamers of a thousand tons could creep in on a high spring tide, drop anchor and wait for the sea to retire. At low tide, stock could be walked and vehicles driven directly to the vessel's side.

For a time the cattle steamers kept coming, meeting teamsters and townsfolk on ground borrowed from the sea, but this unique intertidal handshake merely delayed the inevitable. In December 1911, *The Hedland Advocate* would record Condon's arrival at a point of no return.

S.S. Minilya *at Condon, c. 1905.*

Old residents of Pilbarra have had their minds thrown back through the vista of years by one happening at Monday's Licensing Court— there was no application for a renewal of the solitary wayside house license at Condon. At one time Condon boasted of the best-stocked stores in the Nor'-West, when fully licensed and unlicensed hotels did a roaring trade, steamers called, a large number of teamsters plied between the port and the inland fields, and quantities of wool annually left there. The place was so flourishing that in Sir John Forrest's halcyon days a large sum of money was voted and plans prepared for building a huge jetty, but (tell it not in Gath!) the residents petitioned against it. Port Hedland was opened up, to Condon's ruination—it will not now support a sly-grog shop. Vale Condon![35]

Koombana's detour around Bedout Island cost a little in coal but nothing in time, because both her departure from Hedland and her arrival in Broome required a high tide. It was a leisurely passage of 24 hours, by the grace of the moon. Vindex wrote:

> On a sea continuously calm, the ship glides on northward, passing Bedout Island, on which the new lighthouse shows prominently, and 24 hours after leaving Hedland has slipped into Roebuck Bay, while the tide is favourable, and tied up to a typical Nor'-West jetty. The ship, drawing 18ft. of water, is riding buoyantly as the discharge of cargo commences, yet six hours later passengers are walking round the boat and snapshotting her as she squats on the firm sand of the ocean bed. Every resident who comes down to meet the ship is in spotless white suit, and beyond in the bay coloured men are sitting on the decks of luggers and eating their midday meal. We are now at the show-place of the North-West, and the trip has been a breach of confidence if the stay of the boat does not allow of a run into town by the inevitable tramway, and an inspection of the semi-oriental settlement. But of Broome and its pearls more anon. Suffice it that at this point we are within three or four days of Java, and that the intervening sea scarcely shuts out the atmosphere and colour of the purpling East.[36]

Like Vindex, Jim Low was intrigued by Broome. To Peggy he wrote:

> I like this coast very well, or rather the section that we saw. The scenery isn't much to boast of principally sand hills and small scrub and the various towns we touch at are somewhat primitive nearly all the buildings are of corrugated iron. Broome is the best of the lot there are some trees there, it is the big centre for the pearling industry of the Nor-West and there is a big fleet of pearling luggers there inhabited by a most cosmopolitan crowd. The smell of the pearl oysters isn't so bad there as they open them at sea coming into port for the weekends. It

S.S. Bullarra high and dry at Broome, c. 1908.

is principally the shell they dive for. They don't get so many pearls on the local banks but the shell is worth £150 to £200 a ton. A good deal of our cargo along the coast is shell, done up in cases and bags, for the home markets.[37]

On her second Nor'-West run *Koombana* carried Premier Newton Moore, who came to the Nor'-West to see the ports for himself and to receive the pleas and petitions of the residents. Moore's presence delivered a practical benefit to the crew: the schedule was relaxed a little to give the premier time to complete business and to attend events organised in his honour. At Broome, Jim took some time off and caught the tram into town. He later told Peggy:

A couple of us went ashore for a quick look around there one Sunday and met the Mayor in his shirt sleeves, drunk as an owl, insisted on doing the honours and showing us all the sights. We had a tremendous job to shake him. In the end he had to see the Premier a couple of hours afterwards and make a speech. I would like to have heard that speech.[38]

In 1909 and 1910 Broome was at the peak of its prosperity. There was money to be made and every opportunity to spend it. Ships from north and south brought luxuries from afar: fine foods, whisky and champagne,

Landing pearl shell, Broome, c. 1909.

cigars, silk, porcelain, furniture. Tropical fruit from Singapore sat beside grapes and peaches from the vineyards and orchards of the South-West. Japanese merchants imported from Japan for Japanese customers. Travelling salesmen called regularly and all local businesses, including the gambling dens and brothels, seemed to be thriving. The condition of the town made a lasting impression on Jim Low. A young engineer, he thought, could do very nicely here. Harriet Lenehan was also impressed; indeed, she could find no fault.

> Prosperity seemed to suffuse the very air, and everyone was in good spirits. Even the great gangs of chained natives who passed me on the road seemed to be in gleeful mood. It is true that these chains are very little of a burthen, a fact to which I can bear personal witness, as the superintendent of Carnarvon Gaol kindly let me try them on. I bade good-bye to Broome—lovely, prosperous Broome—with regret.[39]

FROM COSSACK TO PORT HEDLAND TO BROOME, *Koombana*'s passengers had noted the ever-increasing rise and fall of the tide, but only those continuing north to Derby would witness its most spectacular manifestation. South-east of Cape Leveque, a chain of islands blocked the entrance to King Sound. Derby-bound steamers could detour around the islands and enter though the Sunday Strait, or negotiate one of the narrow channels separating the islands.

The Adelaide Steamship Company's preference was for the narrow, fast-flowing Escape Pass.[40] This was not reckless cost-cutting; it was a balancing of risk. Although the pass required skilful navigation, the shorter travel time allowed the ship's master some flexibility. He could choose his moment. The steamer would enter the Pass on the first of the incoming tide and clear to open water before the maelstrom of "full flood," when the current might reach ten knots and the sea rise two inches in a minute. Vindex wrote:

> The ship is entering on a flowing tide, which at "high springs" rises and falls a maximum of 40ft., and the sea is like a vast mountain torrent as it rushes and swirls through the islands and over the reefs. You may see it on the weather side of a rock 3ft. higher than on the lee side, and it is a giddy sight to watch the boiling of the waters on all directions, as the immense volume of the tide rushes over the submerged obstacles.[41]

Having gained the relative calm of the sound, a gentle four-hour run would bring the steamer to Point Torment, sixteen miles from the Derby pier. The ship would drop anchor here, to wait for the high tide needed to complete the journey. Derby boy Tom Ronan would later write:

> There was no radio, of course, to inform of exact time of arrival, but the blacks up the Gulf at Point Torment would light fires when they

MAP 4 • *The entrances to King Sound.*

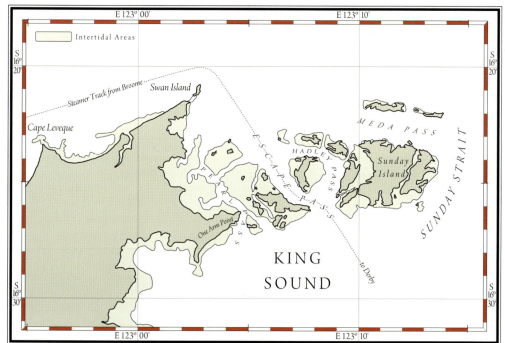

saw a ship in the offing, someone in town would notice the smoke and inform the necessary authorities. The doctor would be told, and the shipping agent; the wharfinger, and the police corporal, who was also customs officer.[42]

As *Koombana* slid through the last few miles and came alongside the pier at high tide, the scene failed to impress. There was no town to be seen, just a long jetty across what to Jim Low looked like "somebody's orchard flooded."[43] Within a few hours even this picturesque image would escape, as if down some unseen plughole. "When the steamer tied up," Vindex wrote, "the jetty was almost awash, but now the eye rests upon as ugly a picture of mud and mangrove as the imagination ever conceived."[44]

On *Koombana*'s first arrival Jim Low was struck by the keenness of the locals to come aboard. To Peggy he wrote:

At the various ports nearly everyone turns out to greet us. The droughts all line up for a cool drink while the ladies get shown round uttering incoherent ejaculations as each fresh marvel is displayed, potatoes peeled by electricity, dough mixing by electricity, knife cleaners, grub hoists, the automatic egg boilers where you set a little pointer to the number of minutes, and punctually to the second the egg is hoisted out of the water, till at the end they gasp like fish out of water.[45]

Derby Jetty, c. 1909.

The main street of Derby, 1913.

Was it the boiled eggs or the young ladies left gasping? No matter! Mood and moment are captured in a wonderful letter from the young adventurer to the girl he would marry.

For Harriet Lenehan it was not mud and mangrove that made her first visit to Derby memorable. The schooner *Namban* had brought the news that native patients coming home from the islands would arrive by *Koombana*. Word had spread quickly. The jetty "swarmed with blacks," she wrote, "sons were there to meet mothers, lovers to meet their old sweethearts, and sisters to meet sisters or brothers."[46]

Derby was always keen to present itself to visitors. Whenever the length of a ship's stay permitted, passengers and crew were encouraged to travel into town. Vindex was pleasantly surprised by what he found at the end of this tramline.

> The jetty and the marsh lead one to expect the worst, but instead here is a pretty little settlement whose one long street is filled with native trees. Trees and vegetation are on all sides, and in the private gardens one sees such exotics as cocoanut and date palms. But the most interesting of all vegetable adornments is the stately baobab tree, with its umbrageous branches, and butt of immense girth, tapering into a narrow neck until it bears resemblance to a giant ale bottle. The large nuts which the tree bears are fancifully carved by the natives, and sought after by curio-hunters. Truly there are worse places on the coast than Derby, the capital of West Kimberley.[47]

Once it was known that Vindex was recording his impressions of the Nor'-West, and that his impressions would find their way into the pages of *The West Australian*, the citizens of Derby made sure that this visitor was well looked after, and well briefed on the district and its fertility. A few weeks later, their targeted kindness was repaid.

> The gold rush to the Kimberleys in the eighties gave Derby its first lift, but now its dependence is on grazing, solely. Magnificent cattle

stations are in the back country which the port serves, and thousands of head of stock are shipped here annually. The town has the best domestic water supply on the coast, and the soil, it is generally agreed, will grow anything with water and the approval of His Majesty The White Ant. The country at the back grows cattle faster than the consumer wants them, and the pastoralists are now considering a proposal to establish canning works at Derby to treat the surplus stock.[48]

Harder times lay ahead. The people of Derby had learned to live with heat, white ants and crocodiles but, like their counterparts in Wyndham, would soon recognise the mosquito as the single greatest threat to their health and happiness.

KOOMBANA FIRST CALLED AT DERBY in April 1909 but the residents of Wyndham, 500 miles further north and east, would wait another six months for a glimpse of the new ship. The final outpost was in an unusual situation: being closer to Singapore than to Fremantle, it received most of what it needed from the north. But as summer approached and the demand for southward passage increased, *Koombana* came to town.

For Harriet Lenehan, the voyage to Wyndham was entrancing.

> Time after time we passed through narrow straits into a splendid expanse of sea, which narrowed again to a channel hardly wide enough, it seemed, to permit of the vessel's passage. After passing this labyrinth of islets and rocks, the lovely scenery continued, but with wider spaces of open sea, so beautifully clear and calm that it seemed as if one could walk over it to the rocks.[49]

Of the town she wrote:

> The surroundings of this capital of the Furthest North looked very striking and picturesque, towering hills sheltering the little town, which nestles at the foot of one of these eminences. The township is only a small one—just a few houses, a store or two, an hotel, a post office, and a gaol—but like all the North-West, full, apparently, of an abounding prosperity. Doubtless, in the days to come this part of Western Australia will carry its teeming thousands, but to-day it is the great lone land, awaiting the touch of the enchanter's wand to awaken it to its destiny.[50]

Wyndham owed its "abounding prosperity" to two products of a great savanna grassland: beef and wool. Sheep and cattle had come to the Kimberley in the 'eighties, but from opposite directions. The first sheep were landed at Derby; the first cattle were pushed overland across the top of Australia in a droving enterprise of singular resolve and audacity.

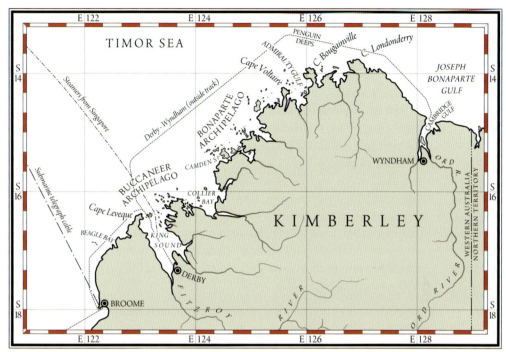

MAP 5 • *Broome – Derby – Wyndham.*

Thirty years on, the pioneering families still dominated the industry.[51] The Kimberley, said Doug Moore of Ord River Station, was all "Sacks, blacks and Duracks."[52]

The pastoral leases were vast and unfenced. Noonkanbah and Liveringa each ran about 100,000 sheep on a million acres. There was no possibility of shearing such a flock using local labour, black or white, but the seasonal rhythm was fortuitous. Southerners could leave their properties at a quiet time, catch a steamer to Derby or Wyndham and support their own ventures by shearing for the magnates of the far north.

With its money-makers so widely scattered, the town of Wyndham would never match Broome for vibrancy, but its night air had a hum no less remarkable. To the light of every candle or lamp came a great jamboree of winged creatures; evening verandahs were shared with moths, resplendent beetles and even tiny bats. And after rain, flying ants in great swarms would alight upon anything and anyone, to crawl, skip and trip over one another, as if for the sole purpose of discarding their wings.

Balmy nights notwithstanding, station life in the remotest of locations was not for the faint-hearted. Doug Moore recalled:

> The year 1911 was a very bad one for sickness. Malarial fever and Blackwater fever—the white men were all down to it and we lost 20

natives. Quinine we had plenty of, McKenzie's fever mixture and we would mix up Gulf mixture—a recipe given us by Mrs. McAuley of the Stud Station. My mother became very sick—hot and feverish—and it was a great shock to my sister and I to see her slowly failing. Both of the rivers were running, and we sent a boy who swam the river and walked 90 miles to the post office at Turkey Creek with wires to the Doctor asking for instructions and what to give her. By the time the boy returned it was too late; my mother had died.

Never in my life have I seen men more helpful and sympathetic. The blacksmith and carpenter made a wonderful coffin out of the side boards of a new wagon, lined it with pure calico and all these men showed out in their true colours and deserve far more credit and thanks for their kindness to people in trouble than I could give and to white women they could never do enough for. They will always have my thanks and both my sister and I will never be able to thank these stockmen enough.[53]

Of desire or necessity, the locals travelled south for relief from the fierce summer heat. Vindex wrote:

The squatter who deals in the golden fleece, migrates with the seasons as regularly as the swallow. In November and December, when the ardour of the sun begins to get oppressive he comes southward, and here he remains till the summer's heat is past. Then, when Nature is throwing a mantle of green over the plains, when the flies have gone

Wyndham Jetty, c. 1910.

into retirement and the mosquitoes are at rest, when the north is said by northerners to be the mildest and balmiest in the world, when the flocks are being mustered and the garnering of the wool commences, the wealthy squatter goes north again to the land that pays him well.[54]

As surely as life was tied to the seasons, it was shaped by the comings and goings of the steamers. In a late-summer letter to his mother, station manager Roy Phillips wrote:

> Everything in the doldrums the last few weeks but people are all coming in for the Koombana now . . . Patsy Durack and his wife arrived last night and Lillas will leave for South on Saturday. She has the same affliction as assails most newlyweds and Patsy will be buying fizz to celebrate in a month or so. Her sister, Nellie, came in with them and is to marry Jack Martin, Manager of Ascot, on the day the boat sails.[55]

When *Koombana* cast off from Wyndham jetty on February 16th, 1910, "Missie" Lenehan's work was done. She later wrote:

> As the last of my dusky charges filed off at Wyndham, each one carrying his or her government blanket, the girls resplendent in new gowns and bright ribbons, I said good-bye for ever to those whom I had watched and cared for for two years. Though to anyone taking up such work, the daily round is a dangerous and disagreeable one, yet I found that there were many bright points in the life of a savage, many fine qualities in the character of the Western Australian aboriginal. And when at last the Koombana steamed out from Wyndham on her return voyage south, and the last little band of my black girls waved me a last good-bye, and danced me a farewell dance, I felt, appalling as had been the work and the life, that I was well repaid by the affection of my blackfellow exiles.[56]

After two eventful Nor'-West trips, Jim Low also travelled south in high spirits, confident that his work on this coast would be challenging and interesting. The settlements, it seemed, were as different each to the other as to the world from which they stood apart. *Koombana*'s arrivals would be keenly anticipated; he and his shipmates would be welcomed everywhere, as honoured guests or simply as friends. He had also found a town which appealed to him greatly, and in which he might one day settle.

For Vindex the southward journey was an opportunity to enjoy all that *Koombana* had to offer. His political reporting done, he could now write subjectively of all he had seen. He would gather his thoughts and confide to his readers that he too had been swayed by the rhythm of the north.

4

OF FEAR AND FASCINATION

IT ALL SEEMED DECIDEDLY ODD. How was it that the experienced Captain John Rees, on his first approach to Denham in the new *Koombana*, had mistaken a black buoy for a red one, missed the navigation channel altogether, and driven the ship under full power onto a mound of sand? The oddity did not end there; the ship had struck at high tide, a day or two after 'springs'. All hope of early release had simply ebbed away.

Everywhere, the Shark Bay incident was discussed, but before anyone could explain the grand alignment, the newcomer was in trouble again. The word was about that *Koombana*, on her second trip north, had struck a rock off Gantheaume Point.

ON THE NIGHT OF APRIL 28TH, 1909, *Koombana* left Broome for the terminus port of Derby. Captain Rees, as master of *Bullarra*, had taken this track many times, but this was his first attempt to steer *Koombana* around Gantheaume Point in darkness. Less than two hours into the journey, and within a mile of the Gantheaume Point lighthouse, he struck something. The ship rode up, slewed sideways and then slid free. Rees figured that he must have hit an uncharted pinnacle of rock or coral. And because the impact had only been felt amidships, and not at the stern where the ship's draft was greatest, he thought it likely that the top of the pinnacle had been sheared off. After establishing that the ship was not taking water, he decided to continue to Derby rather than re-enter Broome on the next day's tide.[1]

By a combination of design and circumstance it was impossible to assess the damage immediately. *Koombana*, like all steamers on the Nor'-West run, had a flat double bottom. Even a gash in the outer skin would not be obvious while the bottom ballast tanks were pressed up with seawater. At either Broome or Derby the hull could be examined while the ship lay hard aground at low tide, but even that uncommon opportunity had its limitation. Damage at the chine would be plainly visible but any injury nearer the keel would remain hidden.[2]

One thing was certain: news of this latest incident would not long be contained. In a sense, the Adelaide Steamship Company was the victim of its own success. *Koombana*'s navigational debut had been inglorious, but her social debut had been spectacular. At every Nor'-West jetty, townsfolk flocked to the ship to mingle with passengers in what was, without doubt, the classiest saloon in town. Mesmerised by iced drinks, electric light, polished walnut and purple plush, visitors drank and talked freely, accepting shipboard gossip as keenly as news from north or south. All details of the Shark Bay grounding were common knowledge from Fremantle to Derby; Rees had little doubt that this debacle would be enjoyed in the same way.

On May 4th, a private telegram received in Fremantle gave rise to a rumour that *Koombana* had struck a rock and was taking water. The story grew in stature by the hour; indeed, some early-afternoon incarnations declared the ship a total wreck. At that point, the Adelaide Steamship Company's local manager William Moxon contacted the press. He wished to assure the public that the incident had been a minor one. Yes, he conceded, *Koombana* had touched something near Broome, but little or no damage had been sustained. When the ship returned to Fremantle, a diver would be sent down to inspect and report.[3]

Koombana's second Nor'-West run was completed without further incident. At Fremantle on May 10th, fourth engineer Jim Low took advantage of a little free time to finish a long letter to his friend Peggy back home. Of *Koombana* and her recent 'touches' he wrote:

> We have been very unfortunate these two trips, first in Shark's Bay we ran on a sandbank at full speed and stuck there for over a fortnight, had to send down to Fremantle for a ship to help us off it was a long hard job. Then this last trip shortly after leaving Broome we struck a reef, at full speed again and bumped clear over it knocking at least one hole in the bottom, of course we are built with a double bottom which was the only thing that saved us from going right under. I was on watch at the time and the third time she struck it was right under the engine room nearly stopping the engines up dead then the stern lifted up and she raced off and lay over on her side, I thought it was all up with her but she righted up again. There has been a diver down today to find out the damage but we don't know yet how serious it is. If he can't fix it off we will have to go round to Melbourne or Sydney to dry dock.[4]

Next day, before posting his letter, Jim added a few lines:

> The diver reports no serious damage to the bottom so we leave tomorrow for the run up again. The diver may be right. You'll notice we don't get much time in port.

On Wednesday, May 12th, 1909, *Koombana* commenced her third Nor'-West run. Before she returned to Fremantle she would have two more incidents to add to a fast-growing scrapbook. Both occurred at the port of Geraldton, and each was revealing in its own way.

Koombana was by far the biggest ship that would visit Geraldton regularly. The harbourmaster decided that whenever possible she would be directed to the more frequently used western berth, where the constant scour of propeller wash kept the water a little deeper than on the other side. But when *Koombana* arrived on May 13th, the steamer *Largo Law* was occupying the western berth. The plan was changed. No problem was anticipated, however; *Koombana* was drawing 19 feet and even on the shallow side the gauges indicated 21 feet. To Captain Rees's annoyance, the gauges were wrong. After an hour of scraping the seabed, *Koombana* was still eight feet from the wharf and defying all attempts to bring her nearer. After further consultation it was decided to accept the situation. A slow, difficult unloading was completed across the gap.[5]

When *Koombana* southbound returned to Geraldton on June 2nd, she immediately ran into strife again. The western berth was free this time—the harbourmaster had made sure of it—but a hard easterly wind was blowing and Captain Rees found it impossible to keep the ship close and parallel while lines were thrown. A smaller vessel might have managed, but *Koombana*'s height above the waterline made her extremely susceptible to crosswind. After breaking two steel hawsers, Rees gave up. He accepted the shallow east-side berth as the lesser of two evils.[6]

ON JUNE 4TH, 1909, when Perth's *Daily News* received the Adelaide Steamship Company's advertisements, the copy included a late change to the schedule. *Koombana*, it appeared, would depart for Sydney in a couple of days. In her absence, the Huddart-Parker liner *Burrumbeet* would take up the Nor'-West running. In its evening edition, the newspaper admitted that it had been unsuccessful in its efforts to ascertain the reason. *Koombana*'s officers had been reluctant to answer questions, and manager William Moxon was out of town and unavailable for comment.[7] The truth was that *Koombana*, on her third Nor'-West run, had been inspected again as she sat on the mud at Broome. Some strained rivets and a broken cement seal were visible, and a leaking ballast tank suggested other, hidden damage. It was decided that after returning south, she would go east for repair.

In the days before his departure for Sydney, Captain Rees was informed that he would make two appearances before the Court of Marine Inquiry. An inquiry into the Shark Bay grounding would be held immediately, and a similar inquiry into the Gantheaume Point incident would convene upon his return from Sydney, when the full extent of damage to the ship would be known. Thus it happened that just two days after the crosswind fiasco at Geraldton, John Rees came to the Fremantle Court to relive the fortnight spent on an isolated mound of sand in Shark Bay, and to defend his right to remain in command.

A case of negligence could easily have been prosecuted, but Rees was saved by the fact that although the loss to the company had been significant, there was no serious damage to the ship itself. Although he was criticised for insufficient caution in hazy conditions, he received no fine or suspension. "Considering the past good record of the master," declared Chief Harbourmaster Charles Irvine, "and the fact that the vessel did not sustain any injury, I recommend that no further action be taken."[8]

With one inquiry behind him, Rees took *Koombana* east to Sydney. The damage to the hull, as Jim Low and others had suspected, was much more than a few popped rivets. Dry-docking revealed a seventy-foot gouge in the bottom of the hull, with a split a few feet long at the keel. The repair took twenty days. Thirteen plates were removed and replaced, and a six-foot steel strap was used to reinforce the keelson.[9]

Koombana arrived back in Fremantle on August 5th. The next day, John Rees was back in court. Although the Gantheaume Point incident had resulted in a much smaller loss to the company than the Shark Bay grounding, Rees's personal situation was more difficult. He needed to explain how an uncharted rock, which was less than a mile from the lighthouse and which must have been visible or at least awash on a low spring tide, was only discovered when *Koombana* ran into it. An alternative explanation, presented by Chief Harbourmaster Irvine, was that the rock was not new at all. Irvine hypothesised that Rees, due to laxity in navigation, had been a quarter-mile off his intended track and had struck a well-known danger.

Somehow, against the odds, John Rees emerged with his master's ticket intact. If there had been injury or loss of life, or a loss incurred by another shipping line, the result must surely have been different. But in this case, as in the last, Rees's error had been costly only to his employer. The court found misadventure rather than negligence.[10]

In the court of public opinion, *Koombana* did not fare so well. Since her Western Australian debut in March, she had been involved in four incidents, two major and two minor, and had been the subject of two formal inquiries. The superstitious declared her ill-fated; the pragmatic wondered if she was simply ill-suited to the work. Whichever the rationale, 'unlucky *Koombana*' was now a matter of newspaper fact.[11]

Although the judgment was harsh, there was a sense in which *Koombana* was certainly ill-fated. Her misfortune was to look very similar to a steamship whose disappearance would preoccupy the nation for almost two years.

ON JULY 1ST, 1909, THE BLUE ANCHOR LINER WARATAH, with 300 passengers and with Captain Joshua Ilbery in command, left Port Adelaide on her second voyage to the old country. At 6.30 a.m. on July 27th, after leaving Durban the previous evening, *Waratah* passed the steamer *Clan McIntyre*. Without the benefit of 'wireless', greetings were exchanged using signal lamps.

> Clan McIntyre: "What ship are you?"
> Waratah: "The Waratah, for London."
> Clan McIntyre: "I am the Clan McIntyre for London.
> What weather had you from Australia?"
> Waratah: "Strong south-west and southerly winds across."
> Clan McIntyre: "Thanks, good-bye, a pleasant voyage."
> Waratah: "Thanks, the same to you, good-bye."[12]

This casual, cordial exchange, entirely without portent, was the last coherent message ever received from the *Waratah*. Across the day and into the evening, the weather deteriorated rapidly. *Clan McIntyre* encountered fifty-knot winds and thirty-foot waves; Captain Weir was probably too busy to wonder how *Waratah* was faring. At about 10 p.m., the Union-Castle liner *Guelph*, south of Cape Hermes, sighted a steamer and signalled. There was a reply, but the visibility was poor and most of the flashes were lost behind the crests of a rising sea. Only the last three letters of the vessel's name were caught: "-t-a-h." So began one of the great mysteries of the sea.[13]

Waratah and *Koombana* were Clydebank cousins. *Waratah* had been launched by Barclay Curle & Company on September 13th, 1908, as *Koombana* was nearing completion at Alexander Stephen & Sons, at Linthouse directly opposite.[14] *Waratah*, intended for transoceanic service, was a much larger ship: a twin-screw steamer of almost 10,000 tons. Although differently targeted, *Koombana* and *Waratah* were both designed for asymmetrical runs. *Waratah* was specially configured for the strong and growing emigrant trade, with cargo holds that could be converted to large-scale dormitory accommodation for outbound voyages, and then reorganised for the carriage of Australian produce on the trip home.[15] *Koombana* was built to carry people and machinery north, and to bring wool and cattle south. On the shoulders of the seasons she would carry many more passengers, southward when the heat became oppressive, and northward to the lands of profit at summer's end.

In shape and design philosophy, *Waratah* and *Koombana* were very similar indeed. Each was ultra-modern, by the standards of its intended trade, and each reflected the new emphasis on passenger comfort and experience. Significantly, both ships were higher than their predecessors; they offered spacious saloon cabins or staterooms on upper decks. Indeed, *Waratah*'s owners advertised: "No first saloon cabins are situated

Koombana *(above) and* Waratah *(below); comparisons were inevitable.*

lower than the bridge deck, so that passengers will be able at practically all times to leave their cabin ports open."[16] Once newspapers had printed photographs of the missing *Waratah*, comparisons were inevitable.

ACCOUNTS OF STORMS were often many weeks in delivery. The steamer *Marere* had left London on June 30th, 1909; she reached Melbourne on August 13th. Interviewed on the day of his arrival, Captain Firth reported that this latest run from the Cape of Good Hope was one of the worst experiences of his seagoing life. He had rounded the Cape on July 22nd, four days before *Waratah* left Durban. *Marere* had then encountered south-westerly gales that persisted until the 28th, when the ship was hit by a terrible storm from the east-north-east. Mountainous seas swept the decks, breaking deck fittings and carrying away one of the lifeboats. There was nothing to be done, Firth said, but to 'heave to'; for the next twelve hours, the ship drove into what he described as "hurricane squalls of snow and hail."[17]

Captain Firth understood that the preoccupation of his interviewer, and the public at large, was not with *Marere*. Regarding *Waratah*, he was as much in the dark as others, but it was too early, he said, to dismiss the presumption that the missing ship had merely broken down. Not all commentators agreed. The misgivings of former *Waratah* passengers had already come to light. The ship had a very long roll, they said; she took a very long time to return upright. Moreover, on her first Indian Ocean crossing, she had carried a persistent list.

Beside the idle speculators were a few well qualified to voice concern. Professor William Bragg, who could claim both membership of the Royal Society and some knowledge of ship stability, had travelled with *Waratah* on her maiden voyage. He had concluded that the ship's "metacentre" was just below her centre of gravity. When slowly rolled over towards one side, he argued, she would reach a point of equilibrium, and stay leaning over until sea or wind pushed her upright.[18] With less erudition but equal persuasiveness, other passengers confirmed that there had been times when the ship was over at such an angle that water would not drain from the bathtubs.

In the wake of any disaster, there will be those who recast hindsight as perceptiveness or premonition. Aboard *Waratah* for her second voyage was one who could not be accused of that particular self-deception. Experienced sea traveller Claude Sawyer had booked through to Plymouth, but as *Waratah* crossed the Indian Ocean he was so troubled by the ship's behaviour that he disembarked at the first opportunity. To his wife in London, he sent a short telegram: "Thought Waratah Top Heavy. Landed Durban."[19]

For a time, the metropolitan dailies did not canvass the awful possibility—indeed the likelihood—that *Waratah* had capsized. But the harmony of mistrust could not be ignored indefinitely. In its long report on August 10th, 1909, *The Sydney Morning Herald* quietly declared:

> Our cablegrams yesterday tended, perhaps, to diminish hope, since it was reported that 300 tons of coal had been shipped at Durban and placed upon the bridge deck.[20]

Within days of *Waratah*'s disappearance, the Royal Navy cruisers *Pandora* and *Forte* were sent in search. A third, H.M.S. *Hermes*, would follow. For three weeks, in weather consistently foul, the navy vessels ranged south and east from Durban. Nothing was seen. The discovery of wreckage would have ended the suspense, but the ocean did not oblige.[21]

From barren ground came a single bloom of optimism. On Monday, August 9th, the agents of the Blue Anchor Line at Durban received the following telegram:

> East London Signal Station. Monday. Blue Anchor vessel sighted a considerable distance out, slowly making for Durban, where she will probably arrive Tuesday.[22]

Waratah's Durban agents enthusiastically conveyed the news to their Melbourne counterparts, John Sanderson & Company. Their cable read:

> Blue Anchor vessel sighted a considerable distance out. Slowly making for Durban. Could be the Waratah.[23]

Sanderson's were delighted. They released a statement:

> Blue Anchor Line.—Agent East London reports Blue Anchor steamer making slow progress towards Durban. It is thought this can only be Waratah.[24]

That evening, in the Australian Federal Parliament, Chairman of Committees Charles McDonald rose to speak:

> I think members will excuse me if I interrupt them to make an announcement which I am sure will give pleasure. I have been told, on good authority, that the Waratah has been sighted, steaming towards East London.[25]

Cheers and applause filled the parliament, but no Blue Anchor liner appeared at Durban.

Late in the afternoon on August 13th, another sensational despatch emanated from the port of East London. Captain Moore of the Hall-Russell liner *Insizwa* had reported that he and his officers had seen human bodies floating in the sea. In a flurry of press interest, Moore was asked why he had not stopped to retrieve them. He offered two reasons, one more satisfactory than the other. The sea, he said, was running so high that it would have been dangerous to turn across it. And out of respect for his lady passengers, he thought it better that the bodies be not brought aboard.[26]

Two boats were despatched to investigate the *Insizwa* sightings. A few days later, Adelaide newspaper *The Advertiser*, quoting telegraphic despatches from London, reported the results:

REASSURING REPORTS.
NOT HUMAN BODIES, BUT A DEAD SKATE.
LONDON, August 14.
The rumor that human bodies have been found in the Great Fish

River is officially denied. The tugs dispatched from East London in search for traces of the Waratah have returned. The voyage was fruitless excepting that those aboard saw floating objects most deceptive in appearance, resembling the bodies of women attired in dressing-gowns, and which investigation proved to be portions of a dead skate.[27]

During the navy search, Lund's (the owners of the Blue Anchor Line) had argued that the awful conditions at the time of *Waratah*'s departure were reason for cautious optimism. They speculated that *Waratah*, pitching in heavy seas, had suffered damage to her running gear and was merely disabled. They pointed to the experience of *Waikato*, which in 1899 had drifted for 103 days after breaking her tailshaft south of Cape Agulhas. *Waratah*'s drift, they suggested, would parallel that of *Waikato*: east-south-east toward Australia, rather than south into sub-Antarctic waters.[28] Nevertheless, even the remote possibility that *Waratah* and her complement might languish in fields of ice was, to the relatives of the missing, a powerful argument for a further search. At the beginning of September, Lund's agreed. They chartered the Union-Castle liner *Sabine* for a three-month search of the southern Indian Ocean: that great, unfrequented expanse from which a few cold islands rise.

Sabine left Cape Town on Sunday, September 12th, 1909; she returned on December 7th, having steamed 14,000 miles and seen nothing. Interviewed on his return, Captain Owen admitted that fog had for many days hampered their efforts and prevented his planned landing on four small islands.[29] For some among the relatives of the missing, that shortfall was sufficient reason to continue the quest. At a public meeting held in Melbourne on December 22nd, a motion was passed to organise yet another search, more thorough and even more wide-ranging. The broad view among experts and underwriters was that further effort was futile, but by the close of the Melbourne meeting, the committee had already secured most of the money it needed. Among the pledges were £1,000 from Neil Black Junior, son of a *Waratah* passenger, £500 from the Government of South Africa, and £500 from the Government of Victoria.[30]

Within a week, tenders were called for a steamship willing to go in search. In the second week of January 1910, the steamer *Wakefield* was chosen from five contenders. Although the committee had shown surprising agility, a delay was now inevitable; *Wakefield* was not expected at Durban until the middle of February. While the committee waited, all details of the operation were worked out. Lieutenant Seymour of H.M.S. *Hermes* would be in command, and five Lund Line officers from the *Sabine* search would go to sea again.[31]

Wakefield departed from Durban on February 26th, 1910. A few days later, *The Sydney Morning Herald* reported:

THE LATEST STORY.
EXTRAORDINARY REPORT BY STEAMER'S OFFICER.
BODIES SEEN IN THE SEA.
Wellington (N.Z.), Feb. 25.
An extraordinary story bearing on the loss, or disappearance, of the big steamer Waratah was made the other day to the Press Association's agent at Westport, New Zealand, by Mr. Day, late second officer of the steamer Tottenham, which called recently at Westport for bunker coal, and sailed for Ocean Island. He says the Tottenham left Durban about 10 days after the Waratah, and steamed over the same course, bound for Antwerp. While off East London at noon one day, an apprentice at the wheel reported to the third officer, who was in charge of the bridge, that he saw float past the ship the body of a little girl clothed in a red dressing-gown. The officer looked round but did not see the body. He, however, went down to the chart-room, where the captain and second officer were laying off the ship's position, and reported that bodies had just floated past. The captain and second officer rushed on to the bridge, and the second officer said he saw something white floating on the water. The captain gave the order "Hard a-starboard," and the vessel steamed round in the vicinity of floating objects. They did not catch sight of the body reported to have been seen fully dressed, but saw what appeared to be portions of human bodies. The weather being very heavy, the steamer was unable to make a thorough examination, so she proceeded on her voyage.[32]

Other members of *Tottenham*'s crew backed up Day's story.[33] On that gruesome day, several among them had seen bodies floating, but not all had seen the same bodies. The chief officer confirmed that a little girl in a gown had floated past, and the second engineer had seen the body of a woman, in a nightdress, with an albatross sitting upon it. Others reported human body parts drifting just below the surface, and one of *Tottenham*'s Chinese firemen had later exclaimed: "Plenty people in sea!" To claim that the sightings were parts of a dead skate was simply untenable; one corpse was said to have passed so close to the ship's side that water from the main discharge had fallen on it.[34]

Day was asked why he had kept his silence for so long. All aboard the *Tottenham*, he said, were under strict injunction from Captain Cox to "keep the thing quiet." Now that he had left the ship, he felt free to say what needed to be said. What made his revelations more newsworthy, and far more disturbing, was the fact that Captain Cox had brought *Tottenham* to Melbourne on January 19th, when the preparations for the *Wakefield* search were very much in the news. He must have known that a new search, funded in large measure by the relatives of the missing, was about to begin. And yet he said nothing.[35]

For four months, *Wakefield* ranged the southern Indian Ocean. The ship visited Prince Edward Island, Marion Island and The Twelve Apostles. She continued to Hogg Island, Penguin Island, Possession Island, Kerguelen Island, Herd Island and the Crozet group. From Amsterdam and St Paul she zigzagged across open sea, making her way back to Australia. It was a search of epic proportions, and monstrous futility.

WARATAH MADE HER ABSENCE FELT. The long uncertainty left many wondering if with this new breed of luxury steamship came a new breed of oceanic disaster. People looked at all ships differently. In Western Australia, *Koombana* was also accused of top-heaviness, and some questioned her suitability for service on a cyclone-prone coast. In *Koombana*'s defence, a curious fact should be recorded. Rumours of her instability flourished at three ports in particular. At Port Hedland, *Koombana* could only cross the bar at the harbour entrance on a high spring tide, and only by emptying some or all of her ballast tanks. Of necessity she was high in the water for every arrival, and often showed a slight list to starboard. For departure she was often higher still, because her heaviest cargo had been discharged. Invariably, ballast tanks were pressed up after leaving the port, but by then the visual impression had been taken.

At Broome and Derby, rumours of top-heaviness had more to do with tide than trade. Twice daily, extreme tides left even the largest steamers sitting on mud. If *Koombana* looked a little high when afloat in light trim,

Low tide at Broome: Koombana *and* Charon *side-by-side at the jetty.*

she looked absurdly so when deprived of water altogether, and especially when she shared the jetty with a smaller or older vessel.

John Rees must have wondered how *Koombana* would fare in a storm like that which had apparently swallowed *Waratah*. On February 8th, 1910, he received a troubling indication. For four days, the Nor'-West coast had felt the influence of a monsoonal depression. As *Koombana*, northbound, passed Depuch Island, she was hit by a severe squall. According to passenger Doug Moore, the ship lay over to a frightening angle and took an uncomfortably long time to straighten up.

Koombana, like most of the steamers visiting Port Hedland that year, was carrying rails and sleepers for the Pilbara railway. Rees made a quick decision to unload the sleepers but not the rails; he would keep the rails as ballast until he returned to Port Hedland on his way south. By circumstance, he never needed to defend his decision. On arrival at Port Hedland he learned that because of an industrial dispute affecting wharf labour, it would not be possible to discharge all Port Hedland cargo. The strike provided the perfect alibi. *The Northern Times* reported that in the absence of the wharf workers, *Koombana*'s crew and even a few passengers had helped to unload railway sleepers, so that the ship could make the next day's tide and continue north.

Koombana's susceptibility to the wind had worried Captain Rees, just as it had worried Doug Moore. He was glad to have 150 tons of iron at the bottom of the hold. Not only did he carry the rails to Wyndham and back; he held onto them for the entire voyage and only delivered them on his next trip north.[36]

If Nor'-Westers stared at *Koombana* and wondered about her safety, it did not stop them buying tickets. By the middle of 1910, she typically left Fremantle fully booked and heavily laden.[37] As her popularity rose, there emerged something that might be called "Koombana anxiety." It began with the observation that *Koombana* was a little too large and luxurious for the trade; it grew into a fear that the ship would be stolen away for service on the more populous eastern seaboard. Every incident, every missed stop, and every departure for annual overhaul led to the same, nervous questioning: "Will *Koombana* be coming back?" "Will *Koombana* remain on the run?" The Adelaide Steamship Company's reassurance was always the same: *Koombana* had been designed specifically for Nor'-West service and no other thoughts were entertained.[38]

WITHOUT DOUBT, the mystery of *Waratah* sharpened a morbid fascination with disaster at sea. Speculation filled newspaper columns. The dispassionate saw things one way; the relatives of *Waratah* passengers quite another. And while the ship and her complement remained in a strange existential limbo, a rash of message-in-a-bottle hoaxes broke out on Australian beaches. From Western Australia to Queensland, hasty scribbles on scraps of paper pleaded for salvation. A bottle picked up at Streaky Bay, South Australia in May 1910 was typical:

August 18th, '09. Waratah sinking rapidly, west coast of Africa. Steamer on fire. (Signed) W. Scott, 18. Elizabeth street, Sydney.

Another found near Wilson's Promontory, Victoria in October 1910 was a little more creative:

At sea. latitude 40 south. Steamer Waratah broke down on August 23, 1909; drifting south.
All well, but anxious. Engineers busy.
J. G. Jones, passenger.
Doubt if this will be picked up.
If so, write to Mrs. J. J. Jones, 28, George street, Sydney.[39]

In November 1910, a message found in a returned bottle at the Castlemaine Brewery in South Fremantle was delivered to the local police. In blue pencil on a tiny scrap of paper was scrawled:

/9/1909
May God have Mercy on us. We are now in a terrible Storm.
1st Officer Waratah[40]

And so it went on, bottle by bottle. After half a dozen cases, the metropolitan dailies ceased printing the stories, although there was a little resurgence of interest in March 1913 when a bottle bearing the stamp of a Melbourne soft-drinks manufacturer was picked up near Tanna, New Hebrides. The message, by *Waratah* standards, was conventional: "We are lost. There is no hope. G. W. E., Waratah." What distinguished this hoax was the confidence with which the ship's agent in Sydney dismissed it. Mr P. Fawcett Storey declared that the bottle could not have come from the missing ship. *Waratah* served only Schweppes waters, he insisted.[41]

One final case should perhaps be cited, if only to demonstrate that the phenomenon was not uniquely Australian. In January 1914 a bottle was found at Bird Island, near Cape Town. The message read:

Ship in great danger. Rolling badly. Will probably roll right over. Captain is going to heave her to.
Later. If anything happens, will whoever finds this communicate with my wife, 4 Redcliffe-street, South Kensington, London.
(Signed) John N. Hughes.[42]

Needless to add, no John N. Hughes appeared on *Waratah*'s passenger list, and no grieving wife was found on Redcliffe-street.

AT 1 A.M. THURSDAY, OCTOBER 20TH, 1910, dense smoke was seen issuing from the ventilators above *Koombana*'s Hold No. 1. The ship was at the time southbound from Broome to Port Hedland.[43] When the hatch was opened, it was discovered fire had broken out among bales of wool loaded at Shark Bay on the run north. The smoke was too thick and the heat too intense for the men to reach the seat of the fire, so Captain Rees ordered them out. The hold was sealed and Clayton's Patent Fire Extinguishing and Fumigating System was activated. When passengers woke on Friday morning to the smell of smoke in their cabins, they sought and received an almost full explanation. Rees told them what he firmly believed: that the fire might still be burning when they arrived in Port Hedland, but would be extinguished before they left.

The Clayton's system consisted mainly of a combustion chamber and a large fan. In the combustion chamber, rolled sheets of sulphur, placed on trays, were ignited to produce a large volume of sulphur dioxide gas which was then forced into the sealed hold to starve the fire of oxygen. For most fires the method was extremely effective. If time were allowed for the hold to cool before fresh air was admitted, total extinguishment was the usual result. But spontaneous combustion in wool or fodder was notoriously difficult to extinguish, because the seat of the fire was hidden somewhere within a steaming, smoking mass. The problem for the Clayton's apparatus, or for any system that relied upon a retardant gas, was that the gas did not always penetrate to where it was most needed. Naked flames on the outside of a wool bale would be quickly suppressed, while the glowing source remained hidden and insulated, like the buried ashes of a camp fire.

After ordering the system activated, Rees allowed it to run continuously for thirty hours before opening the hold to check the results. As fresh air flowed in, the fire quickly re-established itself. He ordered the hold resealed and the process begun again. *Koombana* was not the first vessel on the coast to deal with a fire that had begun in wet wool, but being the largest ship visiting these ports she was the most susceptible. Having a larger draft, her arrivals and departures were more tightly bound to the tides. Wet or dry, bales were loaded when *Koombana* had water enough to present herself.

After two openings and two flare-ups, Rees decided that he could not extinguish the fire. He could, however, contain it—all the way to Fremantle if necessary. Because the bulkheads adjoining Hold No. 1 were now dangerously hot, he ordered some cargo from Hold No. 2 moved to cooler space. He then told his passengers that the fire was under control and that *Koombana* would leave Port Hedland at midnight. The Clayton's apparatus was then run continuously for five days until *Koombana* reached Fremantle.

At Victoria Quay on Thursday, October 27th, with the local fire brigade standing by, the No. 1 hold was opened. After a few minutes of optimism, smoke again began to issue. In exasperation, Rees ordered the hold flooded. Fire be damned! The insurers could take it from there.

A BOARD OF TRADE INQUIRY into the disappearance of *Waratah* was finally convened in London in December 1910, sixteen months after the ship had disappeared.[44] Although several expert witnesses testified that *Waratah* was well designed and well built, diverse misgivings outnumbered votes of confidence. One former passenger declared that on *Waratah*'s first return to England, the ship's persistent list had been a topic of breakfast conversation. Why was it happening? Could the captain not do something about it? The witness recalled that spirits had risen when the ship unexpectedly straightened up, only to slump as she settled down to a similar list on the opposite side.[45]

Among Australian affidavits received by the court was one by Walter Merry, of Adelaide, who stated that he had been warned by members of the crew not to sail in her again, as the ship had nearly 'turned turtle' at the wharf in Sydney. Merry's statement would probably have carried little weight, had it not been corroborated by Sydney Harbour pilots who stated that *Waratah* without cargo or ballast was so unstable that she could not be moved, even from wharf to wharf.[46]

The court also heard from the officers of *Insizwa* and *Tottenham*. That bodies had been seen floating was quickly placed beyond doubt. *Insizwa*'s third officer testified that his commander had enjoined silence, declaring that the owners would have a poor opinion of him if he took time out to collect bodies when dedicated search vessels were already at sea.[47]

FOR ALMOST TWO YEARS, the directors of the Adelaide Steamship Company had dealt with *Koombana* as parents might deal with a gifted but troubled child. In popularity and profitability the ship had exceeded expectations, but rarely had a month passed without some report of mischief in the West. For his part, Western Australian manager William Moxon had become adept at delivering bad tidings to Adelaide by telegram, briefly and without adornment.[48] It should be noted, however, that his was a hard-won composure. After *Koombana* had remained hard aground at Shark Bay for ten days on her maiden Nor'-West run, the social columnist of *The Sunday Times* had quipped:

> The savagest man in this savage State is Adelaide Steamship Co. manager Moxon. The fizz wasted on the send-off of the Koombana boils like a geyser in the memory of all concerned. Don't say Shark's Bay to Moxon if you don't desire to see fur fly.[49]

On Christmas Eve, 1910, the editor of *The Northern Times*, with a twinkle in his eye, hinted that history had very nearly repeated itself.

KOOMBANA AGROUND AGAIN.

Possibly the headline is wrong, but it supplies the most satisfactory solution. The Koombana left Carnarvon jetty on Tuesday night, with the idea of making Denham anchorage soon after daylight on Wednesday. She arrived at 7 a.m. on Thursday instead. The local agents suggest that a dense fog overhung the bay for 24 hours, and the captain deemed it prudent to anchor; otherwise they are unapproachable on the subject. A large number of telegrams were despatched from Carnarvon yesterday, congratulating several of our residents, who are tripping South, on a pleasant day spent fishing for sharks from the Koombana's deck.[50]

December 30th, 1910 was the second anniversary of *Koombana*'s departure from Glasgow. After two tumultuous years, John Rees needed a holiday. The company approved his request for leave and announced that when *Koombana* returned to Fremantle, her popular master would take a well-earned break.

John Rees brought *Koombana* to Victoria Quay at lunchtime on Thursday, January 19th, 1911. Perhaps his wilful mistress resented the prospect of abandonment, even for a month. At eleven o'clock on Saturday night, while Rees was still officially in command, smoke began pouring from the ventilators above Hold No. 2. Five tons of fodder had caught alight, and spontaneous combustion was again blamed. There was no recourse to sulphur dioxide this time. With the prompt attendance of the Fremantle Fire Brigade, passions were cooled in the old-fashioned way.[51]

Captain P. Hurrell took the helm on January 24th, 1911. His temporary captaincy began well, but on *Koombana*'s arrival at Derby he received disturbing news. At Legendre Island, which *Koombana* had passed a few days earlier, the Russian barque *Glenbank* had been destroyed in a cyclone. The ship had been at the Depuch Island anchorage for a month, loading copper ore. When the wind rose on February 6th, *Glenbank*'s anchors held for a time, but by late afternoon she was drifting toward a rocky shore. Captain Morberg decided to make a dash for the open sea. It was a dangerous undertaking, because the bags of ore were not properly secured. Four hours out, the load shifted; control was lost and the ship capsized.[52]

More harrowing still was the fact that news of the disaster had come to hand from a single survivor, Antle Katola. Through an interpreter, the Russian-speaking Finn explained that he had been aloft when the ship rolled. He did not see any of his shipmates again. It was about nine in the evening when he hit the water, and daylight when he reached the shore of the island. For two days he foraged for food; on the third, he sighted a boat. Even then, his ordeal was not quite over. Only by swimming 400 yards to a reef, to make himself visible, did he succeed in attracting the attention of Cossack pearler William Banger.[53]

From Derby, Captain Hurrell guided *Koombana* north and east through the intricate filigree of the Kimberley coast. Paradoxically, it was only after the ship was 'all fast' at Wyndham jetty that his skills and composure were severely tested. A short, sharp summer storm swept in across open water and struck the town. For fifteen minutes heavy hail accompanied a swirling wind so strong that all but one of *Koombana*'s five hawsers parted. With only a single bow line remaining, the crew managed to keep the ship's stern in the stream until the wind dissipated. Within an hour, *Koombana* was resting quietly again. Only to the hawsers—and perhaps to Captain Hurrell's confidence—was any damage done.[54]

When John Rees returned to work on February 22nd, 1911, maritime disaster was very much in the news. Captain Hurrell had brought the *Glenbank* survivor to Fremantle, to recuperate at Fremantle Sailors' Rest before being repatriated to Europe. On the day that Antle Katola's remarkable tale of survival appeared in the local papers, the Board of Trade in London released its verdict regarding *Waratah*.[55] The finding was surprisingly candid. Because the Blue Anchor Line had already been declared bankrupt, the company's survival was not an issue that the court needed to consider. It found that *Waratah* had, on balance of probability, "capsized in the first great storm she encountered."[56]

Captain Rees must have been glad that the saga was finally over. Perhaps now, after two years of guilt by association, *Koombana* might succeed in distancing herself from disaster. A month later, however, that hope was dashed when *Koombana*'s east-coast counterpart went missing in a severe late-summer cyclone.[57] The S.S. *Yongala* was on a voyage from Melbourne to Cairns via ports. On Thursday, March 23rd, 1911, she left Mackay in threatening conditions, and without the benefit of cyclone warning that arrived a little too late. She was last seen by the lighthouse keeper at Dent Island.

This would be no mystery of months or years. On March 28th, all hope was extinguished in the space of a few hours. At Cape Bowling Green, the lighthouse keeper reported that pumpkins and bags of bran and pollard were coming ashore. The company's agents confirmed that these were part of the ship's cargo, and that all had been stowed in the No. 3 lower hold. The tug *Alert*, sent out by the Queensland Government, found artefacts similarly ominous. A basket of parcels from Brisbane must surely have come from *Yongala*'s mail room on a lower deck, and cases of kerosene could only have escaped from a ship catastrophically damaged. A distinctive panel from *Yongala*'s music-room door, and pillows emblazoned with the company's insignia, completed *Alert*'s grim harvest.

At Townsville, *Yongala*'s destination, residents did not wait long or travel far for confirmation of their worst fears. On the same day, wreckage was found floating in Cleveland Bay near the city baths.

FOR REASONS NOT ENTIRELY CLEAR, John Rees's relationship with *Koombana* came to an end in August 1911. In conversations with the press, the Adelaide Steamship Company's manager William Moxon confirmed that *Koombana*, in Sydney for annual overhaul, would return to Fremantle under new command. The change was not part of a broad reshuffle, or forced by any retirement; rather, two of the company's most experienced shipmasters had agreed to an exchange of ships.

For Tom Allen, master of *Winfield*, the exchange was an opportunity for advancement. *Koombana* was considered by many to be the finest ship in Australian service, and the Nor'-West run was broadly acknowledged as the most demanding. For John Rees, the exchange had different merit and meaning. After two years of firefighting—literal and metaphorical—he had seen enough of the Nor'-West and its narrow seas. He sought cooler air, wider shipping lanes, and harbours that remained open for business on any tide.

AT MORT'S DOCK IN SYDNEY HARBOUR, work went on above and below for 25 days. *Koombana*'s engine and boiler were serviced, hull damage inflicted by the S.S. *Pilbarra*[58] was repaired, and Marconi wireless telegraphy apparatus was installed in a custom-built cabin on the boat deck. Inside, deck by deck, a hundred minor matters were attended to.[59]

For Rees it had been a long journey. He had seen *Koombana* launched. He had witnessed her sea trials and brought her out from Glasgow. He had completed sixteen round trips to Derby, eleven to Wyndham, and three to Sydney for repair and overhaul. He had driven the ship onto a mound of sand, and had 'discovered' an uncharted rock. He had battled a wool fire that refused to be extinguished. He had been neaped at Broome and locked out of Port Hedland. He had scraped paint, destroyed wicker fenders and broken steel hawsers. He had almost lost count of the occasions on which he and *Koombana* had found the bottom.

At 3 a.m. on August 16th, 1911, the overhaul was completed.[60] With a final entry in the ship's log, John Rees closed a remarkable diary of misadventure—and left *Koombana*'s new master to write his own.

5

This Latest Marvel of Science

To many, the string of inventions that came together as 'wireless' seemed like a piling of miracle upon miracle. Those who marvelled that etheric vibrations could somehow dart through empty space were further astonished to learn that on a clear, still night a message could skip lightly across the domed roof of the world. And how was it possible that a jumble of messages sent simultaneously could be picked apart by a wireless receiver, permitting a lone voice to be lifted from a crowd?[1] All the while, Marconi's Wireless Telegraph Company, masters of careful attunement, dazzled the public with announcements and confident predictions.

On March 11th, 1905, South Australian newspaper *The Register* joined the chorus of praise. Its editorial began:

MARVELLOUS MARCONI AND HIS WIRELESS WONDERS.
The way in which Mr. Marconi has kept his promises in the past justifies the assumption that he was not 'romancing' the other evening. He told his audience at the Royal Institution that he is confident that before long he will be able to transmit messages to the antipodes more economically than is now done by means of cables stretched across the bed of the ocean! This seems too wonderful to be true, and yet it merely means an extension of a system which has not only stood every scientific test, but has firmly established its claims to recognition, for employment for commercial purposes and other everyday requirements.[2]

Across the northern hemisphere, the spread of the new technology had indeed been remarkable. Wireless stations had sprung up in England, Belgium, Holland, Germany, Italy, and Montenegro; even the Congo Free State could boast two. And in America, the De Forest Company had announced plans for a grand network of transmitters, spanning all of North America and reaching across the Pacific.[3]

In part, *The Register* hailed the achievements in Europe and America to highlight the lack of progress in Australia, where distance and isolation marked the way of life, and where the value of the new technology was plain for all to see. It wondered about the government's failure to act:

> It has been hinted that there has been a scepticism born of jealousy on the part of the Federal Telegraphic Department towards the "wireless" system—a fear that the days of the ocean cable and overhead wires on land are numbered, and an idea that the new invention ought to be as rigidly excluded from this "exclusive" continent as are sunburnt or otherwise tinted immigrants.[4]

By 1905, many trans-Atlantic liners carried wireless telegraphy equipment. Shipmasters received weather forecasts and predicted their arrival times, operators exchanged news with vessels within range, and First Class passengers received printed news bulletins with their breakfast. Increasingly, the Marconi rooms of ships looked and functioned like the familiar telegraph offices, with passengers sending "Marconigrams" almost as freely as they despatched cablegrams on land.[5] Perhaps surprisingly, another four years would pass before wireless telegraphy placed its life-saving credentials beyond doubt, and staked its claim for universal adoption by ships at sea.

ON FRIDAY, JANUARY 22ND, 1909, the White Star liner *Republic* left New York for Gibraltar and Mediterranean ports. Early the next morning Captain Sealby was at the helm, proceeding slowly through a thick fog that had settled like a blanket over Nantucket Island and the sea to the south. Suddenly, a dozen blasts of a fog siren came in quick succession. Before Sealby had even ascertained the direction from which the sounds had come, a steamship reared out of the fog to starboard and struck *Republic* amidships. The impact was sickening; the sharp prow of the other ship sliced through *Republic*'s steel-plate hull and into the engine room. According to one description, the intruder then "pulled away, righted herself, and staggered off into the fog." Seawater rushed through the gaping hole left behind; in a matter of seconds, *Republic*'s fires were out.[6]

Republic's 'Marconi man' was 24-year-old Jack Binns. He had been at his desk sending a message when the collision occurred. By the time the captain called him to the bridge, the first "CQD"[7] distress message had already been sent. It had been caught by the land station at Siasconset, on the eastern tip of Nantucket Island; the operator then stood by until Binns returned with his captain's instructions.

> Binns: "The Republic. We are shipwrecked. Stand by for captain's message."
> Siasconset: "All right, old man. Where are you?"

Binns: "Report Republic rammed by unknown steamer 26 miles N.W. Nantucket lightship; badly in need of assistance but no danger of life. Sealby."[8]

Within minutes, Siasconset had made contact with three wireless-equipped ships within easy steam of the accident. *Republic*'s White Star stablemate *Baltic* had also picked up the transmissions; her master J. B. Ranson had turned his ship around without waiting for a specific request. Binns, now on emergency power, remained at his post, guiding rescue vessels through the fog to the scene of the accident, while Sealby on deck prepared for the evacuation of his passengers and crew.

The ship that had crashed into *Republic*'s side was the incoming Lloyd Italiano liner *Florida*. She soon re-emerged from the fog to declare herself ready and able to receive *Republic*'s passengers. There was some doubt that the much smaller *Florida* could safely accommodate 700 evacuees, but the rescue flotilla certainly could. The evacuation commenced immediately.

Although four passengers had died in their cabins at the moment of impact, the evacuation was completed without further casualty. *The New York Times* concluded its first report by declaring:

> This was the news which reached this city in a series of fragmentary wireless messages yesterday and last night. Seafaring men declare that had it not been for the same wireless the story of the accident, when it finally reached this city, might have been far different.[9]

The *Republic* sank very slowly; indeed, Captain Sealby was not convinced that her loss was inevitable. Once his passengers and crew were secure he proposed that Jack Binns and several officers return with him to the ship, to work out if and how the ship might be saved. Although the late salvage attempt ultimately failed,[10] the rescue of the ship's complement was hailed a spectacular success. Significantly, it was Jack Binns rather than Captain Sealby who enjoyed the greater acclaim. That wireless telegraphy could be used to declare an emergency had long been recognised; that it could be used so effectively to *manage* an emergency was a revelation.

Just eight days after the celebrated rescue, Reuters reported that a bill to make "ethergraphs" compulsory had been introduced to the United States Congress.[11] Eighteen months later, on June 24th, 1910, Congress approved "An Act to require apparatus and operators for radio communication on certain ocean steamers." The *Wireless Ship Act*, as it came to be known, declared that from July 1st, 1911, at all U.S. ports, wireless telegraphy equipment would be compulsory for all vessels carrying fifty or more passengers. Similar legislation was introduced in France and elsewhere,[12] but Great Britain proceeded more cautiously. Replying to a question in the House of Commons on September 7th, 1909, a young Winston Churchill (in his capacity as President of the Board of Trade) said that he did not think that the time had come for the equipment to be made obligatory, though he would be pleased to see it more widely used.[13]

ON THE DAY THE WIRELESS SHIP ACT PASSED INTO LAW, the Orient liner *Otranto*, newly equipped with Marconi apparatus, was passing through the Suez Canal on her way to Australia. Although wireless-equipped vessels both military and mercantile had been visiting Australian ports for a few years, *Otranto*'s arrival was destined to be remembered. The Marconi company had decided that the time was right to extend its southern-hemisphere influence, and the Orient Line was determined to extract full market advantage from its recent decision to equip all of its liners. *Otranto* became the flagship for the initiative, and her 23-year-old wireless operator, Ernest Fisk, became its unofficial ambassador. Fisk was a careful choice: both a capable technician and a natural spruiker, as comfortable with the business as with the science. At Fremantle, Port Adelaide, Melbourne, Sydney and Brisbane, he entertained members of the press in his 'high office' fifty feet above the sea on *Otranto*'s boat deck.

In his first Australian interview, at Fremantle on July 12th, 1910, Fisk waxed lyrical about the rise of the new medium. Two days later, *The West Australian* responded in kind.

> At the time when all good people had resigned their cares to the keeping of Morpheus on Sunday night, the Marconi operator on the Orient liner Otranto was consulting his Marconi chart—a confusion of latitudinal and longitudinal lines, intersected by oblique dotted tracks. To a layman it might represent some abstruse problem in trigonometry, but to his practical eye, it showed him the positions of various vessels fitted with wireless apparatus from day to day, and the radius in which their messages could be detected. For some days his transmitter had been speaking in monosyllables to the vast unhearing ocean, but the lines on the chart told him that the "voice" of his transmitter would soon be audible. A little later and the powerful induction coil of his transmitter was emitting a torrent of sparks causing the etheric waves to radiate to a distance of some 900 miles. Within that radius were the P. and O. liner Macedonia, and the White Star liner Persic and almost in an instant the presence of some unusual disturbance in the ether was communicated to the operators of both vessels by means of the receiver. Much as the eye intercepts the etheric vibrations we call light, so the receiver detects the etheric vibrations peculiar to wireless phenomena.[14]

Fisk told the reporters that *Otranto*, since London, had been in contact with no less than 23 shore stations and 45 steamers. He did not need to hint that Australia was being left behind; the newsmen were left to draw that conclusion for themselves.

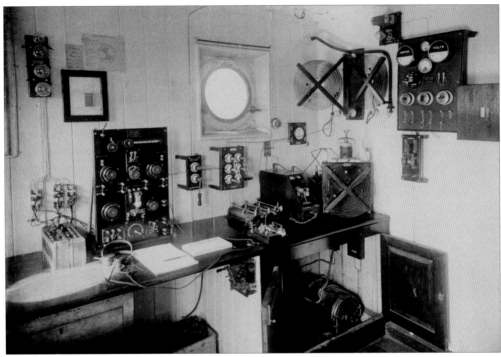

An early Marconi marine installation.

In the course of his first interviews, Fisk found it necessary to explain that he was not an employee of the Orient Line. He was, rather, an employee of Marconi International Marine,[15] assigned to a particular company and ship as part of a comprehensive service agreement. To illustrate, he outlined the progress of his own career. In the course of five years, he had been deployed to several ships in different parts of the world. Indeed, before joining *Otranto*, he had been sent to the Arctic to participate in the annual seal hunt. Noting the interest of his audience, Fisk did not miss the opportunity to explain how wireless had proven its worth among the ice floes of the Arctic. Of the nineteen vessels that had ranged the pack ice, he said, only two were wireless-equipped. Not only had wireless messages been critical to reaching a vessel caught and crushed by the ice, the wireless-equipped vessels had outperformed all others in hunting success. Of the 603,000 seals taken by the fleet, his own ship *Florizel* had secured 46,000! Clearly impressed, *The West Australian*'s reporter wrote: "Despite the extreme cold, Mr. Fisk spent a most enjoyable and interesting time, and he has now in his possession a splendid series of photographs depicting the denizens of the icy regions in their natural habitat."[16]

At each Australian port, Fisk refined his promotional pitch. There was always a simplified explanation of the equipment and its capabilities, and some reference to the celebrated *Republic* rescue. But the Marconi man understood, as did the newsmen, that it was only in the aftermath of disaster or near-disaster that safety devices became newsworthy. In good times it was the non-emergency uses of wireless that would carry the readers of the dailies to a second column of print. From this standpoint, the timing of *Otranto*'s arrival was perfect. Fisk was able to tell reporters that the highlight for passengers on the trip out had been the blow-by-blow reporting of the World Heavyweight Boxing Championship contest between Jim Jeffries and Jack Johnson. Not only had the result of the contest been received, he said, but reports of each round had been posted on noticeboards at three-minute intervals, to great excitement and acclaim.

The young Englishman was probably surprised by the intensity of Australian interest in this American contest. Three ports and several interviews later, he knew a little more of Australia's early, keen interest in the rise of Jack Johnson.

On the last day of November 1908, manager Jim Ronan left the West Kimberley cattle station Napier Downs to take a well-earned holiday. After the 100-mile overland run into Derby, he boarded the old cattle steamer *Minilya* for the 1,600-mile voyage south to Fremantle. He had written to his wife in Melbourne, telling her that he would see her and the children before Christmas. From the ports of the Nor'-West, he sent short telegrams so that she could track his progress south and east. She learned that he would, of necessity, spend a few days in Fremantle, before enjoying a dramatic rise in the standard of his shipboard accommodation. He had booked his eastward passage with the Royal Mail Steamer *Orotava*, passing through Fremantle from London on December 17th.[17]

The message Julia Ronan received from her husband a few days later was not quite what she had expected. Many years later, their son Tom would explain:

> Knowing how he loved sea travel she was agreeably surprised when he wired from Adelaide that he was leaving the ship and coming to Melbourne by rail. It was certainly much easier for a mother with a three-and-a-half-year-old daughter and a yearling son to meet a train at Spencer Street than to traipse down to Port Melbourne Wharf to see a ship come in. When he greeted her at the railway station in Ave atque vale "Hail and farewell" terms, and announced that he was going straight on to Sydney she was astonished; when he explained that this journey was not in any way a business trip but a foray to see the Burns–Johnson fight, her indignation was understandable.[18]

Jim Ronan had not seen his wife or little daughter for almost two years, and had never until that day set eyes upon his son, but Tom Ronan would admit that he admired his father for that decision. Few men, he mused, "could truthfully boast that their moral courage would have been equal to such a gesture."[19] His father, he insisted, was affectionate and loyal but maintained sensible priorities. After all, the Burns–Johnson fight was the first World Heavyweight Boxing Championship to be decided in Australia, and the purse the largest ever offered in the history of the sport!

What Jim Ronan and 20,000 others watched in bright sunshine at Rushcutter Bay on Boxing Day, 1908 was a lopsided contest. The much-heralded Negro challenger dominated from the start. Jack Johnson taunted Canadian Tommy Burns, drawing him in, even dropping his guard to attract punches that he knew he could counter. As the fight proceeded, Johnson's dismissive superiority troubled even erstwhile admirers. Many hoped that fight would end early, either by knockout or by the referee's intervention. The latter seemed unlikely, since referee Hugh McIntosh was also the fight's promoter. It was his money that had brought the fight to Sydney.[20]

The World Heavyweight Boxing Championship, Rushcutter Bay, Sydney, December 26th, 1908.

Vested interests notwithstanding, the fight did not run its course. It was stopped during a brutal fourteenth round, not by McIntosh but by the local constabulary. It is not known how the police justified their invasion of the ring. Were they defending public morals? Were they quelling civil unrest? Whatever the interpretation, the crowd seemed more amused than aggrieved. To all eyes, the contest was already decided; the appearance of the boys in blue merely added a theatrical twist at the end of a memorable day.[21]

Without doubt, the emergence of a Negro world champion troubled white Australians far less than it troubled white Americans.[22] In the sport's adopted home, Johnson's victory was invested with a burning racial intensity. Almost immediately, the search began for a redeemer: a great white hope to restore the natural order and shut the mouth of the quintessential "bad nigger."[23] Two months later, former undefeated heavyweight champion James J. Jeffries came out of retirement. On March 1st, 1909, he told the *Los Angeles Times*:

> I feel obligated to the sporting public at least to make an effort to reclaim the heavyweight championship for the white race. . . . I should step into the ring again and demonstrate that a white man is king of them all.[24]

The contest in Reno, Nevada on July 4th, 1910 was billed as "The Fight of the Century." Black hope was with Johnson. White money was on Jeffries. Perhaps surprisingly, many Australians backed Johnson. He was the man they knew; he was their champion, who had staked his claim of supremacy not in Atlanta or Chicago, but in Sydney under Australian sunshine.

From the opening bell, Morse keys were set tapping. Round by round the despatches flew, by cable to Los Angeles, Chicago and New York, and by wireless to liners at sea. Hastily reconverted to plain English, the punches of the assailants were rushed along decks and pinned to noticeboards in smoke rooms and corridors. In London, at 9 p.m., a crowd gathered in Fleet Street to have its news direct from the offices of the newspapers, and in the music halls the usual amusements gave way to onstage readings of ringside despatches.[25]

In Reno, white hope was sorely tested. By the eighth round, Jeffries was in trouble; by the eleventh, it was obvious that this would be no triumphal return to the ring.[26]

> Battered and bashed, but still game and solid, Jeffries dashed desperately into the eleventh round. He landed hard on the nigger, and fought wildly, hoping by main force to beat down the terrible man who had maimed and half-blinded him. Johnson kept cool and calm, and every now and again punctuated Jeffries' wild rushes with a tolling punch. Again in this round the points went to the negro.[27]

The result of the fight reached Western Australia in 23 minutes, partly by ship-to-ship Marconi transmissions across the Pacific. Greatly assisted by its time zone, Perth's *Daily News* became the only Australian newspaper to deliver round-by-round coverage on the day of the fight. It even managed a hasty summary of the last seconds.

> As Jeffries staggered for a foothold after the third time he had been sent to the floor, Johnson sprang at him like a tiger, and with a succession of lefts on the jaw sent him down and out.[28]

Aboard *Otranto*, the passengers may have felt that they were receiving their news at the speed of light. It was not quite so. Their information did not come from Associated Press or Reuters—at least not directly. It was Ernest Fisk's counterpart on the S.S. *Macedonia*, reading from a Melbourne newspaper, who transmitted each round of the fight as a separate Marconi message.[29] Nevertheless, the demise of Jim Jeffries lost none of its poignancy by late delivery, or in translation from the language of the ether.

> As Jeff was helped to his corner he said:—"I am not a good fighter any longer. I could not come back, boys; I could not come back. Ask Johnson if he will give me his gloves."[30]

Interviewed later, Jeffries later admitted that pride had got the better of judgment. White America was not nearly so gracious. Interracial violence erupted in cities across the United States, and especially in the south-east. By one account, two whites and 22 blacks died in the seven days after the fight. Without doubt there were scores of ugly incidents, but some of what white commentators called rioting was probably no more than wild exuberance. In black neighbourhoods there were spontaneous street parties and parades, some of which began very simply when black churchgoers emerged from their Sunday services and kept walking, in congregation. Perhaps the single greatest source of antagonism to the white community was the inability of many black Americans to wipe the smiles from their faces. As poet William Waring Cuney put it:

> O my Lord
> What a morning,
> O my Lord,
> What a feeling,
> When Jack Johnson
> Turned Jim Jeffries'
> Snow-white face
> to the ceiling.[31]

IN FREMANTLE ON JULY 12TH, 1910, Ernest Fisk met little opposition from the press when he declared the possibilities of wireless telegraphy to be almost limitless. Just two weeks later, "marvellous Marconi" was in the spotlight again.

Soon after leaving Antwerp for Montreal, Captain Kendall of the Canadian Pacific liner *Montrose* became suspicious of two of his passengers. There was something about Reverend Robinson and his son that did not ring true. The reverend had boarded with a moustache but appeared in the dining room clean-shaven two days later, and the son's effeminate manner and clinging intimacy left the captain wondering about their relationship. After catching a glimpse of safety pins in the waistband of the lad's trousers, he decided to investigate. Discreetly, the Robinsons' cabin was inspected. The contents of a wardrobe left little doubt that the two were not father and son. Their true identities were soon suspected. After discussion with his chief steward, Captain Kendall asked wireless operator Lawrence Hughes to send a message to the British police:

> Have strong suspicions that Crippen London cellar murderer and accomplice are among saloon passengers. Mustache taken off growing beard. Accomplice dressed as boy. Manner and build undoubtedly a girl.[32]

Canada being still a British dominion, extradition would be a simple matter if the couple could be apprehended before crossing into the United States. Chief Inspector Walter Dew of Scotland Yard acted quickly. He boarded the much faster S.S. *Laurentic* and telegraphed ahead to have Montrose slowed sufficiently to ensure that he and *Laurentic* arrived first.

In the St Lawrence River the inspector, disguised as the ship's pilot, boarded *Montrose*. The arrest was a simple matter. Kendall and Crippen were standing together, the captain having invited 'Reverend Robinson' to the bridge to meet the pilot. Dew simply removed his cap and said "Good morning, Dr Crippen. Do you know me? I'm Chief Inspector Dew from Scotland Yard." Crippen's reply was as unadorned as the detective's greeting. "Thank God it's over," he said.[33]

On August 2nd, 1910, London newspapers reported that 3,000 people, mostly women, had gathered at the Quebec Police Court, hoping for a glimpse of the man said to have murdered his wife and cut her body into small pieces.[34] From the very beginning the case was destined to titillate and preoccupy. Michigan-born Hawley Crippen, a homeopathic physician, had migrated to England in 1900 with his second wife Cora, a sometime music-hall singer known also by her stage name Belle Elmore. Life in England was not quite as the couple had hoped. Crippen's American qualifications were not recognised, and well-paid work did not come easily. They took in lodgers to supplement their incomes. Although their relationship and lifestyle would later be declared unusual, and much would be made of Cora's succession of lovers, the Crippens of Camden-road drew no particular attention until February 1910. After

a party on the last day of January, Cora disappeared. She had returned
to the United States, Crippen told their friends. His new lover Ethel "Le
Neve" Neave moved into the apartment soon after. Of itself, her sudden
intercession was no ground for suspicion, but her predilection for wearing
Cora's clothes and jewellery raised the ire of old friends. Kate Williams,
better known as the stage-performing strongwoman "Vulcana", made her
suspicions known to the London police.

After a few insinuating reports, Chief Inspector Dew visited Crippen
at home. He found nothing out of order, and accepted at face value
Crippen's explanation of his wife's departure. Dew later admitted that
had Crippen and Le Neve not panicked after his visit, his suspicion might
never have been aroused.

The couple fled to Brussels and then to Antwerp, where they donned
their disguises and boarded *Montrose* for Quebec. As they left the old world
for the new, the police began looking more closely at Crippen's hastily
vacated apartment. Three searches revealed nothing, but a fourth, more
probing, sent London into a spin. From beneath the brick floor of the
basement came human body parts, surgically separated and apparently
deboned. No head or skeleton was ever found.

At sea, Crippen drank heavily, complained of insomnia and spent
much of his time walking *Montrose*'s decks. He became intolerant of
conversation and hypersensitive to the incessant crackle from the
antenna of the ship's Marconi apparatus. He suspected, correctly, that his

Hawley Crippen, escorted from the S.S. Montrose *by Chief Inspector Walter Dew of Scotland Yard.*

movements were being monitored, and monitored on both sides of the Atlantic. When the moment of arrest came, he seemed surprised only by the fact that Inspector Dew was there in person to present the handcuffs.

Following his well-attended extradition hearing, Hawley Harvey Crippen was returned to London and tried for murder at the Old Bailey. He was hanged at Pentonville Prison on November 23rd, 1910. Ethel Neave, tried separately, was acquitted.

AIDED SO ABLY BY JACK JOHNSON AND HAWLEY CRIPPEN, Marconi International Marine enjoyed spectacular growth in 1910. The total number of its shipboard wireless installations rose from 143 to 250, and the number looked set to double again by the middle of 1911, when the grace period of the *Wireless Ship Act* was due to expire.[35]

In Australia, it was the absence of a wireless installation that made the case for universal adoption more compelling. The Blue Anchor liner *Waratah*, which had disappeared in a storm in July 1909, remained in the newspapers for almost two years as search after search failed to reveal any trace of her.[36] In February 1911, as a formal inquiry drew to a close in London, the Adelaide Steamship Company moved to guard its dominance of Australian coastal shipping. To show a commitment to the safety of its passengers—and to distance itself from another company's disaster— it ordered Marconi installations for its three finest steamers: *Grantala*, *Yongala*, and *Koombana*.[37] Incidentally, it was the versatile Ernest Fisk who would fulfil the Adelaide Steamship Company's order. In May 1911 he was transferred from *Otranto* to develop Marconi's onshore facilities in Sydney, and to supervise the first Australian installations.[38]

WHEN KOOMBANA ARRIVED HOME in September 1911, much was made of her new instrument and its capabilities.[39] But as 'Marconi man' Mulholland soon discovered, Western Australia was not the North Atlantic, where operators often struggled to cut through the incessant chatter. Here, on the eastern fringe of the Indian Ocean, many messages went unanswered. From Shark Bay southward, *Koombana* came within range of the Royal Mail steamers. From Broome northward, she conversed with vessels out of Singapore, Surabaya and Batavia. Between Shark Bay and Broome, however, there were days when *Koombana* spoke only to "the sea, the blue lone sea."[40]

The establishment of land stations was long overdue; indeed, there was a widespread perception that the Australian Government had not kept its promises.[41] As early as 1909, the P. & O. company had announced its intention to fit wireless telegraphy equipment to all of its vessels in Australian service.[42] Its decision was predicated upon the government's declared intention to establish powerful land stations at Sydney and Fremantle. Two years later, nothing had eventuated.

By September 1911, plans were in place, but the federal government had a problem that went beyond bureaucratic obfuscation. It was keen to award contracts to the local firm Australasian Wireless, who were supplying Telefunken rather than Marconi equipment, but a recent British court decision—the so-called Parker Judgment[43]—had affirmed the Marconi Company's right to see out the last four years of its patents. Therein lay the problem for the federal government, and for attorney-general "Billy" Hughes in particular: the government could not afford a further delay of four years, but it risked legal action by Marconi if it entered into contracts for the supply of Telefunken equipment.[44]

Australasian Wireless tried to reassure the government that it alone would be the target of any litigation,[45] but Hughes accepted different advice and proceeded very cautiously indeed. On February 10th, 1912, at the formal opening of small land stations in Melbourne and Hobart, the invited guests were carefully chosen, and none were permitted to inspect key pieces of equipment. The thin veil of secrecy achieved nothing. Three days later, the Marconi company issued writs against the Commonwealth of Australia.[46]

Ultimately, the impasse was broken by creative thinking. Hughes and his department recognised that if government contracts were divided between competitors and competing systems, problems of equipment compatibility would inevitably arise. (The national muddle of railway gauges had certainly demonstrated that.) Although the details of informal discussions cannot be known, it is clear that the local agents of Marconi and Telefunken were given a powerful incentive to settle their differences. The message was as clear as it was unofficial: while the government could not predict how its contracts would be divided between competitors, there was a strong possibility that a single, merged entity would win them all.

It seems likely that Billy Hughes brokered—or at least blessed—the local amalgamation of the two firms, solving the government's legal problem at the same time. On July 11th, 1913, the erstwhile competitors came together as Amalgamated Wireless Australasia, or A.W.A., with Ernest Fisk as general and technical manager.[47]

Fisk, now 27, seemed destined to steer the development of wireless telegraphy in Australia. He was the competent operator who had emerged as an articulate spokesperson—for the shipping lines, for the Marconi company, and now for a burgeoning industry. He spoke confidently and often of telegraphy and its accomplishments, but never lost touch with the naive wonder that had drawn him and others to wireless in its scientific infancy. He understood that the medium could still be sold on its magic and its mystery, and may even have wondered if some of that magic was being buried beneath a growing pile of practical achievements. In a review for Melbourne newspaper *The Argus* in November 1910, he recounted the highlights of a few frenetic years, and concluded:

Through fog, through the blackest night, through storm and cloud, our Morse flies, 186,000 miles to the second. If we could speak to the moon, 1⅓ seconds would suffice. Eight and a half minutes would call up the sun. We are trammelled by no retarding induction, like the deep-sea cables, and with greater power and more knowledge we may before long send our waves round the world and back again. Often, while the Morse buzzes in the receivers from the ships across the sea, it strikes me suddenly what a tremendous thing it is, and how little we really know.[48]

6

THE GREAT DIVIDE

Surely we cannot see these people, whom we have ruthlessly dispossessed (without any compensation or obligation favorable to them or theirs) die out for want of humane thought, and action? Let the fair-minded among us evolve something. We must admit the wrong: then let us right it.[1]

Walter Barker, "The Native Question", *The Hedland Advocate*, May 14th, 1910.

IT WAS AN ARGUMENT that grew into a lifelong friendship. In the last week of July 1900, Mrs Daisy Bates called upon Matthew Gibney, the Roman Catholic Bishop of Perth.[2] Polite disagreement was inevitable. Gibney, a long-time campaigner against the mistreatment of Aborigines, had been in and out of controversy for twenty years.[3] Never afraid to raise his head above the parapet, he had at different times delivered sharp criticism, triggered fiery debate, and received stern rebuke. He saw defence of the Australian Aborigine as a duty of his position. Mrs Bates also had great sympathy for the Aborigines, but there was a key difference. She was also staunch in her defence of the pastoralists, and was not receptive to allegations of widespread exploitation or mistreatment. She took exception to some of the bishop's recent and not-so-recent remarks.[4]

Fresh from her Nor'-West study tour, Mrs Bates came determined to be heard; she found herself disarmed, not by logic or authority, but by natural affinity with her new acquaintance. In Gibney she found a kindred spirit: an intelligent, affable Irishman, as vehement as she was. She argued that cases of cruelty and exploitation were anomalies, and that the pastoralists as a group were honourable men. The bishop did not contradict her, but spoke of mistreatment he had personally witnessed. He argued that both the best and the worst of human nature could be found by looking, and pointed out that in her recent travels she had remained very much within her social circle. By accepting invitations rather than choosing her own destinations, she had only visited stations that were recognised as models of humane treatment. If she were to range more widely, he suggested, she might come to a different conclusion.[5]

Daisy Bates and Bishop Matthew Gibney.

The warmly defiant Daisy Bates was perfectly capable of resisting his argument, but she had no defence against the opportunity that came with it: to travel with the bishop and his associate Dean Martelli to the mission at Beagle Bay, for a very different perspective on relations between black and white.[6]

To Daisy, ever the adventurer, the invitation was not merely exciting; it was irrefusable. She was a risk-taker; Gibney was certainly another. Was this not the priest who twenty years earlier had taken confession from the injured Ned Kelly? And who against police orders had entered the burning Glenrowan Hotel to minister to any of the Kelly gang that might remain alive?[7]

After ten years of struggle, the Trappists[8] had announced their intention to abandon the Beagle Bay Mission. Its future hung in the balance. For Bishop Gibney, the practical problem centred on an unsettled agreement regarding the mission lands. The state government had promised that the church would be awarded freehold title to the 10,000-acre site, once fixed improvements to the value of £5,000 had been demonstrated.[9] To secure that title was now critical; without it, there was little incentive for another Catholic order to continue what the Trappists had begun.

Beagle Bay had proved more challenging than any had anticipated, and the mission was in no fit state to be assessed. The authorities, however, would not budge on the terms of the agreement and, as if to bring the matter to a convenient close, had set a date for the valuer's visit.

Unwilling to let it all come to nothing, Bishop Gibney determined to go north himself, to see what could be done before the day of material reckoning. He may have had second thoughts about his invitation to Mrs Bates, but he did not withdraw it. Instead, he left her in no doubt that she would come not as an observer but as a spade-carrying member of his team. He warned that £5,000 in improvements would not easily be demonstrated; she should expect to work hard.

On Friday, August 17th, 1900, Mrs Bates joined Bishop Gibney and Dean Martelli aboard the steamer *Karrakatta* for the eight-day voyage to Broome.[10] A few days later, Father Nicholas Emo and his novices sailed south from Beagle Bay to meet them. Their schooner *Sree Pas Sair* would remain at Broome for several days. There were tools and supplies to be bought and loaded before the combined party could sail north and begin its work.

When *Karrakatta* arrived at Broome, there was a great surprise in store for Father Nicholas. There had been no opportunity for Bishop Gibney to tell him that Mrs Bates would be joining them at Beagle Bay. Deprived of any opportunity for contemplation, Emo was quite undone by the news. In French, he tried to explain that there was no accommodation whatever for a woman at the mission; in fact, church law permitted only a queen or the wife of a head of state to enter its grounds. Bates struggled to hide her amusement:

> However, there I was, and the dear little acting abbot took it upon himself to grant a dispensation, and went out to see what furniture he could buy for me, making wild guesses at what a female might need. His bewildered and exaggerated idea of hospitality filled me with astonishment.[11]

His consternation notwithstanding, "the dear little acting abbot" would rise rapidly in her estimation.

NICHOLAS MARIA EMO, of an influential Spanish family, studied medicine before entering the priesthood. After twelve years of service as a missionary in Patagonia, he returned to France and entered the Trappist monastery at Sept-fons as a novice. There, at 45 years of age, he declared his wish to devote the remainder of his life to the cause of the Australian Aborigines.[12]

In 1894 he came to Western Australia, hoping to minister to un-corrupted humanity. His superiors saw his role differently. He was sent to Broome, where a Spanish-speaking priest was urgently needed. Emo found himself confronting the same mix of disease and demoralisation that had dampened his missionary spirit in Patagonia. Nevertheless, he accepted his instructions and went to work. At first, his Trappist attire and observances were a source of amusement to the locals, but in Broome's Filipino community he found affinity and support. Broader acceptance would follow; seen to be respected by some, he was soon helped and heeded by many.[13]

The reluctant parish priest set his evangelical aspirations aside to deal with humanitarian imperatives. He opened a school for black orphans, and from donations paid a part-Aboriginal schoolmistress. With early success came a setback: when town gossip regarding the girls and their guardian forced the school's closure,[14] Emo saw no alternative but to place the girls in domestic service and send the boys to Beagle Bay. Over time, Emo won the respect of the pearlers; by their subscriptions he was able to build a church and a residence for himself. With money remaining he bought seven or eight town allotments near the church, and handed ownership of the land to mixed-race couples whose conversions and Christian marriages appeared authentic.[15] Increasingly, the plight of part-Aboriginal children drew his attention. Aware of cases in which half-caste[16] babies had been killed by their Aboriginal mothers, he began visiting the outlying camps, advertising his willingness to accept—and if necessary, barter for—any child not wanted.[17] His foster family grew rapidly, as did his circle of dependants. After a few years he had established a new school, a home for half-caste girls, and a quiet seaside camp for the old and the sick.

Although Emo remained supportive of the mission at Beagle Bay, he hoped that a second mission might be established in even remoter parts. To that end he travelled the coast with his Filipino friend and supporter Filomeno "Pat" Rodriguez; together, they chose a site near the mouth of the Drysdale River.[18] But before Father Nicholas could prepare a formal proposal, he was made superior of the Beagle Bay mission—not to further its work, but to superintend its abandonment. It was a heartbreaking promotion. To Bishop Gibney he wrote:

> Well, dear Father, although ignorant of the cause of this order, I confess that it has grieved me profoundly, especially because of the love I profess for the blacks for whom I have always sacrificed myself. I came to Australia for the secret attraction that I felt for this unfortunate race and for whose benefit I made the sacrifice of my life to God. . . . To receive the present order that put me at the head of all, not to build and consolidate, only to destroy, that is to say, to disband the community, has been a hard blow to me and one I will not easily forget. And who would believe that the charge of Superior in such circumstances could be in any way enviable?[19]

After baring his soul, Father Nicholas wondered if his superiors understood the possible consequences of their decision.

> The only thing I fear is to receive a new order to proceed immediately with the liquidation. In such a case would it not be better for his

Lordship to come to an understanding with me to buy for himself, from the government, the mission territory with its springs and gardens and existing stock to save our natives from falling into the hands of Jews and Protestants?

THAT DAISY BATES was excited and enlivened by the prospect of visiting the mission cannot be doubted. A diary energetically kept reveals a buoyant spirit undulled by three days at sea in the once palatial but now dilapidated *Sree Pas Sair*. After the anchor was dropped at Beagle Bay, time moved slowly for her. As the tide fell, the schooner settled down on the seabed and canted to starboard. Only after the sea had retired and the mud had hardened was there any sign of activity. Horses and a wagon came across the seabed to the schooner's side.

Bates recalled an interminable ride across the pindan: nine miles of nothingness, in strange counterpoint to her vivid incantation of it: the shimmering heat, the incessant buzz of flies, and the Bishop intoning the rosary with a few straggling natives joining in whenever they knew the words. Even the horses were subjects of her wry observation. No thoroughbreds these, she mused, but "Trappists, too, skin and bone in their poverty, and stopped so often for their meditations and devotions that the bullock-team arrived before us."[20]

The first indication of nearness was a great wave-like rise of birds, apparently from water. The Bishop, as if woken, looked up. "They're swearing at us!" Mrs Bates quipped, but Bishop Gibney was oblivious to her mischief. A decade earlier, he and the Spanish Trappist Dom Ambrose Janny had chosen this site for the mission. They did not claim to have discovered it. Friendly members of the Njul Njul tribe, who remembered with affection the pioneer missionary Father Duncan McNab, had brought them to this special place: an open parkland of paperbarks and spreading white gums with spring-fed pools, fertile soil and prolific bird life.[21]

If the works of nature commanded reverence, the works of man did not. "When I arrived," wrote Bates, "the Mission was but a collection of tumbledown, paper-bark monastery cells, a little bark chapel and a community room of corrugated iron, which had been repeatedly destroyed in bush fires and hurricanes."[22]

WITH THE VALUER'S VISIT less than three months away, the restoration of the mission began in earnest. With black helpers, Gibney, Emo, Martelli and the novices repaired buildings, restored wells, straightened fences, and attended to anything with a declarable monetary value. Daisy Bates, meanwhile, with an entourage of black women and children, set about transforming the gardens. "I worked like a Trojan," she wrote, "but the force of my example failed dismally. Day after day those women played

Beagle Bay, 1900: the women and children who worked under Mrs Bates's supervision.

with the babies, and laughed both with and at me, full of merriment and good feeling."[23] Bates admitted that to have their help, she had resorted to all manner of trickery. Seeking to keep the children entertained while their mothers worked, she had introduced the game of Ring-a-ring-a-roses, only to have the adult women down tools and join in. And their delight was not feigned any more than it was momentary; thereafter, work proceeded in short shifts, with breaks for games. Ring-a-ring-a-roses was the new smoke-oh.

It is safe to declare that in the course of three months, powerful bonds of friendship and respect were forged, and that those bonds were further strengthened on the day of formal valuation. The government valuer, it seems, was surprised and impressed by what he found at the end of a desolate track from the ocean. Recognising the sheer determination that had brought it about, he approached his task more as a friend of the mission than as the agent of a distant government. Bates wrote:

> He was surprised to see a thriving property where he had expected ruin and decay. Every screw and post, every fruit and vegetable, buildings, wells, trenches and implements were meticulously valued, and with the livestock on the run, the supplies in the store, the sorghum and sugar-cane fields, the tomato and cucumber patches, and the orange, banana, coconut and pomegranate groves, the sum reached over £6,000. Even one Cape gooseberry bush and one grape-vine had to be valued. The Mission was saved for the natives.[24]

Bishop Gibney understood that the award of freehold tenure was but the first step in a long process. No Catholic order had yet declared a willingness to take over the mission. Still, the transformation of the 10,000-acre site was a great accomplishment.[25] Their endeavour had not only satisfied the valuer; it had created new determination and new optimism. "All together and in much jubilation," wrote Bates, "we made the first bricks of sand and loam and a clay for the new convent and monastery."

AT BEAGLE BAY IN THE SPRING OF 1900, Matthew Gibney, Daisy Bates and Nicholas Emo became influential in each other's lives, but it was the influence of Nicholas Emo on Daisy Bates that would emerge as the most striking legacy of the Beagle Bay visit. Bates recognised that Emo's keen interest in Aboriginal culture, custom and legend set him apart. He was not primarily an evangelist; rather, he drew sustenance from humanitarian service. Her enduring memory was of a humble man "sitting on the ground in the midst of his aged and decrepit natives, making homely jokes as he tended their sores and administered medicines." Importantly, Emo had told her that in any clash of tribal law and Christian teaching, tribal law would win, and that only by earning the respect of the natives would he—or she—be listened to.[26]

Although Nicholas Emo could not have known it, Daisy Bates would soon devote herself to the study of Australian Aborigines, as he had devoted himself to their care. For the next fifty years, she would immerse herself in black culture and language, adopting key elements of his vision as her own.

IN LATE 1902, after an unsuccessful return to the role of wife and mother, Daisy Bates moved to Perth, took up residence in a city hostel, and tried to build a career as a freelance journalist. There was some early success. For *The Western Mail* she wrote a series of articles on the Murchison goldfields. For the state government she wrote a paper on the Trans-Australian Railway. And for a few months the avowed Protestant was afforded her own page in *The Western Australian Catholic Record*. But all of this was not enough to sustain her; she supplemented her income by the sale of picture postcards on Nor'-West and Aboriginal themes, printed from her own photographs taken at Beagle Bay and elsewhere.[27]

While taking whatever work came her way, she remained keen to document Aboriginal customs and language. It is known that she received encouragement from Bishop Gibney and Dean Martelli, and also from former state premier and now federal parliamentarian John Forrest, whose interest in the Aborigines was, like her own, characterised both by great sympathy and great pessimism. This was urgent work, they agreed, to be undertaken before it was too late.[28]

Almost two years would pass before an opportunity arose. How it arose is not entirely clear. On May 3rd, 1904, Bates became an employee of the state government. She had been hired by registrar-general Malcolm

Fraser, on a junior clerical wage of eight shillings a day, to compile basic vocabularies of the state's Aboriginal languages. In an office in the centre of the city she began by reading the works of historical commentators. There was George Fletcher Moore's *A Descriptive Vocabulary of the Language in Common Use Amongst the Aborigines of Western Australia*, and a French translation of Bishop Salvado's *Memorie Storiche dell' Australia*. There were also the diaries of explorers who had taken time to study those whose lands they crossed.[29]

The work of compiling vocabularies began almost immediately. Questionnaires were sent to post offices and police stations across the state. Only upon their return did serious problems begin to surface. Not only was there inconsistency among the survey responses; there was no agreement between the responses and the reference works. Worse still, there were irreconcilable differences between the so-called authorities. Serious about her work, and never shy, Bates began corresponding with English anthropologist Andrew Lang and with the Australian surveyor and self-taught anthropologist, Robert Mathews. Once appraised of her situation, Mathews offered advice direct and simple. "Get out among the blacks," he wrote.[30]

The opportunity—or rather, the push—came incidentally. On August 10th, 1904, after a motion of no confidence was passed in state parliament, Henry Daglish became Western Australia's first Labor premier. Some reorganisation of departments was inevitable; a few months later, Bates learned that her city office was to be requisitioned. Rather than risk the work for which she had waited so long, and which she had begun with great zeal, she put to Malcolm Fraser a bold proposal: that she be permitted to set up camp at Maamba, an Aboriginal reserve on the outskirts of the city, to live and work among the last living speakers of some south-western dialects. Her determination prevailed, and her boss agreed. Biographer Elizabeth Salter would later write:

> On a winter's day of July 1905, she set out with a police escort for Cannington. The men remained long enough to choose her site and pitch her tent for her. When they had seen her safely settled in they left her, a lone white woman, her tent a hundred yards away from the Government huts of her black neighbours. Impressed by the power of this white woman who could dismiss from her presence the policemen of whom they were so much afraid, the black people watched proceedings from a discreet distance. Daisy stood at the edge of her breakwind and smiled at them. Little by little they came closer. She did nothing to encourage or discourage them. Waiting patiently for her moment, she invited them to visit her. Then, speaking in the dialect of the Bibbulmuns, she asked them if they would care to join her for a cup of tea.[31]

WHILE MRS BATES SCOUTED FOR AN OPPORTUNITY to study Aboriginal languages and customs, Bishop Gibney continued to campaign against black exploitation and mistreatment. He and other churchmen had long advocated the establishment of a royal commission to inquire broadly into the condition of the Aborigines.[32] In 1904, their perseverance was rewarded. Colonial Secretary Walter Kingsmill thought that Queensland's *Aboriginals Protection and Restriction of the Sale of Opium Act 1901* might be a model for new legislation in Western Australia. He invited Queensland's Chief Protector of Aborigines Walter Roth to Western Australia, to tour with his local counterpart and advise on which elements of the Queensland law might be replicated.

In Queensland, Roth had come to the role of Chief Protector as a well-established anthropologist. His *Ethnological Studies Among the North-west-central Queensland Aborigines*, published in 1897, had been followed by a series of ethnological bulletins, written and published in the course of his wide-ranging work.[33] Most importantly, Roth had been influential in the drafting of the Queensland law, and had supervised its implementation. The value of his visit to Western Australia was broadly recognised, and plans for a royal commission survived the sudden change of government. On Saturday, August 27th, 1904, Roth was interviewed by new premier Daglish and his colonial secretary George Taylor.[34] A few days later, Perth's *Daily News* reported:

> THE ABORIGINES OF THIS STATE.
> A ROYAL COMMISSION APPOINTED.
> In this week's "Government Gazette" the appointment of Dr. T. W. Roth, the Chief Protector of Aborigines in Queensland, as a Royal Commissioner to inquire into the conditions and treatment of the aborigines of this State, is notified. The Government's desire is that the inquiry will be conducted on an entirely independent basis, and Dr. Roth will be empowered to take evidence on oath from any persons whose testimony may be deemed of value. . . . Dr. Roth, during his tour of the State, will not be accompanied by any local official, as it is the intention of the Government to obtain, as far as possible, an unbiassed report as to whether the allegations which have been made in regard to the treatment of natives in this State are justified or not.[35]

Roth's appointment was not welcomed by all. Many in the Nor'-West bristled at the prospect of being interrogated by an outsider. They knew that Roth had sharply divided opinion in Queensland; they had little doubt that he would do the same in Western Australia, and along the same lines. Almost immediately, the commissioner was under attack, and to his great irritation an old controversy was revived and recirculated.[36] In Queensland's parliament two years earlier, the conservative far-north member John Hamilton had alleged that Roth had offered some kind of inducement to have an Aboriginal man and woman demonstrate a particular sexual position, and that he had photographed the couple in coitus. Having obtained a copy of the photograph, Hamilton declared Roth's behaviour disgraceful and called for his dismissal. Fortunately for the anthropologist, Hamilton did not have all of the facts at his fingertips. Roth, seeking redress from the parliament by letter, called attention to three facts: firstly, that Chapter XIII of his *Ethnological Studies* included an illustration identical to the offending photograph; secondly, that the publisher of his 'pornographic' work was none other than the Queensland government printer; and finally, that His Royal Highness the Prince of Wales had graciously received a copy as a gift!

With hardly a raised eyebrow, Roth had shifted the spotlight back upon his accuser, and when it emerged that Hamilton had obtained the photograph by lying to a public servant, the matter was all but settled. Nevertheless, when Roth came to Western Australia to interrogate, perhaps to uncover, a vague reputation for indecency came with him.

During November 1904 the commissioner travelled widely. He took evidence at Wyndham, Derby, Broome, La Grange Bay, and elsewhere. The parallels with North Queensland were striking, but one phenomenon seemed peculiar to Western Australia. For a few years, the number of natives imprisoned for killing cattle had been rising sharply. To explain that anomaly was an early priority. At Derby, Roth called Police Constable John Wilson of Isdell River to the witness stand, to explain how the rules of evidence were applied at the edges of civilisation. Roth asked:

> Do you arrest every black you find in the camp?— Not on all occasions. Sometimes we do when we have sufficient evidence against them.
> You mean aboriginal evidence?— Yes; and with what evidence we have seen ourselves.
> By looking at the carcase of a beast that has been killed, do you mean to tell this Commission that you can tell whether one black or one gin or 20 blacks or 20 gins have killed the beast?— The tracks are there to go by. We see the tracks of a large number of natives where the beast has been killed.
> Does it follow that because you see a large number of tracks in the neighbourhood of a carcase that all these blacks have had a hand in it?— They usually do. There is usually a large party of blacks assembled at the time one of these beasts has been killed.
> How do you know this—by aboriginal evidence or not?— We have the tracks to go by and we have the evidence of the gins who accompany the blacks.
> Is this evidence of the gins obtained before or after you arrest the men?— Before we arrest them. On some occasions we secure the men

first and get the information from the gins afterwards.

You may really be arresting men who are not guilty?— There is no other way of arresting them. These natives will not stand until we get the information from the gins unless we detain them. Civilised natives would certainly.[37]

Constable Wilson's testimony was as remarkable for the answers he gave willingly as for those he did not. Roth asked:

Do you ever arrest the gins?— Yes.

Do you accuse them of cattle-killing?— No.

Do you arrest them as witnesses?— Yes.

Have you any legal authority to arrest these women as unwilling witnesses?— No. Not that I am aware of.

How do you detain them? With neck chains?— They are chained by the ankles.

Do you mean that their two legs are chained together?— No. I fasten the gin to a tree with a handcuff and then fix the chain to one ankle with another handcuff—one handcuff for each prisoner.

Is it only at night that they are chained like this?— It is necessary to detain them sometimes in the day when going through scrub or rocky country where they might get away. It is very rare that they have to be secured in the day time.

The Commission has received evidence that these witnesses are generally young gins or young children. Is that so?— I have never brought in female children as witnesses, that is, what I have considered children.

Have you brought in young women?— Yes.

Have you brought in old women?— Yes.

Is it true that more young women are brought in as witnesses than very old ones?— I think there would be an equal portion of each.

Do you allow your trackers or the assisting stockmen to have sexual intercourse with the gins whose relatives or friends you have arrested?— They may do it without my knowing it.

Do you take any precautions at night that these assisting stockmen or trackers do not have connection with the women when chained to the trees?— No.

Does such intercourse go on?— I suppose so. It could go on in the camp at night and I would know nothing about it.

Roth was a skilled interrogator who moved witnesses quickly to matters of interest and substance. He pressed Constable Wilson to explain the economics of this remote police work.

How much do you receive per day for escorting each aboriginal prisoner or witness?— 2s. 5d. each per day.

Do you get the same amount for returning the witnesses to their native homes after the trial is over?— Yes.

Are they always taken back again, without exception, to their native homes?— I have sent them out on one or two occasions when they have not had far to go.

Do you receive payment for this?— Yes. I have given them the amount in supplies to carry with them sufficient to take them to their own country.

Have any of the accused prisoners you have brought into court been found "not guilty"?— I do not remember any.

How many have you secured a conviction against during the same period?— There may be about 100, or perhaps over. I am not certain.

Is there any name given by your Department to this special allowance for aboriginal prisoners and witnesses?— Yes. It is called "prisoners' rations."

Are these rations paid for by the Police Department or the Aborigines Department?— By the Police Department, until the prisoners are disposed of to the Gaols Department.

Do you actually spend 2s. 5d. per day on each prisoner or witness?— No, but each native has sufficient food.

How could you make up 2s. 5d per day for rations for a young female aboriginal witness, for instance?— They have the same rations as the men.

You say that they only receive flour, tea, and sugar, and that you kill kangaroo sometimes, and that they some times collect lizards and roots. I want to know how you can spend 2s. 5d. per head on each one?— (No answer.)

If the apprehension of black suspects was a travesty, their court appearances were a farce. Aboriginal offenders were often so compliant as to exasperate those who sat in judgment. The accused cattle thief might declare "Me killum bulliman all right" but show no regard whatever for the consequences of his admission. The result was darkly ironic: having so freely admitted guilt, he took to prison an unassailable innocence. He could be made to suffer, but could not be made to feel guilty.

For the most part Roth's advice to the Western Australian Government was measured and pragmatic, but with regard to arrest and incarceration he cast aside all reserve.

Your Commissioner has received evidence which demonstrates the existence of a most brutal and outrageous condition of affairs. The number of aborigines brought in being the great desideratum, each having a money value to the escorting officer, it is not surprising to find that little boys of immature age have been brought in to give evidence; that children, varying in age between 10 and 16 years, are charged with killing cattle; that blacks do not realise what they are

Black prisoners, Roebourne Gaol, c. 1908.

sentenced for; and that an old and feeble native arrives at the end
of his journey in a state of collapse, and dies 18 days after admission
into the gaol.[38]

In the capital, the finding of endemic police corruption enraged the
Commissioner of Police, Captain Frederick Hare. He launched a personal
attack on Roth, claiming that in support of preconceived notions he had
secured evidence from "the riff-raff of the north." Roth did not contradict
the police chief; he simply affirmed that he had taken testimony from
sergeants, constables, magistrates, gaolers, doctors, and from Captain
Hare himself.[39]

The published testimony was so revealing, and the finding so stark,
that many in the south expected immediate governmental action. Surely
Roth's "outrageous condition of affairs" could not continue. And yet it
did: for another three years, incarceration rates continued to rise. As far as
can be told, the increase did not lead to any soul-searching on the part of
white settlers. The prevalent view was that the increase in imprisonment
was due entirely to the black man's enjoyment of it. Even the state's new
Chief Protector of Aborigines, Charles Gale, in his annual report for 1908,
acknowledged the lack of a deterrent effect.

> During the year 156 natives were convicted from East and West
> Kimberley of cattle killing, or being in unlawful possession of meat.
> These figures represent an increase of 54 prisoners over the previous

year, and somewhat point to the fact that our present system of punishment is not acting as a deterrent to this form of crime; many holding the opinion that natives look upon a term of imprisonment as more of a holiday than anything else. One has only to compare the condition of natives brought in from the bush before being committed to gaol with their healthy, fat, and sleek condition after being fed on prison rations, to realise that they fared better under civilisation than in their own country. The scale of rations per day allowed to native prisoners, as laid down by prison regulation, is as follows:—1lb. bread, 1lb. meat, 1lb. vegetables, 1oz. rice for soup, 3 pints tea, 1½ oz. sugar, ¼oz. salt, ¼oz. soap. With this plentiful supply of good food cooked for them and being made to do but light work, there is every encouragement given to natives to further commit depredations in the hope of returning to prison after their release.[40]

By 1909, the transfer of black prisoners by coastal steamer had become quite an industry. In a letter home in May 1909, *Koombana*'s fourth engineer Jim Low wrote:

We brought 200 fat cattle down from there this trip and 3,500 sheep from Cossack. The 'tween decks of this ship are a sight sometimes. There is always a lot of dogs, generally a dozen horses or so, sheep,

Chained black prisoners in transit.

cattle, fowl of all sorts in crates, parrots and other birds in cages, black
prisoners either being taken to jail or just let out, we had 25 coming
down last time. It is like a menagerie generally.[41]

While the targets of Roth's criticism angrily defended their reputations
and morality, others gave careful thought to how the lucrative "nigger
catching industry"[42] might be eliminated. They recognised that between
the police and the pastoralists, an unhealthy symbiotic relationship
had grown. In effect, the police were now guarding the Kimberley cattle
herds on wages furnished by the state government. There seemed little
likelihood that change would be brought by persuasion, but what could
not be preached could still be demonstrated. In 1908, new administrative
arrangements, quietly enacted, removed the financial incentive for police
to arrest natives for cattle-killing. No longer would officers be reimbursed
for the expense of providing for suspects and witnesses on the road;
instead, the actual cost of stores and supplies would be charged to the
Colonial Secretary's Office.

If the rise in prison populations had been dramatic, the fall was even
more so. For the State of Western Australia, in 1908, the total number of
Aborigines imprisoned was 664; in 1909, the total fell to 344, with Derby
and Wyndham accounting for almost all of that 47 per cent reduction.
In his annual report, Comptroller-General of Prisons, Octavius Burt,
expressed satisfaction at the result but repeated his assertion of two years
earlier, that far too many natives were being imprisoned upon their own
admission of guilt. Lamenting the lack of response to his earlier plea,
Burt expressed himself plainly: "I do not think a plea of guilty should be
accepted from an untutored savage."[43]

So effective was the change to policing arrangements that when
Colonial Secretary James Connolly toured the Nor'-West aboard *Koombana* in June 1910, he was surprised by the rebalancing of local priorities.
Journalist George Romans travelled with him, covering the tour for *The
West Australian*. Under his *nom de plume* "Vindex", Romans wrote:

> But unfortunately for the municipalities—and it was the subject of
> complaint everywhere—the native prisoners were not as numerous
> as they used to be. None of the gaols is full, and Derby prison was
> stark empty. It is not that the native has become virtuous. He is
> probably today just as black and no blacker than he was twelve
> months ago, but possibly the law is more just to him. The fact of the
> matter is that the police system has been changed. Tales told to Mr.
> Connolly by authoritative people during his northern trip need not
> be here repeated.[44]

As the gaols emptied, and a popular opinion became untenable, a grain
of truth remained. To some extent the cooperation of pastoralist and
policeman also extended to the man arrested. For while the policeman

Colonial Secretary James Connolly and journalist George Romans, a.k.a. "Vindex".

had a great incentive to deliver the cattle-killer to justice, the gaoler had no comparable incentive to keep him there. The accused might be sentenced to a year in prison but was often out after a month or two. Few among the white settlers believed that short periods of imprisonment were harming the natives. Even Vindex acknowledged the emergence of an odd relationship.

> But if such practices had prevailed, would the native have minded? Not at all. For a while at any rate prison life was a real "pink-eye" to him. In gaol he was fed and got tobacco, and if he was not loaned too frequently to the municipal bodies he became fat and lazy. Except that in time he would be yearning to get back to his own country, gaol was no hardship, although it might be a very grave injustice.[45]

If complaints about the lack of free black labour left Colonial Secretary Connolly smiling inwardly, he must have been tempted to laugh out loud at a new quarrel between the pastoralists and the police. The cattlemen now openly criticised the police for their unwillingness to act upon reports of cattle-killing. The police rose smartly in their own defence. Surely it was unreasonable, they argued, for wealthy pastoralists to think that a million acres could be managed by two or three white men. Perhaps they should hire some boundary riders.[46]

IN POLITE REPORTING, it was sometimes softened to "loathsome disease" or, as one commentator circumscribed it: "the major physical evil of the north-western blacks, who have suffered severely from contact with Afghans, Chinese, Malays, and Japanese."[47] To those responsible for identifying sufferers it was syphilis, although with some symptoms peculiar to the Australian Aborigine. By 1905, the disease was widespread; by 1907, few doubted that it had the potential to decimate the black population of the Nor'-West. Even in remote parts the disease was making its presence felt. Whites had long marvelled at the stealth and mobility of the blacks: their ability to vanish silently into the bush and cover great distances. Few predicted that this ancient gift would be reincarnated as a curse. With consummate ease the natives came to the ports to barter; with equal ease they carried syphilis and other ailments to their homelands.

It is difficult to judge whether members of the white community took an interest in the matter out of sympathy for the Aborigines or concern for their own health. Whichever the motivation, the state government had a problem it could no longer ignore. Sexual contact with sufferers had to be prevented. Isolation hospitals seemed the only solution, but the government faced a dilemma. If Aboriginal patients were to be confined for months, perhaps even years, the hospitals would need security measures similar to those of a prison. But if the natives viewed the hospitals as prisons, they would not submit willingly to medical examination. Somehow, by education or deception, sufferers had to be persuaded that isolation and treatment were necessary.

In June 1907, at a meeting of doctors chaired by the state's Principal Medical Officer, Thomas Lovegrove, it was decided that two isolation hospitals, one for men and one for women, should be established not on the mainland but on uninhabited islands. There was a strong consensus that only by that degree of separation would the primary objective be met. Bernier Island, thirty miles west of Carnarvon across sheltered water, had been gazetted as a pastoral lease but had been used mainly as a summer holiday camp by the lessee. Having the advantage of some existing buildings, it was chosen as the site for a women's hospital. Barrow Island, three hundred miles farther north and sixty miles out from Onslow, had abundant fish and game; it was thought particularly suitable for the men.[48]

By far the greater burden of syphilis was carried by women. Female patients being greater in number and need, a women's hospital on Bernier Island was established quickly. The pioneering staff consisted of medical superintendent Dr Frederick Lovegrove (a nephew of Thomas Lovegrove), nurse Harriet Lenehan as matron, three orderlies (two with carpentry skills) and a cook. The first patients—about 55 in all—arrived by schooner in the spring of 1908. Some were so weak that they had to be carried ashore, and some would never leave the islands.[49]

Although opinions varied as to the likely success of the venture, few doubted the government's broad humanitarian aim. In pre-emptive defence, Colonial Secretary Connolly declared:

> This is the first attempt made not only in this State but in the whole of Australia to give the natives fair treatment, and it certainly provides a decisive answer to the criticisms made regarding the treatment of natives in this State.[50]

A few months later, invited guests and newsmen were permitted onto the islands to judge the work for themselves. Although the impressions taken were mostly positive, some were surprised by the lack of conventional hospital facilities. "The buildings are unpretentious," declared *The Northern Times*, "and certainly no charge of extravagance can be levelled against the Department in connection with them."[51] Chief Protector Charles Gale was quick to respond.

> Every effort has been made to introduce on the island conditions as nearly approaching those to which the natives are accustomed on the mainland as possible. Hence, instead of what would elsewhere be regarded as orthodox hospital buildings, here they take the form of tents, breakwinds, and small canvas-sided and iron-roofed cubicles, the natives having an excellent chance of leading the simple life to which they have been used.[52]

No men's hospital was ever established on Barrow Island. Early in the planning, a cheaper alternative emerged. By housing the afflicted men on Dorre Island, adjacent to Bernier Island to the south, one doctor and one bacteriologist could serve both exiled communities, and a single chartered vessel could keep both hospitals supplied.

In June 1910, at the end of his Nor'-West tour, Colonial Secretary Connolly visited the hospitals for a second time. Newsman George Romans observed, as others had done, that the women preferred their own bark shelters to the canvas and corrugated-iron structures provided for them, and that tribal divisions did not seem to be the great source of alienation that some had predicted. Certainly, they camped in groups according to their home districts, but with no more than a schoolyard separation. It seemed that the islands, and the affliction that brought the women together, granted some dispensation from the usual rules of interaction. As far as could be seen, they co-existed peacefully, aided by the shared experience of suffering and dislocation.[53]

None among the visitors to the island doubted that the women were getting enough to eat. Vindex wrote:

> With flour they make a damper which makes a good showing on the scales, and they get other stores, including occasional jam. In the

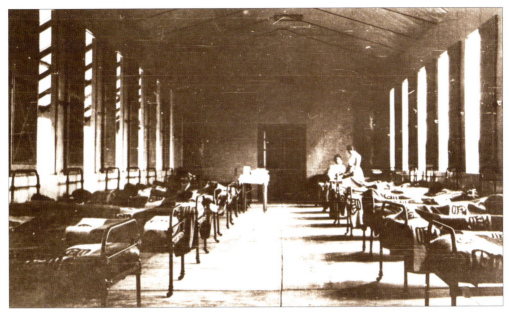

The new hospital ward, Dorre Island, 1910.

matter of supplies they sometimes show a dainty fastidiousness, as, for instance, when one lady of precise tastes returned her tin of black currant jam saying, "No want black stuff; gib em white jam." They prefer their native game, and as some of the tribes are particularly good hunters they feed plentifully on wallaby, boodie rats, and fish, and turtles when in season. The treatment of the women does not require very studied dieting, and the consequence is that the majority range from fatness to positive corpulency. The pride of the island is Rosie, who tips the scales at 15 stone.[54]

The colonial secretary's party also made the crossing to Dorre Island, where the circumstances of the men were a little different. Most were well enough to work; indeed, several certified "cured" were awaiting repatriation. For a few months, the men had been engaged in building a new women's hospital ward and surgery. An exchange of islands was planned: when the buildings were complete, the women would come to Dorre Island, and the men would move to Bernier.[55]

For the touring party, the visit to Dorre Island was largely recreational. Vindex wrote:

When the official duties were completed, the party moved over to the west side of the island, where the sea breaks in magnificent anger upon the reefs, and where oysters that would gladden the heart of an epicure may be collected by the hundredweight from the reefs. Good fishing, too, was enjoyed, and the day's catch included a couple of groper weighing upwards of sixty pounds each. After dinner the natives, whose black bodies had been ornamented with fearsome designs in plaster of Paris cribbed from the building materials, danced a corroboree.[56]

Vindex reported that after the sticks and feet had fallen silent, one black man seized a rare opportunity. He stepped forward, buttonholed the Colonial Secretary, and declared: "You good boss fellow, but me wanta my country go."

WHILE FRED LOVEGROVE AND HARRIET LENEHAN worked in isolation from white society, Daisy Bates in the southern capital was dividing her life between her black friends at Maamba and a growing band of liberal white admirers. Word of a white woman living among the blacks on the edge of the city had spread. There was recognition of the unique grass-level fieldwork, and rising celebrity for its audacious originator. By 1909 Mrs Bates was recognised as an authority on the Western tribes and their customs, and much in demand as a public speaker. By all accounts she excelled in that role. Part evangelist and part *raconteuse*, she was lyrical, entertaining, and highly responsive to the interests and ideosyncrasies of an audience.[57]

Such was the local regard for Mrs Bates that when it became known that the state's Aborigines would soon be studied in the field by an English party led by anthropologist Alfred Radcliffe-Brown,[58] many simply presumed that she would be involved. Indeed, *The Western Mail* went so far as to suggest that the expedition was the direct result of her endeavours.

> The credit of being the historiographer of the customs of Western Australian aboriginals is due to Mrs. Daisy Bates, whose work in the field of local ethnology is well known. What Howitt, Spencer, and Gillen have been to the vanishing races of Eastern Australia Mrs. Bates has been to the natives of this State. So much has her work attracted attention in the old world that a special expedition is being fitted out under the auspices of the Universities of Oxford and Cambridge (England) to win some further knowledge of the peculiar customs and institutions of our imperfectly known native races in the North-West. This expedition will be here about June next, and it is possible that Mrs. Bates may be permitted to accompany the expedition, and so render it the assistance that her previous experience will enable her to give.[59]

Soon after Radcliffe-Brown arrived from London, an invitation was indeed extended to Daisy Bates and local interest in the project rose suddenly as a result. Brown's financial position was also dramatically improved, as *The West Australian* of October 1st, 1910 reported:

> Mr. Alfred R. Brown, the leader of the Cambridge Ethnological Exploring Party, lectured before a large audience at the Museum last

night on the subject of "Primitive Man in Western Australia." His Excellency the Governor presided. Mr. Brown announced at the close of an interesting lecture . . . that through the generosity of Mr. Samuel McKay, who had placed the sum of £1,000 at the disposal of the expedition, they would be enabled to spend nine months or so longer than they had originally intended in the work of anthropological research in Western Australia. He felt bound to mention that to a lady they owed much in connection with this gift. Mrs. Daisy Bates had been enthusiastic over the matter, and by her urgency the generous action of Mr. McKay was largely prompted.[60]

Radcliffe-Brown was keen to investigate Aboriginal rules of intermarriage: the so-called four-class marriage system. The sanctity of tribal law had been dramatically demonstrated just a few weeks earlier. At Darlot on September 11th, nine Aborigines had been killed and 27 wounded in punishments exacted for marriage-law and other violations.[61] From an anthropological perspective the killings were interesting; Brown decided that the troubled district would be the expedition's first destination.

It was a party of four that went east by train from the port of Geraldton. Travelling with Brown were zoologist Elliot Grant Watson, self-described government attaché Daisy Bates, and Swedish cook Louis Olsen, recently hired. Bates wrote:

A few miles from Sandstone township, we pitched our tents among the natives gathered there, a travelling menage that consisted of a large fly for our dining and community room, furnished with folding chairs and other luxuries, the men's tent, Louis's portable kitchen, and my quarters. We were surrounded by nearly 100 natives, from Darlot, Barrambi, Sandstone, Laverton, Mt. Magnet and other nearby districts, and there was obvious ill-feeling and friction among the groups. I spent the afternoon making new friends, greeting old ones, and, with their assistance, digging out some honey-ants, which I proffered to the professor for supper. Grant Watson would have none of them. It took some time to convince the natives that my companions were not policemen, of whom, for their own reasons, they lived in an unholy fear at the time. After some vain endeavours at explanation, I found it easier to introduce them as my two sons.[62]

Despite simmering tensions between tribal groups, the work began well. For Brown and Grant Watson, it was not only their first engagement with Australian Aborigines; it was also their first opportunity to observe Daisy Bates in her 'native' element. Grant Watson in particular was struck by her extraordinary rapport with the subjects of their study. Years later, he would write:

Mrs. Bates probably knew more about the Australian Aborigines than anyone else alive. She was not primarily an anthropologist, but an enthusiast, who has given all her love and sympathy to these outcasts from their own land. Her guiding spirit was not a missionary spirit, but one of charity and compassion, and she presented in her person, so neat and dapper, and so much cut after the pattern of an Irish county lady, a strange example of symbiosis with these stone-age men and women, who accepted her with trust and appreciation.[63]

At first light on about October 24th, everything changed. Mounted police, on the trail of the Darlot murderers, galloped through the camp shouting, swearing and shooting in what Grant Watson would describe as "quite a cinematograph manner." The ill-conceived raid achieved nothing. In the chaos, most of the natives simply vanished into the bush. Radcliffe-Brown emerged from his tent, closed the flap behind him and stood his ground, furious. He scolded the police, telling the officer-in-charge that if it were of any satisfaction to him, their work in the area was ruined. The police soon departed, disturbed more by their failure to apprehend the suspects than by any harm done to the emerging science of anthropology. A little while later, two of the accused murderers emerged from Brown's tent. When the troopers came, they had dashed for what they considered the right kind of cover. They had thrown in their lot with the white boss who to their minds was "close up 'longside o' God."[64]

Mrs Bates was amused and impressed, both by Brown's willingness to harbour the alleged criminals, and by the mix of bluff and authority

Anthropologists Walter Roth (left) and Alfred Radcliffe-Brown.

that had kept them safe. Paradoxically, the raid led to her first serious disagreement with Brown, and his authority was at the very heart of it. Brown believed that the raid had destroyed any possibility of further work; Bates was equally insistent that the natives would soon return, and that they should wait and watch. Neither gave way. Each by a different criterion expected deference from the other. Mrs Bates was 47, knowledgable, and determined; Radcliffe-Brown was 29, talented, and egotistical. He was also the leader of the expedition. Daisy's challenge was too direct for his character and, arguably, his maturity. Without consultation, and with no apparent regard for Bates's success in trebling the expedition's finances, he announced that they would relocate to Bernier Island, where hospital patients from many tribal groups could be studied at leisure.[65]

If Brown had any reservation about his decision, it related only to the correctness of leaving a woman behind. In the end he decided that he should treat Mrs Bates exactly as he would treat a man in the same circumstances. He reaffirmed his intention to decamp and left Daisy to decide if she was coming with them. Of Grant Watson's allegiance, there was never any doubt. Years later, in his autobiography, he would describe the Sandstone incident as "the cause of our first breach with Mrs. Bates."[66]

Within three weeks, Radcliffe-Brown and Grant Watson had set up camp on Bernier Island and begun work in conditions they found surprisingly agreeable. Under a canvas awning on the beach they interrogated their captive subjects, taking regular breaks to bathe and fish. For Bates, things did not run so smoothly; almost a month passed before she reached the island. In his memoir, Grant Watson would recall a string of misfortunes for which Radcliffe-Brown and "Henrietta", the hard-drinking skipper of the government supply boat, would be held accountable.

> She arrived, very tired and very cross, for she had had a terrible time. She had stayed for some days at Sandstone, then had been forced to follow, first to Geraldton then to Carnarvon. At Carnarvon the yearly race-meeting was in full swing. Every house, every bed, every chair was occupied. Crowds of drunken, swearing men, and no place for a lone woman. Henrietta was in a blissful state of continuous intoxication. Nothing on earth, or from heaven, would move him till the end of the races. He drank and slept and drank again, and Mrs. Bates had to live how and where she could, sometimes on a table for the night, when she was lucky. And when at last the hated races were over and Henrietta sober enough to sail *The Shark*, they had the worst crossing on record. Thirty-six hours of being tossed and buffeted and buffeted and tossed on a small boat, and wet through all the time,

and very sea-sick. This undeserved suffering was put down, not quite logically, to Brown's account. It must have been galling, also, to find us so comfortably established and happy in our work. There followed an ever-widening estrangement.[67]

While Brown and Grant Watson worked among the male patients on Bernier Island, Bates spent more time with the women confined on Dorre Island. She also worked to refine and reorganise her manuscript of *The Native Tribes of Western Australia*. Perhaps surprisingly, she was still receptive to having Radcliffe-Brown edit and criticise her work. Disagreements aside, she recognised his ability to help her toward a leaner, more academic publication. Brown, for his part, saw great value in the work but did not quite know where to begin. His comments—pleas for reorganisation for the most part—often overflowed the margins and overran the text. There is no doubt that he confided his frustration to Grant Watson, who wrote:

> The trouble was that Mrs. Bates's knowledge, collected through many years of close contact with the natives, was not in a condition that Brown considered easily available for the ends of science. Indeed, he found it to be in a most hopeless tangle. The contents of her mind, in his estimation, were somewhat similar to the contents of a well-stored sewing-basket, after half a dozen kittens had been playing there undisturbed for a few days. At first he optimistically thought he might disentangle some of that rich medley, but in this he proved mistaken.[68]

Although Bates and Brown were still working with Aboriginal patients on the islands in February 1911, their collaboration in the field was effectively over. By different routes, they arrived back in Perth in the second week of April. That both were interviewed by *The West Australian* on the same day was probably due to the newspaper's assumption that their partnership was alive and well. Indeed, in their respective statements, there was no hint of disharmony. Radcliffe-Brown indicated that he would soon go north again for six months of work in the Ashburton district.[69] Mrs Bates declared herself "fit as a fiddle" and eager to resume the work disrupted by the Darlot killings. She would travel alone to Meekatharra.

The newspaper described Mrs Bates as "brimming over with enthusiasm over what had already been accomplished."[70] She was very happy with the work she and Brown had done, and also impressed by the humanitarian work being done on the islands. She was particularly struck by the affection that had grown between the natives and their nurses.

> Men and women alike revere their nurses, and I am convinced that when the time comes for the natives to return to their tribes this affection will be found to be a happy means of inducing other affected men and women to go to the hospitals before they become very bad.

The nurses, too, although they lead a lonely life, seem to be throwing themselves heart and soul into the work, and their attention and devotion to the sick natives is every bit as marked as the attitude of the natives towards them. Nothing more could, I am sure, be done for the natives than is now being done there.[71]

Radcliffe-Brown told the press that upon the advice of the Cambridge University committee overseeing his work, Mrs Bates's services would be retained for the duration of the expedition. And in a sense they were: when Brown with new assistants left for the north, he took with him Mrs Bates's 800-page manuscript. That he continued to edit the manuscript is certain. Its influence on his work, however, is difficult to judge.

IT IS NOT KNOWN WHO HAD THE IDEA to send the cured patients home as cabin passengers aboard the elegant *Koombana*, but the merit of the suggestion was immediately obvious. Since the hospitals had been established, the greatest challenge had been to convince afflicted natives that to be sent to the islands was not a death sentence. Managed well, the repatriations might soften the blacks' view of the hospitals, and lead more to accept the need for treatment.[72] There were issues to be considered. If the natives aboard ship were intimidated by their surroundings, any positive effect might be nullified. It was decided that Harriet Lenehan, who had recently left the islands, would be the perfect chaperone. Lenehan—or "Missie" as she was known to the black women she had cared for—was remembered with great affection.[73]

Having accepted the high cost of cabin accommodation, the Colonial Secretary's Office was determined to extract full value from its investment. If possible, the families and friends of those released would hear of their homecomings in advance. Before the repatriation, message sticks from the islands would be carried across to Carnarvon and sent north with the government-owned ketch *Namban*. There was no doubt that a lasting impression would be made upon those who came into town for *Koombana*'s arrival. The long-missed would arrive home in new clothes, looking well, and considerably fatter than when they left. Moreover, they would step ashore in the white way, down the gangway, from a ship that few imagined they would ever travel by, except perhaps in chains on the 'tween decks.

As far as can be told, Connolly and his department were willing to stand any criticism of the repatriation arrangements. The plan was pragmatic, but cynical it was not. If more diseased natives were willing to submit to medical examination, the benefit would outweigh the inevitable grumblings about the cost, and any amount of tut-tutting from the leafy suburbs of the capital. The programme went ahead. At Carnarvon jetty on February 5th, 1910, Harriet Lenehan and 37 Aborigines boarded *Koombana* for the run north.[74]

In the great scheme of things, a few cured patients were of little consequence: mere specks of light upon a great, dark dome. But for black and sympathetic white, there was no alternative but to draw breath from optimistic moments, so few and so widely spaced. To focus upon the present was to guard hope and guard it jealously, against overwhelming odds.

At Cossack, Hedland, Broome, Derby and Wyndham, Harriet Lenehan saw two years of difficult humanitarian work come to modest fruition. From *Koombana*'s rail she shared her girls' delight as down the gangway they tramped, overweight and over-pleased, with a government blanket under one arm and waving wildly with the other. And below, on the jetties of the Nor'-West, black faces responded with joy and wide-eyed fascination as their abducted kin crossed from the white world back into their own.

7

A Sea Change for Sailors

On November 11th, 1911, a frivolous little piece appeared on page ten of *The West Australian*.

> Chief Steward and Baker at Loggerheads.
> There was a considerable attendance of the public at the Fremantle Police Court yesterday to listen to the evidence in a case in which Frank W. Johnson, chief steward of the s.s. Koombana, was charged with having used abusive and insulting language towards Edwin Albrecht. . . .[1]

Albrecht was a 28-year-old Berliner who had completed one Nor'-West voyage as *Koombana*'s baker. He alleged that between Shark Bay and Geraldton on the previous Monday, the chief steward had come into the bakehouse and had, without provocation, broken a loaf of bread on him, abused him verbally, and torn his shirt.

When Albrecht was cross-examined by Johnson's solicitor Frank Unmack, he said he was not aware that there had been numerous complaints about his bread. He was, he insisted, a competent baker and a member of the Bakers' Union. To the amusement of the gallery, Unmack then produced two loaves of bread which Albrecht acknowledged as examples of his work. Unmack declared: "Fine stuff, aren't they? If the chief steward broke one of your loaves on you he must have had some trouble in doing it." Laughter continued in ripples through the gallery as Unmack led Albrecht toward a begrudging admission that if his bread was soft and light, so too was his case. If, on the other hand, the loaf had caused pain or injury as it broke, there might well be complaints about his bread.

After corroborative evidence from other crew members, Frank Johnson took the stand. He admitted that, having been irritated by repeated complaints about the bread, he had called Albrecht a "German cow," but he denied using other, more virulent expressions. Unsurprisingly, Fremantle's Resident Magistrate Edward Dowley decided that the court's time was being wasted. He dismissed the complaint without kind words to either party.

The matter should have ended there, but it did not. Albrecht, it appears, had friends in low places. The following day, after a meeting with their counterparts from the stokeholds of *Suva*, *Kyarra* and *Kurnalpi*, *Koombana*'s firemen called upon William Moxon, local manager for the Adelaide Steamship Company, to advise that the vessel would go nowhere while Frank Johnson remained aboard.[2] They cited the poor quality of the food and the chief steward's lack of respect for his fellow crew members. Moxon told the men that he would not, indeed could not, do what they asked. To remove the chief steward before any investigation would be a denial of natural justice, if not outright persecution. He asked the men to keep working while the matter was investigated.[3] They refused, and so began the Koombana Firemen's Strike of 1911.[4]

At face value this squabble deserves neither a title nor a place in history. It might have been forgotten had it not coincided with, and threatened to derail, a critical industrial negotiation taking place on the other side of the country.

Relations between steamship owners and seamen had never been harmonious. Theirs was a history of fundamental disagreement and disputation, punctuated by interim agreements and brief respite. By 1910, the lines were very sharply drawn: the Commonwealth Steamship Owners' Association represented all of the larger companies and their ships, while the Federated Seamen's Union of Australia represented about 98 per cent of the seamen and firemen working on those ships. Battle lines notwithstanding, the political pendulum had swung in favour of the seamen. A government with clear sympathy for the worker now enjoyed a majority in both houses of the young Federal Parliament, and the Commonwealth Court of Conciliation and Arbitration had by its recent rulings shown a keen interest in social justice. The time was right for the new industrial machinery to be tested. In the first week of December 1910, the Seamen's Union reported that it had failed to reach agreement with the shipping companies, and that because the current agreement would expire at year end, the ships from January 1st would no longer be manned.[5]

The union expected a response from the Arbitration Court and did not wait long to receive one. Court president Henry Higgins ordered a compulsory conference of the parties and scheduled it for New Year's Eve. There would be no adjournments.

Certainly much work was done in the interim, but by any measure the eleventh-hour conference was a success. A draft agreement was tabled, the strike was called off before it began, and the parties agreed to submit to arbitration. Higgins must take some credit for this, but it was not his eloquence that kept the union at the table. It was his reputation as a reformer that persuaded the seamen to submit to his further influence.

Henry Bourne Higgins had been appointed president of the Arbitration Court in November 1907. Within a few weeks of his elevation, he had reserved a place in Australian history with a landmark judgment. In 1906, the Australian Labor Party had sought to introduce measures which would protect the interests of low-paid workers. But there was a problem: under the Australian Constitution, it was beyond the discretion of parliament to legislate on such matters. Undaunted, the legislature sidestepped the Constitution and introduced a strange, potentially troublesome piece of legislation. The *Excise Tariff (Agricultural Machinery) Act 1906*, which passed with the remarkable support of the Protectionist Party, created a new excise on locally made machinery which would be waived if the manufacturer paid wages considered "fair and reasonable."[6]

As expected, more than a hundred local manufacturers applied for the waiver on the grounds that the wages they paid were already fair and reasonable. And as expected, the applications made by larger companies were opposed by the unions. One of the largest was Hugh McKay's Sunshine Harvester Company; its application became the test case.

The new law and the court case placed McKay in an invidious position. His company had no alternative but to apply for the waiver, because its liability for the new excise would exceed £20,000. Similarly, the court and its president were imposed upon, because at its heart the case was not about Sunshine Harvester or any company; it was about whether the wages paid in the industry as a whole were fair and reasonable. From Henry Higgins's displeasure came a new direction. At the outset he declared that there would be no assessment of Sunshine's profitability or of any employer's ability to pay. Rather, he would establish a minimum wage based on "the normal needs of an average employee regarded as a human being living in a civilised community."[7]

The choice of words was new, but the principle was not. Higgins drew heavily from Pope Leo XIII's encyclical *Rerum Novarum*, which in 1891 had defined the position of the Catholic Church on the rights and duties of capital and labour. Although *Rerum Novarum* defended the institutions of private property and inheritance, and did not reject the wage system, it insisted upon the worker's right to fair reward. "There is," it had declared famously, "a dictate of natural justice more imperious and ancient than any bargain between man and man, that remuneration should be sufficient to maintain the wage-earner in reasonable and frugal comfort."[8]

In Melbourne, Higgins turned to the practical challenge of defining a wage sufficient to keep an Australian family in "reasonable and frugal comfort." Evidence was taken from wives as well as workers to roll a swag of necessities, contingencies and little luxuries. Clothes, boots, heat and light, furniture, life insurance, union dues, sickness, books, newspapers, alcohol, tobacco, transport: all were counted, as the basic needs of an Australian working family received scholarly consideration.[9]

Sixteen years after *Rerum Novarum*, the first legal minimum wage was declared. Higgins ruled that an adult male Australian worker should receive no less than seven shillings per day, regardless of the employer's circumstances. The sum of £2 2s., for a six-day working week, was deemed adequate to support a wife and three children.[10] This was possibly the first such decision anywhere in the world. Although later overturned upon appeal, the Harvester Judgment remained tangible and influential, and the basic wage marked Higgins as a champion of the common man.

IN OCTOBER 1911, almost a year after the New Year's Eve conference, the case of Federated Seamen's Union of Australia v. Commonwealth Steamship Owners' Association came to court. As hearings proceeded, the unionists became more comfortable with the process and authority to which they had submitted. In Justice Higgins they had found a sympathetic arbiter. By early November, as judgment approached, they were confident of success, but this *Koombana* trouble was reflecting badly upon the union and proving difficult to resolve.

When *Koombana*'s stokers declared that they would not work while Chief Steward Johnson remained aboard, the company quickly found men who would.[11] On November 16th a new crew arrived from South Australia aboard the little steamer *Karoola*, but from that point forward, things did not proceed to plan. The new recruits had signed agreements in Adelaide, but upon arrival in Fremantle they declined to board *Koombana* until they had heard the views of the striking men. At a meeting attended by both old and new hands, most of the newcomers decided not to serve.[12]

The show of solidarity may have buoyed union spirit in Fremantle, but had precisely the opposite effect in Melbourne, where the union executive was actively involved in the court proceedings and knew how much was at stake.[13] In particular, the extension of the Fremantle strike raised the ire of Robert Guthrie, who was well placed both to form an opinion and to see that opinion prevail. Glasgow-born Guthrie was near the end of a long career as seaman, unionist, member of the Legislative Council in South Australia and now federal Labor senator. He was also general secretary of the Seamen's Union. The executive had turned a blind eye to the shipping company's attempt to recruit strike-breakers, but now had no alternative but to declare its hand. On November 21st, Guthrie delivered a blunt message to the Fremantle branch of the union and released the text of the message to the press:

Robert Storrie Guthrie (left) and Henry Bourne Higgins.

The Adelaide Council has decided that the Koombana should be remanned, leaving the dispute regarding the Chief Steward for investigation.

The members' action is detrimental to the best interests of unionism. A special meeting of the men cannot reverse the decision of the Executive.

The Fremantle meetings were informal, and the men who signed the agreement in Adelaide and afterwards broke it are liable to suspension and expulsion from the Union.[14]

Condemnation of the strike was now almost universal. Even Walter Barker, the partisan editor of *The Hedland Advocate*, joined the chorus of criticism.

This unfortunate strike has resulted in supplies being short from Onslow to Wyndham, and that phase of the question alone is not likely to rebound to the credit of the men. Apart from the pros and cons of the men's grievances over the food supplied them, it must be apparent to all well-wishers of the Labor party that the task of Labor ministers and others will not benefit by tactics of the kind the Koombana men have been guilty of: the Labor members of parliament for W.A. (Federal and State) asked these men to go back to work and allow their grievances to be investigated, but they refused to do so unless the chief steward was removed. No class of employer (even with the strongest sympathies for Labor) will submit to the principle involved in the attitude adopted by these men, and we are pleased to see that the union executive in the Eastern States has repudiated the action of the Koombana men.[15]

It is remarkable that the striking men, thus arraigned before the court of public opinion, did not capitulate.

Friday, November 24th was a day on which newspaper men east and west would have plenty to write about. In Fremantle, the offices of the Adelaide Steamship Company were busier than ever. Some strikers had finally dropped their objection and had agreed to serve, and new strike-breakers were being groomed. Thus far it made no difference; the company still could not muster a full crew.[16] There were also meetings with Frank Johnson. Although the company had asserted publicly that it would not transfer him, it is almost certain that the advantages of a voluntary departure were impressed upon him. Late in the afternoon, it all became too much for the chief steward. He collapsed from stress and was driven away to a private hospital.[17]

In Melbourne, it was judgment day in the Court of Conciliation and Arbitration. When Justice Higgins spoke, the confidence of the union executive was fully vindicated. To the consternation of the shipping companies, the union received almost everything it had asked for. It had won the right to an eight-hour working day at sea,[18] and all of its proposed rates of pay had been accepted. The new monthly wages would be:

Ordinary Seaman, £6
Able Seaman, £8
Trimmer, £8
Boatswain, or A.B. employed as lamp trimmer, £9
Fireman, £10
Donkeyman, £10
Greaser, £11

One small variation resulted from Higgins's decision to introduce what might be called a youth wage. He ruled that an ordinary seaman under eighteen years of age should receive £5 per month.[19]

There were other changes long sought. For a few years seamen had been paid monthly, but only by grace and not by any formal obligation placed upon the shipowner. They would now receive payment on the first of each month, as of right. So ended the age-old regime under which a sailor's wages did not accrue until the end of his term, even if that term was for two or three years. Also welcomed was the ruling that any seaman could apply to have up to 75 per cent of his wages paid directly to dependent family.[20]

In his judgment, Higgins wrote:

> There is no doubt that in the matter of wages, as well as in the other
> matters, the seaman has had the fag-end of things. Owing, I presume,
> to the difficulty of meeting, of combining, of acting in concert,
> scattered as they are across the face of the globe, in a roving life and
> with scanty leisure, seamen have never been able properly to assert
> their collective interests.[21]

It seems likely that two commencement dates had been pencilled in for
the introduction of the award. The new wage rates would apply from
January 1st, 1912, with the introduction of the eight-hour working day
set back to July 1st to give shipowners six months to complete a radical
redesign of their shipboard rosters. For both the court and the union,
the *Koombana* dispute was a festering sore. Higgins knew that criticism of
his judgment would be sharper and more difficult to deflect if the strike
were to continue—if the striking firemen, having lost public sympathy,
continued to flout the instructions of their leadership. If, on the other
hand, the union leadership were to end the *Koombana* trouble and end it
quickly, criticism of the award would be blunted and the reputations of
both the union and the court would be enhanced. Higgins told the press:

> The detention of the ship is serious, especially as the owners are
> under contract to carry mails. . . . I shall have this case put down for
> Thursday and if the trouble be not over by that time I must consider
> what I should do. I had hoped to make the increased wages in the
> Seamen's Union award apply to December work . . .[22]

By touting "December", Higgins created a powerful incentive for the
union to act decisively. The new deal so surpassed the old that early
commencement would be a windfall for its members. But just as Higgins
raised the possibility, he also raised the stakes.

> I am inclined to think that, even after an award has been made, the
> Court has power to strike out wholly or in part the relief granted to
> a union if it appears that the men of the union, although taking the
> benefit of the award, are not prepared to take up the burden also.[23]

Higgins's public pronouncements were philosophical, almost circum-
spect, but his challenge to the union executive was simple and direct: the
award would not be declared until the union could inform the court that
Koombana had resumed regular service with a full crew. Thus, with both
the prize and the measure of success now defined, and with December a
few days away, the Seamen's Union was left to prove itself worthy of the
new paradigm.

For a union to intervene to break a strike by its own members was
almost unheard of, but none who had followed the award proceedings

doubted that this intervention would be for the greater good. Guthrie wasted no time. He cabled the Adelaide Steamship Company's manager William Moxon to request that no further attempt be made to recruit or persuade. A full replacement crew would be delivered to *Koombana* in the shortest possible time, at union expense.[24]

That afternoon, sixteen firemen left Melbourne. By express train they were whistled across Victoria to Port Adelaide to catch the steamer *Riverina* for Fremantle. Travelling with the men were two union officers, doubtless to ensure that upon this arrival in Fremantle there would be no hiccup, no hesitation, and no unsupervised breathing of the local air.[25]

On the last day of November 1911, *Koombana* departed for the Nor'-West with passengers and mail scrambled, her chief steward somewhat chastened, and a full, fresh complement of firemen.[26]

The deal was done.

8

THE DREAD VISITOR

The weather becomes unsettled a day or two previously and a long rolling sea sets in from where the storm is. The barometer begins to fall, the thermometer to rise, as the atmosphere becomes more sultry, and ultimately the appearance of a dense bank of cloud betokens that the dread visitor is at hand.[1]

"A Catechism of Cyclones", *The Sunday Times*, March 31st, 1912.

BY 1912 THE RESIDENTS of Onslow, Roebourne, Port Hedland, and Broome had accepted that cyclonic storms were an inescapable fact of Nor'-West life, but that acceptance was the product of seventy years of difficult, defining experience. When a wild wind swept in from the sea at Shark Bay in February 1839,[2] members of George Grey's exploring party were left to wonder if this low coast might, like the islands of the Caribbean, be especially vulnerable to hurricane. Although their suspicions would ultimately be confirmed, the blow of 1839 was an anomaly. Shark Bay was too far south to be hit frequently by the storms of the tropics. Only after a settlement had been established further north—near Nickol Bay in 1863—did the getting of wisdom begin in earnest.

In March 1867 the coastal trader *Emma* left Tien Tsin Harbour for Fremantle in restless, late-summer heat. The little ship and her complement disappeared entirely.[3] Beside the cataclysmic events of a troubled world, the tragedy was microscopic. In Bengal, the death toll of the Orissa famine[4] had passed one million, and in China fifteen times that number had been cut down during two decades of bloody rebellion.[5] But here on the coast of Western Australia, the 42 who disappeared with *Emma* represented almost one third of the white population north of the Tropic of Capricorn. The loss was profound.

In 1868, 1869 and 1871, summer storms narrowly missed the nascent North-West Settlement. The pioneer residents watched the sky and wondered what the results of a direct hit would be. The speculation ended on March 20th, 1872, when Roebourne received its first catastrophic visitation. A month later, when news of the disaster reached Fremantle, the *Perth Gazette and West Australian Times* began its coverage by declaring: "We have been favored with many personal descriptions of the fearful hurricane which ravaged, and completely erased from the map of Australasia, our Northwest Settlement."[6]

In his despatch to Colonial Secretary Barlee, Government Resident Robert Sholl described the storm at its height.

> Shortly the native came and said that the roof of the Residency and kitchen had been blown off, and that the walls were falling. We had pushed against the door, which faced the wind, and kept it closed, but felt the front wall of the place gradually yielding. The timber was blowing about us from the Residency, and fearing some of it might penetrate our frail screen, I proposed going to the offices, which still stood. The children went with me, but Mrs. Sholl distrusted the offices and remained. We reached the offices with difficulty, crawling on hands and knees. If it had not been for the native I should not have made way against the wind; the children managed better. We could not (luckily for us) enter the building, and got under the lee of the back verandah. In the course of a few minutes, during a fearful and continued gust of wind, the building was unroofed and we had to flee. I was scarcely outside when I was driven before the wind, knocked over, and rolled along, the roof of the office falling around me, and small pieces striking me. Here I must have been struck heavily, but do not recollect it. When I recovered from insensibility I was lying on my face with my fingers dug into the ground. I found I could not move easily, or without pain. Attempted to go towards the bush hut, but in the haze, and with the rain beating in my face, went in the wrong direction, and was finally blown back. As I was rolling along, caught hold of a rock, and with difficulty got to leeward of it. I was here several hours, several attempts to get to the bush hut being unsuccessful, with the gale still at its height, and in my disabled condition. During this time the wind had not abated, but had gradually shifted from S.E. to E., thence N.E., and later, to the northward, when it diminished in force. It was moonlight, but the dense clouds and driving rain rendered it impossible to distinguish objects within a few feet. When the wind had veered North, and there was a partial lull, the sky was sufficiently clear to enable me to see by the misshapen shadows in the haze that every building was down.[7]

In the wake of near-annihilation, townsfolk launched into rebuilding, but that first flurry of activity spoke more of confidence lost than of confidence retained. Even Sholl wondered if stouter construction would, in conditions like those just experienced, make any difference at all.

From what I can learn it appears that all the buildings in Roebourne were destroyed within half an hour of each other. No matter how they were built, or of what material, they went in the direction of the wind. As a general rule the roofs were the first to yield. My watch, broken by the fall of the office walls, had stopped at 6.55 p.m. At about that time, the ruin of Roebourne was effected.

Pessimism notwithstanding, the town was rebuilt quickly by settlers who saw no alternative. And if the buildings seemed different, so did the builders. The old stoicism was there for all to see, but superimposed upon it was a new fatalism: a shrugging acknowledgment that their homes and institutions would periodically, inevitably, bow to the will of the wind.

IF MARCH 20TH, 1872 WAS ROEBOURNE'S DAY OF RECKONING, Christmas Eve of 1875 forced a similar change of outlook upon the pearlers of Exmouth Gulf. From fragmentary accounts, two days of utter chaos were reconstructed. From the Fortescue River west to the Ashburton and beyond, boats were sunk or smashed. About sixty men—Europeans, Malays, and Aboriginal divers—were lost in a storm of almost indescribable intensity. The most troubling aspect was that large vessels had fared no better than small. The schooner *Agnes*, having stood out to sea, was swept from end to end, thrown on her beam ends and dismasted, but somehow survived. Further west, *Lily of the Lake* and the former coastal trader *Wild Wave* were run south into the Gulf, where their masters believed they would be safe. They were not; both vessels were overcome as the changing wind turned the enclosed water into a vast, confused expanse of rolling surf.[8]

The storm was reported as a hurricane but to the battle-scarred pearlers this imported label now seemed inadequate, and not merely because the storms of the Nor'-West rotated in the opposite direction to those of the Caribbean or the South China Sea. The phenomenon they were coming to know was more than a whirlwind of the open sea; it was a peril made unique by the work in which they were engaged and by the deceptive embroidery of the low coastline. In the end, the pearlers' choice was natural and just. Their native divers already had a word for the spinning wind, and an uncanny sense of when it was needed. If the barometer fell and the black boys began chattering about *wili wili*,[9] their masters paid attention.

By 1880, "willy-willy" had all but replaced "hurricane" and "cyclone" in the Nor'-West lexicon. Its first appearance in print appears to date from February of that year, when the pearling correspondent for *The West Australian* reported:

We have forsaken Exmouth Gulf, partly on account of the threatening aspect of the weather—for the Gulf is an ugly place in a 'willi-willy,' as was proved towards the end of 1875—and partly on account of the superior attractions of our kind old friend Kate Carney Island, which always has something for us.[10]

Whether *wili wili* was traditional Yindjibarndi dialect or some kind of pidgin may never be known, because it was the pearler rather than the anthropologist that first showed a keen interest in the Nor'-West native. Either way, a visitor's impression of Roebourne, dating from 1885, confidently attributes the term to the original inhabitants.

> Upon approaching Roebourne a stranger is struck with the peculiar aspect of the buildings, which are of a varied and motley description, and nearly all presenting a low squab appearance. They are chiefly of wood, with roofs of corrugated iron fastened down with stout battens firmly bolted through the rafters. Upon closer examination the rafters will be found bolted to the wall plates, and in turn the latter are clamped down to the uprights. When inquiring why such a quantity of iron is used, the reply is, "willy willy," the native word for cyclone, the meaning of which is very clear to all who have resided a few years in Roebourne.[11]

By 1880, many Nor'-Westers believed that they had the willy-willy figured out. The townsfolk of Roebourne had seen their buildings fall and rise again, and pearlers had lost boats and men to phenomenal seas. But none had yet seen the landscape transformed by a sudden, dramatic rise of the sea.

On Thursday, January 6th, 1881, twelve pearling boats were gathered at Mary Ann Patch, about thirty miles west of the mouth of the Fortescue River. As the weather looked threatening, John Brockman took his lugger *Kate* into Coolgurra Creek, where he dropped anchor in company with the schooner *Ethel*. The creek, he thought, would be perfectly safe in any weather. Twenty-four hours later, chaos reigned.

> The gale had now increased to a hurricane, and we could only get about by crawling on our hands and knees. The glass was now below 27 deg. and still going down, and though not yet noon it was so dark that it was difficult to distinguish objects at more than a few yards distance. We now began to drag, and entered the Mangroves about 200 yards up the creek. Here we lost our rudder. The mangroves were now all round us, and waving ten or twelve feet above our heads, and the vessel was grinding and crushing them on all sides. All at once I heard the vessel give a great roll, and the water came up along the deck to the combing of the main hatch. She, however, righted again, and I then noticed that the mangroves had entirely disappeared.[12]

His boat now a plaything of the elements, Brockman could only hope that his wild ride would end on dry land. It did not.

A few minutes after this she gave another roll, and capsized. This must have been in the height of the gale. After clinging to the wreck until about five in the afternoon, it suddenly fell a dead calm, and the darkness cleared away enough to enable us to make out the land. After some difficulty we succeeded in righting and partially bailing out the only dinghy that had fortunately been lashed to the mast by a strong new painter, and got those of the hands into it who were unable to swim. We all managed to get ashore, with the exception of one poor fellow (a native) who we found next day entangled in the chain.[13]

By Friday evening, Brockman had reached some conclusions about what had occurred.

In thinking over the whole matter, and judging from the appearance of everything this morning, I am quite convinced that we must have had a large tidal wave which carried us over the mangroves, and then overturned us, as it was done so suddenly—one minute they were waving many feet above the deck, and the next had entirely disappeared. . . . I have no means of ascertaining the fate of the other vessels which were lying near the Mangrove Islands, as the dinghy we got ashore last night was blown away by the wind in the night, and where we landed is now an island.[14]

The toll was high indeed. All but one of the twelve boats had been destroyed. Three white men and several Aboriginal divers had drowned. All stores, shell and pearls had been lost. But for Brockman and the others who survived to see the sun rise, the storm was a revelation. Several tiers of sandhills had simply disappeared. From high land, they saw that the sea had penetrated miles inland. And where rivers in reverse had cut paths to the interior, great tongues of sand were littered with the bodies of turtles and sharks, and fish in strange, petrified shoals. It was, *The West Australian* concluded, "altogether unprecedented."[15]

OVER THE NEXT FEW YEARS, Nor'-West pearling changed dramatically. The year 1882 marks the beginning of a gradual northward and eastward migration of the industry, from Onslow and Cossack to the Eighty Mile Beach and Roebuck Bay.[16] Methods changed, too: in 1884, the first copper diving helmets appeared. By 1886, about three quarters of the pearling boats were using 'diving dress' and with each passing year the fraction increased.[17] In most conditions the native diver could not compete with the man in copper helmet and heavy boots. While the native dived and dived again, hoping to surface with a shell in each hand, the dress diver could remain below, studying the seabed, developing and following his intuition. Moreover, he could communicate: short tugs on the air line relayed his view and guided the boat above.

The transition to diving dress was rapid but not acrimonious. While the price of shell remained high, there was good money to be made using either method, and "native swimming boats"[18] often worked alongside the mechanised luggers of the new order. In 1886, when Chris Coppin and Jack Shepherd decided to give pearling a go, they chose the old way. They chartered the 60-ton schooner *Jessie* and engaged 21 native divers.[19] With George Woolbeck as skipper, they set out from Condon at the beginning of November 1886. Until Christmas they ranged south and west, but after returning to Cossack for supplies, they turned north and east, following report and rumour to Cape Keraudren and beyond. In the last weeks of the summer season they fell in with a large fleet of boats working a fine patch of shell off the Eighty Mile Beach.

When *Jessie* first joined the gathering, Coppin was surprised to see that none of the boats using diving dress were working. In broken English, the Lascar divers told him that the visibility below was too poor. This was a situation in which the 'swimming boat' had a distinct advantage, because the Aboriginal divers searched with their eyes close to the seabed. The dress divers worked standing up; they walked the seabed, stooping and scooping when shell was found. If the visibility dropped to six feet or less, they had trouble making out the seabed, let alone what clung discreetly to it.

In unsettled conditions, *Jessie* and her divers did extremely well: in one excellent day, they collected 1500 pairs. The first-time pearling entrepreneurs were in no hurry to return to port, but laws recently enacted required that the influenza-prone Aborigines be returned to their homelands by March 31st. On Thursday, March 21st, Coppin and Shepherd decided to work two more days and then sail for Condon. Within hours their plan was obsolete. Before dawn on Friday, a strong easterly wind sprang up. When the anchor line parted, the skipper set one sail and allowed the wind to take *Jessie* off the shore.

Their diving prowess notwithstanding, Australian Aborigines are not seafarers. At first light the black divers were terrified by the waves and became agitated. In a huddle on deck they stripped naked and made ready to swim. The coast was now fifteen miles away, into a fifty-knot wind, but Coppin could not convince them that to swim for the shore was impossible. Only by making light of the predicament did he persuade them to stay aboard. That was a life-saving outcome, for both black and white. For eighteen grim hours, twenty-four men pumped and bailed to keep the schooner afloat.

By dawn on Saturday the wind had swung to the north-west and abated. The exhausted crew steered toward the coast and, after sighting Mount Blaze, ran along the coast to Condon. Having no anchor to drop, they ran into the creek and secured *Jessie* among the mangroves. With their boat, crew and eleven tons of shell all safe, the men congratulated one other, but lightness of spirit would soon be overcome by grim news from the pearling grounds.

When the schooner *Sree Pas Sair* arrived off Cossack, dismasted and in tow behind the S.S. *Australind*, her master J. H. Haynes immediately telegraphed the colonial secretary in the capital.[20] An easterly gale, he reported, had caught the pearling fleet off the Eighty Mile Beach. Of 48 boats, very few had come through unscathed. There were drowned men floating about, he said, and more than five hundred crewmen remained to be accounted for. Of the boats still at sea, most were disabled, short of food and water, and drifting toward Rowley Shoals. He recommended that *Australind* be despatched immediately, to deal with whatever she might find.

The tragedy was not quite as Haynes had reported; indeed, the chaos at sea was almost matched by the confusion and speculation it spawned. As the days passed, the toll of boats and men steadily fell. The schooner *Dawn*, carrying sixty Aboriginal divers, had been seen on her beam ends during the storm but somehow survived to reach port. Other boats also limped home, some bringing lucky men plucked from the sea. And several, like *Jessie*, emerged from their refuges in mangrove-lined creeks to report themselves safe and tell their stories. By later estimates, six large vessels, twenty luggers and 250 lives had been lost in the single worst day in the short history of the Nor'-West.[21]

THE TROPICAL STORMS OF SOUTHERN LATITUDES often travel in a south-westerly direction. As the latitude increases, the westward progress may slow; the storm may then 'recurve', tracking to the south-east. For Western Australia, the positive aspect of this tendency is that severe storms often cross the coastline perpendicularly. Some of the worst have affected one town only, or better still, a small section of uninhabited coastline. But while the Nor'-West cyclone may have a nature, it is not in that nature to be corralled. Between sea and sullen sky it may choose any direction.

When a tropical storm remains over sea but tracks parallel to the shore, damage may be widespread indeed. Such was the case in February 1893, when a cyclone approached the coast near the mouth of the Ashburton River, but paused and did not cross. It turned right and followed the coastline of Western Australia for six days and a thousand miles. From the Ashburton the storm swept south-west across the Exmouth Gulf, catching the pearling fleet at sea. About fifty vessels, large and small, were sunk or smashed to pieces. The cutter *Florence Hadley Harvey* disappeared with two white men and seventeen Aboriginal divers, and one crew member from *Smuggler* survived 36 hours in the water to tell of his ordeal.[22]

Tropical storms decay quickly as they travel over land, but this unruly serpent was determined to be different. At the head of the Exmouth Gulf, it slithered across the peninsula and returned to the open sea.

In the town of Carnarvon on Sunday, February 25th, the locals noted the falling barometer and prepared for a blow. They had seen it all before. When the wind came, some sought refuge in the Government Residency, while others took their chances in the bush. Here, the storm was severe but not catastrophic; an early report from the town indicated that almost all buildings had been "more or less damaged" but the clean-up had already begun. The distances that parts of houses had been transported by the wind was the source of some amusement and distraction, but of greater community interest was the news, from stations upstream, that the storm had brough heavy rain to the interior. The Gascoyne was on its way and flooding was inevitable. There was nothing for the town to do but to wait for the wide embrace of its great, ephemeral river.[23]

A little further south, the storm struck Shark Bay. The settlement at Hamelin Pool was spared the worst of the wind but had a particular vulnerability to a storm passing to its west. It was situated near the end of a long shallow bay opening to the north. As the northerly gale came, the sea came with it. Very soon there was a foot of water in and around the police station. None could recall such a tide, but the incursion was more an inconvenience than a mortal danger. Upon this broad expanse, unmarked by ridge or ravine, there was little chance of drowning and even less of finding higher ground.

To the west, in the path of the storm, the pearling fleets at Dirk Hartog Island and Monkey Mia fared worse. Trapped on what sailors call a "lee shore," boats were thrown ashore or sunk at their moorings.[24]

By almost any measure the cyclone of 1893 was different. It confounded fifty years of observation and anecdote by holding its course and travelling far beyond the Tropic of Capricorn. Residents of Perth and Fremantle were already reading accounts of destruction in the Nor'-West when north-easterly winds brought great plumes of orange dust from the interior to cloak their town and port.[25]

For a few hours on Monday, February 27th, shipping chaos reigned at Fremantle. The port was well used to the hard north-westerly winds of winter storms, but this assault came from a different quarter. Three steamers—*Saladin*, *South Australian* and *Flinders*—were caught on the weather side of the jetty. As the wind and sea rose, the ships repeatedly struck hard against the fender piles, risking damage to themselves and to the jetty. *Saladin* was the first to move; she cast off her springs and steamed out to sea. *South Australian* prepared to do the same, but was called to render assistance to *Flinders*, which had not raised enough steam to help herself. The little steamer was now rising almost to the top of the fender piles and crashing hard against the jetty with every fall. With great difficulty a towline was passed. *South Australian* took up the load but as she neared the head of the jetty the line parted and both ships were again thrown against the wharf. *South Australian* stove a plate in just above the waterline, while the jetty took a further battering from *Flinders* until a new line was secured. To universal relief the second line held firm; the pair cleared the harbour and, with *Saladin*, rode out the storm at anchor.[26]

The great ocean traveller was not quite spent. Toward evening, wind and rain lashed the southern town of Bunbury, where a normally well-behaved estuary flooded orchards, filled wells with seawater and forced some residents to leave their homes for camaraderie if not comfort at the Good Templars' Hall.[27]

SOME STORMS ARE REMEMBERED for particular human drama rather than for greatness in the scheme of things. At midnight on Friday, March 27th, 1896, the postmaster in Perth received a telegram from his counterpart in the little port of Condon:

WILLY WILLY RAGING HERE.
WIND SO HIGH THAT SPRAY COMING THROUGH EVERY ROOM.
CANNOT HEAR INSTRUMENT.
MUST ATTEND TO SAFETY OF OURSELVES AND HOUSE.
SERIOUS RESULTS EXPECTED BEFORE MORNING.[28]

In the capital, there would be no further news until the steamer *Albany* arrived from the north a week later, bringing full particulars.[29] Throughout the afternoon of March 27th the wind had risen, but it was well after dark when the situation became serious. Traini's Condon Hotel lost its roof at 10 p.m., and most of its walls soon after. Among the guests were Mr Paton, commercial traveller for the furniture and homewares firm Sandover & Company, and his wife, who had decided to accompany him on this tour.

To lose the roof from their hotel room would have been bad enough, but the Patons suffered the added indignity of losing two of their four walls at the same time. They could do nothing but huddle together in the one remaining corner. Exposed to the full force of the wind and rain, and debris being hurled about, it must have seemed that things could not get much worse. Not so: Condon, like Hamelin Pool in Shark Bay, sat at the head of a narrow inlet which opened to the north, from which direction the first hard wind had come. As the gale rose to hurricane force it dragged the rising tide with it, along the channel, over the jetty and into the town. In a matter of minutes the water reached the floor of the hotel and kept rising. For three hours the Patons sat in water to their waists, with little protection from wind, rain and sand.

Other residents could do nothing to assist. From the relative safety of a government building they heard the wind tearing strips from the buildings still standing. A little way along the street, a private house was demolished and all of its contents blown or washed away. Nothing was spared; even the piano, with part of the floor on which it had stood, was picked up and hurled against the wall of the post office.

Had the eye of the storm passed directly over the town, there would have been some brief respite, and an opportunity to rescue the Patons before the wind returned. But there was no lull; although the wind shifted, it did not ease. At about 1 a.m., publican Traini and local resident Matthews took their chances. They negotiated the wreckage of the hotel, reached the stranded guests, and brought them to safety. How the Patons coped with their ordeal is not known. It may have haunted them for a very long time. But as the furniture salesman and his wife sat in tight embrace with the homewares of Condon flying all about, some positive thoughts may have intruded.

The change in the direction of the wind brought another dramatic change: the water withdrew as rapidly as it had risen. Dawn revealed sodden ground and the full extent of the destruction. The deck of Tiffany's Jetty was lying a hundred yards from its snapped piles. The receiving sheds had been levelled. The Condon Hotel had lost its roof, most of its walls, also its kitchen, stables and outbuildings. And beyond the settlement, the telegraph line lay flat on the marsh for miles.

THE WILLY-WILLY AT CONDON was the first of four direct hits upon coastal towns in the space of three years. The greatest, and one of the first to be recorded in photographs, was the Cossack Blow of 1898.

For the crews of pearling vessels and coastal traders, a visit to Cossack was keenly anticipated. In other places, loading and unloading could be tedious, with goods transferred by lighter to beach or jetty. By contrast, the Cossack township was neatly stitched to the bank of a tidal inlet. Having enjoyed the modern convenience of a masonry wharf with a tramway and holding sheds, sailors could choose between drinking establishments immediately adjacent.

There was comfort here, too. After a few hours at the Weld or the White House, a sailor could look forward to undisturbed sleep. At other places boats bumped, scraped and canted over with every ebb of the tide. But Cossack's wharf projected into a deep, natural pool. Any vessel with a draft of seven feet or less could drop anchor and remain afloat—with masts vertical and bunks horizontal—for the duration of its stay.

Few among Cossack's drinkers and sleepers ever gave much thought to the natural forces that had shaped Butcher Inlet. The body of water was not only a tidal estuary; it was also one outlet of the Harding River. At first sight, it did not look like the mouth of any river. There was no permanent freshwater flow, and the braided channels of the hinterland seemed strangely ambivalent. And yet it was to the river that thanks were due for the luxury of a good night's sleep. The ebb and flow of the ocean had attended to the landscaping, but it was the periodic flooding of the Harding River that had done the dredging.

If residents or visitors had followed that line of thought a little further, they might have seen mortal danger hiding behind convenience and comfort. If a willy-willy from the north-east were to deliver heavy rain to the interior before crossing the coast west of Cossack on a high spring tide, the results would be catastrophic. The ocean would meet the floodwaters of the Harding in the middle of town.

That extraordinary alignment occurred in the late afternoon of Saturday, April 2nd, 1898.[30] *The West Australian* later reported:

> The jetty has sunk down many feet and the goodshed is frightfully torn about by the storm. The sea burst in the door facing the creek and swept a quantity of cargo out. Fearful damage has been done to shipping. The s.s. Beagle is piled up on the rocks on the south side of the jetty in front of the Weld Hotel with her stern resting on the fallen wall of the jetty and her bows on the rocks. The schooner Maggie Mollan is a total wreck on the beach toward Japtown. The dilapidated jetty was fully loaded with general merchandise for Condon. The cargo is now strewn along the strand from one end to the other. The schooner Harriett is high and dry on the beach close to the north side of the jetty. The s.s. Croydon, which was moored near the stock jetty, on the opposite side of the creek, was carried fair on to high land. The cutter Rose has been washed up between the residences of A. Rouse

Cossack, 1898: the wreckage of the schooner Maggie Gollan *on the beach by the wharf.*

Cossack, 1898: S.S. Beagle *aground upon the wreckage of wharf and tramline.*

and A. S. Thompson. . . . The only boat that remained at her moorings was the police boat. Not a single boat other than this is safe. Tee and Co's. office, H. Wilson's residence and buildings, the Weld and White House hotels and Paxton's boarding house are scattered in all directions. The new Customs-house and the residence of J. Meagher have been unroofed. A great deal of other damage has been done. The buildings of the Nor'-West Mercantile Company were flooded, and the company are heavy losers through the damage done to their merchandise, which is floating about the stores. Japtown is one heap of ruins. The houses which are composed of wood and iron flimsily put together were felled like skittles.[31]

As residents surveyed the damage in disbelief, a camera bought for family amusement became a powerful tool of record and reportage. What its lens brought to unprecendented focus was not common mayhem; it was Cossack's vulnerability to a once-in-a-century confluence of water and circumstance.

IT HAD ALWAYS BEEN BELIEVED THAT BROOME was situated too far north to be susceptible to cyclone, but two disastrous events in the space of six months demanded change in theory and practice.

On April 26th, 1908, almost four weeks after the end of the official cyclone season, the first of the two storms struck south of Broome. The combination of location and time could not have been worse. Most of the pearling boats had left port for their first foray of the new season, and most had sailed south to work along the Eighty Mile Beach. Complacency and poor understanding contributed to a terrible toll of men and boats. When the wind rose from the east, many stayed inshore where the sea was manageable, only to be caught on a lee shore when the eye of the storm passed and the wind reversed in direction. Almost forty boats and a hundred men were lost.[32]

The disaster brought new intensity to the discussion of tropical storms and the natural laws that might govern them. Some speculated that the latitude of greatest danger might migrate with the sun, moving south and then north as summer progressed, making Broome more prone to assault at the beginning and end of the season. When disaster struck again on December 8th, that view received tragic endorsement: another six vessels and forty men were lost less than a hundred miles from the scene of the earlier disaster. Heading the list of shipping casualties in the second storm was Mark Rubin's beautiful 140-ton schooner, *Kalander Bux*. Her master Ancell Gregory survived hours in the water to reach the beach alive, but most of his elite crew did not.[33]

When the second storm struck, most boats had already returned to Broome for the summer lay-up. The master pearlers were acutely aware that had the storm come two weeks earlier, the death toll would have been horrendous. Without delay, the Pearlers' Association issued new advice to its members.

> Your Committee desires to draw your attention to the following observations that would, in their opinion, considerably reduce the disastrous effects of these hurricanes if attended to in time:
>
> (1) To carry on no pearling operations between the 1st December and the 30th April, except in those waters from which shelter can be easily reached.
>
> (2) To carefully note the barometer night and morning during these months, as it is an unfailing guide to the weather in the tropics.
>
> (3) The barometer has two tides in the tropics, just the same as the ordinary water tides. It rises about 1-10th from 4 a.m. to 10 a.m.; falls about the same from 10 a.m. to 4 p.m.; rises again from 4 p.m. to 10 p.m.; to fall again about the same from 10 p.m. to 4 a.m. High water by the barometer, 10 a.m. and 10 p.m. Low water by barometer, 4 a.m. and 4 p.m. Any variation from the above pearlers should view with the greatest care.
>
> The normal summer reading of the barometer is 29.90. A fall in the barometer of say 2-10ths below normal should always be taken as a danger signal, and this more especially if the wind is in the east. During the summer months—December to April inclusive—an

easterly wind and a falling barometer is a sure indication of abnormal conditions in the weather, and pearlers should at once seek shelter. The one great lesson of the last two 'blows', however, has been not to work away from the place from whence shelter can be easily obtained, and, secondly, not to seek the shelter of an open beach because the wind is in the east. Owing to Broome's position, the centres of these dreaded hurricanes have invariably passed to the westward, and this means that as the storm progresses the change of wind will be from east to north-east to north to north-west to west. This places luggers seeking shelter of an open beach (merely because the wind is east) in a position of grave danger, and has undoubtedly been the cause of the great losses the industry has suffered during the past year.[34]

ALTHOUGH THE VISITATIONS OF 1908 were disastrous for Broome's pearlers, neither storm did any great damage to the town itself. Indeed, Broome had never in its 25-year history been struck by a blow like those which had ravaged the towns further south. For a time it seemed that the pretty, poinciana-lined showpiece of the Nor'-West enjoyed some natural immunity.

Broome's halcyon days ended abruptly. On Saturday, November 19th, 1910, the town took a direct hit from a storm with a devastating combination of features: it was large, intense and slow-moving.[35] Before dawn, an easterly wind rose to hurricane force but continued to strengthen for another ten hours. By midday, much of Chinatown had been levelled and the telephone system lay twisted and draped over fallen trees. By 2 p.m., uprooted trees were rolling before the wind and pearling boats were piled one upon the other. The wind that had so ruthlessly dismantled the camps and shanties now hurled corrugated iron through the better parts of town, where even trusted refuges were opening to the rain.

At 5 p.m. a sudden stillness descended. For a short while, in the eye of the storm, the sky was clear and Broome's desolation was bathed in yellow late-afternoon light. But as darkness fell, the wind returned from the north-west. The second half of the storm was as powerful and persistent as the first, but chose different targets. Of the buildings that had survived the day, many fell to the night. And whereas the first assault had raked the pinions of the town's prosperity into a pile on the east-facing foreshore, the second chose Cable Beach to display a grim harvest of the open sea.

Three weeks later, *Koombana* arrived in Broome on her regular Nor'-West run. As the ship came alongside the jetty at high tide, disembarking passenger Len Knight wondered what kind of place he had come to. Protruding from the water at odd angles were the masts of some forty sunken luggers. The scene was gaunt and apocalyptic. Along the tramline and in the town, naked trees and perversely twisted telegraph poles continued what the sunken boats had begun. Knight wondered if he should turn around, reboard the steamer and leave. He did not. He stayed and made Broome his home.[36]

By the end of summer some colour had returned to the town's streets, but like Roebourne in 1872 and Cossack in 1898, the community had been altered in character and confidence by its first great visitation. For the young Irish engineer Jim Low, who had left *Koombana* to settle in Broome a few months earlier, the cyclone—his first—was something he would never forget. Two years later, in a letter to his sister Jane in England, Jim wrote warmly of life and opportunity in Western Australia, but added:

> Between Carnarvon and Onslow is the southern limit of the cyclone storms and let nobody come to the conclusion that I am talking through my hat when I say that I will have no hand in advising any of my friends to settle down within cooee of them. You can judge for yourself.[37]

9

The Lore of Storms

On land, a great tropical storm may be terrifying; at sea, it is another experience entirely. For while the landsman may take refuge and wait for the tumult to pass, the seafarer must deal. The seafarer must *negotiate*.

On December 27th, 1897 the aging steamer *Albany*, northbound on her regular coastal run, sighted the North West Cape. For smaller vessels the high promontory was the turning point for the eastward run to Onslow. The pearling boats and little coasters would cross Exmouth Gulf and then weave among fringing islands to reach the mouth of the Ashburton River. But *Albany* was the mainstay of Nor'-West trade; her master was under instructions to follow a wider, safer track. After continuing north to round the Muiron Islands, sightings of the outermost islands would be taken from the prescribed comfort of deep water. Only after Anchor Island had been made out would the cautious run to the anchorage begin.[1]

On most trips the turn to the east brought a sudden and remarkable softening of travelling conditions. Passengers conditioned to the long swells of the southern Indian Ocean would emerge from cabin or saloon to feel the warmth of the air and to gaze upon a calm sea alive with sea snakes and turtles.[2] But this trip was different: *Albany* turned to meet a hard south-easterly wind and a short, sharp sea. Captain Odman stood on his track but watched his barometer carefully. He knew that a hurricane from the north was a distinct possibility. At Anchor Island the wind rose alarmingly; he turned the ship around and steamed out to sea. Although the storm now lay in his path, the decision was not a difficult one. Onslow offered no safe harbour; it was an open roadstead. If a hurricane were to be faced, it would not be faced here among reefs and islands. *Albany* would roll with the punches of the open sea.

And roll she did. For twelve hours, heavy punches came in flurries. Machinery was damaged and the superstructure was strained as the ship was swept from end to end by seas which, Odman later declared, "rose mountains high." Not all of *Albany*'s cargo was stowed below;

S.S. Albany, c. 1900.

chained to her deck were eight iron tanks weighing 800 pounds apiece. All were torn free and washed overboard. Water percolated everywhere: down the companionway, across the floor of the saloon and into the cabins. To passengers in fear of their lives, the ship at times seemed to be more submerged than afloat.[3] But suddenly, when the assault seemed unsurvivable, the wind fell away to nothing.

At the centre of a whirlwind, the first impression taken is of uncanny stillness. Not of silence, but of stillness. The wind may be altogether absent or come from any quarter in flukes and swirls that die away as quickly as they arise. A sailor may recognise the opportunity to speak and be heard, and yet stand spellbound and say nothing. He may light a cigarette and find that the match, held aloft, continues to burn. And from the bridge, an officer may look down upon smoke hanging in the air, clinging to wet machinery, refusing to disperse.[4]

The crew of *Albany* quickly learned that there was more to this strangeness than the sudden dissolution of the wind. Second engineer C. R. Hunter would recall:

> We steamed through the first portion of the storm into the centre, where all was calm so far as the wind was concerned, but where the water was simply a seething, boiling cauldron.[5]

The English sea captain and author John Macnab had described more precisely the unique agitation of the sea to be found at the centre of a circular storm:

The centre has a peculiar sea of its own, the water rising in great pyramidal heaps, and literally throwing itself about in all directions, making it difficult for a ship to live.[6]

Perhaps appropriately, the most engaging of all descriptions would come not from science but from well-versed imagination. Two years after *Albany*'s encounter, merchant seaman Joseph Conrad began writing the novel *Typhoon*, in which the fictional steamer *Nan-Shan* meets a great storm of the South China Sea. Like the officers of *Albany*, Conrad's men are delivered to a place beyond their experience.

Through a jagged aperture in the dome of clouds the light of a few stars fell upon the black sea, rising and falling confusedly. Sometimes the head of a watery cone would topple on board and mingle with the rolling flurry of foam on the swamped deck; and the Nan-Shan wallowed heavily at the bottom of a circular cistern of clouds. This ring of dense vapours, gyrating madly round the calm of the centre, encompassed the ship like a motionless and unbroken wall of an aspect inconceivably sinister. Within, the sea, as if agitated by an internal commotion, leaped in peaked mounds that jostled each other, slapping heavily against her sides; and a low moaning sound, the infinite plaint of the storm's fury, came from beyond the limits of the menacing calm.[7]

Typhoon was fiction, but a hundred years of fact and folklore were honoured by its transparent prose.

Conrad touched lightly upon what *The Times* had described as "that singular phenomenon, termed by Spanish sailors *El ojo*, or the storm's eye, when in the midst of a black and lurid mass of clouds there appears a luminous circle in the zenith."[8] From within the eye the seafarer may look upward as if from the bottom of a well, to a narrow circle of starry sky. For those made captive to the eye in daylight, the experience is different but no less remarkable. In place of a saucer of stars, a patch of blue sky may be seen. For the master and crew of the *Marmion*, sailing from Liverpool to New York in 1849, the spectacle was bright indeed. In the ship's log, the captain wrote:

At noon it was quite moderate, and a beautiful clear, blue sky, and the sun shining beautifully, but this is in the treacherous centre. From meridian to about 0-40 it remained quite moderate and clear. At 0-40 there rose up a thick impervious cloud or haze, and it became quite dark, comparatively speaking, though there was no black cloud; and in a very few minutes we were involved in a terrific storm.[9]

There was a simple reason why from the deck of *Marmion* the great escarpment of cloud did not appear dark and threatening in the usual way. The ship had sailed into the eye of the storm as the sun passed over. Both ship and cloud were bathed in sunlight, and the cloud was seen as if from above.

For the men of *Albany* there was an unexpected addition to the strangeness of their circumstances. When the wind dissipated, hundreds of birds appeared as if from nowhere. Spiralling downward, they landed and sat motionless on the wet deck. Many were unfamiliar, even to crewmen who had travelled this coast for years. A few of the hapless creatures were picked up. With eyes open they lay soft and warm in the sailors' hands, exhausted beyond resistance—not beyond fear, but beyond any display of it.[10]

Within the eye, fascination is tempered by inescapable fact: the second half of the storm has still to be endured. With the return of the wind comes a great assault upon composure; it is rarely well recorded. Some describe the sound emanating from the approaching eye-wall as a low groan that rises in pitch only to be overtaken by something akin to a shock wave. And behind that invisible curtain, a great shearing of waters demands frantic effort to turn the ship to face an altered sea. So it was for *Albany*: the wind caught the ship on her port side and, as her head was swung, a torrent of seawater over the bow swept the birds into a compact ridge below the starboard gunwale.[11]

There is hardly a tale of storm at sea that does not draw out the metaphor of nature's fury; indeed, the lore of storms is built upon the attribution of rage and enmity. But as the fictional *Nan-Shan* steamed into great elemental strife, her creator was alert to a different danger. Rather than exploit a myth, Conrad chose to explore it.

> It was something formidable and swift, like the sudden smashing of a vial of wrath. It seemed to explode all round the ship with an overpowering concussion and a rush of great waters, as if an immense dam had been blown up to windward. In an instant the men lost touch of each other. This is the disintegrating power of a great wind: it isolates one from one's kind. An earthquake, a landslip, an avalanche, overtake a man incidentally, as it were—without passion. A furious gale attacks him like a personal enemy, tries to grasp his limbs, fastens upon his mind, seeks to rout his very spirit out of him.[12]

By gift of circumstance, the men of *Albany* would also glimpse the greater truth. As another great wave raked the deck, the officers watched as the birds now lifeless were disentangled and discarded to the sea. Here, in a few moments, the metaphor of wrath was stripped bare. The men were held, briefly transfixed, by a simple illustration—a reminder if not a revelation—that nature is not vengeful. Nature is utterly indifferent. They had little time to think on this because their ship was once again in great danger. Fight now they must, and with new, cold clarity: this storm would run its course without reference, without regard, and with neither malice nor mercy.

Seamen's lore warns that the second half of a circular storm is often worse than the first. So it was for *Albany*, and especially for the men below decks: the engineers and firemen.

In fair weather, conditions in a ship's engine room are not too bad. Cool air is drawn in through the ventilators, forcing hot, stale air out through an iron grating called the fiddley. In a storm, however, it is imperative to keep a full head of steam; the comfort of those below will be sacrificed to keep the engine room dry. With the fiddley covered by tarpaulin, the air quickly becomes stale and the temperature may rise to 120 degrees Fahrenheit.

On the latest steamers the fiddley was large, rectangular and raised above the level of the deck; it could be battened down quickly when the need arose. Not so, old *Albany*; she was of unusual design. For twenty years she had served as the combined sail-and-steam vessel *Claud Hamilton* before her acquisition in a takeover by the Adelaide Steamship Company. Her new owners cut her in half, added 31 feet amidships, straightened her cutwater bow, removed one mast altogether and shortened the other two. She would serve out her remaining years as a dedicated steamer, and one that was almost impossible to keep dry.[13]

In the gloom and oppressive heat of the stokehold, unique camaraderie may grow among men who never have cause to question the value of their work. For these blind guardians of the heartbeat, the rolling rhythm of the ship's engine is a thing of beauty and a source of pride. Their reward—and their gift to all on board—is that precise mechanical reassurance which may be seen or heard or felt.

There is among sailors a fear of dying below deck, akin perhaps to the landsman's fear of being buried alive. Whether on land or sea, the best known antidote for fear is distraction. In a great storm at sea, the engine room has its appeal, for nowhere else is distraction so complete. Its sensations may not be pleasant, but while the crankshaft turns, all senses are engaged. Dappled twilight, oppressive heat, the smell and taste of coal dust, the clang of the firebox door and the hiss of steam combine to pervade and preoccupy. But if the fire is ever extinguished, all warmth and consolation are lost; the engine room becomes a hideous place: cold and cavernous, with a pitch and roll governed only by an unseen sea.

Engineer Hunter described the second half of *Albany*'s ordeal:

> The Albany was an open "fiddley" ship, with only an iron grating around her funnel base, instead of being closed in. When we got our second dose we shipped huge seas, which poured down into the engine room and flooded the place out. In less than no time there was a depth of 9ft. of sea water in the engine room, and the fires were out

for over 24 hours. During that time we had relays at work bailing the ship out with canvas buckets, and eventually we were able to get the fires going again.[14]

At noon on December 29th, 1897, *Albany* arrived at Onslow in dilapidated condition. Her officers were greatly affected by an experience they hoped and expected would never be repeated. But just three months later, the *Albany* again found the centre of a great storm at sea. In the first week of April 1898, the *Northern Public Opinion* interviewed Captain Odman to report:

> At noon on Friday Bedout Island was passed about 6 miles out. The barometer then fell rapidly. The wind changed to the N.E., gradually increasing to cyclonic force. At 11 o'clock that night a fearful hurricane set in. The ship was headed N.N.W. and stood on the same course until 10 a.m. on Saturday, when she suddenly became becalmed with the barometer down to 27.80. This state of affairs continued until 11 a.m. Reverse winds were then got into and blew harder than before. The barometer started to rise, and at noon stood at 28. The violence of wind did not show signs of decreasing until 4 a.m. on Sunday, though the barometer read 29.1 at 1 a.m. After it had moderated it was discovered that the steamer had lost her rudder, but no other damage had been done. . . . The position of the ship was determined at 70 miles due north from Cossack. Her head was put southward and sails set to a fairly light sou'-wester. In the absence of the rudder the trysails and staysails were employed in steering.[15]

For the southward run to port, men were stationed fore and aft, port and starboard to trim the improvised sails. By Sunday morning, when Jarman Island lighthouse was sighted, the new navigational regime was working very well: *Albany* moved a little this way and that as Odman, more field marshal than helmsman, barked instructions from the bridge. At noon in Cossack Roads the ordeal ended; the order was given for the anchor to be dropped. And as the chain slid through the hawsepipe, a vibration instantly recognised passed along the deck. The crew cheered.

Although none aboard ship knew it, Cossack had been torn apart by the greatest storm of its short history.[16] For residents dumbstruck by destruction, *Albany*'s arrival was both a relief and an amusement. Her comical flapping of canvas wings lifted spirits greatly. At the end of the day, for the enlivenment of the locals, Odman told his story in a salty, matter-of-fact way, brushing off homage for his seamanship. "No," he said, "the old ship knew her way into port too well to need any guidance."[17]

A year later, on March 21st, 1899, *Albany* was again fighting for survival in a Nor'-West willy-willy. Again she lost her rudder, but this time Odman was unable to control her. She lay broadside to the wind for four hours with passengers and crew working shoulder to shoulder to bail her out. Again the old ship survived, but her recent form was troubling. For the third time in less than two years she had met strife at sea and had responded by steaming into the middle of it.[18] To some, it was incomprehensible that ships' masters were failing to take evasive action when science had been offering guidance for fifty years. Had they no knowledge of the Law of Storms?

ALTHOUGH THERE HAD BEEN EXPLICIT REFERENCES TO "WHIRL-WINDS" as early as 1698,[19] the scientific explanation of these great storms can be traced to a chance meeting in 1831 between an amateur meteorologist and a professional scientist. The amateur was New York engineer William Redfield; the learned professor was Denison Olmsted. Redfield had read Olmsted's work on hailstorms and, keen to ask a few questions, had introduced himself. Many years later, at the end of a lifelong association, Olmsted recalled that first meeting:

> I was soon made sensible that the humble enquirer was himself a proficient in meteorology. In the course of the conversation he incidentally brought out his theory of the laws of our Atlantic gales, at the same time stating the facts on which his conclusions were founded. This doctrine was quite new to me, but it impressed me so favourably that I urged him to communicate it to the world through the medium of the American Journal of Science. He manifested such diffidence at appearing as an author before the scientific world, professing to be only a practical man, little versed in scientific discussions, and unaccustomed to write for the press. At length, however, he said he would commit his thoughts to paper and send them to me on condition that I would revise the manuscript and superintend the press. Accordingly, I received the first of a long series of articles on the law of storms and hastened to procure its insertion in the Journal of Science. Some few of the statements made in the earliest development of his theory he afterward found reason for modifying, but the great features of that theory appear there in bold relief.[20]

The "great features" of Redfield's theory were: that the storms of the tropics are great whirlwinds; that the rotation is clockwise in south latitudes, anticlockwise in north latitudes; that the axis of rotation may be vertical or inclined; that the winds spiral downward toward the centre and rise upon reaching it, and that only at sea level do the winds blow horizontal; that the barometer falls toward the centre, and falls with increasing rapidity toward the centre; that the storms advance as they revolve, following curved paths; and that "great uniformity exists in respect to the path pursued."[21]

The year 1831 is salient for another reason. On August 11ᵗʰ, the island of Barbados was struck by its greatest ever hurricane. The damage was daunting and the death toll horrendous; one conservative source reported that 1477 lives were lost in the space of seven hours. In the storm's aftermath, the Scottish soldier-engineer William Reid was sent to the island to superintend the reconstruction of government buildings. During his two-and-a-half-year civil assignment Reid began a systematic study of Atlantic storms.[22] He collected data, corresponded with William Redfield, and in 1838 published *An Attempt to Develop the Law of Storms by Means of Facts*. Its clumsy title notwithstanding, 'Reid on the Law of Storms' was keenly read, widely discussed, and reprinted within a year. Importantly, Reid had formulated simple rules that mariners could apply to avoid being drawn into the vortex of a storm at sea.

The first weapon of a tropical storm is deception, for with the wind and waves comes an assault upon common sense. With a gale in one's face it is difficult to accept that the greatest threat must lie in another direction entirely. The objective of Reid's first rule was to establish the direction to the storm's centre. In simple non-nautical terms, the rule states:

> In the southern hemisphere, tropical storms revolve clockwise. If the seaman turns to face the wind, the eye of the revolving storm will lie to his left and, moreover, slightly behind him, because the winds spiral inward as they rotate.

Having established a direction to the centre of the storm, the next objective was to understand its progress over the sea. The mariner was instructed to note any shift in the direction of the wind before applying the second rule:

> If, as a storm approaches, the shift in the direction of the wind is clockwise, the storm should pass to the right. Conversely, if the shift in the wind is anticlockwise, the storm should pass to the left.

The value and appeal of this second rule was its surprising simplicity. Somehow it distilled the essence of the 'un-obvious'. A few minutes with pencil and paper was usually sufficient to convince a bright young officer that the rule was universal: it would hold true in either hemisphere, regardless of the direction of a storm's rotation.

From knowledge came strategy. Reid explained that once the location and progress of a storm were established, positive action could be taken to avoid or escape what was called "the dangerous quadrant," which in southern latitudes is that area to the front and left of the advancing whirlwind. To be caught here is doubly dangerous: not only are winds strongest where the storm's rotation and its advance are aligned, but the direction of the wind in this quadrant is directly into the storm's path.[23]

A revised, expanded edition of 'Reid on the Law of Storms' appeared in 1850 under a title even more cumbersome than the first: *The Progress of the Development of the Law of Storms, and of the Variable Winds, with the Practical Application of the Subject to Navigation.* Reid's first edition had been theoretical but his second was greatly strengthened by the testimonies of ships' masters who in the intervening years had tested his contentions and found them sound. One early advocate was Captain Hall of the *Black Nymph*; in September 1842, he had found it necessary to test Reid's principles.[24]

Black Nymph was three or four days' sail from Macau. The weather was fine and clear and the crew, who had been smartening things up in preparation for their arrival in port, were greatly surprised to receive orders to prepare for a storm. Hall had been watching the barometer and had noted its fall.

> Toward evening I observed a bank in the S.E. Night closed in and water continuing smooth, but the sky looked wildish, the scud coming from N.E., the wind about North. I was much interested in watching for the commencement of the gale which I now felt sure was coming, considering that Colonel Reid's theory being correct, it would point out my position with respect to its centre.

When the wind came, Hall consulted his charts and diagrams and concluded that *Black Nymph* was on the southern and western verge of a typhoon. His account, first published in the *Nautical Magazine* in 1847, would also swell the body of evidence in Reid's new edition.

> The wind rapidly increased in violence, but I was pleased to see it veering to the N.W., as it convinced me I had put the ship on the right tack, viz the starboard, standing, of course, to S.W. For five hours it blew with great violence but the ship being well prepared rode comparatively easy. The barometer was now very low, the wind about W.N.W., the centre of the storm passing doubtless to our right.
>
> Thinking it a pity, as the gale sensibly decreased, to be so far out of our course, I wore to N.W., and made sail, but in less than two hours heavy gusts came on and the barometer began to fall. I now thought we were approaching the storm once again, and doubtless the theory is not mere speculation. I wore again to the S.E., and to show more clearly how great a difference a very short distance nearer to or farther from these storms makes, the weather rapidly improved.
>
> When we arrived at Hongkong two or three days afterwards, we found they had had a gale, and its centre lay between the ship and Hongkong, through which centre I might have had the pleasure of passing if, regardless of the indications of the barometer, and the results of the scientific comparison of the data of other storms, I had been eager merely to keep on the tack nearest my course.[25]

The revised edition was much heralded and warmly reviewed. In London, *The Times* devoted several columns to Reid's theory and case studies and then, as if apologising for not extending its salute, declared:

> We have already, we trust, made it evident how far the domination of science may be extended over these hitherto intractable operations of nature.[26]

From Britain, Europe and America, a flood of new publications came. Works by Dove, Birt, Meldrum and Ley were all reprinted.[27] There were practical offerings too: Henry Piddington's *The Sailor's Horn-Book for the Law of Storms* was sold with transparent storm cards which, when laid upon a chart and aligned with the prevailing wind, could be used to locate the centre of a storm.[28] By the 1880s, science had become syllabus. At Board of Trade examinations, all candidates for first officer or master were now required to demonstrate an understanding of the Law of Storms. It is hardly surprising that the best known of all books on the subject was also the slimmest. John Macnab's *Catechism of the Law of Storms* was little more than a bundle of sample questions and answers that helped a generation of ships' officers to meet the Board's requirements.[29]

Conrad's *Typhoon* was fiction, but fiction well founded upon the facts of life at sea. At the time of its publication, most young officers were well versed in the Law of Storms,[30] but many older masters remained sceptical of both the science and the policy of avoidance. It is hardly surprising that Captain MacWhirr, master of the *Nan-Shan*, was cast as one such.

> "A gale is a gale, Mr. Jukes," resumed the Captain, "and a full-powered steam-ship has got to face it. There's just so much dirty weather knocking about the world, and the proper thing is to go through it with none of what old Captain Wilson of the Melita calls 'storm strategy.' The other day ashore I heard him hold forth about it to a lot of shipmasters who came in and sat at a table next to mine. It seemed to me the greatest nonsense. He was telling them how he outmanoeuvred, I think he said, a terrific gale, so that it never came nearer than fifty miles to him. A neat piece of head-work he called it. How he knew there was a terrific gale fifty miles off beats me altogether. It was like listening to a crazy man. I would have thought Captain Wilson was old enough to know better."[31]

Like Conrad's MacWhirr, Olaf Odman was an old-school master forced by experience to accept the need for change. His career would continue, but *Albany*'s hat-trick of near disasters had sealed the old ship's fate. At Fremantle on a Saturday afternoon in March 1900, invited guests gathered in the saloon of "the magnificent new Bullarra" to toast Queen, colony, company and progress, and to pay tribute to a vessel that had grown old with the colony and in her service.[32] For Nor'-Westers, *Albany* was an institution; many of her passengers had known no other steamship. On the threshold of a new century, her retirement was also tinged with sadness for the many who thrived upon thrilling tales of survival at sea. In the new world, would science disarm nature? Would all avenues to adventure and heroism be closed?

The eye of a hurricane may be a strange, mystical place but for those who emerge to speak of it there is no desire to return. For while the outsider may taste its fascination, the insider knows also a visceral fear: a tight, encircling constriction in which wonderment struggles for breath. The men of S.S. *Albany* counted their 1897 experience among the worst of their lives, but readers of fact or fiction will see things differently. They will carry a quiet conviction that the survivors of great storms at sea are a privileged few, chosen to be tested and chosen to bear witness. Conrad knew this. In the first chapter of *Typhoon* he sketched the character of a man soon to be so tested.

> Captain MacWhirr had sailed over the surface of the oceans as some men go skimming over the years of existence to sink gently into a placid grave, ignorant of life to the last, without ever having been made to see all it may contain of perfidy, of violence, and of terror. There are on sea and land such men thus fortunate—or thus disdained by destiny or by the sea.[33]

The schooner Enterprise, *lightering copper ore to steamer.*
Depuch Island anchorage, 1910.

10

The Koombana Blow

On Tuesday, March 19th, 1912, Depuch Island anchorage was busy. Lighters of the Whim Well Copper Mining Company were delivering ore to two large sailing ships at anchor. The 1800-ton iron barque *Crown of England* had recently arrived from Natal.[1] She had been built at Workington in 1883, but after years of service to Britain had been sold to Norwegian interests. Her new owners decided that although she would fly the flag of Norway, she could keep her imperious name.[2] German-built *Concordia* was a little smaller and a few years younger, but her path to this remote place was remarkably similar. She too had been built to carry cargo that few steamships could accommodate, and she too had been sold away from her homeland.[3] On both ships, Norwegian was now the language of the mess room.

The crews of *Crown of England* and *Concordia* had time on their hands, because loading copper was a tedious business. At the mine twelve miles inland the heavy green ore was crushed, bagged and loaded onto flat rail trucks. From there it rattled across marshland to the railhead at Balla Balla where a short jetty jutted into a mangrove-lined pool of a tidal creek. At the jetty the bags of ore were slung, hoisted and manhandled into the company's lighters for open-water transfer to the holds of the waiting ships. It would be a month at least before either ship would hoist sail.

During the morning, the company's lighter *Steady* broke from its routine; it returned to the jetty to collect stores and passengers. Several Whim Creek locals, who had witnessed a fatal fight at the Federal Hotel, were under instruction to proceed to Roebourne for the trial of two Italian miners.[4] At the anchorage they would wait for the steamer *Bullarra*, which would divert from its regular track to collect them.

With a light easterly wind, *Steady* made easy passage. She delivered stores to *Crown of England* and then dropped anchor to wait for the steamer. *Bullarra*, they believed, was due that evening, but after *Steady* had left Balla Balla the postmaster received a wire from Port Hedland. *Bullarra* had missed the morning tide and would be delayed a full day.[5]

Steady was a heavy workboat; she offered little in the way of comfort or protection, even for a crew of three. She now had eleven aboard: three Norwegian sailors, seven witnesses to alleged murder, and one intending *Bullarra* passenger, Charles Turner, making his way home to Perth. When the steamer failed to appear, all settled down for an uncomfortable night among bags of copper ore.

In the early hours of Wednesday morning, a breeze sprang up from the north-east. It was stronger at sunrise and rose further as the morning passed. There was little to do but sit tight and watch the comings and goings. At lunchtime, all loading of copper ore ceased. The lighter *Clyo* dropped anchor a little way away from *Concordia*, and the schooner *Enterprise* remained near *Crown of England*. Three pearling boats arrived and also dropped anchor, but after an apparent change of mind, moved on. They rounded the southern tip of the island and disappeared.

MAP 6 • *Depuch Island and Balla Balla.*

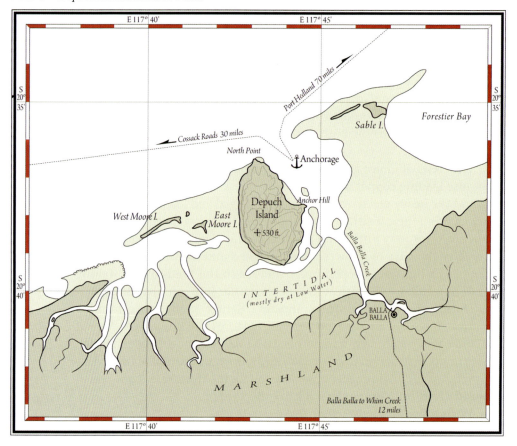

Aboard *Steady*, eleven men were now hungry and cold. During the afternoon, two attempts were made to beat back to Balla Balla but the boat twice missed stays while attempting to come about. On the first occasion the boat drifted dangerously close to rocks; on the second, she came so close to *Clyo* that she was obliged to drop anchor once more. *Clyo* and *Steady* were now only fifty yards apart. By day end, none aboard either vessel was in any doubt that they were in for a rough night. Charles Turner would recall:

> A heavy sea was running, and to crown everything rain began to fall. The lighter had no hatches, and we therefore had no place in which to shelter. The copper which we carried was loaded on the deck, and there was only a small hatchway down the forepeak which we had to nail up in order to keep the water out. We tried many times to fasten the mainsail over the deck but as often as we did so the force of the wind broke it adrift again. The rain soon drenched us to the skin. Through the storm we could see the two ships, Concordia and Crown of England, being tossed hither and thither much as we were ourselves. We next discovered that the Steady was dragging her anchor, so we dropped another, which held her again. Still the wind increased, and the raging seas continually broke over the vessel's bows, and wet us again and again. There were on board only sufficient provisions for one day, with the result that on the second day we had only one tin of salmon and one potato each. During the afternoon we had a chance of getting ashore in daylight, for if we had let go the anchors the wind and tide would have taken us in. But the skipper thought he could save the boat, so we held on. With the rain came a thick mist, and it was only at intervals that we could see even the Clyo.[6]

As daylight faded, the men were surprised to see a motor boat approaching. *The West Australian* later explained:

> On Wednesday afternoon, the motor launch which is used for towing and carrying mails and passengers from the steamers to Balla Balla left the wharf at Balla Balla to take out the last of the passengers and mails for the Bullarra. Amongst those who went out were Messrs. Maginnis (wharfinger), Slaven, Thomson (of the mine staff), and Hill (licensee of the Federal Hotel). When the launch left a very strong wind was blowing, and some doubt was expressed as to whether it would be possible for the launch to reach the steamer, but as the news of her departure had been received from Port Hedland, and no intimation given as to her not coming in to Balla Balla, Mr. Maginnis considered it necessary to keep faith with the steamer, more especially as the witnesses concerned in the case at Roebourne were under a penalty to appear.[7]

After a difficult passage the launch reached *Clyo*, which sent a dinghy to collect the passengers. Maginnis, Thompson and Hill were the first to go. They boarded safely but all those who watched the transfer thought it too dangerous to be repeated; indeed, some of the trial witnesses said they would have none of it. While waiting for conditions to moderate, the launch made the short crossing to the schooner *Enterprise*, where Captain Vallianos had been discussing the weather with Captain Eriksen of *Concordia*. The two men, who had been watching their barometers for 24 hours, knew that no abatement was likely. In fading light, they boarded the motor launch to warn of worse to come. By their action the two captains were simultaneously vindicated and confounded: conditions deteriorated so rapidly that neither was able to return to his own ship. At about 9 p.m., Eriksen hailed *Clyo*. The launch was in danger of swamping, he said; they would return to Balla Balla.[8]

The men aboard *Steady* had seen boats come and go but were isolated from all conversation. It hardly mattered. There was little prospect of any rendezvous with a steamer, and nothing to be done but to batten down. Charles Turner described the evolving ordeal:

> Night brought down with it an inky darkness. I do not think one soul on board will ever forget it. All the while the storm was gathering in fury. Very few words were spoken except when a wave would sweep over the deck and nearly swamp us. The cold was intense. There was no galley on the ship, and all we had was a firepot to light a fire in, which was impossible. So we spent the night. Just after daylight the gale appeared to lessen, but the next moment it was blowing harder than ever. We could hear the cables straining against the boat, and feared every moment they would carry away. There was one thing to be thankful for; we had no croakers on board.[9]

On Thursday morning, with the wind gusting to seventy knots, there was one simple objective for every vessel at the anchorage: to hold fast. All would endeavour to keep their vessels off the shore. All would fail. *Concordia* was the first to drag her anchors but her early surrender was doubly fortuitous: not only did she come to rest upon sand rather than rock; she settled beside a little headland which would provide some protection from the hurricane still to come.

A little to the north, *Crown of England* had two anchors out, but at about 8 a.m. she also began to drift toward the shore. A third anchor was let go. This held for a while, but within an hour she began to drag again. More chain was let go, and a heavy wire hawser was played out along one of the anchor lines. At 11 a.m., when the drift recommenced, there was nothing more to be done. The lifeboats were made ready. Close to the rocks, the drift stopped; a strong ebb-tide current was working against the wind. Although his ship hung in this precarious balance for a long while,

Captain Olsen knew that she could not be saved. When the tide turned, wind and water would co-operate to drive her ashore.[10]

Aboard the schooner *Enterprise*, first mate Nicholas Pappastatis had reached a similar conclusion. By mid-afternoon the easterly wind was beyond resistance. In the absence of Vallianos, he made a master's decision: while daylight remained he would sacrifice the schooner to save the passengers and crew. At 4 p.m. the anchors were slipped, but the landing was not what he had hoped for; *Enterprise* caught rocky ground and stopped short. With the tide falling, it would be dark before she moved again. After some discussion, Greek sailor John Scordese volunteered to swim ashore to secure a lifeline. Somehow, against the odds, he succeeded. Across the gap he took a light line which he then used to pull a heavy rope from ship to shore. Once the heavy rope was secured to rocks, the human transfer began. The three sailors still aboard were sent first; all completed the crossing and joined Scordese onshore. Pappastatis then matched the courage of his countryman: leaving *Enterprise* to her fate, he took to the water with the schooner's two passengers, both poor swimmers afraid to face the ordeal alone. All landed safely.[11]

As Captain Olsen had predicted, *Crown of England*'s fate was sealed by the turn of the tide. At 6 p.m., under the combined action of inflowing water and onshore wind, the vessel took rocky ground stern-on. Olsen told his men that there was nothing any of them could do to save the ship; she was doomed. Lifebelts were issued and the men were asked if they wished to swim ashore while there was still daylight. Together, they decided to wait until morning.

Aboard *Steady*, eleven men were keeping close, damp company at the bow of the boat. An hour or two after dark there was a sharp crack as one of the anchor cables parted. The lighter then dragged its one remaining anchor and drifted stern-first toward the shore. The men had been wet, without sleep and almost without food for 62 hours but all knew that concentration and composure would be needed for the next few minutes. The shore of Depuch Island is predominantly a rocky scree, with little sandy beaches between blunt headlands. *Steady* was already half-full of water. If she were to ground upon rock, she would not ride up; she would break apart. But if she found sand, the men's prospects would be good. Their drift in darkness was a simple heads-or-tails wager with the highest possible stakes. The men gathered near the stern, ready to jump when the crunch came. The lead was kept going, and the first calls were encouraging: "Sand . . . sand . . . sand." And then, recalled Turner:

> All at once the lead gave rock. For the first time I felt my heart sink. But only for a moment. I remembered that some of the others could not swim, whereas I could, so I began to think that after all matters might have been worse for me. We drifted on, passed over the rocky

zone, and in a trice grounded on the sand. The ensuing wave shot us up to within 10 yards of the beach, and the next within a few feet of dry land. More than one of us said, "Thank God."[12]

ABOARD CROWN OF ENGLAND the men now gathered in the mess room. As the drama unfolded they must have regretted their decision to stay aboard. The ship had a thousand tons of copper in her holds; after an hour of heavy bumping, water began to seep in. All the while the wind kept rising. At 11 p.m. it reached a screaming pitch that none could ever have imagined. After the lifeboats, the chart-house and everything loose on deck had been torn away, Captain Olsen issued to each man a short length of rope to secure himself in the mizzen rigging. He then stripped naked and advised his men to do the same. The advice was sound but all declined, each man acutely aware of his vulnerability but none prepared to make so primal an admission of it.

The men took to the rigging, but after two hours, the masts had swollen and the pounding from below had damaged their steps. Olsen ordered them down. Within minutes, his judgment was vindicated; in rapid, cracking succession the three masts failed and went overboard. The men now clung to the rail and to each other, but briefly. With a great groan the iron hull divided, both forecastle and poop departing before the hull split down the centre into two. Some men were thrown into the sea; others chose their moment and jumped.[13]

Several of the *Crown of England* men would never be seen alive again, but the deliverance of first mate Matthias Holst was, by his own account, miraculous. Thrown into the water on the weather side, he found himself in the worst of predicaments. Caught between huge breaking waves and a wall of iron, there was every possibility that he would be knocked unconscious and drowned. But the first wave that picked him up was so large that the iron hull rolled over as it struck. Holst was swept clear over the top of what remained of the ship. As he surfaced on the lee side, a second great wave swept him high onto the rocky shore, beyond the reach of those that followed.[14]

By contrast, Captain Olsen's struggle was painful and protracted. After saluting two men who declared that they would not leave before him, he dived into the sea. In quick succession, three huge waves caught him and took him under. As he came up he managed to get hold of some timber, but was sucked down again. He managed to get the timber beneath him but even with some support, several attempts to reach the shore failed. After being tossed about like a cork, he was unceremoniously dumped upon the rocks, bruised and badly cut. He crawled to a sandy spot and sat naked and cold from 2 a.m. until daylight, with the rain and sand beating in his face. It was too dark to move, he later said, and the wind too strong to stand against.[15]

On the shore of Depuch Island the men of *Steady* had much to be thankful for, and more to confront. Charles Turner would recall:

> The flying sand and shell travelled with such speed through the air as to almost bury themselves in our flesh. We climbed over the sand ridge with difficulty, and with some wet blankets over us lay down to await the dawn. It seemed an eternity before daylight appeared. Somewhere about three in the morning I heard voices calling out, but could not tell from which direction the sounds came. All through the night we could hear the Crown of England breaking up on the rocks. It reminded one of some big foundry and steam hammers at work upon steel plates.[16]

At first light, Turner woke to a grey sky and a north-westerly gale that seemed like no wind at all. Mounds of sand, each marking a spot where a comrade lay asleep, surrounded him. Climbing to the crest of a sand ridge, he looked down upon the little beach and headland. *Steady* was high and dry where they had left her. A hundred yards offshore, the masts of sunken *Clyo* stood clear of the water with scraps of sails flapping toward Balla Balla. On the beach, *Concordia* was aground but not fast; she would swing parallel to the shoreline and be carried higher when the tide turned. A little to the north, upon rocks in shallow water, lay *Crown of England* unrecognisable: a contortion of skin and spine, picked and parted like the frame of some great, fallen carnivore.

From the beach Turner saw on one of *Clyo*'s masts what appeared to be a clump of sail. It was not; Greek crewmen Con Celezis and George Carlos still clung to the rigging. With men on the beach ready to assist, the exhausted men were encouraged to leave their perches and to swim ashore. On the beach, they were reunited with their countryman Dimitris Chandros who, having fallen from the rigging at the height of the storm, had managed to wrap his arms around a floating spar. He and his consort had come ashore together.

From fragments, *Clyo*'s pitiable story was reassembled. At around 5 p.m., on the last of the ebb tide, her anchors had also been let go. It seemed that the wind would push her directly onto the little beach but, like *Enterprise*, she did not reach her destination. About a hundred yards from shore, *Clyo* stuck fast on a sandbank. There was some consolation: the lighter was intact and perfectly upright. The men climbed into the rigging; here they would stay, clear of the waves, until the incoming tide lifted her. Although *Clyo*'s deck was above water, she was swept by breakers that partly filled her hold. She floated again, but only briefly. At 7 p.m., having moved just a few yards, the lighter settled down on the same bank with her deck still visible below the water. For the moment, the men felt safe in the rigging. Two hours later, chaos reigned. One crewman lost his grip and went overboard. Captain Maginnis was struck on the head by

Clyo *sunk and* Concordia *ashore, Depuch Island, March 1912.*

some part of the rigging; without any cry of pain or anguish, he simply fell and disappeared. A little later, Thomas Hill apparently decided to swim; he freed himself, called out "Good-bye" and jumped. Of Robert Thompson or John Pitsikas, nothing was known.[17]

Having helped the *Clyo* survivors to come ashore, the men from *Steady* walked toward the wreck of *Crown of England*. Turner would recall:

> We had not gone far before we came across the first body, that of the only Englishman on board, who had a life belt on. A little further on we found another body, also fully dressed and with a lifebelt. Further on again we picked up what was left of the unfortunate cabin boy. Then we came to a pile of rocks on which were huddled together the captain and the remainder of his crew. They presented a pitiable sight, and had been very roughly handled by the waves and rocks. They had another body with them on some timber just below where they were sitting.[18]

In grey morning light Martin Olsen had assembled what remained of his crew. While staring in disbelief at the wreck of their ship, someone had seen movement. To the amazement of the men cast ashore, the two seamen left clinging to the stern rail had survived the night. They were helped to dry ground, utterly exhausted.

From *Crown of England*, eight men were missing. All were found dead on the shore. The survivors, close to exhaustion, needed help to place the bodies of their shipmates beyond the reach of the sea. Charles Turner again:

Crown of England *wrecked, Depuch Island, March 1912.*

The bodies were removed above high water mark, and we set about collecting some of the provisions which had been washed in. Returning to camp we had our first good meal for four days. We had not known that tinned dog could be so appetising.[19] After a brief spell we renewed the search for bodies, and found those of Messrs. Macguiness and Hill, and the steward and second mate of the Crown of England. The last two named had evidently come ashore on two hatches, which were lying beside them. Mr. Hill, a fine specimen of manhood, had only his boots on. He must have put up a game fight.[20]

A FEW MILES AWAY, the settlement at Balla Balla had met the full force of the storm. The jetty had been seriously damaged, but for the most part the town still stood. The government buildings, razed to the ground in April 1898, were now made of sterner stuff. North and south, the telegraph lines were down, but the news most keenly sought—and the subject of greatest anxiety—was the fate of the fleet at the anchorage.

On Friday afternoon, the stranded captains of *Enterprise* and *Concordia* teamed up with four locals to ascertain the fates of ships and men. In the mangroves near the settlement, a pearling lugger was found to be seaworthy but its Malay crew refused to make the trip. The boat was commandeered.[21] The straight-line distance to the island was only three miles, but a hard nor'-wester now blew directly into the mouth of the creek. Tacking all the way, the lugger made the crossing in three hours.

By chance, the inquirers came ashore just a few yards from where the bodies of Maginnis and Hill lay high on the beach. A little further along, they found the bodies of two men they did not recognise. Only after carrying the four bodies to the lugger did they learn the greater scale of the tragedy; only then did they realise that it would be impossible to bring all of the dead to the mainland. After a brief conference with the two Norwegian masters, it was decided that six men would be buried immediately. Charles Turner recalled a simple, improvised observance.

> A spot for the island graves was selected on the highest part of the sand ridge under a hill of rock, and with shovels taken from the Steady a number of us soon had an extensive grave dug. The bodies were then carried up the hill, and placed side by side, the two skippers reading the burial service in Norwegian. As the bodies were being placed in the grave I noticed that the Englishman seemed almost to clasp hands with the Norwegian next to him. The thought flashed through my mind, "Brothers in death." The grave was then filled in, and a door from one of the ship's cabins was erected to mark the spot. It was an awesome sight to see those poor mangled bodies lying side by side. I shall never forget the scene, neither I think will any of the others.[22]

In fading light and upon a falling tide, the lugger carrying the bodies of Maginnis, Hill, Andriasen and Gron set out for Balla Balla. Although the wind was now following, the water was so thick with sediment that it was impossible to distinguish deep from shallow. The lugger ran aground. After four hours with the larger waves breaking over the stern, the boat was released by the incoming tide. It was after midnight when the bodies were finally brought ashore, but for assistant wharfinger Hugh McDonald and the others, the long day was not quite over. There remained the awful duty of calling upon Maude Maginnis to tell her that her husband was dead.

The death of Captain E. P. "Eddie" Maginnis was especially poignant. Maginnis had lost his first wife in 1902, when he was only 26. The young widower continued his seafaring career on both sides of Australia, as an officer of *Grantala*, *Yongala* and *Koombana*. But in November 1909, remarried and with a child on the way, the popular sailor took a 'shore job': he accepted the position of wharfinger for Point Samson and Cossack. There he remained until the end of 1911 when H. R. Sleeman, the manager of the Whim Well Copper Mining Company, offered him the role of wharfinger at Balla Balla. Sleeman's offer was too good to refuse: the salary was more than Maginnis had been accustomed to, and the accommodation excellent. Maginnis wrote to his mother in Queensland, whom he had not seen for several years, to suggest that at summer's end she should come to Western Australia and live with them. Ellen Maginnis arrived at Depuch Anchorage on Monday, March 18th, 1912. Five days later, on a little rise between the Balla Balla jetty and the flooded causeway, her son was laid to rest.[23]

LATE ON SUNDAY MORNING, two Japanese crewmen from the missing lugger *Clara* walked into Balla Balla. The diver Nagga Nitsia and sailor Yama Cooa had taken advantage of a very low tide to walk and swim from the south-western corner of Depuch Island to the mainland. They had then trudged through marsh and mangrove to reach the settlement. Another story was told.

After coming into the anchorage on Wednesday morning, *Clara*, *Karrakatta* and *Britannia* had sought protection on the western side of the island. They had been close together at anchor when the storm came. *Karrakatta* and *Britannia* had been seen in great difficulty before being lost to sight. *Clara* had capsized. After three hours in the water and three days alone on the western shore of Depuch Island, the two Japanese believed that they were the only survivors of the little fleet.[24]

The news was shocking; a further loss of twenty lives was now feared. *Clara* had carried six Japanese and a Malay. *Karrakatta* had carried James Scanlon and a crew of six; *Britannia*, skippered by his brother Hugh, had the same. Worse still, it was thought that Scanlon Senior was with them, on one or other of the boats.[25]

After four days without food, the two *Clara* men could fairly have expected a little rest. But even this relief was to be postponed. After water, brandy and a few sandwiches, Constable Fred Growden asked the men if they would come aboard the cutter to assist in the search for the Scanlons and any other survivors of their fleet. They agreed.

At 6 p.m., a dinghy was sighted near East Moore Island. In it were three other Japanese sailors from *Clara*, naked, emaciated and taking turns to row the boat with broken deal boards. Like Nagga Nitsia and Yama Cooa, they had spent some hours in the water but they, along with much of the wreckage of the lugger, had been swept south-westward over the shallows to the mainland. After two days wandering here and there, they had found the dinghy, full of sand but intact.

From *Clara* there were still two men unaccounted for. In broken English the Japanese explained to Constable Growden that their Japanese shipmate Shi Raata was almost certainly dead. When the storm came he refused to put on a lifebelt. He went below and never returned to the deck before the lugger capsized. Of their Malay shipmate Bin Ahmat, the news was a little better. After hours in the water, he had met up with them on the shore, but when the salvaged dinghy was ready to be launched he refused utterly to set foot in it. He would walk to Roebourne along the telegraph line, he declared.[26]

The five Japanese believed that *Karrakatta* and *Britannia*, like *Clara*, had been overwhelmed, but by day end there was cause for optimism. Having instructed his deputy to take the starving men back to Balla in the cutter, Growden teamed up with local beachcomber Fisher to continue the search. In failing light the two sighted four luggers, including one dismasted and in tow, sailing eastward toward Port Hedland. In their haste to intercept, they ran Fisher's boat onto a sandbank and failed to make contact. Time and tidings await no man.[27]

BY SUNDAY NIGHT, NEWS OF THE DISASTER had reached the capital. The following morning, *The West Australian* printed all it had gleaned. Its long report began:

> Once again the Nor'-West coast has been brought into sad and sudden prominence by the visitation of one of those terrible cyclones which from time to time sweep down so ruthlessly and play such havoc with life and limb as well as with property on land and sea. It is barely fourteen months ago since a gale off Cossack sent the fine barque Glenbank to her doom, permitting one man only out of her crew of 21 to reach the shore alive. And only four months before that Broome was visited by the most awful cyclone the town has ever known, causing damage estimated at over £30,000 and a loss of life that in the case of one small fleet alone accounted for 23 men. On that occasion practically the whole length of the 90-mile beach was strewn with wreckage, and for many days after the sea continued to give up its dead. And now again the roll has been called, and to the name of many a sailor, perchance not a few landsmen too, there is no response.[28]

The chronicle of destruction included some good news. At noon on Saturday a battered S.S. *Bullarra* had limped into Cossack. Her passengers and crew were all safe. Captain Upjohn was later asked if he considered *Bullarra* lucky to have survived. "We escaped by a miracle," he said.[29]

Bullarra, southbound, had called at Port Hedland to load 190 bullocks. After missing Tuesday's high tide, she found herself sharing the jetty with *Koombana*, northbound for Broome and Derby. The next morning, *Bullarra* had left Port Hedland about twenty minutes behind *Koombana*, and had kept the larger vessel in sight for a time before turning south-west for Depuch Island. Over the next few hours, conditions deteriorated dramatically. A "very nice fresh breeze" at the harbour entrance stiffened to an east-north-easterly gale and continued to rise. At 4 p.m., in horizontal rain and with the glass falling, Captain Upjohn discarded any thought of calling at the anchorage. He turned *Bullarra* around and made for the open sea.[30]

Four weeks would pass before the first detailed account of the *Bullarra*'s ordeal appeared in *The Western Mail*.

> At 8 o'clock that night the ship was labouring in a full hurricane with tremendous seas buffeting her about. The crew were kept at work hoisting canvas sails on the weather main rigging aft to keep

the ship's head to sea and so prevent her from turning broadside on to the storm. The work was hard, and the blinding spray and rain cut the men's clothing, while the wind tore the canvas sheets in the rigging from time to time. At midnight the funnel crashed down on the deck, and created havoc among the superstructure. Luckily no one was to leeward of the funnel when it fell, but the third mate was steadying himself on the weather wire when it snapped as the gear tumbled to the deck and commenced thumping about as the ship lurched to and fro.

With the cyclone hustling in from the east, at 2 a.m. on the 21st, the ship was helpless in the grip of the storm, and Captain Upjohn ordered the port anchor to be let go, and 120 fathoms of cable run out to keep the ship's head to the wind, the engines being set at three-quarter speed steaming up to the anchor. Everything regarding the hatches, was done commensurate with safety, and in order to give the frantic cattle below every chance, four of the hatches were kept open for ventilation purposes, men being stationed alongside to be ready to batten down if necessary. There was no rest for anybody aboard the tortured ship, and all hands were at work, constantly engaged in securing fittings, which were torn away by the weather and in replacing the canvas screens aft, which had to be renewed every hour or so in order to keep the vessel head-to.

At noon the glass read 28.00, and the hurricane was blowing with unabated force, darkness being everywhere. The blinding rain and spray from the mountainous seas battered the bodies of the ship's company with a constant tattoo and stinging like "a handful of pebbles flung in one's face." It was impossible to face the weather, and speech was only practicable by shouting in one another's ears, while progress along the deck was made with the utmost difficulty. The seas were running two and three times the size of the ship itself, which resembled to the officers "a pigmy in a mountain range." Five men were engaged constantly in passing oil from the engine room forward to where a bucket perforated with holes was used to pour oil into a downpipe. The oil streamed out on to the sea, and had a wonderful effect in preventing the waves from breaking. A huge wave, however, struck the bridge and the captain's cabin 34ft. above normal sea level, and strained the superstructure. The impact started the drawers in the captain's locker, and the sextant was tumbled out from one of the apartments on to the floor, where it was washing to and fro in the water until rescued. From stem to stern the fittings of the ship were sodden, and water percolated everywhere.

At 2 p.m., with the glass reading 27.80, the force of the wind ceased, and the vessel was in the centre of the storm, where light variable breezes were encountered. The seas, however, were high and dangerous, and instead of rushing down on the gallant ship from one quarter they hurled themselves in conical shape from all directions, "flopping up and down." The engines were slowed down, so that the ship would be ready to meet the second half of the storm when it should, as it inevitably had to, hurtle in from the other direction. At 6 p.m., wind and sea rose again from the W.S.W. to W., increasing in force until at midnight the cyclone in all its fury had the ship again in its toils. All night long it blew, the Bullarra labouring heavily in the mountainous seas. At 6 o'clock the following morning the ship was lying like a derelict in the troubled waters, thrashed about in the gale which was abating. From 8 a.m. the weather cleared up, and the crew were engaged all day in dumping dead bullocks overboard.[31]

From *Bullarra*'s bridge the wild sea had been something to behold, but for the men below deck the maelstrom could only be imagined. One fireman declared:

We thought we were gonners pretty nearly every minute, for a long while. But we sang no hymns. We did have some sing-song when she looked like going down, but it was not hymns—no d--- fear. It was more cheerful. I forget what it was now, but it went all right.[32]

Here was a lead that cried out to be followed. After probing a little deeper, the correspondent for *The Northern Times* was able to report:

In the thickest of the hurricane, when a sudden and calamitous end to the desparate struggle of the ship for life seemed inevitable, some called for a hymn. But it appears that none of them knew any hymns—none of those who had any opportunity for singing, at any rate. Then, in the midst of the terrible anxiety, a fireman struck up, "I Wonder Who's Kissing Her Now?" And to the accompaniment of the roaring of the hurricane, the crew joined in most lustily, and howled the chorus in the vigor of men seeking distraction from desparate peril. And as they sang they grew cheerful. "But I never want to hear that tune any more," said the man who told me about it. And he looked as though he meant it.[33]

On his return to base, Constable Growden wired Roebourne with the latest information and asked his colleagues in the neighbouring town to render assistance to a Malay seaman proceeding to Roebourne on foot along the telegraph line. Impossible, they replied; the rivers had broken their banks and the land was impassable. Floodwaters notwithstanding, Bin Ahmat covered the forty miles unassisted. At seven o'clock on Monday evening, after five days without food, he walked into the town and asked for something to eat.[34]

In some respects, the storm that had annihilated the Depuch Island fleet was like no other, but the characteristic bloom of rumour and speculation had been seen before. At first the imagined death toll rose sharply, only to fall steadily as battered boats reached port and resourceful men rejoined the ranks of the living. And when repaired telegraph lines brought news from neighbouring towns, the broad landscape could again be seen.

From Port Hedland came the news that *Karrakatta* and *Britannia* were safe.[35] Moreover, the wind that had caused such havoc to the north and to the south had somehow bypassed the town. Although Cossack had suffered some damage, there was mischievous satisfaction for those who had wagered that the Point Samson jetty would fall to the first great storm that struck it.[36] In Roebourne, two Italians charged with murder had faced trial but had been spared the harmonised testimony of men who wanted them dead.[37] And in Perth the Norwegian consul, upon learning of the tragedy of *Crown of England*, had offered to receive the personal effects of the dead men, only to be told that there were none, that the ship and all it contained had been destroyed utterly, and that the living and the dead had come ashore naked or nearly so.[38]

Place by place, piece by piece, the elements of a great disaster were quietly interlocked. But just as coastal accounts reached stark consensus, the focus of public attention shifted from the known to the unknown, from the irresistible will of the wind to the stubborn silence of the sea. Of *Koombana* there was no word. The pride of the fleet had failed to reach her destination.

11

Tom Allen's Dilemma

In a very real sense, Tom Allen's seafaring career began on the day his father's ended. As Tom Allen Senior watched the barque *Contest* go to pieces on the beach at Rockingham, Western Australia, he decided to call it quits.[1] The year was 1874 and the 58-year-old Cork Irishman had been at sea for forty years. He had carried the last convicts to Hobart,[2] been falsely accused of smuggling in California, and had traded coffee through South-East Asia during the Crimean War.[3] It was time to settle, and time for his eldest boy to assume the mantle.

Tom Allen Junior, born at Port Adelaide in December 1859, first went to sea in 1861 when his father became master and part-owner of the barque *Schah Jehan*. A year later, he had a younger brother with even greater reason to claim the sea as his native element. Sarah Allen, who had sailed with her husband for most of their married life, was not troubled by the prospect of giving birth at sea, but the timing of the second boy's arrival could not have been worse. On April 29th, 1862 she went into labour during a fierce electrical storm off South Australia's Cape Northumberland. The storm was so severe that Captain Allen was unable to leave the bridge; he had no alternative but to leave his wife in the care of *Schah Jehan*'s steward and a thirteen-year-old girl passenger. The birth, although dramatic, was trouble-free. According to family folklore, little Seaborn Allen arrived to thunderous applause and a magnificent display of St Elmo's Fire along the ship's wires and masthead.[4]

Four years later, the birth of another boy was similarly commemorated. Marmion Allen was born at the Emerald Isle Hotel in Fremantle,[5] and proprietor William Marmion, later the Honourable William Marmion of the John Forrest Ministry, became the child's godfather.[6]

Thomas Maurice Allen, conservative by nature, was probably grateful that by the ordinary circumstances of his own birth he was spared a lifelong reminder of his parents' eccentricity. Within a few months of his father's retirement, he had left the Port Adelaide Grammar School and signed on as ordinary seaman aboard the *City of Madras*. Or was it *City of Ningpo*? Or *City of Benares*? Across the span of years, his mother could not remember exactly which of the Glasgow 'Citys' had taken her boy from home. More precisely recalled was his return as able seaman of *Northern Monarch*, which delivered 400 British immigrants to Port Adelaide on June 12th, 1876.[7]

Northern Monarch, *c. 1884.*

It was in May 1878 that Tom Junior, as a quartermaster of the Orient liner *Cuzco*, faced his first major challenge at sea. On a voyage from Plymouth to Melbourne, *Cuzco* called at Cape Town for coal before steaming further south to take full advantage of the 'roaring forties,' the boisterous but reliable westerly winds south of the 40th parallel. For eight days *Cuzco* made wonderful progress, running at full speed under both steam and canvas, but on the morning of May 23rd, about 600 nautical miles south-west of Cape Leeuwin, her main propeller shaft broke.

Captain Murdoch immediately ordered more sail set. *Cuzco*'s size, speed and disposition to the sea were all fortuitous; her conversion from sail-assisted steamer to fully fledged barque was accomplished quickly. Notices were posted at several locations, advising passengers that there was no cause for alarm. Disruption would be minimal, Murdoch insisted; the ship's fine masts and good sailing qualities would carry them all safely to port.

The captain's reassurance was a little premature. After further inspection, chief engineer McDougall told his commander that the break had occurred very near the sternpost; precisely how near, he could not say. There was a possibility that the propeller, with what little of the tailshaft remained attached to it, might slide aft and be lost. And if the propeller were to break free, it could take the rudder with it.

Later that evening a decision was taken. In daylight, an attempt would be made to secure the propeller by passing a heavy cable beneath it. As the fine detail of the operation was worked out, new advice was transmitted to the passengers. Their journey, Captain Murdoch now conceded, was likely to be of longer duration. Short ration allowances would apply in all classes while uncertainty remained. By all accounts, the passengers accepted the revised outlook very well, some even going so far as to send messages of support and condolence to the bridge.

If a line were to be slipped beneath the hub of *Cuzco*'s great propeller, it would first need to be fed through the gap between the sternpost and the rudder. On a ship with the rudder visible from the stern rail, that could be a straightforward operation, but *Cuzco*'s graceful rising stern extended some forty feet beyond the sternpost. Her propeller and rudder were far below and out of sight. The officers decided that two men—volunteers, if volunteers could be found—would be lowered over the sides, one from the port quarter and the other from starboard. At the rudder post, just above the waterline, one would use a pole to feed a light line through the gap; the other would endeavour to catch it with a hook. The light line could then be used to pull a heavier, weighted line into place. It was hoped that by keeping lines taut and vertical by means of carefully placed weights, a loop could be guided around the blades and hub of the propeller. Once that was done, a heavy cable could be made to follow the same path.

One of the men lowered over *Cuzco*'s side, for a different experience of the southern Indian Ocean, was eighteen-year-old Tom Allen. The identity of the other man is not known. That they succeeded in passing the line is remarkable. Although it would later be shown that the propeller had remained secure after the accident, and could never have eloped with the rudder, the visible restraint delivered peace of mind to a captain whose ordeal was far from over.[8]

On Tuesday, May 28th, the weather turned. For the next twelve days *Cuzco* met storm after southern storm, culminating in a gale on June 8th that Captain Murdoch described as the worst of his 27 years at sea. "The sails were blown clean out of the bolt-ropes," he later told a reporter from *The Sydney Morning Herald*.[9]

After sixteen difficult days, *Cuzco* found refuge at Portland, Victoria, where residents were surprised at the sight of an immense steamer coming into the bay under canvas. A few days later, upon a more compliant sea, the ship was towed to Williamstown for repair. She was the largest vessel ever to enter the graving dock, and Melbourne newspapers reported the progress of her repair in surprising detail.

> It was discovered that the outer or propeller section of the shaft had broken only about a foot inside of the stern post. The adjoining section was disconnected . . . and the great rod of iron, about 10ft. in length and 18in. in diameter, was drawn out of the tunnel, and lifted

H.M.V.S. Nelson, *open for inspection at the Alfred Graving Dock, Williamstown, Victoria. Date uncertain.*

Sorata *at Port Melbourne, March 22nd, 1884.*

into the hold. The remaining 9ft. of the broken shaft is that portion which passes out through the stern, and holds the propeller. This will be removed from the exterior. In order to effect this the vast propeller is to be taken to pieces, four fins, each weighing about two tons, being unbolted separately and taken off.[10]

As repairs went on below, the local agents for the Orient Line opened *Cuzco* to the public. A correspondent for *The Argus* joined the throng.

Yesterday afternoon the graving dock was visited by thousands of people, the steamer Gem conveying a large number across the bay. The visitors were courteously permitted to inspect the ship, and her saloon and excellent appointments generally excited considerable admiration. The P. and O. Company's steamer Assam was lying at the graving dock jetty, and H.M.V.S. Nelson was moored across the end of the dock. Both were open to inspection, so that visitors had an opportunity rarely offered of gratifying their curiosity in respect to naval architecture, both ancient and modern.[11]

Tom Allen Senior must have been delighted by the progress of his son's career. At twenty years of age Tom Junior left South Australia again, as bo'sun of the Pacific liner *Sorata*.[12] While away he completed his Board of Trade examinations, and in 1883 returned home as first mate of the *Meeinderry*, a little 200-ton coasting steamer built for the Sydney–Shoalhaven run.[13]

Meeinderry, c. 1900.

The early experience of Tom Allen Junior was broad but not unusually so. His formative years were the years of transition from sail to steam, and he learned his craft aboard vessels that sported both masts and funnel. Without doubt, there was much to be learned. No aspiring commander could ignore the new machinery of motion, but respect for sea and sky still defined the age-old vocation.

It appears that Tom Allen Senior lived just long enough to see his son rise to the rank of master. Tom Junior's first command—the first of many—was a brief elevation. In August 1884 he took the helm of the old barque *Verulam* when her captain was injured in a late-night fall from the Wallaroo Jetty.[14] *Verulam* had been trading on the coast since 1858. Although the old ship now earned her keep carrying coal, she had in her prime been one of the crack clippers of the home trade. It must have warmed the heart of a proud but ailing father to learn that his son would cut his teeth exactly as he had done, in a ship that conversed sweetly with the wind and paid no heed to the modern ways.

Only for one short period of his adult life was Tom Allen Junior wholly disengaged from the sea. When alluvial gold was discovered at Teetulpa in October 1886, Tom was one of about 4,000 optimistic South Australians who set up camp on the new field.[15] But gold prospecting was mere dalliance for a young man happily married to the sea. By late February, he was back in the arms of his long-time love.

A dozen ships later, Captain Tom Allen would freely have admitted that he had benefited greatly from the discovery of gold, but not in the way he had imagined as a restless 26-year-old. When the Western

Australian goldfields opened up, the Adelaide Steamship Company struggled to meet the demand for westward passage, especially from Melbourne. It chartered two ships: *Buninyong* from Melbourne and *Tekapo* from New Zealand. With the new vessels came opportunities for advancement; indeed, the sudden expansion of the fleet forced a wholesale reorganisation of the company's officers and engineers. Tom Allen was perhaps the single greatest beneficiary of the reshuffle; on April 15th, 1894, he took command of *Tekapo*. The 2,400-ton steamer was no glamour ship but she answered the needs of both her young master and her impatient gold-seeking clientele.[16]

By the judgment of their peers, two classes of mariner are considered most accomplished: the masters of large cargo vessels, and the pilots who guide large and often unfamiliar vessels in and out of a major port. But these acknowledged experts enjoy very little public recognition compared to the ever-popular masters of passenger liners. And strangely, although frequent travellers may treat the captain as a personal friend, it is those who travel rarely who may feel the stronger bond. Like doctors, priests and midwives, ships' masters rise to prominence at significant moments in their passengers' lives. In October 1895, Tom Allen assumed the command that would guarantee such recognition. For several years the graceful, reliable S.S. *Marloo* had been a passenger favourite in all the ports of southern Australia, and some of that popularity was immediately accorded to her new master.[17]

S.S. Marloo, *Sydney Harbour, c. 1900.*

Tom Allen probably looked forward to a long association with the ship, but a terrible shipboard accident was to end his captaincy after only fifteen months.

It scarcely needs to be stated that if a ship has two decks above a cargo hold, hatchways one-above-the-other must pass through them. *Marloo* was such a vessel. Whenever she arrived in port, it was the responsibility of the chief officer to supervise the opening of the hatchways, and to ensure that stanchions were placed to prevent any passenger or crew member from falling into an open hold. The hatchways were a well-recognised danger, and cabins or bunks near them were often assigned to crew rather than passengers. On *Marloo*'s 'tween deck, however, no such reservation was feasible. A ring of double bunks surrounded the forward hatchway, and strict protocols were needed to keep passengers away until loading was completed and the dangerous openings were 'trunked over.'

When passenger Francis Blackwell boarded the ship at Fremantle on the morning of Saturday, December 12th, 1896, things went terribly wrong. The 48-year-old had just arrived from the goldfields, to sail east and spend Christmas with his wife and five children in Ballarat. Although the ship was not due to sail until mid-afternoon, he came aboard at 8 a.m. and asked fore-cabin steward Tom Connor if he might have a particular bunk on the 'tween deck. Connor escorted him there.

Neither man knew that the stanchions directly opposite Blackwell's chosen bunk had been removed and not replaced, and that only a heavy canvas curtain divided the narrow corridor from the open cargo hold. As Connor and Blackwell conversed, two men entered the corridor through an open door. As the steward turned to speak to them, Blackwell out of courtesy stepped backward to let them pass. The canvas curtain gave way as he lent on it; he fell backwards and head-first into the cargo hold, fracturing the base of his skull as his head struck the wheel of a traction engine. He never regained consciousness.[18]

The inquest held in the Fremantle Courthouse on January 7th, 1897 was a strange affair.[19] Although Coroner Thomas Lovegrove presided, a jury of three non-nautical men would deliver the verdict. Across two sittings, Lovegrove conducted the investigation in a purely interrogative way, as if he alone would determine its outcome. Very quickly, three members of *Marloo*'s crew were shortlisted for blame.

Captain Tom Allen was not on duty at the time of the accident; he had handed command of *Marloo* to his chief officer upon their arrival in port. But that fact, he knew, was insufficient to absolve him. Under cross-examination he testified that no person was allowed to take down the stanchions without the permission of the chief officer, although it was frequently necessary and frequently done. The stewards, he insisted, were under strict orders not to permit passengers to enter the dangerous areas while loading continued.

Chief officer Tom Truscott testified that when heavy cargo was being lifted, it was often necessary for crewmen to remove some of the stanchions so that the cargo suspended by derrick could be guided in or out of the hold. On the night before the accident, he had issued orders to the stewards to close off the dangerous areas, and to admit no passengers.

Fore-cabin steward Tom Connor testified that, under orders from the chief officer, he had secured the access doors the evening before the accident. The following morning, however, he had found the doors open; observing some passengers already in the area with their swags, he had escorted Francis Blackwell to the bunk he had asked for.

Whether Tom Allen expected any censure or suspension is difficult to judge, but when Coroner Lovegrove delivered his final summing-up, he focussed almost entirely on the actions of Tom Connor. To the jury he said: "The question you have to consider is, whether it was on account of neglect or laxity on the part of the fore-cabin steward that the deceased met his death." Having framed the question so prescriptively, Lovegrove then proceeded to tell the jurors how it should be answered. In his opinion, the conduct of Connor had resulted in Blackwell's death. In the eyes of the law, therefore, Connor was guilty of a very serious offence. "It is hardly necessary," he declared, "for me to tell you what that offence is. I will leave the matter in your hands."[20]

In criminal proceedings, there is no question whatever about who is on trial. Here, there was no such simple premise. The jury understood its broad prerogative and chose to exercise it. After retiring for only 35 minutes, the three men concluded that a serious criminal offence had indeed been committed, but not by Connor. They returned a verdict of culpable negligence—tantamount to manslaughter—against both Captain Allen and his chief officer.

Police Sergeant Houlahan, it appears, had been brushing up on his procedures in expectation of a finding against Connor. As soon as the jury foreman resumed his seat, the sergeant sprang to life. "In view of the verdict of the jury," he declared to the bench, "it is my duty to apply for a warrant for the arrest of the captain and chief officer."

Coroner Lovegrove was taken aback. "In view of my directions to the jury," he replied, "I am surprised that you ask for it."[21]

Barrister Matthew Moss, who was present as legal observer for the Adelaide Steamship Company, could not contain himself. Suddenly aware that two long-time servants of the company might be shackled and led away, he burst forth: "Do I understand that the sergeant is making an application for a warrant? The idea of the police attempting to take any further action after the strong expression of opinion which fell from you, Mr. Coroner, is inexplicable. . . . As a matter of fact, you would be stultifying yourself if you did issue a warrant."[22]

Moss's point was clearly made, although his choice of words was odd.

The sergeant's application was unforeseen, certainly, but "inexplicable" it was not. History records that Coroner Lovegrove stood his soft ground. No warrant for the arrest of Allen or Truscott was ever issued.

IN QUICK SUCCESSION, Tom Allen Junior left the witness stand, the courtroom, the *Marloo*, and the Adelaide Steamship Company. The adverse finding, it appears, damaged neither his reputation nor his prospects; within a year he had accepted a position of unquestioned responsibility as a Port Adelaide pilot.[23]

There is here a remarkable parallel between the careers of Tom Allen Junior and his father. Both men joined the Port Adelaide Pilot Service in the immediate aftermath of a questionable finding of negligence. In May 1862, in heavy weather, Tom Allen Senior had scuttled *Schah Jehan* beside the Wallaroo Jetty. Although the action was taken to save the vessel and to limit damage to the jetty, the Court of Marine Inquiry saw things very differently. The court's criticism of the master was severe indeed, but one aspect of its finding was silly enough to cast doubt upon the rest. Tom Allen Senior had a 25 per cent stake in the vessel and was bankrupted by its loss, and yet the court condemned his "gross inattention to the interests of the owners."[24]

Although father and son came to the Port Adelaide Pilot Service in similar circumstances, their respective engagements would end very differently. In September 1866 the steamer *Coorong*, with Tom Allen Senior in command as pilot, ran down the mailboat *Mercury*, slicing it in two. Two men including a fellow pilot were killed. Although the subsequent inquiry found that the skipper of the mailboat had erred in attempting to run across *Coorong*'s bows, there was broad agreement that the steamer had been travelling too fast. All censure was reserved for Tom Allen Senior; he was dismissed from the Pilot Service and forever banned from holding a similar position at any South Australian port.[25]

The cautious, teetotalling Tom Allen Junior determined never to make his father's mistake. For ten years he safely guided vessels large and small into and out of Port Adelaide. It was a decade of service that established his reputation and delivered what he would remember as a highlight of his career. On July 4th, 1901, Adelaide newspaper *The Advertiser* reported that Tom Allen, the youngest member of the Port Adelaide Pilot Service, had been chosen to pilot the royal yacht *Ophir* into Port Adelaide.[26] The royal visit had been a long time coming. More than two months earlier *Ophir* had slipped quietly by, carrying the Duke and Duchess of Cornwall and York to Melbourne for the opening of Australia's first federal parliament. Since that great ceremonial day, the future King and Queen had toured Brisbane, Sydney, Auckland, Wellington, and Hobart. Only now, near the end of their six-month southern sojourn, would the couple step ashore in South Australia.[27]

The royal yacht Ophir, *Port Adelaide, July 9th, 1901.*

Tom Allen's honour was greatly extended by *Ophir*'s early arrival at the anchorage. He had expected to board the vessel early on Tuesday morning, but the call to service came on Monday evening. When the launch left the dock, conditions were far from ideal, but wind and rain played a part in making the night memorable. Against a sky coal-black and starless, white *Ophir* was dazzling: "one blaze of light from stem to stern," the scribe from *The Register* would later declare.

Once aboard, Allen learned that arrangements had been made for his overnight stay. After being escorted to a fine cabin, he was told that the ship would receive other visitors during the evening, and that at 9 p.m. there would be a concert attended by the duke and duchess.[28] The young pilot probably thought that a brief introduction at the evening's soirée would be his only direct contact with the royal couple. It was not so; his dealings with the duke would continue, on ground more natural and familiar. George had been a naval officer and remained a keen sailor. When the time came for *Ophir* to be guided into port, the future King George V joined Captains Winsloe and Allen on the bridge for the run up the river. And when *Ophir* was secure at the overcrowded dock, he complimented the pilot on his handling of the vessel and presented him with a scarf pin bearing the emblem of the White Rose of York. For Tom Allen, that accolade was next-best to a knighthood. Friends said that he treasured that pin and wore it often.[29]

Among the most sought-after assignments for an Australian ship-master was to be sent to the old country to bring out a new vessel. It was just such work that drew Tom Allen back to the Adelaide Steamship Company in 1906. In late October he boarded the Royal Mail Steamer *Oruba* as a passenger, bound for London and Glasgow to collect the new cattle steamer *Junee*. Six months later, after trouble-free trials and an easy delivery voyage, he handed the ship over to another master.[30] Just ten weeks later he was England-bound again, for a delivery assignment of even greater interest and prestige. His second trust was the innovative cargo carrier S.S. *Echunga*, nearing completion in the Middlesbrough shipyard of Sir Raylton Dixon & Company. Such was the early interest in *Echunga*'s design and capability that the ship was fully booked in advance. There would be no delivery voyage as such; she would proceed direct to New York to load general merchandise and only then make her Australian debut. *Echunga*'s ability to manage more than 3,000 tons of water ballast gave her officers extraordinary control over draft and trim, and cantilevered framing created a huge, unobstructed cargo space. Indeed, on the eve of her first arrival in Sydney, *The Sydney Morning Herald* hailed *Echunga* as "the largest cantilever steamer in the world."[31]

Tom Allen probably expected to retain command of *Echunga*, but not long after her commissioning, international demand fell so sharply that

Innovative design: Echunga*'s cargo hold and water-ballast compartments.*

the company saw no alternative but to lay the vessel up.[32] The commercial uncertainty lasted only a few months, but by the time *Echunga* returned to service, her first commander was otherwise engaged. Tom Allen had settled back into the steady, reliable work of carting coal from New South Wales to South Australia. As master of *Winfield*, he plied between Newcastle and Port Pirie for most of the next three years. Although there were brief secondments to other ships,[33] it seemed that the 45-year-old, now as accomplished as any man in the mercantile marine, was biding his time.

It is not known when John Rees, master of *Koombana*, and Tom Allen, master of *Winfield*, first discussed the possibility of swapping ships. Perhaps Captain Rees made a formal request to be transferred from the Nor'-West run, or perhaps the two men reached private agreement and only then approached the company. At a glance, it seemed odd that Rees was willing to trade fast, elegant *Koombana* for coal-smudged *Winfield*. After all, he had been present at *Koombana*'s launch, had taken part in her sea trials and had brought her out to Australia. He was to *Koombana* what Tom Allen was to *Echunga*.

For Tom Allen, the swap was an opportunity. *Koombana* was considered by many to be the finest ship in Australian service, and the Nor'-West run was broadly acknowledged as the most demanding. Whatever the private thoughts of the protagonists, the company did not object to the exchange. In Sydney, during the last week of August 1911, the two experienced masters traded places.[34]

To her new master, *Koombana* delivered a difficult initiation, just as she had to his predecessor. On his first run into Port Hedland, Tom Allen grounded the ship on the western bank of the channel. He was not greatly troubled; the seabed was soft and there seemed very little likelihood of damage to the hull. He ordered one starboard-side ballast tank pumped out, and within an hour was afloat and on his way to the jetty. He noted the occurrence in the ship's log, recorded *Koombana*'s draft fore and aft, and determined not to make the mistake again.[35]

Four weeks later he approached Hedland from the south for a second time. Using his first approach as a guide he raised the ship higher by emptying tanks both port and starboard. But once again he found the bottom. This time the contact was a mere scrape; *Koombana* slithered over the bar without any need to stop or reverse.[36]

What Tom Allen quickly learned was that *Koombana*'s schedule was not moulded to client demand or company convenience; it was tightly bound to the cycle of the tides at two particular ports. For about three days in every fourteen, at Port Hedland and Broome, there was insufficient water for *Koombana* to reach the jetty, even at the top of the day's highest tide.

A round trip from Port Hedland to Derby took seven days, and therein lay an intractable problem. Seven days is one quarter of the lunar cycle;

it is the gap between the spring and neap tides. If *Koombana* were to leave Port Hedland on high spring tide, with water to spare beneath her keel, she would almost certainly be locked out of the port on her return. This quirk of geography was the bane of *Koombana*'s working life. Tom Allen could not choose a different track to Derby any more than he could sway the cold mistress of the night sky. Like his predecessor, he recognised that the only viable option was to negotiate Port Hedland on the shoulders of the spring tides, when the depth of water over the bar was marginal at best. If the port could be reached three or four days before 'springs', he would have just enough to get in on his way north, plenty of water at Broome in both directions, and just enough to re-enter Port Hedland on the way back. It was a delicate arrangement, and any delay could break it.

Not all of *Koombana*'s Nor'-West voyages terminated at Derby. It was also her mission to serve the tiny settlement of Wyndham, five hundred miles further north and east. On the longer run, the problem at Port Hedland disappeared because the time between northbound and southbound arrivals increased to fourteen days. That was half of the lunar cycle, and perfect for managing the tide. *Koombana* could leave Hedland on the full moon and return for the new moon, or vice versa, gliding into port with ease on both occasions. But as one problem faded away, another rose to prominence. From Fremantle, the 4,000-mile round trip to Wyndham could not be completed in the 28 days of the lunar cycle. If *Koombana* were to visit the last outpost on every trip, she would soon be hopelessly out of phase. The company's schedulers arrived at a simple solution. The Derby trips would average 23 days, they calculated, and the Wyndham trips 30. If *Koombana* were to visit Wyndham on alternate months, time lost on the longer run could be made up on the next. From a purely logistical standpoint this solved the problem, but the regime placed absurd demands on the crew. After four weeks at sea in tropical heat, members of the crew were often permitted only two or three days of shore leave before *Koombana* was northbound again.

AFTER HITTING THE HEDLAND BAR on his first two Nor'-West runs, Tom Allen was determined that the third would be different. And different it was. Of the protracted firemen's strike which tied *Koombana* up at Fremantle for three weeks, much is elsewhere written. What is important here is that the delay was not 14 days or 28 days, which would have left *Koombana* in harmony with the tides, but 20 days. In a single stroke, all synchronicity was lost.

Koombana's Trip No. 34 of December 1911 was her worst ever. On her way into Shark Bay on December 4th, she scraped a sandy ridge at Heirisson Flat, less than a mile from where Captain Rees had run her hard aground three years earlier.[37] Just twelve hours after that scrape, *Koombana* was aground again, near the Carnarvon jetty. She floated off on the high tide.[38] Port Hedland was reached on December 9th, three days after the full moon. There was barely enough water for the ship to gain admission, and because the tides were becoming less generous with each passing day there was a distinct possibility that she would be trapped inside for several days. By pumping out most ballast tanks, Captain Allen made his exit the following day, but his difficulties continued. The extension of the run to Wyndham meant that *Koombana* would face similar conditions when she returned to Port Hedland on the run south. At any other time, he might have cut Wyndham from the itinerary, but the strike had left all Nor'-West ports short of food. Although Wyndham had received some supplies from Singapore, the town was desparate for fresh produce from the south. To call there was imperative.

Koombana scraped back into Port Hedland at 'dead neaps' on Christmas Day 1911. The following day, all ballast tanks were emptied to give her the best chance of escape. She left the port riding so high that the top of her propeller was fully eighteen inches clear of the water.[39]

Tom Allen had been at sea for almost forty years but had never experienced such enslavement to the rise and fall of the sea. *Koombana* and the Nor'-West, it seemed, were partners in adversity. It is likely that he now saw his exchange with John Rees in a different light. He had come to *Koombana* wondering why a senior colleague had been so willing to give her up. Now he was aggravated by the Nor'-West: its heat, its dangers, and the extraordinary demands its so-called ports placed upon *Koombana* in particular.

After six months of pumping out ballast tanks and pressing them up again he also knew that *Koombana*, so well-behaved when deeply laden, was far from reassuring when riding high. He must have wondered how she would fare in a storm like that which had swallowed *Yongala* and her complement a year earlier. In a letter dated March 8th, 1912, he told an east-coast colleague that the worst of the Nor'-West cyclone season was over. "I just kept clear of a blow last trip," he wrote, "but as soon as I got round the North-West Cape it started, so my luck was in that time."[40]

AFTER SEVERAL DAYS OF OPPRESSIVE HEAT, Wednesday, March 20th, 1912 dawned grey and windy. Port Hedland was unusually busy. For the first time ever, *Koombana* shared the jetty with *Bullarra*, the vessel she had replaced in 1909. The Adelaide Steamship Company had decided to introduce a fortnightly service and 'the old Bull' was back in town.[41] She had been scheduled to leave for Fremantle on Tuesday, but her shipment of cattle had arrived late and she had missed the tide. *Bullarra* would now follow *Koombana* out of port.

No one was quite sure what to make of the weather. For three days the barometer had been falling, but not sharply. The wind had come in hard for a couple of hours overnight, but by daylight had eased to a moderate nor'-easter. Some of the locals were preparing their houses for a possible blow, but that was something they did more than once in an average summer, to be safe rather than sorry. At the harbour entrance the sea seemed a little flustered, with white-caps riding along the crests of a low swell from the north-west.[42]

As the passengers of the two ships mingled with townsfolk on the jetty, a few noticed that Captain Allen seemed ill-at-ease; indeed, he gave some inquirers the impression that he did not want to leave port. "Twenty-four hours here will not hurt," he told local newspaper man Walter Barker, "I might bump the outer bar going out on a sea like this."[43]

Captain Thomas Allen.

Allen's concern about the sea at the entrance was well founded. After a few scrapes and bumps it had become his practice to study the tide charts, predict the depth of water for departure, and adjust the ship's draft as soon as the discharge of cargo was complete. It is likely that he had trimmed *Koombana* on Tuesday, anticipating the tide but making no allowance for a rough sea at the entrance. This was a difficult situation: *Koombana* would certainly pitch and roll when she felt the wind and the sea on her starboard side, but if time were taken to reduce her draft, the peak of the tide would be missed. By delay, the problem could easily be made worse.

There was a second strong argument for remaining in port. With a top speed of fifteen knots, *Koombana* was a fast ship; in fair weather she could make Broome easily between tides. But on this day the wind was east-north-east; after rounding Bedout Island, *Koombana* would be punching into a short, sharp sea. For the comfort of passengers, speed would have to be reduced, and the noon high tide in Broome would almost certainly be missed. There was another high tide around midnight, but he had never brought the ship to the Broome jetty in darkness, and was not keen to attempt it in rough weather. By his reckoning, a full day would be lost regardless of whether he left port, and regardless of any further deterioration of the weather.

To Tom Allen's consternation, there were also good reasons for leaving. *Koombana* was running late. She had entered Port Hedland two days after the new moon; she now had to reach Derby and be southbound before the neap tides made the Broome jetty unapproachable. If *Koombana* were forced to remain outside at Broome, southbound consignments would be delayed by a full month.

It is difficult to know if the possibility of a cyclone influenced Tom Allen's thinking. Every shipmaster would prefer to face a storm on the open sea rather than among reefs and islands, but a choice between Port Hedland and the open sea was not nearly so clear-cut. The harbour was little more than a mangrove-fringed tidal estuary with a jetty projecting into a deep pool. If *Koombana* were caught there in a cyclone, she would almost certainly end up in the mangroves, perhaps permanently. In this scenario, the interests of passengers were clearly at odds with the interests of the shipping company. The passengers would be safer upon dry land— or wet land, flooded land, any land—than at sea in a tropical storm.

According to Walter Barker, Captain Allen appeared to change his mind after a conversation with Captain Upjohn of the *Bullarra*. "I am going out," he then told the newsman. "The Broome passengers, who think they will get to Broome to-morrow, will be lucky if they get there on Saturday—I'm going straight out to sea, and will fill my tanks when I get outside."[44]

Tom Allen remained uneasy. During the morning about forty luggers had come in from the pearling grounds. When some of the boats blocked the channel, he asked the Harbourmaster to have them cleared away, and when one remained, he declared bluntly that he would not leave unless it was removed.[45]

Port Hedland's method of indicating the depth of water over the bar was simple but effective. Large wicker spheres were lowered one by one from a yardarm at the top of a steel tower on the foreshore near the Port Hotel. On March 20th, 1912, it was nineteen-year-old Bert Clarke who climbed the tower to deliver the signals.[46] At about 10.20 a.m., when the tower indicated 19 feet, *Koombana* began her run to the entrance. Twenty minutes later, *Bullarra* followed her out. It is difficult to judge whether it was Bert Clarke or *Bullarra*'s officers who kept *Koombana* in sight for the longest, but Bert certainly had the better view. "Normally," he recalled, "ships going northbound were out of sight within 30 or 45 minutes, but this day as the storm was getting stronger I stayed up there in the tower watching the *Koombana* pitching and rolling for nearly two hours."[47]

After crossing the bar without contact, Tom Allen may have permitted himself a sigh of relief. But that indulgence can only have been momentary. There were important decisions to be made, and made quickly. The master of another steamer may have considered leaving the ballast tanks empty, but if this thought entered Tom Allens's head, it can only have flickered. *Koombana* partly ballasted was difficult to control, even in port.

Port Hedland harbour c. 1905: a navigational challenge for ships' masters.

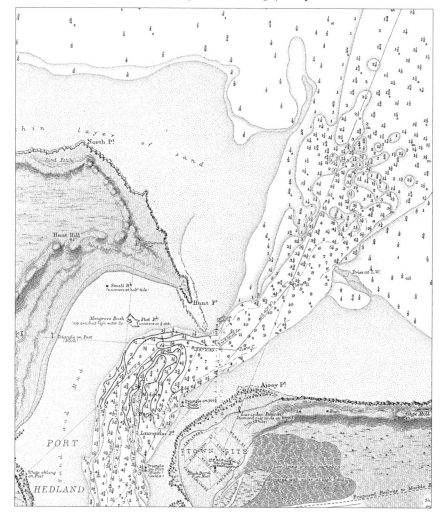

Koombana *departing Port Hedland. Date uncertain.*

Without question, the tanks had to be filled. And once the pressing-up was commenced, it had to be completed, because a sloshing, half-full tank could be more detrimental to the ship's handling than an empty one.

The next question was how to accomplish the refilling. In calm conditions it was a simple if time-consuming operation, but this day seemed determined to be different. Because the usual course to round Bedout Island was due north at first, the wind would be 'on the beam' while the tanks were being filled. That would certainly be uncomfortable; if conditions worsened, it could be dangerous. The captain's preference would have been to put *Koombana*'s head to the wind and steam slowly until the re-ballasting was complete. But all eastward progress was blocked by reef and shoal water. He may even have considered dropping anchor, but to take that option was to lose at least three hours without making any progress at all. If the weather were to deteriorate, that decision would be difficult to defend.

It appears that Captain Allen and his officers reached an intelligent compromise. Firstly, by steering a little east of north, the ship's roll was limited by keeping the wind as much on the bow as the beam. Secondly, by reducing speed and allowing the ship to 'sag away' on the wind, an approximate northerly course was maintained. To Bert Clarke, atop the Hedland tower, *Koombana* appeared to be struggling. She was not. Her slow progress and rolling motion were merely symptoms of the necessary work in which she was engaged.

Tom Allen may have permitted himself a second sigh of relief when the reballasting was completed. But this relief must also have been short-lived. For *Bullarra*, conditions changed alarmingly in the middle of the afternoon.[48] *Koombana* would have encountered something similar. By 4 p.m. Captain Allen must have suspected that he was feeling the influence of a cyclone to the north-west. An hour later, with a rising north-easterly sea crossing a long north-westerly swell, he must have known it. Although he may have regretted the time lost in pressing up the tanks, he cannot have regretted his determination to accomplish it.

ON MONDAY EVENING and through the early hours of Tuesday the storm had tracked southward over Rowley Shoals. Had it continued on this course it might have crossed the coast near Cape Keraudren at the western end of the Eighty Mile Beach, but under some unknown atmospheric influence its southward progress was thwarted. Across the daylight hours of Tuesday it made a broad right-hand turn, to sweep westward past Bedout Island in the late evening. In the early hours of Wednesday morning the wind blew hard in Port Hedland, but by the time *Koombana* and *Bullarra* left the port it had eased to what Captain Upjohn of the *Bullarra* would later describe as a "very nice fresh breeze."

If the storm had continued to track westward across open water, the winds at Port Hedland would have gradually shifted anticlockwise, from east-north-east to north-east to north. They did not; over 24 hours the wind strengthened steadily but shifted little. And the same was true at Wallal and Whim Creek and Cossack, although the direction of the wind was different at each place. The explanation was unusual but simple: by 10 a.m. on Wednesday, the westward advance had ended. At about S 18° 20′ E 117° 40′, the storm eased back a little to the east and then simply hovered.[49]

It is dangerous to think that a storm which fails to advance also fails to thrive. Often, the atmospheric influences that steer a cyclone are antagonistic to its development. By contrast, a storm unguided may intensify rapidly, at least for a few hours until the upwelling of cool seawater begins to suck the life force from it. So it was for this monster-in-the-making: throughout Wednesday, it drifted a little this way and that, gathering its resources, as if pausing to decide where the greatest damage might be done.

Mariners may prefer a storm that moves slowly enough to be outrun, but the cyclone that hovers and intensifies creates two distinct problems. Firstly, it cannot be told apart from the storm that approaches the vessel directly. In each case, the shipboard observations are the same: a falling barometer, a rising wind, and a wind that shows little sign of swinging. Secondly, the wind by its stubborn consistency may produce a truly phenomenal sea.

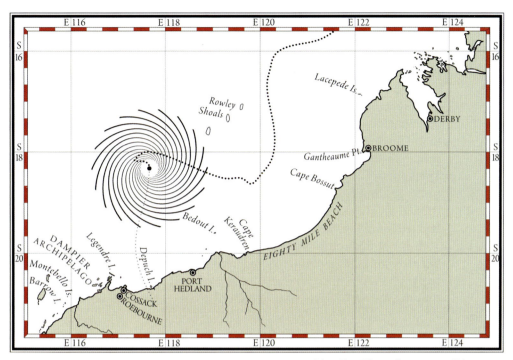

MAP 7 • *The early progress of the storm.*

THE EYE OF THE STORM was to the north-west; that he knew. How far to the north-west, he could not say. With most points of the compass foreclosed by islands and shoal water, Tom Allen was left to decide between three courses of action, all difficult and all dangerous.

He could turn *Koombana* to port and steam due west, with the wind on his starboard quarter. He would enjoy deep water and navigational freedom but would steam directly into disaster if the storm should recurve toward the land.

Alternatively, he could gain sea room very quickly by steaming nor'-nor'-west. But by so doing, he would move closer to the storm's centre and, moreover, place the ship in 'the dangerous quadrant': that area to the front and left of an advancing storm, where wind speeds are greatest and where the wind tends to sweep a vessel directly into the storm's path. Worse still, progress in that direction could only be made with the wind and the sea fully on *Koombana*'s beam.

Finally, he could continue on his track to Broome, taking the shortest safe path around Bedout Island before steaming east-nor'-east out of harm's way. Here too, the complications were daunting. Two hours at least had been lost in pressing up the tanks; *Koombana* would be abeam of Bedout at low tide and in failing light. Sighting the island's unattended beacon would be more important than usual because the ship's slow, crabbing track had made it difficult for his officers to establish the ship's position by what is called "dead reckoning." Tide would be critical too, especially if *Koombana* had strayed a little to the east. Along the intended deep-water track, the state of the tide was of little consequence, but closer to the reef the rising seabed could mould and magnify the deep-ocean swell. On this day, no master could predict what sea and land might together contrive.

What anguish must there have been for the conservative commander whose every contemplation sought the safe way. Suddenly that principle—nay, that vocation—found no outlet. There was no safe way. The ships of a long career had carried him to this place, but nothing in his résumé could contain the present danger or light the way. And therein lay the essence of Tom Allen's dilemma: the sum of all decisions had led him here, yet none nor all could guide him hence.

It is not difficult to imagine that the dominant emotion was not fear but profound exasperation. Locked in a game of chess he had never sought to play, he was pinned, in check, on a board left sparse by the sacrifices of the day, and with an invisible opponent awaiting his next move.

12

THE STUBBORN, SILENT SEA

ALGY COLLINS was purser of the Blue Funnel steamer *Gorgon*. In Singapore on Thursday, March 21ˢᵗ, 1912 his Chinese boy—"a stripling of sixty summers, by the way"—told him that he had heard of a big blow on the Nor'-West coast, and that a steamer had gone down. When Collins told his commander of the rumour, Captain Townley would not dismiss it. "There is often truth in these Chinamen's tales," he said. Both men made inquiries, the captain to Blue Funnel's local agent, and the purser through a friend at the Eastern Extension Telegraph Company. Nothing was known. Nothing was learned.[1]

When *Koombana* failed to arrive in Broome on Thursday morning, little was made of it. She had certainly left as planned on Wednesday morning; a wire from the company's agent in Port Hedland had confirmed that. But Hedland and Broome were both tidal ports; even a stiff headwind could result in a tide being missed and a full day being lost. It was not until Friday morning, when the steamer again failed to appear, that anxiety gained a foothold. And when word spread that Ted Hunter's lugger *Constance* had been wrecked south of Broome on Tuesday night, a nervous waiting began.[2] Inquiries to the telegraph office yielded little information, except that Port Hedland was unreachable. The lines were down, north and south.[3]

For a brief time there was a sense that news of *Koombana* would arrive as soon as the wires were restored, but Saturday delivered deeper anxiety. A thrice-relayed message brought the news that *Bullarra* had limped into Cossack after a terrible ordeal at sea. The facts were incomplete, but compelling nonetheless. After following *Koombana* out of port on Wednesday morning, *Bullarra* had steamed into the worst conditions her master and crew had ever experienced. By streaming two anchors and 120 fathoms of chain they had kept *Bullarra*'s head to the sea, but her funnel had been torn away by the wind and her superstructure strained by a wall of water that hit the navigating bridge 25 feet above the waterline.

For those with wives, daughters, brothers and friends on *Koombana*, this was more than mere drama. On Sunday they came together to plan, and ultimately to plead.

THREE VESSELS, each provisioned for a month, left Broome in the early hours of Tuesday, March 26th. Each would take a different, agreed track and all would converge upon Bedout Island in six or seven days.

The largest and fastest was the schooner *Muriel*, under the command of Broome wharfinger Oswald Dalziel. Assigned to the 'outside track,' *Muriel* set course for Rowley Shoals which, all masters agreed, presented a particular danger to any vessel that had lost power or steering. Two hundred miles west of Broome, three exquisite coral cays sat atop volcanic pillars which rose steeply from blue-black depths. If *Koombana*, disabled, chanced upon them, no anchor would hold her off.[4]

Assigned the 'middle track' was another stalwart of Broome pearling: the lugger *Mina*. Captain Bennie would be in command but pearler Hugo Harper, whose brother George was aboard *Koombana*, would share the long hours on watch. *Mina*, it was agreed, would sail west-south-west across open water to a point north of Bedout. She would then tack southward in daylight to fix her position from the island.[5]

Joining the tried and true was a vessel that had passed only a single test: its delivery voyage from Fremantle. Hastily christened "McLhennan", the brand-new lugger was placed under the command of Robert White and assigned to the 'inside track': south and west along the Eighty Mile Beach, and then north-west across the Amphinome Shoals to Bedout.[6]

The citizens of Broome had good reason for choosing Bedout Island for particular attention, and for the rendezvous of its little fleet. The low dome of sand and scrub, home to countless seabirds, seemed harmless enough, but the island's south-western reef was more than decorative edging. Honed over time by converging ocean currents, a blade of rock and coral extended five miles into the sea, into the path of coastal steamers.

It was not known precisely when *Muriel*, *Mina* and *McLhennan* would reconvene, or which vessel would arrive at Bedout first. Each was instructed to circumnavigate the island, taking advantage of any abatement of the sea to run close along the edge of the known danger.[7]

IN THE SOUTHERN CAPITAL, Premier Scaddan may have expected that his morning meeting with Chief Harbourmaster Charles Irvine would consider the redeployment of the government steamer *Penguin* and perhaps the charter of another vessel to search for *Koombana*. However, a bundle of cables including two from Broome had arrived during the night. Broome's first despatch was a plea for immediate action; the second, a few hours behind the first, delivered a plan as bold as it was broad. The steamer *Moira*, the cable declared, was loading cattle at Wyndham; she could search Rowley Shoals on her way south. *Bullarra*, after effecting repairs, should return north without delay. *Minderoo* was northbound from Geraldton; Captain Mills could receive instructions at Carnarvon. And *Gorgon*, south-bound from Singapore, could be intercepted by cable at Batavia or Surabaya.[8]

In essence, the contention was simple: that every steamer within 500 miles should join a search for *Koombana*. If the premier was surprised at Broome's effrontery, he must also have been impressed. Broome's mayor and magistrate had pointed out that there was no time to wait for *Penguin*; she was too far away, and she alone could not scan the vast area in which *Koombana* might be found. Scaddan knew that the residents of Broome, with a dozen of their own among the missing, had incontestable reasons for urgency. He sought the harbourmaster's advice. The Broome plan was understandable, but was it rational? Was it intelligent? In the course of a short discussion, the two men recognised that the proposal could be assessed by one simple criterion: the government's willingness to bring coastal commerce to a standstill. If that outcome was acceptable, the Broome plan was the right one.

To his credit, Scaddan made the decision without hesitation and turned to a new challenge: to gain the support of the shipping companies whose vessels could not simply be co-opted. Scaddan recognised that while a single shipowner might baulk at the prospect of suspending normal operations and sacrificing trade, an assemblage of competitors would more easily be enjoined. Thus, the agents of the shipping lines were immediately called together. The government would leave no doubt of its commitment to the search, and let all know that the high cost of the search would be broadly shared.[9]

From the Adelaide Steamship Company came manager William Moxon; his support at least could be counted on. James Clarke of the Singapore line[10] came authorised to release *Minderoo*. Similarly, the Australasian United Steam Navigation Company spoke for *Moira*, and the Ocean Steam Ship Company for *Gorgon*. When the meeting was over, the wires were set humming again.

The citizens of Broome had been most keen to secure the services of *Minderoo*'s master, Andrew Mills, said to know the coast as well as any officer in the mercantile marine.[11] Because *Minderoo* had already left Geraldton, and was not wireless-equipped, instructions were sent to Carnarvon, for hand-delivery to the captain upon his arrival. The cable read:

> Government request you to make thorough search for Koombana. I authorise you to use your discretion and do what you consider best in the interests of life and property. Captain Irvine suggests you proceed Cossack, driving ship utmost speed, examining Montebello as far as possible. Will wire you further at Cossack.[12]

At Point Samson, the crew of the battered *Bullarra* had wasted no time in preparing for a return to sea, whether to continue south or to go in search. With no opportunity to have a new funnel delivered, the men fashioned a rectangular one of timber and corrugated iron. It was a strange sight to nautical eyes, but Captain Upjohn was pleasantly surprised by its effectiveness. "It answers very well," he told the chucklers and the sceptics.[13]

In Fremantle, William Moxon informed the harbourmaster and the press that although repairs had been effected, *Bullarra* was now critically short of water, and there was none to be had at Point Samson or Port Hedland. The nearest source was Broome, 400 miles away. "This," he added, "is one of the disadvantages we have to contend with on the Nor'-West trade."[14]

A plan for *Bullarra* was quickly worked out. She would proceed to Port Hedland but remain outside. By launch or lighter she would deliver the mails and check for new instructions. She would then proceed to Broome for water, searching the Turtle Islands and Bedout Island en route. From Broome, she would return to sea, and remain at sea for as long as necessary.[15]

An early impression of how the search for Koombana *would proceed.*[16]

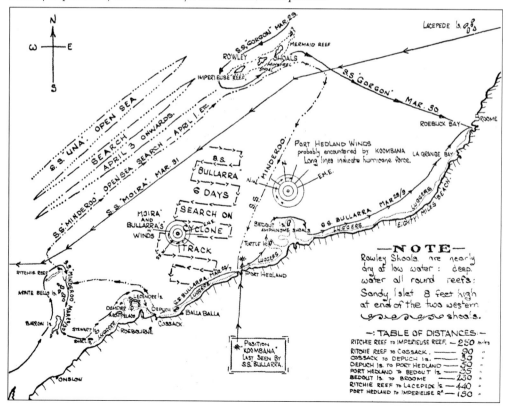

At Wyndham, *Moira* had been delayed waiting for cattle, but she was now loading. It quickly became obvious that offloading the stock served no useful purpose. She could search the Lacepede Islands, Rowley Shoals and the Montebello Islands, all of which she would pass on her direct run to Fremantle. And if some discovery should force a change of plan, the cattle could go along for the ride.[17]

Instructions for *Gorgon*, telegraphed to Surabaya, were hand-delivered to Captain Townley. He was advised not to disembark passengers or discharge cargo, but to search Rowley Shoals thoroughly on his way south and then divert to Broome for further advice. When Algy Collins came to the bridge, he found the commander holding a folded paper and staring out over the foredeck. Townley turned, passed the cablegram to his purser and said: "What do you make of this, Collins?"[18]

ACROSS AUSTRALIA, daily newspapers faced a new challenge: their readers craved news of *Koombana*, but there was none to be had. For a few days, the storm that had ravaged the coast became the story: the annihilation of the fleet at Depuch Island, the battering of *Bullarra*, and the inundation of the land by a downpour that had treated rain gauge and riverbank with equal contempt. Remarkable accounts of survival sat beside practical reports of damage to infrastructure: telegraph lines laid flat for miles, a tramway all but destroyed, and a noble deep-water jetty left swaying between splayed piles. The stories were newsworthy in the common way, but this was no common calling. Paragraphs came in pilgrimage to fill an abhorrent vacuum.[19]

Also proffered by the dailies was a bloom of speculation that *Koombana* was merely disabled. *The West Australian* declared:

> Many well-known seafaring men at the Port, who have had considerable experience of the Nor'-West coast, are firmly convinced that the Koombana will be reported within a day or two. It is very probable, they state, that she has received such a terrible buffeting that she is lying off the coast awaiting a complete abatement of the storm before approaching the land. Others are of the opinion that she has met with a mishap to either her propeller or to the machinery. The Koombana is never very heavily laden on the trip north, and after leaving Port Hedland she would have only the Broome and Derby cargo in her holds. She would thus be in very light trim, and the theory has been advanced that during the storm an accident occurred to the shaft or propeller as the result of the vessel pitching in the tremendous seas.[20]

Damage to *Koombana*'s propeller or tailshaft was indeed a possibility. When a steamship pitches so heavily that her propeller is alternately immersed and exposed, the strain upon her machinery may be extreme.

The propeller will race when it breaks clear of the water, only to stall when the blades bite and disappear. Although mechanical failure could reasonably be considered a positive outcome, it was ironic that *Koombana*'s light condition should be offered as ground for optimism. It was also possible that *Koombana*, riding high, had been overwhelmed by the sea and had capsized, but few commentators were yet willing to place that private thought in the public domain.

Interviewed for the *Broome Chronicle*, former chief engineer Jock McDonald was adamant that *Koombana* could deal with almost any eventuality.

> My opinion is that she has met with some minor disablement, such as a mishap to the rudder, in which case she would be unmanageable, and repairs would have to be effected at sea. They have all the necessary appliances and facilities on board for doing such work. I have every hope that she will turn up partially repaired. You cannot do much in a week at sea in the way of repairs. Those who are anxious should take heart, because the Koombana is a splendid sea vessel, and well equipped in every way.[21]

There is little doubt that talk of disablement kept spirits high. On the afternoon of Thursday, March 28th, the *Geraldton Guardian* declared:

> We understand that on news being received concerning the missing steamer, it will be posted up at the post office, and Mr. Faulkner (manager of the local branch of the A.S.S. Company) states immediately he hears the steamer has been found, the house flag of the company will be run up.[22]

In the newspapers, as on the streets, there was much interest of *Koombana*'s recently installed Marconi wireless apparatus. If she were merely disabled, why had no message been received? After all, the device had been touted as essential and life-saving in circumstances just such as these. In the spirit of optimism, many fell back upon a simple explanation: that the storm which had torn away *Bullarra*'s funnel had also damaged *Koombana*'s antenna. Day after day, the Marconi men of other ships tapped out *Koombana*'s call sign "MZP", hoping all the while that some crackle of reassurance might be received in reply.[23]

Inevitably, Captain Townley and Algy Collins pondered the intuition or information of the Chinese servant. *Gorgon* was not wireless-equipped, but several of the ships working the Straits[24] now were; perhaps a distress message—even a garbled distress message—had been picked up by someone. In theory, *Koombana*'s transmitter had a range of 1,500 miles; it was certainly powerful enough to ruffle the ether along the Indonesian archipelago. But it was one thing to send a message skipping across the sky on a night clear and calm; it was quite another to transmit from wet equipment in the middle of a Nor'-West willy-willy. Time would tell. Certainly, it was too early to pay homage to the wisdom of the ancients; there was every chance that this Chinese whisper owed more to Marconi than to Confucius.

ACROSS THE DAYS OF EMPTINESS the opinions of seafaring men were keenly sought and widely published, but if the editors of the dailies thought that the opinions of master mariners would lend clarity to the discourse, they were quickly re-educated. The result was an epidemic of disagreement that left most readers none the wiser.

Interviewed by *The West Australian*, Captain Richardson of the *Paroo* insisted that there was no simple rule regarding the Nor'-West willy-willy.

> Occasionally they will work in the same direction as the hands of a watch—that is to say, they will come in from the N.W. hard, and swing round to die away in the S.W. At other times they will work from the N.E. back to the S., and into the S.W. That is what the recent one did, so far as I can gather.[25]

Richardson's remarks left better-educated shipmasters shaking their heads. The change in the direction of the wind, they knew, was not a characteristic of the storm at all; it related only to the observer's position in relation to it. On one side of a storm's advance, the winds shift clockwise as the storm passes; on the other side, anticlockwise. It was perhaps fortunate that the state's most accomplished shipmasters were out searching for *Koombana*, beyond the reach of *The West Australian*.

When asked about *Koombana*'s predicament and the decisions her master may have taken, Captain Richardson declared:

> There are two things that Captain Allen would do—in fact, what any master would do under the circumstances. I take it that he was between Port Hedland and Bedout Island when he began to feel the cyclone . . . the wind would then be about E.N.E. That is, to all intents and purposes practically in his course for Broome. Is he going to go with the wind on his starboard bow and plug through it, or run to the N.W. with it on his quarter? The latter plan is scouted, by reason of the fact that we have not heard of him.[26]

This speculation sent one nautical man searching for his copy of John Macnab's *Catechism of the Law of Storms*. Having found it, and refreshed a memory that dated back to his Board of Trade examinations, he scurried off to *The Sunday Times*.

> The gentleman who loaned us the "catechism" remarks:— "Richardson in the West Australian says there is no hard and fast rule. What nonsense! The Koombana as last seen by the Bullarra was in the dangerous quadrant, and the instructions are you must not let the

centre pass over you. Therefore the Koombana should have run south-west to escape. When one sees in cold print this talk about 'plugging through' it makes one exasperated at such ignorance."[27]

But as one gentleman professed exasperation, his words spawned new exasperation in others. It was already known that the storm had crossed the coast west of Depuch Island, and had swept in not from the north-east but from the north-west. Had *Koombana* "run south-west to escape" she would have followed *Bullarra* directly into the path of the storm. Indeed, Captain Allen would have accomplished by strategy what his colleague had suffered merely by chance.

Perhaps the most constructive contribution came from a man with powerful reasons to deal only in fact. Facing the possible loss of his wife and two stepdaughters aboard *Koombana*, master pearler Sydney Pigott recognised that one ship, and one ship only, had encountered the storm from the opposite side. On her northward run from Fremantle to Wyndham direct, *Moira* had taken a wide track outside the Montebello Islands and the Lacepedes. Because the storm had passed between his ship and the coast, Captain Ward's observations would be critical to understanding the progress of the storm over the sea, and critical to understanding *Koombana*'s plight, then and now. Pigott spared no effort to place this new information in the hands he considered most capable. From Broome he had telegraphed to Wyndham, where *Moira* was delayed awaiting cattle. As soon as the reply came, it was relayed to Perth, and from there to Carnarvon, for Captain Mills of the *Minderoo*.

The cable, dense with detail, contained *Moira*'s hour-by-hour observations—the direction of the wind, the condition of the sea, and the state of the glass—for twelve hours from the time of *Koombana*'s departure. By careful analysis it could be concluded that although *Moira* had endured a rough trip, she had never been close to the eye of the storm. Indeed, when the conditions she encountered were at their worst, the storm was closer to the land than to the ship. That, of itself, was useful information.[28]

By the morning of Friday, March 29th, all optimism had begun to yield. While daily newspapers across the nation struggled for a new angle, *The West Australian* found resonance in the void. Under a simple, powerful headline, it spoke directly to universal anguish.

> THE KOOMBANA.
> ANOTHER SILENT DAY.
> With an immense coastline to patrol and an area of sea that must take days to cover, news from the search fleet is necessarily slow in coming to hand, and the passage of each hour without a single word has begun to dispel the belief that no news is a bulwark to which those in suspense can cling. Optimistic endurance of the silence from the

seas has almost reached its breaking point in the public mind. It is probable that the first tidings will come through from Broome to-day, where the Bullarra, herself scarred by the hurricane, is expected to arrive at daylight.[29]

For the first time, the likelihood of grim news was stated barely. *The West Australian* told its readers that the little coasting steamer *Una* had been chartered by the government "for a cruise in what may be termed the catastrophe zone."[30]

As THE NEW PESSIMISM WENT TO PRESS, the lugger *Mina* reached her first waypoint. Hugo Harper estimated their position as sixty miles due north of Bedout Island. That was ideal; he could now tack southward, scanning a large area in favourable conditions before fixing his position at day end.

Late in the afternoon Bedout was sighted, but as *Mina* ran toward the land she was caught by what Nor'-Westers call a "cock-eyed bob": a pint-sized but nonetheless dangerous open-water whirlwind. As the lugger skirted the island to the east, fading light confirmed the crew's suspicion that the island's unattended beacon was not burning. All wondered how long it had been out, but that was not the pressing concern. With no beacon, Bennie and Harper were unwilling to risk a close approach. They turned the lugger around and returned to deep water, choosing the fickle wind in preference to a reef as unyielding as it was invisible. Within an hour the cock-eye had blown itself out; *Mina* rode comfortably through the night under minimal sail.[31]

At daylight on Saturday, March 30th, the search was resumed. After scanning the sea for four days without the slightest reward, *Mina*'s crew had sunk into a shared belief that nothing would be found. However, at 9 a.m., ten miles to the west of Bedout Island, a small piece of painted wood panelling was plucked from the water. On close inspection, it seemed to have come from the inside of a cabin, but little was made of it. Alone and uncorroborated, against the sea's blank denial, the first artefact of disaster struggled for significance. It was stowed below and did not rate mention in *Mina*'s log.[32]

WITH HER NEW CORRUGATED-IRON FUNNEL, *Bullarra* looked more shack-shape than ship-shape, but her arrival at Broome on Friday afternoon was cause for relief and excitement. Buoyed by the prompt acceptance of their earlier proposals, the citizens convened again in the evening, to finalise and despatch a detailed plan for the steamer's redeployment.

In Perth, Premier Scaddan was becoming accustomed to receiving the thoughts of Broome with his breakfast. The latest cable read:

> After consultation with master mariners and the master of the Bullarra we consider it advisable that the Government should endeavour to

induce the Adelaide Steamship Company to issue instructions to the
Bullarra to discharge her cattle here, arrange if necessary to obtain
coal supplies from the Gorgon, and proceed to a position off Turtle
Island, bearing east six miles, from which point she might commence
a systematic search across the track of the storm as follows:—From
the point of departure proceed due west 75 miles, then due north 15
miles, then due east 75 miles, then due north 15 miles, and so on for
six consecutive days, the search only to be conducted during daylight
and with an officer at the masthead.[33]

Once again the premier and the harbourmaster conferred, and once again
Broome had its way.

AT 2 P.M. ON SATURDAY, *Minderoo* arrived at Cossack. From the telegraph
office a brief progress report was despatched to Fremantle by passenger
and parliamentarian Joseph Gardiner:

> Arrived Cossack in Minderoo today. Captain Mills made thorough
> search through Mary Ann Passage, along the east side of Barrow
> Shoal, round Barrow Island, and round Montebello Island and Ritchie
> Reef. Then steered east 25 miles, then south again to Sholl Islands.
> Searched the islands and then along the coast to Cossack, through
> the whole of the Dampier Archipelago. No trace of the Koombana.[34]

Captain Mills had dropped anchor in the roads, but on receipt of new
instructions from the chief harbourmaster he brought *Minderoo* to the
Point Samson jetty, to expedite preparations for the next phase of the
search. His urgency was due in large measure to his belief that the real
work, with genuine prospects of success, had yet to begin. Precious time
had been lost to what he considered a fruitless exercise. He and his crew
had scanned a vast expanse of ocean in which *Koombana*, he felt sure,
would not be found. Like Dalziel and Bennie, Mills had reached the
conclusion that Bedout Island was pivotal for the search, as it must have
been for Captain Allen ten days earlier. Whether *Koombana* ran north-
west or north-east was difficult to judge; it all depended on the conditions
her master had faced as he approached that difficult and dangerous turn.

The second set of instructions for Captain Mills was, like the first,
finalised without the benefit of his experience. This time, however, the
thoughts of shipmaster and searchmaster were fully aligned. From a point
north-east of the Montebello Islands, *Minderoo* would begin a systematic
sweep of the ocean, steaming north and south on lines thirty miles apart,
working steadily eastward towards Bedout.[35]

IN OCTOBER 1906, Bedout Island rose briefly to prominence, not through
any maritime disaster upon reef or shore but by a remarkable consensus of
shipmasters that the island carried such potential. The state government

had announced that four new lighthouses would be built along the Nor'-West coast, at locations yet to be decided. The plan included a novel element: senior shipmasters of the Nor'-West would not merely be consulted; they would be invited to cast votes on where the new lights should be placed.[36]

The opportunity was broadly embraced. To the government's table came Andrew Mills, then master of the *Paroo*, also Townley of the *Sultan*, Richardson of *Minilya*, Hurrell of *Moonta*, and nine others. The particular form of lighthouse democracy was simple: each master would cast four votes, and the results would be tallied: 13 masters, 52 votes in total. The "shipmasters' consensus" left little doubt that a coralline islet north-east of Port Hedland was held in dark regard. Let the votes tell the story:

Bedout Island   12
Cape Leveque   8
Point Cloates   7
Cape Inscription   7
Cape Ronsard (Bernier Island)   5
Cape Vlaming (North West Cape)   4
Shoal Point   3
Cape Londonderry   2
Low Point   2
Montebello Islands   1
Bassett Smith Shoal   1

Each captain was asked to provide concise remarks in support of his choices. Captain Mills wrote: "Bedout Island, on account of island being low-lying with extensive reefs and strong currents running athwart the usual course of vessels." Captain Townley echoed Captain Mills, and Captain Airey did not waste words. "Of undoubted necessity," he wrote.

Interestingly, several shipmasters explained that the danger of Bedout was not primarily the work of nature; it was, rather, an accident of human history. In round steamship terms, the settlements of Port Hedland and Broome were 24 hours apart, and both ports were tidal, meaning that they could only be entered or left on a high spring tide. The problem arose because the travel time and the cycle of the tides were closely matched. For all but the fastest steamers, catching the tide at the destination port was a close-run thing. There was no time to dilly-dally or to take a wider, safer line around an inconvenient island.

Several of the captains also explained that because Bedout Island was closer to Hedland than to Broome, it was the southbound steamer that faced the greater risk. Typically, the northbound boat would slip out of Hedland on a morning tide and be clear of the danger by nightfall. The southbound boat, leaving Broome on the same tide, had no alternative but to make the dangerous turn in the middle of the night.

The decision to place a light on Bedout created a new problem. Of the sites chosen, the island was least suited to conventional lighthouse construction and to human occupancy. The island's highest point was less than twenty feet above the high-water mark, and there was evidence that it had, on occasion, been swept from end to end by the sea. An automated light seemed the only practical possibility.

The state's first unattended lighthouse, an acetylene-burning, occulting beacon of Norwegian design, entered service on Bedout Island in December 1908. Pleasantly surprised by its rapid completion and low cost, the government declared the innovation a great success.[37] The shipmasters, however, reserved judgment. They welcomed the new beacon, looked out for it, and bent their courses by it, but none was quite ready to place his trust in a new-fangled contraption—and a new-fangled Norwegian contraption to boot.

ON THE MORNING OF MONDAY, APRIL 1ST, as *Bullarra* made final preparations for her departure from Broome, a crew member dashed off a postcard to a friend:

> Dear Sinclair
> Had an awful time in the Cyclone passed thro the centre never expected to see anybody again. Just about fed up of the sea now—wouldn't take much to make me chuck it up. The old ship is a marvel she is badly knocked about. Just off again for an 8 days search for the Koombana—hope we will meet with success. This is a photo of the jury funnel nearing completion in haste. Yours, E.T.B.[38]

The card sent ashore for posting did not travel far. Someone, probably the Adelaide Steamship Company's agent in Broome, took exception to the line "Just about fed up of the sea now—wouldn't take much to make me chuck it up." After running a blue crayon through the offensive content, the self-appointed message-manager apparently thought better of sending the card at all. It was filed away not with material relating to *Bullarra*, but with passenger lists and correspondence relating to the missing *Koombana*. And there it would remain.

WHEN GORGON ARRIVED OFF BROOME and signalled "No News," her tour of duty was officially over. She would remain at anchor overnight and then resume her regular running, albeit with officers maintaining a lookout across all daylight hours. It was under these instructions that *Gorgon*, steaming south for Cossack, made the discovery that would change everything.

At 10 a.m. on Tuesday, April 2nd, twenty miles north of Bedout Island, the lookout saw something floating. In a sense it was a chance sighting; the wind had fallen away to nothing and the sea was like glass. After

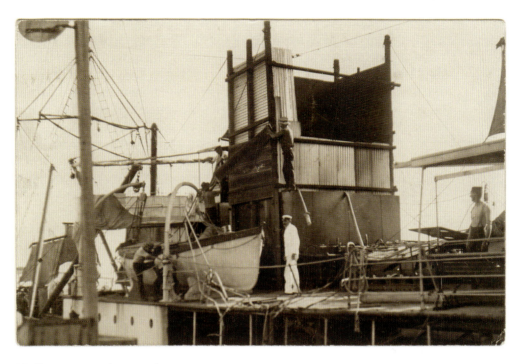

A Bullarra *crewman's postcard,*
sent ashore for posting at Broome on April 1st, 1912.
The photograph, taken at Point Samson a week earlier,
shows crew members fixing the last corrugated-iron panels
of a makeshift funnel.

ss Bullarra E.T.B. 19/3/12 ?note Mr Nairn   Compliments Mr ?

Dear Sinclair

POST CARD

Had an awful time in
the Cyclone passed thro the centre
never expected to see anybody again
just about fed up of the sea we
wouldn't take much to knock me
chuck in ?. The old ship is a marvel
she is badly knocked about just
off again for an 8 days search for
the 'Koombana' hope we will meet
with success This is a photo of the

Gorgon's engines were reversed and then stopped, purser Algy Collins watched from the rail as a boat was lowered. What appeared at first to be wooden panelling turned out to be a cabin door, still hinged to its broken stile. The scene was something he would remember for a very long time, and two things in particular remained vivid in that memory: the silence broken by the screeching of seabirds, and the colour and opaqueness of the sea.[39]

A great Nor'-West storm leaves its mark. The rains that escort the whirlwind to shore may be torrential and transformative. As if startled by the splash of water, dry land seizes brief opportunity; it sucks up what it can and sends the surplus red and iron-rich to the sea. Delivered into the custody of the tide, the desert's complexion may be carried far offshore, to blend with plumes of pale, coralline silt that wind and waves have drawn up from the seabed. Here, eighty miles from land, ten days beyond calamity, the fate of *Koombana* was pulled not from clear water (which a few calm days might otherwise produce) but from a strange, mushroom-coloured milk. Captain Townley recorded the discovery in *Gorgon*'s log:

> April 2, 10.15 a.m., Lat. 19.10 S Long. 119.6 E. Ship steering S 6 W. true. Sighted white painted piece of wood. Stopped and picked up same. Description: Painted door painted white one side, polished on other. Silver fittings marked cross-flags Walker and Hall (W. & H.). Fingerplate both sides ornamented with Grecian urn, with hanging wreaths each side. Door apparently had been forced by pressure. Handle on white side, and on reverse side drawn in. Builder's joiner written with hard pencil, 'Stat---- First-class entrance 429 J.D.' The lock is marked 'N. F. Ramsay and Co., Newcastle-on-Tyne. Several small leatherheads attached, about half-inch long.
> 10.40 a.m., Proceeded.
> 10.45 a.m., Stopped. Passed through several very small pieces, one a painting stage, and others apparently small pieces of board. Unusual number of birds about.[40]

Among *Gorgon*'s crew were several who had travelled by *Koombana*, and who knew the ship well. None doubted the door's provenance. Captain Townley looked closely at the word scribbled in pencil on the back of the stile. He was almost certain that it was "State". As *Koombana* was the only vessel on the coast which offered staterooms, her loss now seemed beyond doubt.

GORGON'S UNSCHEDULED LATE-AFTERNOON ARRIVAL sent Port Hedland into a spin. The unusual import of her visit was sensed; even before Captain Townley reached the telegraph office, word spread that she carried evidence that *Koombana* had foundered. At 7.45 p.m., the Port Hedland postmaster sent a telegram to his counterpart in Perth.

Portion of Koombana found 50 miles from here by the s.s. Gorgon. Lots of small wreckage about Bedout Island.[41]

Perhaps the message was meant to be confidential, but it could not possibly have remained so. *The Sunday Times* reported:

The news of the arrival of this message spread like wildfire through the city, and people attending the theatres and other places of amusement that evening lost all interest in the various entertainments through the sudden gloomy pall which enveloped everybody and everything.[42]

In Port Hedland, locals and visitors asked to see the evidence of disaster for themselves. Some were ushered aboard, for what they would remember as something akin to an autopsy. While *Gorgon* was steaming for Hedland, the stateroom door had been examined minutely by her officers; they had tipped it, turned it, studied its handle and its lock. Now, with some authority and with a sense of ownership, they led inquirers below to where the door lay on a bench under canvas, and where by the light of a bull's-eye lantern, its 'injuries' could be revealed and interpreted. A reporter for *The Northern Times* later wrote:

It clearly told its own tale. It had given before the force of an even pressure from outside, and in falling in had smashed the inside handle against a bunk or some hard object. When the pressure came, the catch began to give (the door was closed but not locked) and the lock was being forced through the woodwork when the hanging stile—the upright post to which a door is hinged—came away, and with the door fell into the cabin. On the inside, and therefore unpainted, part of the stile, was the joiner's note in pencil, the number "429" doubtless being his registered number on the job, followed by his initial. Captain Townley says it is the door of a port cabin and judges that it belonged to the cabin 1-2-3 opposite the music room.[43]

The reporter remarked that all stood quiet and attentive as the explanation was offered. "We could not but be solemnly impressed," he wrote, "by the sight of this silent but eloquent witness of the ocean tragedy."

THE NEXT MORNING, *Minderoo* also reached Port Hedland; Captain Mills took advantage of the high tide and brought the ship in. Townsfolk came in congregation to the jetty, to ask and to tell in equal measure. When Mills stepped ashore and left for the telegraph office, locals were struck by his jaded appearance. *Minderoo*'s passengers confirmed that for four days he had rarely left the bridge.[44]

A precise account of *Minderoo*'s discoveries was telegraphed to the ship's owners:

Searched within the following positions by running parallel lines 30 miles apart:—Latitude 20.15, longitude 116; latitude 18.40, longitude 116; latitude 18.40, longitude 117.40; latitude 20, longitude 118; from the last position steering east ten miles, then north thirty miles, then east fifteen miles. Stopped to pick up smoking-room settee cushion and part of cabin drawer in latitude 19.36, longitude 117.53; and in latitude 19.32, longitude 118.10, picked up bottom board of boat and small teak panel. Abandoned further search at sunset on Tuesday, and consider the ship is lost in the vicinity of Bedout Island.[45]

Although the fact was not noted in the despatch, the board from the bottom of a lifeboat also carried the number "429". It was soon realised that 429 was not the number of a shipyard worker, but of the ship itself. "Koombana" was ship-building project No. 429 for Alexander Stephen & Sons, at Linthouse on the south bank of the Clyde.

If there be one coincidence worth recording, it is that the first two significant discoveries of *Koombana* wreckage were, after so many empty days, pulled from the water within minutes of each other. While the crew of *Minderoo* retrieved a waterlogged cushion, the crew of *Gorgon* lifted the stateroom door. The two ships were at that time 70 miles apart, each below the other's horizon.

It is not surprising that the two captains dealt differently with their respective finds. Although the discovery of a red morocco-leather cushion from *Koombana*'s First Class smoke room was ominous, it did not prove disaster. The stateroom door, by contrast, spoke clearly of violent separation from the ship.

For Hugo Harper, the discoveries of *Gorgon* and *Minderoo* settled the issue: *Koombana* and her entire complement, including his brother George, were lost. He telegraphed his brother Gilbert in Broome:

Fear worst.
Found some wreckage myself
but did not place much importance in it.
Gorgon in Hedland with cabin door.
Minderoo has bottom of lifeboat,
cabin fixings, and smoke room Morocco settee.
Personally now fear disaster.
Returning to-night by Minderoo.[46]

ON THE AFTERNOON OF WEDNESDAY, APRIL 3RD, the schooner *Muriel*, which had searched for eight days but found nothing, was drawn toward a ragged tail of smoke on the horizon. The wind had fallen away and progress was slow; more than an hour passed before Captain Dalziel recognised *Bullarra*. At six in the evening, he boarded the steamer to speak with Captain Upjohn.[47]

Bullarra, he learned, had made three discoveries which pointed to disaster. Part of a smashed boat, bearing the badge of the Adelaide Steamship Company, had been recovered north of Bedout Island. A distinctive piece of ceiling panelling had also been retrieved, and Captain Upjohn had seen what had appeared as the outline of a submerged ship, but which turned out to be a slick of oily, greasy water. Samples had been taken for analysis.[48]

After a brief discussion, it was decided that *Bullarra* would remain at sea and continue the search, leaving *Muriel* to convey the grim news. In isolation from the conversation of the port, neither captain knew that *Koombana*'s fate was already sealed.

IN GERALDTON on the morning of Thursday, April 4th, 1912, the flag of the Adelaide Steamship Company rose slowly at the local shipping office, and stopped at half mast. A message posted in the window read:

> S.S. KOOMBANA.
> With profound regret the company have to announce that they consider the discovery of wreckage by the s.s. Gorgon and s.s. Minderoo (which has been identified as belonging to the s.s. Koombana) is evidence that the Koombana was lost with all hands, in the vicinity of Bedout Island, during the cyclone which raged on the 20th and 21st March. The vessel evidently being caught in the vortex and overwhelmed by the sea, which no human agency could prevent. The loss of the passengers, Captain T. Allen and his fine crew is deeply deplored.[49]

In Carnarvon, *The Northern Times* extended sympathy to the relatives and friends of her passengers and crew.

> The presence on the boat of well-known North-Westers returning from their summer holidays caused a wave of general apprehension and deep regret in Carnarvon, and all news to hand from day to day was eagerly inquired for. We trust that even if the disaster is complete, some indication will be found to mark the resting place of the victims of the hurricane and the last anchorage of the palatial steamer whose presence was a compliment to our coast and a source of much comfort and satisfaction to passengers.[50]

Although *The Northern Times* was gracious in its commiseration, there was a late change in the texture of its reporting. It appears that when all hope was extinguished, all restraint was extinguished with it.

> With a little imagination we can picture the disaster: the rapidly incoming tide at Hedland Jetty, the crowding indications of an unusual weather disturbance, the anxious consultation of the captain and officers of the two Adelaide Company's steamers, the decision

to face the storm in the open sea, the breezy assurances to troubled passengers, the good-byes to friends and earth; forging into the rising sea, hatches battened down, and passengers cooped up amid protest and alarm, the burst and roar of the hurricane, the vessel dropping in troughs fearsomely deep, shaking herself free from the deluge upon her, and lifting and heaving upon hill-tops; the bridge carried away, the steamer at the mercy of the storm, a list, the roar of waters, and then the great darkness.[51]

As it happened, the only vessel specifically chartered to search for *Koombana* arrived too late to play her intended part. The little coaster *Una*, having steamed from Geraldton to Cossack direct, received new instructions by wire:

> Cossack
> Captain Rantzau "Una"
> Wreckage found 25 miles north by west Bedout Island.
> Proceed at once to that island.
> See if any wreckage about reef
> then proceed to spot where wreckage discovered
> and after searching in the vicinity for one day
> put into Hedland and report for further instructions.
> The Bullarra is searching east of Turtle Island
> Should you sight her, signal master return Cossack at once for orders.
> Harbour Master
> 3rd April 1912 [52]

Captain Rantzau was thus given the thankless task of determining, as nearly as possible, the location of the disaster. On the morning of Friday, April 5th, he steered *Una* slowly north-north-west from Bedout. Late in the morning, after the island had disappeared astern, a few pieces of wreckage were seen floating.[53] The engines were stopped. In the course of an hour, while *Una* drifted on the tidal current, Captain Rantzau decided that the search for *Koombana* was over. His final report to Chief Harbourmaster Irvine records his arrival at that place—and at that conclusion.

> At dinner time stopped in position 19.7 S. and longitude 118.53 E. Wreckage at this place seemed to come from the bottom as within the course of 15 minutes no wreckage would be visible and then it would be seen floating, indicating to me that the ship was lost at about this point. I would also like to state at this place there were a large number of sharks to be seen. Being satisfied that nothing further could be done I proceeded to Port Hedland arriving there at 1.30 am on 6th April.[54]

April 6th. Easter Saturday. It was now seventeen days since *Koombana* had left Port Hedland, and eleven since *Muriel* had left Broome. Anchored overnight in the lee of Bedout, one task remained for Broome wharfinger Oswald Dalziel and his crew. They would endeavour to fix the light.

Ashore on the island, crossing sand ridges littered with dead and maimed birds, Dalziel became irritated. What was Upjohn thinking? *Bullarra*'s master—or at least his chief officer, who had led a party sent ashore—had concluded that because the glass of the light was not encrusted with salt, the island had not experienced the full force of the blow. What nonsense, he thought. Lashing rain could clear the glass as surely as the sea-spray would encrust it, and a couple of dewy nights would erase all evidence of either.[55]

The Bedout Island Light, c. 1912.

After climbing to the platform at the top of the tower, he stared at the sea for a few moments and then set to work. After removing one of the panes shielding the lamp, he thought he could hear and feel the flow of acetylene. That was quickly confirmed; when a match was brought close to the jets, the lamp flared immediately and stayed alight. There seemed nothing wrong with it. After checking the machinery and the rotating screens, he replaced the glass pane, carefully pressed the putty around it, and tightened the screws holding the brass battens in place.[56] He descended the tower none the wiser, but with a keen sense of having locked the gate after the horse had bolted.

The crew stood by until early evening, to be sure that the job was done. Although the light worked perfectly, there was little satisfaction drawn from this final service rendered. There was, rather, the simple wish to be gone, born of sadness, fatigue and vague discomfiture that a beacon so oblivious and unrepentant should now cast its beam, its blessing—its weightless, worthless blessing—upon a softly breathing sea.

With dull desire to be cloaked in darkness, to answer only to the wind, the tired men of *Muriel* set sail for Broome.

13

The Ill-fated Complement

INEVITABLY, THE TRAGEDY OF KOOMBANA settles upon her passengers and crew: the men, women and children who embarked from Port Hedland on Wednesday, March 20th, 1912.

When the discovery of wreckage erased all doubt that the ship had foundered, the Adelaide Steamship Company set out to compile a complete list of the missing. It was no easy task. Many passengers, especially those travelling in Second Class, had not made reservations. They had simply come aboard, called at the purser's office and paid their fares. Because the only complete record disappeared with the ship, the company had no alternative but to rely on the recollections of shipping clerks and disembarking passengers, and the assurances of friends and relatives. For several weeks the list slowly grew; more than a dozen names were added. There were also a few crossed off: passengers who had broken their journeys and engaged crew members who had failed to present for work.

Although the company attended diligently to the clerical process, its effort was made to meet the requirements of the registrar-general and to answer questions from the public and the press. Significantly, the company kept no record of next-of-kin, and made no effort to contact the families of the lost. It was easier and less complicated to take no action, admit no liability, and deal only with those who wrote seeking solace or redress.

Perhaps it is time to revisit the men and women of *Koombana*, to pay some late attention to their lives and circumstances. The respect thus paid cannot be complete or even, any more than the records of their lives are complete or even. But we may accept the fragments, and work with them.

First, we walk *Koombana*'s decks to meet the 72 men and two women who comprised her crew.[1]

Directly below the navigating bridge was the cabin of **Captain Thomas Maurice Allen**. We need not linger here. Of *Koombana*'s cautious commander, much is elsewhere written.

From Allen's cabin, steep stairs port and starboard led down to the promenade deck. Three strides from the bottom of the starboard stair, beside the main companionway, was the cabin of his right-hand man. *Koombana*'s chief officer—'first officer' or 'first mate' if you prefer—was **Norman Jamieson**, another long-time servant of the Adelaide Steamship Company. The Daylesford-born bachelor considered himself a lucky man. He had been transferred from *Yongala* in February 1911, immediately before that ship's final voyage.

If the chief officer was stationed below his commander's right elbow, as it were, second officer **Walter Kinley** was similarly deployed below his left. Kinley, the only son of a sea captain, was born at Penola in South Australia but educated at the Semaphore Collegiate School just a few blocks from the wharves of Port Adelaide. At 22 years of age, he seemed a little too young for his cap, but had already proved his worth as a seaman.

Third officer **F. S. Peacock** was on his first voyage with *Koombana*. In a sense, he had taken two backward steps to reach this place. The 27-year-old had already served as a first officer for the Straits Steamship Company of Singapore, and as second officer aboard *Bullarra*. But there was prestige associated with *Koombana* and the Nor'-West run; this new post would not harm his prospects.

Peacock's accommodation was enviable. The third officer's cabin was well aft on the promenade deck, near the footbridge to the poop deck. It nestled among First Class staterooms and benefited greatly from the association; it shared their dimensions and large, rectangular window to the world.

Every merchant vessel has, rolled into one, an administrator, secretary, postmaster, paymaster and custodian of cash and valuables. *Koombana*'s purser was a 28-year-old South Australian, **Francis Hedley Harris**. Although married with a child, "Hedley" had much in common with first officer Jamieson, a few years his senior. They had served together on other ships, in other places, and both had transferred from *Yongala* on the eve of that ship's final departure. Jamieson went to *Grantala*; Harris came directly to *Koombana*, for the different sea and sky of the western coast.

The cabins of a ship's engineers were often placed lower than those of the officers, but the convention was unrelated to status or authority. Because the officers were responsible for the ship's navigation, their cabins often commanded a broad view of the sea. By similar logic, the engineers slept closer to the machinery of motion. So it was aboard *Koombana*: the engineers occupied a cluster of cabins port-side on the spar deck, with the First Class smoke room directly above and cattle stalls directly below.

Chief engineer Jock Innes (front row, far right) with the officers of Yongala.

Koombana's chief engineer was, according to his opposite number on the S.S. *Minderoo*, "a fine stamp of a Scotsman." Aberdeen-born **William Booth Innes**—"Will" to his wife but "Jock" to his shipmates—kept a house for Mrs Innes and the bairns in Hampton Road, Fremantle. His home life was limited to a couple of days each month, of course, but postcards from northern ports punctuated his absences. "This is a photo of the ship at Wyndham Jetty," he wrote on one, "don't let those terrors get a hold of it."

Koombana's new second engineer, in a cabin directly opposite, was perhaps the unluckiest man aboard. **Albert Wassell** and his mate Murdoch Gunn had been the second engineers of *Echunga* and *Koombana* respectively. To improve their prospects by broadening their experience, they had applied to the company to swap ships. The company had agreed.[2]

In the next cabin along, something seemed different on this trip. Third engineer **Walter Kelly** was in love. In Perth before the boat sailed, the Ballarat boy had become engaged to a tall, attractive New Zealander named Kitty Gillies. He had tried to convince Kitty to marry him immediately, but she thought they could wait a month. Her box was not quite ready, she quipped.

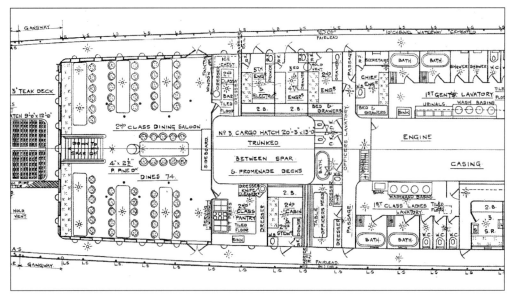

The engineers' cabins, port-side on Koombana's *spar deck.*

Kelly's cabin-mate was fourth engineer **Arthur Christie**, a good-looking 23-year-old from Sydney who, with his parents' pride and blessing, had left the family home for a life at sea. For his age, he was highly accomplished; he had hit his straps as second officer of the *Paroo*, under Captain Richardson.

By contrast, 24-year-old West Australian **James Arrow** was new to the work. Recruited as fifth engineer in January, this was his third Nor'-West voyage.

Sharing the last cabin of the engineering enclave was nineteen-year-old wireless operator **Harry Lyon**, born in England but now living in Victoria. Like his cabin-mate, Harry was learning the ropes. Although he had travelled previously as apprentice, this was his first voyage as 'Marconi man' in his own right.

With twenty passenger staterooms amidships, and with First and Second Class dining rooms fore and aft, there was little space on the spar deck for crew accommodation. Apart from the engineers, only stewards with special roles had their cabins here.

Well forward, in a well-appointed suite beside the First Class dining room, was *Koombana*'s highly strung chief steward **Frank Johnson**. In November 1911, Johnson had appeared in the Fremantle Police Court to answer a charge of assault brought against him by *Koombana*'s then baker, Edwin Albrecht. Although the action was dismissed by the court without kind words to either party, the dispute triggered industrial action by *Koombana*'s firemen, who declared that the ship would not leave port while Johnson remained aboard. Of the dispute and its resolution, much has been written. Perhaps surprisingly, Johnson and several of his erstwhile antagonists were serving together on this voyage.

Koombana had only two female crew members, to attend to "the particular needs of lady passengers." A little way down the corridor, past the First Class bar, they shared a windowless cabin beside the linen room. Stewardess **Anastasia Freer** was a 45-year-old widow with children in South Australia. Her assistant was **Delia McDermott**, a Dubliner who now called Sydney home. At thirty, Delia was still single, but may have found romance at sea. With steward William Burkin, she had transferred to *Koombana* from the old *Marloo*.

Also sharing a cabin, on the starboard side next to the officers' mess, were second steward **Jack Mangan** and fore-cabin steward **John "Jackie" Coughlan**. Mangan, 43, was London-born but now had a wife Minnie, a daughter Maggie and a large extended family in Sydney. Coughlan was younger, and single. Now 32 years of age, he had gone to sea at sixteen. For half of his life he had served in the stewards' departments of Adelaide Steamship Company vessels. It is difficult to say if he maintained any home other than his mother's in Port Adelaide, but he had many friends in Fremantle, and Nor'-Westers treated him as one of their own.

THUS FAR WE HAVE MET ONLY THE ELITE: crew members accorded space and comfort in proportion to their responsibilities. No such recognition was granted to *Koombana*'s seamen, firemen and stewards. Let us now visit the regulars in their cramped accommodation.

From the cabin shared by Mangan and Coughlan, the starboard rail could be followed almost to the ship's bow: past the windows of a dozen staterooms, past the broad foyer at the bottom of the main companionway, and past the curtained windows of the First Class dining room. Where the dining room wall curved away, gentility suddenly gave way to industry. Three heavy steam winches, side by side, stood guard over the main forward cargo hatch. On the far side of this open space was a blank steel wall relieved only by the doors to two large cabins: a port-side cabin for fourteen firemen, and a starboard-side cabin for fourteen seamen.

In the firemen's quarters, space was tight. Along the inside of *Koombana*'s flared bow ran a line of double bunks, head-to-tail like rail wagons on a curved track. A long table with two benches filled most of the remaining space. The personal circumstances of the stokers varied greatly, but most were aged in their late twenties or early thirties. The reason was simple: the work was backbreaking and hot, and the stoke-hold no place for boys or old men. Those who accepted this confinement did so for extra pay. It was a role accepted by men with debts or demons, or who needed every penny for a family far away.

Of the thirteen men who shared this cabin, only three were born in Australia. Tasmanian **Jack Smith** had just returned to work after time in hospital. At 23, he was the youngest man on the stokehold floor, but he held a third engineer's certificate and had worked for the company in different capacities for five or six years. **Albert Bryant** and **Tom O'Loughlin** were both Victorians. Bryant was single with a girlfriend in Western Australia, while 33-year-old O'Loughlin had a wife and five little daughters in the Perth suburb of Bayswater.

Of the Britishers, **William Clarke** was London-born but now had a wife and seven children in Seaforth, Liverpool. He had been "stepping out in Australia" for close on two years, his sister-in-law said. Little is known about a second Londoner, **Henry Offord**, who during his shore leave came and went from a boarding house in East Fremantle.

It was not uncommon for itinerant ship workers to be identified only by a brief entry in a crew list. From that source we learn that **McDermott** hailed from Liverpool, and **Furlong** from Bristol. We wonder who, if anyone, watched out for the young Cork Irishman **Fitzpatrick**.

Among the Scots, **Joseph Downie** had sailed from Glasgow with *Junee* in 1907, while Dundee-born **Tom Taylor** was a raw recruit.

Three Swedes—**Norlin**, **Olsen** and **Andersen**—filled the remaining places.

Firemen's and seamen's quarters at Koombana's *bow.*

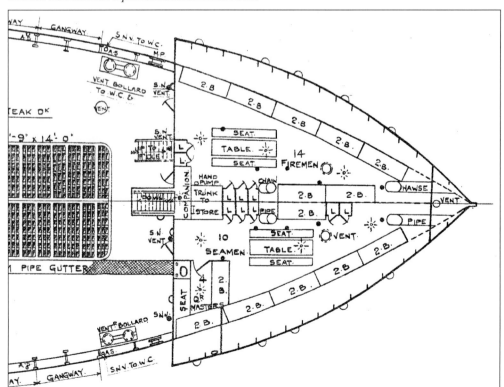

ABOUT HALF OF KOOMBANA'S FIREMEN had been involved in the recent strike, on one side or the other. Offord, Downie and Olsen were among those who had downed tools over their objections to the chief steward, while Clarke, Fitzpatrick, Norlin and McDermott were part of the team sent from Melbourne to break the impasse. The three-week strike would probably not be remembered at all, had it not threatened to bring down the first Australian Seamen's Award on the eve of its declaration. For their part in securing the new award, Clarke, Fitzpatrick, Norlin and McDermott had each received a gold medal and a letter of congratulation from the national secretariat, "for great services rendered to the union at a critical time in its history."[3] It is safe to assume that they did not display their medals in this cabin.

Directly adjoining the firemen's quarters, on the starboard side, were the seamen's quarters. Into this bunkhouse, twelve able seamen and two young ordinary seamen were crammed.

The ordinary seamen, both eighteen years of age, were almost certainly given the last two bunks in this tight and tapering space. New recruit *Fred Herbert*, from Melbourne, was the only Australian in the room. Jokes about convict ancestry were probably part of his introduction to seafaring life. By contrast, *Sid Stewart* from Shepherd's Bush may well have drawn comfort from the mix of accents in this little Britain.

Three of the able seamen were Londoners. *William Farnell* held a second officer's ticket and was probably the most experienced hand. For several years he and his brother Farnell Farnell had sailed together out of London, but after the death of their parents, they left the old country. For another two years they remained together, working the Australian east coast. Their last shared voyage, in August 1908, was with Captain Tyler aboard *Komura*, when the ship lost part of her propeller in a storm off the Solitary Islands.[4]

For *Charles Herbert Stanley*—not to be confused with storekeeper Herbert Bertie Stanley—the merchant marine was something new. After fifteen years with the Royal Navy, most recently aboard H.M.S. *Encounter*, Charlie had come to Fremantle. After a short spell as a wharf labourer, he was back at sea, with *Koombana* on the Nor'-West run.

The third Londoner was 34-year-old *Harry Rea*. Although he had an older brother in the navy, Harry was almost alone in providing for their mother back home in Camberwell.

The circumstances of the two Bristol men could scarcely have been more different. Aboard *Koombana* for the first time was 32-year-old *Fred Gunning*. The death of his wife had left him solely responsible for their daughter; he had left the little girl in care in Adelaide and come west for work. By contrast, things were looking up for able seaman *M. Heffernan*, or M. Ryan as he sometimes identified himself. His wife, their little son, and her 21-year-old daughter were on their way to Fremantle aboard the

Aberdeen liner *Gothic*, to begin a new life in Western Australia. He had not yet told his sister in London that he was a married man. He would surprise her soon.

Fred Wilson, born in North Shields, now called Western Australia home; he and his wife had settled at Woodlupine, south-west of the capital.

Of Harrington-born *J. McGuckin*, little is known.

In all, *Koombana* had ten Irish crew members. It was pure coincidence that three came from the little village of Termonfeckin in Drogheda.[5] Able seaman *Peter "Petie" Clinton* was one. With Heffernan, he had transferred from the old *Innamincka* in August 1911.

Although born in Liverpool, 36-year-old *William Carton* also called Termonfeckin home. His father, also a seaman, had been born there, but worked out of Liverpool. The son not only followed his father to sea; he returned to Termonfeckin with his English wife Amelia.

New to *Koombana* was 25-year-old *Michael "Jack" Dwyer* from Dungarvan. His father was a sailor, still working but not making good money. Mrs Dwyer now relied upon Jack to top up what her husband sent home.

Of Dubliner *Thomas McDonnell*, nothing is known.

The sole Scot among the seamen was Stirling-born *Peter Jenkins*. He had been with the Adelaide Steamship Company for five years and, like his countryman Joe Downie in the stokehold, had signed on in Glasgow for the delivery voyage of the cattle steamer *Junee*. In a letter written from Manila in August 1911, he had told his brother that he might request a transfer to another of the company's ships, "for a change."

One resident of the seamen's quarters had distinct duties and title. Night watchman *Harry Bow* had emigrated from Dorset; he now lived in Western Australia with his wife Florence.

From the spar deck, between the doors to the firemen's and seamen's quarters, a near-vertical stairway led down to the main deck. On the port side, directly beneath the firemen's quarters, was a cabin shared by eighteen stewards.

Gordon Gee, a 25-year-old from Sydney, was *Koombana*'s saloon waiter. He had sailed Australia's southern coast as barman of the *Karoola*, and between ships had maintained his links with the merchant marine by working at Smith's Railway Hotel in North Fremantle. There he made friends as easily as he had at sea. He was, the hotel patrons insisted, "a model of good nature and respectability." With what authority and clarity they spoke is difficult to judge.

Three of *Koombana*'s First Class stewards were English. With his parents and elder brother, 23-year-old *Henry Durham* from Brighton had emigrated to Western Australia a few months earlier. In a sense, he was the trailblazer for his family: before coming to *Koombana*, he had worked the Cape route from Southampton with the Union-Castle

Line. *Percy Farrance*, from Chislehurst in Kent, was also 23; he had an Australian girlfriend now and looked set to stay. And *Claude "Bennie" Benedict* from Bournemouth had been with the company for a few years. He had transferred to *Koombana* from *Moonta* in 1911.

At about £5 per month, there was no fortune to be made as a second-grade steward. Typically, the positions were filled by young men seeking a taste of seagoing life, or easy passage to a new land. It is hardly surprising that very few of *Koombana*'s stewards were Australian-born.

Among the Englishmen was 21-year-old *Jack Blades* from Middlesbrough. His parents were comfortable working folk who made it clear that they expected him to repay the costs of fitting him out for a seagoing life.

The circumstances of *Joe Winpenny* from Leeds were strikingly different. His father had died and his mother in Yorkshire needed help to get by.

Twenty-two-year-old *H. Smith* from Clapham was new to life at sea. *Koombana* was his first ship, and this his first voyage. *Harry Hughes* from Swansea was two years older and one month wiser: this was his second voyage.

From a family of fifteen children in Bootle, Liverpool, *Robert Davies* had left for the sea at seventeen, to support his parents. Their need was unquestionable but it was with an eye to adventure that he set out. Before leaving home he sent a short note to his Sunday school teacher at the Free Welsh Church in Merton-road:

> I regret to state I shall not be in Sunday School next Sunday, or for a good many more Sundays to come. I am about to try my luck in Australia, if I can succeed there, and by God's help I will. Remember me to my class at Sunday School. Good-bye.[6]

Where adventure is sought, it is often sought in company. The two Scots, *Edward Wardlaw* and *William Dick*, had struck out together from the old country and had remained together from ship to ship. After serving aboard the *Ferret*, they had transferred to *Koombana* in August 1911. Dick, who now had a wife and child back home, took his shore leave with his mate at a Scottish-run boarding house in Perth.

Londoner *William Burkin* was one of nine brothers, but only he and George had come to Australia. After working the south coast aboard *Marloo*, he had transferred to *Koombana* early in 1911. Like all first-time visitors to Broome, he had been greatly taken by the sight of large ships left high and dry by the ebb of the tide. Wading in knee-deep water by the jetty, he took a magnificent photograph of his shipmates resting on and around *Koombana*'s great propeller. The boys must have been delighted when the picture appeared in *The Western Mail*.[7]

At 33, Burkin was fully ten years older than most of the stewards, but was popular with all. He looked out for the young ones, too, especially *Arthur Salkild* who, at seventeen years and eight months, was *Koombana*'s

William Burkin's celebrated photograph: Koombana *crewmen, Broome, 1911.*

youngest crewman. Arthur was fresh from the family home in the Sydney suburb of Leichhardt.

If Arthur Salkilld was green, 27-year-old **Stanley Reynolds** from Adelaide was greener still. This was not only his first ship; it was his first working voyage.

Completing the tiny Australian contingent was 27-year-old Queenslander **James Crosbie**. "Jim" to his mates but forever "Jimsy" to his sister, Crosbie had served on *Grantala* before coming west in 1911, following his father who had taken work as a government engine driver at Kalgoorlie.

Koombana's stewards' department was constantly changing. There were fresh faces on almost every run and 32-year-old Dubliner **P. Finnerty** had seen most of them. He had been with *Koombana* almost since the beginning.

The high turnover of recruits had its particular misfortunes. At Fremantle, a few hours before *Koombana*'s departure, **Walter Burrows** had agreed to serve.

Among *Koombana*'s crew were several who could not read or write. The 54-year-old Welsh steward **William Cant** was one. On land, illiteracy was an inconvenience; at sea, it guaranteed alienation from the world left behind. While others thrived on words from home, illiterate sailors wrote no letters and found none waiting. And too often, in tragedy, they left wages that would never be claimed.[8]

FROM THE STEWARDS' QUARTERS on the main deck, corridors either side of the main forward cargo hatch led aft to two steel doors separating the human accommodation from the cattle stalls. At the end of the port-side corridor, past the washhouse, was a cabin shared by bo'sun and carpenter.

Koombana's bo'sun—"boatswain" if you prefer—was 33-year-old Irishman **James "Nish" Levins**. Like able seamen Carton and Clinton, Levins came from the village of Termonfeckin, Drogheda. He had lost his father when he was eight; he now supported his mother Mary from the other side of the world.

Even a steel ship needed a carpenter. Little is known about Glasgow-born **Thomas Grant**, newly hired. Perhaps he came with fine joinery skills from the shipyards of Clydebank, or perhaps he just 'knew a thing or two' and made it up as he went along.

On the starboard side, similarly situated, was a cabin set aside for donkeyman and storekeeper.

While *Koombana*'s engineers took charge of boiler, engine, tailshaft and propeller, the donkeyman attended to all other steam-driven machinery. **John Kearns**, with an ailing wife and two children in Belfast, had come to *Koombana* as a strikebreaking fireman on the promise of promotion to donkeyman after three months. It meant better pay and an end to shovelling coal. It also meant a cabin, albeit one he would share with storekeeper and barkeeper **Herbert Bertie Stanley**, who had been with *Koombana* almost since the beginning. Like several of his shipmates, Stanley had gone to sea as a young man after the death of his father. His mother, living in the Melbourne suburb of South Yarra, was heavily dependent on money her boy sent home.

Further back on the main deck, directly below the First Class dining room, was *Koombana*'s galley. And beside the galley on the port side were the cabins of those whose business it was to keep the passengers well fed.

In the first galley cabin was chief cook **Walter Tutt**. The 41-year-old English widower had only recently joined the ship. As a cook aboard the old *Innamincka* he had travelled the southern and eastern coast of Australia, leaving his two boys in Hobart with their grandmother Annie Worbey. His transfer delivered a much-needed rise in salary, but *Koombana* would take him even further from home. For the present, annual reunions were all he could hope for.

Tutt shared his cabin with pantryman **William Black** who, like second officer Kinley, came from Penola in South Australia. But while the Kinleys were of a seafaring bent, the Blacks turned their talents to horseracing and football.

In the absence of a candlestick-maker, *Koombana*'s butcher and baker had the second galley cabin to themselves. At 5' 0" tall, butcher **Charlie Walker** was as well known for his proportions as for his cheerful disposition. He presented to the world with a smile and a cleaver, standing on a box as necessary. Charlie had a wife and three little kids in South Fremantle, where he had run a butcher shop before going to sea. He had run off with *Koombana* when she first came to Fremantle in 1909; she had been his mistress ever since.

Since the bunfight between Frank Johnson and Edwin Albrecht,[9] Charlie Walker had had a different cabin-mate on almost every trip. *Koombana*'s latest baker, aboard for the first time, was a 25-year-old Englishman, **Albert Deller**. His baking had yet to be proven, but his need for a steady income was not difficult to discern. With both a wife and a widowed mother in London, he had taken the best wage on offer.

There had been changes in the third galley cabin also. Back in July, shock and disbelief had attended the death of second cook William Jones. A fall down the main companionway left Jones in a coma; he died in hospital a few days later.[10] Since then, there had been a string of replacements, and third cook **G. Jones** from Liverpool (no relation) could only guess who would share his cabin on this trip. Indeed, there remains some doubt about who, if anyone, wore the second cook's hat on *Koombana*'s Trip No. 37. Although a Swede named **H. Gainsburg** had signed on in Fremantle, there is doubt about whether he presented for work.[11]

At the bottom of the galley hierarchy, and probably relegated to the cattlemen's quarters, were two recent recruits. **John Jackson**, a 22-year-old from Gilnahirk in Belfast, had signed on as kitchenman, while **Evan Davies** took the exalted position of scullion. Evan was the older brother of Robert Davies, already working in the stewards' department. Back in Bootle, Liverpool, their parents were delighted—and somehow reassured—that two of their boys were together on the other side of the world.

WHEN KOOMBANA LEFT PORT HEDLAND on Wednesday, March 20th, 1912, only two ports of call remained. Among the 82 passengers known to be aboard, ten were directly linked to Broome and its pearling industry. A further eighteen were associated with Derby and its beef cattle. And 22, from all parts of Western Australia, were shearers engaged by their union for seasonal work at Liveringa Station.

The others—32 in all—represented many facets of a distinct Nor'-West life. They included a wharfinger, a police corporal, and a gaoler's wife; two engineers and a surveyor-turned-missionary; a saloon-keeper, a shop-keeper, and two holiday-makers. But these are mere statistics. Let us take this microcosm and unpick it.

It was no accident that *Koombana*'s complement included ten pass-engers whose travels were directly related to the business of pearls and pearl-shelling. In Broome, the summer lay-up was nearing an end and the 1912 season was about to begin.

Saloon passenger **George Harper**, of Harper Brothers Pearlers, was heading north to rejoin his brothers Hugo, Norman and Gilbert for the start of the season. George loved the *Koombana*, or so his friends said; he had delayed his departure from Fremantle to travel by her. The voyage he had looked forward to, however, was very nearly a short one. At Geraldton, he stepped out with old friends from the rowing club, lost track of the time, and very nearly missed the boat.

Master pearler Sydney Pigott, secretary of the Pearlers' Association, had remained in Broome for the summer but had sent his wife and two stepdaughters south to escape the worst of the heat. He now keenly awaited their return. His marriage to Jane Skamp in 1900 had been life-changing. In an instant, he became the head of a family. Jane, widowed about ten years earlier, brought two beautiful daughters everywhere admired but of an age that neither demanded nor countenanced a replacement for the father they had lost.

By 1912, **Jane Pigott** knew *Koombana* well. For this trip north she had booked side-by-side staterooms, amidships on the promenade deck. Alice and Jennie could share one; she would take the other. There was a fair chance, she thought, that she would have the second all to herself, since few women who travelled First Class also travelled alone.

Alice Beatrice Skamp had lost her father at eight and gained a stepfather a few days after her eighteenth birthday. Aboard *Koombana* on the day they left Geraldton, another significant life-mark had been reached. How Alice felt about being thirty and still single is not known.

Alice and Genevieve Skamp.

At 27, younger sister **Genevieve Callanan Skamp** had a little more time to ponder her future.

Broome's pearling aristocracy usually travelled First Class, but on the shoulders of the seasons, demand for *Koombana*'s staterooms often exceeded supply. On this voyage, several of the well-heeled found themselves in steerage, sharing dinner with the boys from the backblocks: the cattlemen engaged to Emanuel's and the shearers bound for Liveringa. One so relegated was **Abraham de Vahl Davis**, well known to all in Broome. Brother-in-law of the "pearl king" Mark Rubin, Davis was the pre-eminent pearl buyer in Western Australia. Success and popularity notwithstanding, he did not relish this latest return to work. A difficult and much-publicised divorce had taken its toll, and it seemed that he had spent most of the last five months at sea, aboard one steamer or another. Of the remarkable man Broome knew as "Abe", much might be written.

Travelling with Abraham Davis and in his employ was Englishman **John Evans**. It is not known whether Evans had been hired as a temporary assistant or was being groomed for a managerial role in Rubin & Davis of London & Broome.

Of no relation to Abraham was the young Englishman **James S. Davis**, the Broome representative of Siebe Gorman & Company, manufacturers and suppliers of diving apparatus. Davis had travelled to Fremantle to welcome—and introduce to an enthusiastic press contingent—eleven

English divers about to try their hand at pearling. The stakes were high, and not only for the divers. Now that the federal government had declared an end date for the use of indentured coloured labour, Siebe Gorman's survival in Broome depended on the success of the "white experiment."[12]

Joining *Koombana* at Port Hedland for the overnight run to Broome were two well-established pearlers.

Colourful Queenslander **Captain Charles Browne Stuart** was near the end of a remarkable career. He had arrived in Brisbane in about 1884, as captain of the sailing ship *Bell*. Ten years later, as a veteran of both sail and steam, he followed opportunities that carried him ever more northward and westward. After an experiment with dugong fishing off Mackay, he shipped railway sleepers to Normanton on the Gulf of Carpentaria. From there, he continued to Thursday Island to take command of one of James Clark's pearling schooners. Everywhere, the captain's competence was recognised; in time, he found himself managing all 'outside' operations for a pearling company in Broome. In 1909, upon the collapse of that enterprise, Stuart established himself as a pearler on his own account, reaping the rewards of independence when Broome's star was at its brightest. All the while, his wife and children—eight at last count—remained in South Brisbane. It is not known how often he saw them—or, indeed, when he had found time to conceive them.

Joseph Johnson was also independent and successful. His operation was tiny compared to that of Mark Rubin or the Pigotts, but it was profitable nonetheless. He and his brother Willie were joint owners of *Eos* and the newly built *Arafura*, and held stakes in several other vessels. While the price of shell remained high, the money would continue to roll in.

The Malay pearl diver **Hassan**, who also boarded at Port Hedland, was almost certainly under engagement to Joe Johnson or Captain Stuart, but very little is known about him.

The same might be said of one **Mr A. McRouble**, who booked through from Fremantle to Broome. In the "Nationality" column of the ship's passenger list, the entries rarely ranged beyond "British", "Colored", or "Aboriginal", but none of these terms seemed appropriate to this well-educated foreigner. The gap would be filled later, from a shipping clerk's recollection: "Dark complexion, like native of Philippines or Cape Verde. Spoke well."

Broome's pearling and pearl-shelling industry was an interesting mix of large and small operations. It had remained so for ten years at least because a particular size of boat had proven most efficient for the gathering of shell. Almost all divers now worked from two-masted luggers of 12–14 tons, regardless of the size of the enterprise. In this respect, the Kimberley cattle industry could not have been more different. Economies of scale had ensured that the beef cattle industry remained the province of a few great pioneering enterprises. Of twenty cattlemen aboard

Koombana, most were employed, directly or indirectly by Forrest Emanuel & Company or by the Kimberley Pastoral Company.

Rob Jenkins was stock agent and representative for Forrest Emanuel & Company in Derby. At 52, the long-time widower and former station manager was one of the most experienced men in the business, and as familiar to the crew of *Koombana* as to the townsfolk of Derby. "Another Dad Fleming," one of the locals called him.

Rob's eldest daughter, 27-year-old **Edith Jenkins**, often travelled with her father for company. Cast into the role of mother upon the death of her own, she had looked after her younger sisters and had grown up quickly. And if her young life in the suburbs of Perth had seemed hard, the remote stations of the Kimberley had changed her perspective. More than once she had been left alone at a remote homestead, to deal with any and all challenges while her father and his men ranged elsewhere.

If Rob Jenkins was delighted to have his daughter travelling with him, Elder Shenton's agent **Fred Clinch** was troubled by his eldest daughter's distress at seeing him go. On March 17th, after *Koombana* had rounded the North West Cape, he wrote to his wife:

> Dear Eliza
>
> This St. Pats "seventeenth of Old Ireland" we are nearing Onslow after a nice smooth run. There are a good number of passengers a good few who are Derby people whom I know.
>
> I can't get over poor Eileen breaking up so at my departure, she said "Don't go away Papa" as though she had some instinctive presentiment of ill-foreboding, no doubt she feels a bit lonely going into a situation . . .[13]

Clinch was proceeding to Derby to supervise the mustering of cattle for shipment, but as *Koombana* steamed northward, his thoughts remained in the south.

Also travelling First Class were two bright, ambitious brothers on parallel pathways. Born in England but raised in Queensland, **George Piper** and **Alfred "Ally" Piper** had learned the cattle business as protégés of Queensland pastoralist James S. Tyson, and had come west to further their careers. George, now thirty and recently engaged to be married, managed Margaret Downs Station; Ally, two years his junior, managed Meda.

If George Piper's mind had turned to romance over the summer break, it was never fully distracted from the business of running a cattle station. Before departure from Fremantle, he had hired four new men to assist with the running of Margaret Downs—four men very pleased to learn that their engagements would begin with twelve days of luxury, travelling First Class aboard *Koombana*.

Of the four, **W. W. Purcell** was the most experienced. For several years he had managed Satterthwaite's run at Alma, north of Geraldton.

Hired as a drover was **William Poor**, from Pyramid Hill in Victoria.

Piper's third recruit was a 'new chum.' The young Englishman **A. S. Taylor**, from Berkshire, had only landed at Fremantle in November, but to his credit he had already been working, on George Gooch's "Cheriton" estate at Gingin.

Finally, young **Pearson** from Perth was pleased to be hired, and pleased that his Uncle Bill—Derby wharfinger Captain William Pearson—would also be aboard for the run north.

Until recently, **Tom Forrest** had been butchering at Tuckanarra, south of Meekatharra, but there was better money to be made as a teamster on contract to Emanuel Brothers. Forrest had a wife and two children in Perth, and had recently bought into a property at Pingelly. Like several of the shearers, he needed money to get his own venture up and running.

One of the few of *Koombana*'s cattlemen not employed by Emanuel Brothers was **James Hayes**. Stepbrother to the pioneer pastoralist Joseph Blythe Senior, Hayes now managed the Blythes' station at Brooking Creek near Fitzroy Crossing.

Travelling with Hayes was forty-year-old **Jim Craigie**, returning from a holiday in the east. Craigie had been a Kalgoorlie butcher in the early days of the 'fields, but for seven years had called Brooking home.

Fred and Eliza Clinch.

The last of the engaged cattlemen was **William Laughton Cowain**, teamster for the Kimberley Pastoral Company. He too had come south for the summer, but the death of his mother a few days before Christmas had greatly altered the character of this latest family reunion.

Also travelling First Class to Derby was nineteen-year-old **Will Smith**. From the port he would make his way a hundred miles east to Napier Downs, where his uncle Jim Ronan was manager.

Of similar age and stage was young Englishman **S. H. Slade**. Having worked in both the London and Fremantle offices of Dalgety's, he was on his way north for station experience.

At Port Hedland, the Kimberley cattlemen were joined by **Frank McGowan**. The purpose of McGowan's visit to Derby is not known.

In any community there are those who seem happiest when taking their chances. At Fremantle, former Queensland drover **William "Billy" Vile** had boarded the ship and bought a steerage ticket to Derby. There is no indication that he knew where or for whom he would be working. The same might be said of teamster **Charlie Matthews**; he had walked a hundred miles to catch the boat at Carnarvon.

In a sense, **Fred Drake** was alone at the bottom of the cattlemen's hierarchy. Not only was he attending to stock to be disembarked at Broome rather than Derby, he was also more like a passage worker than a passenger. When the shippers of livestock placed their own men aboard to tend their animals, the attendants did not enjoy even a steerage cabin. They were accommodated in the cattlemen's quarters under the starboard bow. On this trip, the residents of that bunkhouse were a ragtag lot: two kitchenmen, two late recruits to the stewards' department, one or two shearers working their passage to Derby, and **"Jockey Jack" Dwyer**, who was to Mr Milne's horses what Drake was to the Broome-bound cattle.

THE SO-CALLED LIVERINGA TEAM was *Koombana*'s largest contingent: 22 shearers bound for Liveringa Station, via Derby. There was plenty of work ahead; Liveringa and Noonkanbah each ran about 100,000 sheep on a million acres. There was no possibility of shearing that huge flock using local labour of any colour. Fortunately, the climate favoured shearing in the autumn, when willing men could be engaged in the south.

We now step back a little in time, to meet the shearers port by port as they come aboard. At Fremantle on March 8th, Australian Workers' Union secretary T. L. Brown came to Victoria Quay to farewell the men his union had engaged.[14]

Patrick Smith had a small farm at Bridgetown. At the end of February he had left the property in the care of his mate Jim Drummond and set out for Fremantle. Travelling with him were **Donald McSwain** and **William McKibbin**, who were partners in a nearby property. All three had signed up to shear at Liveringa.

The men who gathered on the wharf found much in common. **Walter Thornton** was married and lived in Victoria Park, but had been working on his brother's property at Wagin. **George Lawrence** was from Woodlupine; he had left his wife to manage their property. From Northam came two brothers: **Richard Quinlan**, 25, and **Thomas Quinlan**, 21.

Of the fourteen who boarded at Fremantle, only four were itinerant professional shearers. Between sheds, **Tom Goddard** lived with his wife Rose and three children at Armadale, on the outskirts of the capital. Of **T. Reece**, **Robert Henry**, or New Zealander **Tom Barry**, little is known.

Most of the men had paid for their passage in advance. On the shoulders of the seasons, when demand was high, it was risky to do otherwise. **George Farrow** from Northam took his chances and secured a berth, but the plans of young **H. Bates** and **William Smith** very nearly came unstuck. Smith had the ticket that his mother had bought for him, but his mate came intending to 'book on board.' When they were told that the ship was full, Smith gave his ticket to Bates and signed on as a passage worker in the stewards' department.

Also at the quay, with his wife and children to see him off, was the Kimberley Pastoral Company's wool classer, **Ernest Dalton**. He too was Liveringa-bound.

At Geraldton, *Koombana*'s first port of call on the run north, another five shearers joined the ship.

Bill Lewis was well known in Geraldton; in a sense, he had married into a town as others may marry into a faith. His chosen partner of later life was the widowed Mrs Wright, one of the town's oldest and best-known residents. Lewis loved the *Koombana*, his friends said; like pearler George Harper, he had delayed his departure to travel by her. He could easily have booked 'saloon' but with twenty shearers in steerage all Liveringa-bound, the camaraderie of the Second Class dining room was not to be forfeited, at least not for a softer pillow or a better class of napkin.

At the pier, Lewis was joined by three men who had come in by train from the mining centre of Cue. The youngest was Englishman **Andy Shiels**, who came as much for adventure as for the pay packet.

The work had a different meaning for 39-year-old **James Clarke**, married with six children. He was engaged in the serious business of carving out a future. He and his wife Elizabeth had heard about good wheat land soon to be released in the Dalwallinu district, but they needed money to make a start. Elizabeth would remain in Cue and keep her position at the hospital; he would go shearing for the winter.

Like James Clarke, South Australian **Robert Scougall** had six children, but his circumstances were very different. His marriage to Flora had ended in divorce in 1904. The children had gone to live with their mother and her new partner, and he had made his own way in Western Australia. In Geraldton, before boarding *Koombana*, he dashed off a letter to his younger sister Mary, telling her that he was with friends and bound for Derby, to shear at a sheep station inland.

For the last member of the Geraldton contingent, shearing represented something of a career change. *Sydney Spencer*, originally from Victoria, had spent fifteen years prospecting along the Murchison River.

Koombana was due at Carnarvon on March 15th, and two men came overland to catch her. North from Wooramel came station manager *C. A. Bailey*, and west from Winderie came 23-year-old *Tom Binning Junior*, who had been working on his father's property. Tom Binning Senior had advised his son not to waste the opportunity to scout for good land in the north. To that end, the son brought equipment for an extended tour of the back country.

The last of the shearers—the 22nd member of the Liveringa team—joined the ship at Onslow. *David Jones* was a native of Geraldton or Northampton, but had been working inland along the Ashburton River. After boarding from a lighter in the roads, he paid his fare and joined the others in steerage.

AMONG KOOMBANA'S PASSENGERS were ten men engaged in government engineering work.

Travelling First Class was 38-year-old engineer *William Milne*, perhaps the most popular civil servant in the Nor'-West. A few years back, the Geological Survey Department had told the cattle breeders that their land sat above an almost limitless source of drinkable artesian water. That was good news, but to have Mr Milne and his drilling party demonstrate it was something else. A chain of spectacularly successful wells along the stock routes was the visible result of three years' work. In January, Milne had come south for a holiday and for the birth of his third child. After ten weeks of family life, he was northbound again.

Milne brought with him new drilling equipment, fresh horses, and a gang of six men. Only two of the men, *A. Baker* and South Australian *William Libby Davey*, had worked with him before. In November last, Davey had gone south to be married. After a long vacation he was now returning to work.

The party included two young Englishmen going north for the first time. Twenty-two-year-old *Fred Martin* from East Greenwich had come to Western Australia to visit his aunt. When work offered, he decided to stay for a while. *Edgar Green* from Wraxall in Somerset told a similar story: he had met a Western Australian girl and decided to stick around.

Of *William Hurford* from Llanelly in Victoria, or last-minute recruit *Maurice Vasey*, nothing is known.

Occupying a stateroom opposite the entrance to the First Class social hall was 46-year-old Public Works engineer, *George Simpson*. Responsible for a major upgrade of Broome's town water supply, George had long divided his time between family in the south and work in the north. During his absences, his wife Amelia did her best to keep a young son and five spirited daughters in check.

It had been reported that Simpson would take two men with him on this trip. By a process of elimination, the likely lads emerge. *Jack Murphy*, recently married to Perth girl Leah Asher, had for a few years been working in the machine room at *The West Australian*. *Garnet Sydney Bailey*, a native of Pill in Somerset, had been working in the south-western farming town of Wagin. He had recently become engaged to a local girl.

Sharing George Simpson's stateroom on the promenade deck was Derby wharfinger *Captain William Robin Pearson*. A long-serving master of the Melbourne Steamship Company, he had tired of life at sea and had taken a shore job. He was close to retirement now; indeed, he had told close friends that he would soon resign his post and join his wife and children on their property at Springfield in Victoria.

Also returning to Derby after a summer break was Pearson's friend and close working associate, *Corporal Frank Buttle*, Derby's senior police officer and gaoler. When *Koombana* crossed the Hedland bar on March 20th, 1912, Buttle had been with the force for nineteen years and a day. He had accepted the Derby post in February 1910, at a time of great change. New rules that removed the financial incentive for police officers to arrest natives for cattle stealing had all but emptied the Derby gaol. Buttle came to the Nor'-West with a mission and a mandate: to present a more humane, civilised face and to disown the excesses of the recent past.

Like Captain Pearson, Buttle took the view that there were better places than Derby for raising a family. When he sailed north, he left his wife Minnie and their two children in Perth.

In Frank Buttle's absence, the Derby gaol had been under the supervision of warder George Gilham, who now awaited the arrival of his wife and 22-year-old daughter. With several Derby residents for company, *Mrs Gilham* and *Miss Gilham* were heading north to join George for the cooler months.

Also travelling First Class were two of Derby's hotelkeepers: wine saloon owner *Dean Spark* and Derby Hotel proprietor *Louise Sack*, whom Doug Moore of Ord River Station would later describe as "old Mrs. Sack, mother of all the Sacks in the country at the time." Louise had gone south for the summer to escape the heat and to spend time with her daughter Evelyn McGovern and baby granddaughters, twins Ruby and Pearl. Her six-year-old grandson *Thomas Crotty* had also come along. It had been agreed that he would return to Derby with his grandmother. But when Mrs Sack tried to book a stateroom cabin for herself and Thomas, she discovered that First Class was almost full. Only a single cabin space— sharing a stateroom with Mrs Pigott—remained available. It seems that Louise Sack spoke directly to Captain Allen, whom she knew well. The captain raised no objection to having the boy bunk in with his grandma; indeed, he seemed more concerned about Mrs Sack's comfort than any breach of rules. "We'll make do," she said.

Travelling steerage, and engaged to Mrs Sack as a domestic, was 21-year-old English immigrant *Florence "Florrie" Price*. It is not known whether she was going north for the first time, or was returning to Derby to complete her engagement. What is very clear is that she had misgivings about the journey. To a family friend she wrote:

> Dear Mrs Lambert
> I am very sorry but I am going by the "Koombana" on tuesday. I don't want to go, but I must. I have engaged myself for twelve months. I would have liked to have come and said good-bye, but it is impossible. I feel very much troubled. You will say good-bye for me to all friends. Good-bye from Flo.[15]

Travelling with greater enthusiasm was forty-year-old surveyor *Robert Main*. The youngest son of a Presbyterian minister, Main was going north to assess several candidate sites for a new Nor'-West Presbyterian

Postcard written by Koombana *passenger Florrie Price, March 1912.*

mission. From Broome, he would travel to the outlying districts with Constable Fletcher, who had taken leave of absence from the police force to concentrate on his work for the church.[16]

It appears that of *Koombana*'s 82 passengers, only two were travelling for recreation or recuperation. For **James Doyle**, owner of the Comet Skating Rink at South Fremantle, the voyage was restorative. He had recently undergone surgery and needed rest and relaxation. Although he had not previously travelled by *Koombana* he had a connection with the ship, albeit one he would perhaps have preferred to forget. On March 5th, 1911 the sporting columnist for *The Sunday Times* had written:

> It is not likely that the manager of the Comet Skating Rink at South Beach will put on any more boxing contests in which one of the principals is an unknown man, such as was Corbett (or whatever his name is), the victim of Black Paddy's furious assault last Monday night. . . . The show put on was a poor one, for the simple reason that Black Paddy's opponent knew nothing about boxing; and it was a disgusted mob which filed out of the rink when the big, lumbering baker from the Koombana was carried to his corner in a state of collapse. Corbett was the softest thing Paddy ever had handed out to him in his natural. The loser is supposed to have won several battles in the East. We have nothing but sympathy for the men he beat there.[17]

Koombana's other holiday-maker was carpenter **Ben Smith**, who had just completed a long, hot stint at the Youanmi gold mine south of Sandstone. After an overland trip of 250 miles, he had arrived in Geraldton and booked return passage to Derby.

To discover each passenger's story, every lead and laneway has been followed, but a few bare names remain.

Fred Cane and **Wallace Ireland** were late additions to the stewards' department. Their reasons for travel are not known.

Of young **Gilbert**, known to have embarked at Fremantle for Broome, nothing is known.

Of Scandinavian labourer **H. Hartel**, who boarded at Cossack and bought a ticket to Derby, nothing is known.

One case of particular poignancy has been left until almost the last. Port Hedland shopkeeper **Harry Briden** had never made a great success of his grocery and general businesses. Although he and his wife Annie had managed to support their four children, they were after six years still in temporary accommodation: a rough cottage of whitewashed hessian and corrugated iron, with a packing-crate floor. In January 1912, Annie Briden became seriously ill. Leaving Harry and the children, she went south by steamer and was admitted to Perth Hospital. In her absence, the financial situation became desperate. On the verge of a second bankruptcy, and with hospital bills looming, Harry saw no alternative but to leave their children with friends and go to Broome for work. Arrangements were made quickly. Of the three youngest children, Dollie and Otto would stay in Port Hedland, while five-year-old Mollie would go to Marble Bar to stay with the Hedditch family. Thus the little girl, who had so recently suffered the alarm of waving good-bye to her mother, found herself walking with her father in pre-dawn starlight to the railway station. It was a memory she would carry for a very long time.[18]

OUR TOP-DOWN TOUR began at the navigating bridge; it ends on the 'tween deck. There seems no doubt that *Koombana* carried at least one **Aboriginal prisoner** and one **Malay prisoner**. Both *The Hedland Advocate* and the *Broome Chronicle* listed prisoners among those who boarded at Port Hedland.[19] But neither in those reports nor elsewhere were the names of the men recorded. It is not known what they were convicted of, or charged with, if indeed they were charged at all. Nor can it be known if they went to their deaths in chains, or were by some act of kindness released for a slim chance at life.

WHEN ALL IS DONE, we stand at *Koombana*'s rail and stare into the sea. Perhaps we came seeking clarity or closure. We leave with neither. But however imperfect this late engagement, we are nonetheless altered by it. By new acquaintance we are admitted to the privilege of personal sadness. We move beyond the mechanics of disaster, and beyond the naked list, to see a tragedy defined not by brief suffering but by the forfeiture of hopes and aspirations: a tragedy not of life extinguished but of life foregone. Thus we join in common prayer, and thus we take communion.

Programme cover, "Koombana" Memorial Concert, Sunday April 21st, 1912.

Allen, Captain Thomas Maurice

Andersen, C.

Arrow, James Grant

Bailey, C. A.

Bailey, Garnet Sydney

Baker, A.

Barry, Thomas

Bates, H.

Benedict, Claude H. (Bennie)

Binning, Thomas Henry

Black, William Patrick

Blades, John Stephen (Jack)

Bow, Harry

Briden, Harry

Bryant, Albert Edward

Burkin, William H.

Burrows, Walter

Buttle, Corporal Frank Taylor

Cane, Fred

Cant, Frederick William (William)

Carton, William

Christie, Arthur Mowbray

Clarke, James William

Clarke, William Job

Clinch, Frederick W. B. (Fred)

Clinton, Peter C. (Petie)

Coughlan, John Francis (Jackie)

Cowain, William Laughton

Craigie, James S.

Crosbie, James (Jim)

Crotty, Master Thomas Charles

Dalton (or D'Alton), Ernest James

Davey, William Libby

Davies, Evan

Davies, Robert W.

Davis, Abraham de Vahl

Davis, James S.

Deller, Albert Ernest

Dick, William C.

Downie, Joseph

Doyle, James

Drake, Alfred

Durham, Henry

Dwyer, Jack ("Jockey Jack")

Dwyer, Michael (Jack)

Evans, John

Farnell, William Alexander

Farrance, Percy

Farrow, George

Finnerty, P.

Fitzpatrick, W.

Forrest, Thomas

Freer, Anastasia

Furlong, G.

Gainsburg, H.

Gee, Gordon Alan

Gilbert, Mr

Gilham, Miss

Gilham, Mrs F.

Goddard, Thomas

Grant, Thomas Millar

Green, Edgar P.

Gunning, Fred

Harper, George N.

Harris, Francis Hedley

Hartel, H.

Hassan

Hayes, James

Heffernan (alias Ryan), M.

Henry, Robert

Herbert, Fred

Hughes, J. (Harry)

Hurford, William Henry

Innes, William Booth (Jock)

Ireland, Wallace Bruce

Jackson, John

Jamieson, Norman C.

Jenkins, Edith Emily

Jenkins, Peter

Jenkins, Robert Henry (Rob)

Johnson, Francis William (Frank)

Johnson, Joseph Madison

Jones, David

Jones, G.

Kearns, John

Kelly, Walter John

Kinley, W. R. A.

Lawrence, George H.

Levins, James ("Nish")

Lewis, William (Bill)

Lyon, Harry A.

Main, Robert William

Mangan, John Joseph (Jack)

Martin, G. Frederick (Fred)

Matthews, Charlie

McDermott, Delia

McDermott, T.

McDonnell, Thomas

McGowan, Frank

McGuckin, J.

McKibbin, William J.

McRouble, A.

McSwain, Donald

Milne, William Patrick

Murphy, John (Jack)

Norlin, Carl

Offord, Henry

O'Loughlin, Thomas

Olsen, O.

Peacock, F. S.

Pearson, Captain William Robin

Pearson, R.

Pigott, Jane

Piper, Alfred Charles (Ally)

Piper, George

Poor, William

Price, Florence Lucy (Florrie)

Purcell, W. W. or W. A.

Quinlan, Thomas A.

Quinlan, Richard C.

Rea, Harry A.

Reece, T.

Reynolds, Stanley Warwick

Sack, Louise Caroline

Salkilld, Arthur Thomas

Scougall, Robert

Shiels, Andy

Simpson, George Nicolas

Skamp, Alice Beatrice

Skamp, Genevieve Callanan

Slade, S. H.

Smith, Benjamin

Smith, H.

Smith, Jack

Smith, Patrick

Smith, Will

Smith, William

Spark, J. D. (Dean)

Spencer, Sydney C.

Stanley, Charles Herbert (Charlie)

Stanley, Herbert Bertie (Bert)

Stewart, Sidney Graham

Stuart, Captain Charles Browne

Taylor, A. S.

Taylor, Thomas

Thornton, Walter Clifford

Tutt, Walter

Vasey, Maurice

Vile, William E. (Billy)

Walker, Charles Gilbert (Charlie)

Wardlaw, Edward

Wassell, Albert

Wilson, Fred

Winpenny, F. J. (Joe)

Prisoner, unnamed, Aboriginal

Prisoner, unnamed, Malay

14

BEYOND HUMAN KNOWLEDGE

TO INQUIRE OR NOT TO INQUIRE: that was the question. Colonial Secretary John Drew decided that given the appalling loss of life an inquiry should be held, but Chief Harbourmaster Charles Irvine wondered what would be learned or gained by it. In the end, he saw no alternative but to accede to the colonial secretary's wish.

There were respectful requests for the inquiry to be held in the Nor'-West,[1] where the loss was most keenly felt and where any number of witnesses to *Koombana*'s departure could be called to give evidence. To say that these requests 'fell on deaf ears' would be something of an understatement. The preliminary inquiry held at Fremantle on Monday, April 22nd, 1912 was no more than a private meeting between Harbourmaster Irvine, Crown Prosecutor Frank Parker, and the Adelaide Steamship Company's barrister, Matthew Moss. Not only did the meeting determine that Nor'-West sittings would be unnecessary, it decided that a full inquiry should commence immediately.[2] It would be over before any Nor'-Wester could board a steamer to participate in it.

Three days later, in the Fremantle Police Court, Resident Magistrate Edward Dowley declared open the "Court of Marine Inquiry into the total loss at sea of the S.S. *Koombana* on or about March 20, 1912, between Port Hedland and Broome." Dowley, broadly experienced but never a seafarer, was assisted by nautical assessors Captains Parkes and Yates. The crown prosecutor appeared on behalf of the chief harbourmaster, and Matthew Moss came to defend the reputation and interests of the Adelaide Steamship Company.[3]

It is probably fair to say that Crown Prosecutor Parker did not quite understand his role. Indeed, it appears likely that he sought the advice of Queensland colleagues who had 'prosecuted' a similar mystery a year earlier.[4] In his opening remarks, Parker told the court that the inquiry was unusual. It did not come about because there appeared at the outset to be negligence, or because the chief harbourmaster had brought any specific charge; rather, an extraordinary loss of life demanded that information be brought to light.[5] In the absence of survivors, he said, the inquiry would focus primarily upon the stability and seaworthiness of *Koombana*, and on the actions of her master, Thomas Allen.

If the crown prosecutor was feeling his way, the company's represent-ative certainly was not. Matthew Moss, King's Counsel, came with a mission: to prevent any finding of negligence that might leave the company liable to pay compensation for lives and property lost. *Koombana* would be presented as a ship well managed and maintained, of superior construction and intrinsic stability, incapable of capsizing. It would be demonstrated that she had left port in fine trim, and that no part of the tragedy could be blamed upon her. Further, it would be shown that Captain Allen had not put to sea under pressure of policy or schedule, but had left routinely, without any indication of an impending blow. Finally, it would be argued that *Koombana* had encountered a storm like no other, and by that singular misfortune had been battered and overcome.

It was a lopsided contest, if it was a contest at all. First to the witness stand was Harry Upjohn, master of the S.S. *Bullarra* and a long-time servant of the Adelaide Steamship Company. He was cross-examined by Frank Parker.

> During the time you were in Port Hedland did you have any conversation with Captain Allen in respect of the weather?— Yes.
> On what date was that?— On the morning of the 20th.
> Will you tell the Court what the conversation was?— It took place on my ship. We had a general conversation and Capt. Allen said "What do you think about the weather?"
> What was your reply?— "It's overcast and a bit dirty but there is nothing in it."
> Can you fix the time that this conversation took place?— It was just before breakfast or just after.
> That would be about 8 o'clock?— Yes.
> What was the state of the weather at this time?— Very nice fresh breeze, overcast and cloudy.
> It struck you as being a bit dirty?— Just overcast.
> What did you expect from the weather?— I expected the same right through: fine if anything.
> Did you have any further conversation with Captain Allen about the weather?— None.
> Was anything said in reference to leaving Port Hedland, whether you would leave or not?— No.[6]

The direction of Parker's questioning related to published reports that *Koombana*'s master had seemed disinclined to leave port, and that only after a conversation with Captain Upjohn on the jetty had he decided to put to sea. It had also been reported that *Koombana* rode so high that her propeller thrashed the surface of the water as she made her run to the harbour entrance. Parker asked Upjohn:

> Where were you when the Koombana left Port Hedland?— I was on the lower bridge and the Chief Officer was with me.
> What were you doing?— We were just looking at the Koombana.
> Did you notice her trim?— She was in excellent trim.
> Did you notice the draft?— No. I noticed how well she behaved and the Chief Officer said the same.
> Have you any reason for that remark?— No, but she looked so well.
> Did you notice her propeller?— It was well submerged.[7]

At the end of the first day, news travelled fast. Almost before the seats of the public gallery were cold, the residents of Port Hedland had heard—by telephone, presumably—that the company's witnesses seemed particularly well briefed, that accounts of *Koombana*'s departure were at odds with local recollection, and that the company's barrister rather than the crown prosecutor seemed to be calling the shots.[8] To those so deliberately but unsuccessfully isolated, the message was clear. At best, the inquiry would reach a vague conclusion; at worst, it would rewrite the history of a tragic day.

On its second sitting day, the inquiry turned to the question of *Koombana*'s stability. The company brought two large exhibits to the court: a large, finely detailed model of the ship, and a "Ralston's Stability and Trim Indicator."[9] The Ralston apparatus, always customised for a particular ship, was *Koombana*'s own. It was usually on board but had not been carried on the final voyage. Captain James Rankin came also, as expert witness, to demonstrate the use of the apparatus and to show that *Koombana*'s "G.M." was perfectly acceptable.

"G.M." may look like an acronym, but it is not. The letters do not stand for "General Manager" or "Greenwich Mean" or even "Good Manners," though G.M. may well indicate acceptable behaviour. It is, rather, the distance between two points, labelled "G" and "M" respectively, on a ship stability diagram.[10] The precise meanings of "G" and "M" are not important here. What is important is that the greater the G.M., the more stable the ship. It is a measure of how quickly and assertively a ship returns upright after wind or waves have pushed her over.

The court watched with interest as Captain Rankin placed weights and made adjustments to simulate various different loading conditions. In all cases the instrument, on *Koombana*'s behalf, showed stability in excess of British requirements. The indications, the court was assured, were an accurate reflection of *Koombana*'s ability to right herself, and much was made of the fact that Ralston, the inventor of the device, was chief draftsman at Alexander Stephen & Sons, where *Koombana* had been designed and built.

For all of Captain Rankin's confidence, there was a gaping hole in his demonstration and testimony. Seafarers and ship designers know that a ship's ability to right herself is only half of the stability picture; the other half is the ship's susceptibility to being knocked over in the first place. It is a remarkable fact of the *Koombana* inquiry that Captain Rankin testified before two experienced seafaring men but never once was pressed to admit that a ship's height above the waterline was even relevant.[11]

To some, the prosecution's lack of tenacity was a revelation. Indeed, there were a few moments when the crown prosecutor appeared to forget whose side he was on. As the discussion of load distribution continued, Frank Parker recalled *Koombana*'s former chief officer Henry Clarke, "for the express purpose of contradicting a rumour circulating in Fremantle." The rumour was that the ship had at one time been ballasted with iron rails to improve her stability. Under cross-examination, Clarke declared that never during his fifteen months with *Koombana* had "ballast in the shape of iron rails" been carried. Company man Matthew Moss could not contain himself. "Another pavement expert's opinion exploded!" he interjected.[12]

Moss had good reason for wanting the matter of ballast dispensed with. Henry Clarke's answer was truthful, but truthful by the barest of margins. From October 1909 until about May 1911, most northbound steamers calling at Port Hedland had carried rails and sleepers for the new Pilbarra Railway. The rails were paying cargo but their value as ballast was recognised by *Koombana*'s first master, John Rees, and must have been recognised by his chief officer also. On February 8th, 1910, *Koombana* had struck rough weather between Cossack and Port Hedland. Passenger Doug Moore, returning to Ord River Station after his summer break, would never forget it.

> One time I was a passenger on her coming to Wyndham. We had about 200 tons of railway iron on board for Hedland. They were then building the line to Marble Bar. Just before reaching Hedland we struck a squall and the ship lay over at an angle of 45 degrees and was quite a long time before straightening up. Johnny Rees was the Skipper and he said to me "there is no loading going off at Port Hedland—we'll hang on to all those rails for ballast and drop them off coming back."[13]

Memories are often reshaped and reimagined as years pass, but a report published a few weeks after the *Koombana* disaster is entirely consistent with Moore's late-age recall.

> Consider the statement of a well-known Nor'-Wester. He was living at Port Hedland the year before last when the Koombana, in common with other vessels, was carrying steel rails for the Port Hedland-Marble Bar railway during what is known locally as the willy-willy season. He

states that the Koombana arrived at Hedland with a cargo consisting chiefly of such rails, of which she discharged all but 150 tons. These 150 tons, he declares, were left on board at the request of the captain of the ship in order to increase her stability on her trip to Wyndham and back. As a matter of fact, the rails were carried, not only to Wyndham but down to Fremantle, and were not landed at their destination until the ship returned to Port Hedland on her next trip northward.[14]

An interesting element of this story is that when *Koombana* arrived back in Fremantle after that memorable trip, her chief officer went job-hunting. He was successful, apparently;[15] after one more Nor'-West run, Henry Clarke left *Koombana* for a position at the Fremantle port. At the inquiry, no former *Koombana* officer was ever asked why he had left the ship.

At a glance, it is difficult to understand why Matthew Moss was so determined to steer the inquiry away from the matter of ballast. A review of recent history delivers the answer. A year before *Koombana*'s disappearance, the company's steamer *Yongala* had been lost off the coast of Queensland, and the finding of the *Yongala* inquiry had included the following paragraph:

> In regard to pig-iron ballast being placed in the vessel whilst in the West Australian trade and subsequently removed when the ship was transferred to the Queensland trade, it was explained by the general manager that this ballast, amounting to 164 tons, became unnecessary owing to cargo being obtainable both up and down the Queensland coast. A letter from Captain Knight to the Company at the time confirmed this view, and stated that the ship rolled less and was more comfortable in a seaway.[16]

There, in sharp relief, was Matthew Moss's problem. *Yongala* and *Koombana* had both been ballasted: in the same way, to the same extent, and for the same reason. The parallel was compelling and Moss did all in his power to prevent it being drawn.

Matthew Moss was also aware of a weakness in the company's argument regarding the cyclone. If the storm was unsurvivable, how then had *Bullarra*, which had steamed into the very centre of it, come through? On the inquiry's first sitting day, Moss launched a pre-emptive strike. He asked Harry Upjohn to explain how *Bullarra* had come within a hair's breadth of disaster. The exchange scarcely deserves the title "cross-examination."

> Do you consider you were lucky in having escaped?— We escaped by a miracle.
> Your boat was in a battered condition?— Yes.
> What occurred to your funnel?— It was carried away in the early part of the blow.
> You went to Broome to effect temporary repairs and for water?— Yes.

That was before you searched for the "Koombana"?— Yes.
Have you been in cyclonic weather before?— Yes, in the China Sea,
when a ship went down alongside of us.
Was it very bad?— Not so bad as this.
This was absolutely the worst thing you have experienced?— Yes.
And it was only by a miracle you came through?— Yes.[17]

It is unfortunate that court transcripts record only the words of the
protagonists. Neither wry smile nor raised brow finds its way to the future.

Late on the second sitting day, Crown Prosecutor Parker asked for an
adjournment. He had been told that one Reverend William Patrick, who
had been in Port Hedland on the morning of *Koombana*'s departure, was
willing to attend and testify. With remarkable effrontery, Matthew Moss
opposed the application. "It is probably just another of those rumours," he
told the court. He could not see why the proceedings should be postponed
on slender evidence that such a person existed and, if he existed, that he
was prepared to say anything.[18] And while he did not wish to shut out
anything that would throw any light upon the matter, he would remind
them all that Mr Moxon was very anxious to see the inquiry through
and return to his duties in Adelaide. Judge Dowley decided that there
was sufficient evidence for the existence of Reverend Patrick. A two-day
adjournment was granted.

After the first sitting day, prominent citizens of Port Hedland, Broome,
and Derby had sent coordinated telegrams to Premier John Scaddan,[19]
requesting that the inquiry be not closed until evidence had been
taken in Port Hedland. Scaddan had worked closely with the Nor'-
West communities during the search for *Koombana*. He understood
their concern but stopped short of recommending that the inquiry be
relocated. Instead, he asked that arrangements be made for evidence to be
gathered in each of the three towns.[20]

Although the inquiry declared its willingness to receive submissions,
and adjourned for a few days, it did little to facilitate the gathering
of evidence. Matthew Moss, sensing that Nor'-West agitation would
probably come to nothing, saw this latest adjournment in a more positive
light. "I am glad that Mr. Dowley has issued that general invitation to the
public," he told the court. "It will give some of those people who have
been spreading the rumours a chance to show in Court what they know
about the subject."[21]

It appears that although telegrams were exchanged between the
Colonial Secretary's Office and the resident magistrate at Port Hedland,
the evidence-gathering process stalled.[22] When the inquiry reconvened on
Friday, May 3rd, no evidence from the Nor'-West was presented. Matthew
Moss, on behalf of the Adelaide Steamship Company, delivered a lengthy
summing-up. Having done all in his power to subvert the inquiry and

hasten its closure, he now sang its praises, but perhaps only as a platform for an extraordinary attack upon Walter Barker, editor of *The Hedland Advocate*. Moss's remarks were reported at length by *The West Australian*.

> Mr. M. L. Moss, K.C., in the course of his address said that there had been a preliminary inquiry held before Captain Irvine, and he thought that as a result of that inquiry the Captain would have been justified in preventing any further inquiry, but he was to be commended on his action in bringing about a public investigation. There had been a tremendous loss of life and valuable property, and it was in the interests of the whole community that the greatest possible light should be shed on the inquiry. The Adelaide Steamship Company, he might mention, was just as anxious as anyone that the strongest searchlight should be thrown on loss of the Koombana, in view of the scandalous remarks that had been made concerning the stability of the vessel by irresponsible persons.[23]

Moss had been particularly upset by the *Advocate*'s claim that on the morning of *Koombana*'s departure, there were clear indications of an impending blow.

> There was nothing unusual to give the slightest occasion for alarm. On that point they had the emphatic statement of Captain Upjohn. Those busybodies who said things to the contrary had been given an ample opportunity to appear before the Court and give evidence, but not one of their number had come forward. He did not want to mention names, but would say that there was at Port Hedland one particular busybody who sought to stir up strife on every conceivable occasion.

Moss's summing-up must have left some in the gallery wondering if they had heard correctly. Busybody! His chosen word was not "troublemaker" or "nuisance"; it was "busybody". Did the company mean to imply that the Nor'-West, with seventy of its own among the missing, was guilty of meddling in this inquiry? Or that *The Hedland Advocate* should mind its own business? Needless to say, the newspapers of the Nor'-West ran the story. None offered any opinion as to whether Moss's outburst was ridiculous or revealing or both; they simply printed it. Indeed, *The Northern Times* ran with the headline:

INQUIRY CONTINUED.
JOURNALISTIC BUSY-BODY.
MYSTERY INSOLUBLE.[24]

Somehow it seems appropriate that Matthew Moss's week of ministration and protestation should end with a cry from the tortured soul of petulance, and with an utterance both so wrong and so right.

ONE WEEK LATER, on Friday, May 10th, 1912, the Court of Marine Inquiry made its finding public. Precisely, point by point, it delivered the exoneration that the Adelaide Steamship Company had sought. No fault was found with ship or crew, and no opinion ventured as to what had befallen *Koombana*.

> In conclusion, the Court simply finds, without indulging in use-less speculation, that the stability and seaworthiness of the S.S. "Koombana" were unassailable, and the competency and carefulness of master, Captain Allen, beyond question, and after being lost sight of at sea on the 20th March 1912, her fate passes beyond human knowledge and remains a mystery of the sea.[25]

The inquiry and its finding were widely criticised. *The Sunday Times* declared:

> It cannot be said that the inquiry into the loss of the steamer Koombana was satisfactory to the public. It was certainly satisfactory to the Adelaide Steamship Company, which, by the finding, escapes any compensatory liability to the widows and orphans and other dependents of the 150 victims who went down in the vessel; but that isn't what we mean. In the first place, the evidence was all one-sided. No attempt whatever was made to produce independent expert evidence as to the stability of the steamer, and by that we mean her ability to live in a cyclone, and not her constructional strength. Mr. McDonald, who supervised her building at Glasgow, was asked with regard to her stability, and he replied—"She was a magnificent vessel, strongly built." But that was not the import of the question, which should have been as to her resistance to a great storm. A steamer may be a "magnificent vessel" in ordinary ocean conditions, but what we want to know is, was she fit to face extraordinary conditions?[26]

If *The Sunday Times* surprised some by its directness, *The Hedland Advocate* took forthrightness to a new level. Walter Barker's long repudiation began:

> The unwarranted attack on the editor of this paper, by Mr. M. L. Moss (solicitor for the Adelaide S.S. Coy. at the inquiry into the loss of the Koombana), calls for a parting shot. We would be the last in the world to wish to say anything which would leave the slightest smudge on the reputations of the capable officers who went down in the ill-fated Koombana, but no mercenary motive would induce us to deviate from the course of justice in the public interests, and we have heaps of company (in the Nor'-West, at any rate) when we assert that the finding of the Marine Board of Inquiry suggests capable handling of the whitewash brush and a prodigal use of lime.[27]

In the course of his refutation, Barker declared: "The whole of the statements find flat denial on every hand locally."

Perhaps it is time for a new arbitration, a careful review of the three points of greatest contention: the weather in Port Hedland on the morning of departure, *Koombana*'s draft and trim, and the alleged conversation between Captains Allen and Upjohn.

On Saturday, March 23rd, 1912, before any search for *Koombana* had begun, *The Hedland Advocate* published a detailed report of the storm that had struck the town.

> As if to palliate the tedium of the scorching, enervating heat, Hedland was visited this week by a cross-bred willy-willy, which, coming with the equinoctal tides, did a fair amount of damage. It is pretty certain that had it been a full-blooded willy it would have spelt disaster to the lowlands of Hedland. It started on Tuesday night, with a strong easterly wind whistling and roaring, and the sea thundering and crumbling on the beach, indicative of heavier and deadlier surges out at sea.
>
> Wednesday morning saw about 40 luggers running to the shelter of Port Hedland, where they were soon safely anchored, with bowsprits swinging up and down in salutation to the dip and rise of each other. These luggers had a rough time on Tuesday night, near Turtle Island, the cutting away of masts on some being seriously contemplated.[28]

The arrival of so many pearling boats in Port Hedland harbour on the morning of *Koombana*'s departure created a problem for the Adelaide Steamship Company, which came to the inquiry determined to prove that there was no indication of bad weather. The company men did not dispute that the pearling boats had arrived; instead, it offered a different explanation. A letter from Joseph Gardiner, the company's agent in Port Hedland, was tendered in evidence. Gardiner had written:

> A large number of luggers came into the creek on Wednesday morning and I spoke to a number of them and they explained that they came in on account of dirty water caused by the strong easterly wind and there was no talk in any way of a blow. In fact many of them have said to me since that the pearling fleets narrowly escaped a disaster which would have been the greatest in their history as they never thought of a blow when they came: it was solely on account of dirty water.[29]

The agent's explanation does not bear close scrutiny. Although poor visibility often interrupted pearling operations and occasionally brought boats home early, it could not explain the arrival of so many boats at Port Hedland in the space of a few hours. The reason was simple: the boats did not belong to a single fleet. Whilst they shared good ground and often worked within sight of one another, they worked independently and took their own decisions. Only in danger did they move as one.[30]

The 'dirty water' argument was not only flawed; it was disingenuous. When Joe Gardiner wrote that careful letter, it was already known that the storm had wreaked havoc north of Port Hedland on the night before *Koombana*'s departure. As early as March 30th, the *Broome Chronicle* had published "Luggers in the Gale," including a dramatic account from Alfred Saunders, master of the lugger *Dona Matilda*.

> Tuesday, March 19th.—Half way between First Wash and Solitary Island got three grs. of shell until midday, when the water got dirty. At 1 p.m. hove up; strong east wind; put like h— for Banningarra; let go about 5 p.m., about 3 miles north of Creek; strong N.E. wind blowing, with a big sea—50f. high; spent a rotten night—had everything cleared off deck, main sail and gaffs taken down and hatches battened down; sewed pearl in handkerchief and tied it round my neck; I saw several boats drifting, and at about 8.30 p.m., the cutter "Kooki", belonging to Pardoo Station, which was anchored close to me—too close to my liking—broke her chain and started to drift towards Mount Blaze. I stood by with diver, tender and crew all night; two big waves got the lugger broadside on, and made things very uncomfortable for a few seconds; about 1 a.m. one of Tommy Clarke's luggers was drifting towards us, we all shouted out and they managed to get their jib up just in the nick of time.
>
> Wednesday, March 20th.—Big sea with N.E. wind, strong; 11 a.m., hove up and made for the Creek under double-reefed mainsail and jib; just before heaving up big sea caught Voladora taking away dinghy, dress, starboard rail and bulwarks; heard afterwards from "Bob" that he lost a basket containing 1½ cwt. of shell, together with his cabin awning; the Voladora and Aurora both lost their anchors heaving up. I got well up the Creek and made fast to the mangroves; put out three mooring lines for'd and 3 aft., also put two anchors with two fathoms of chain aft and for'd. About 26 boats here; lugger Elsie got foul of the mangroves about quarter of mile from entrance to Creek and bumped two small holes in her bills; glass not too low but not working; went out to Mt. Blaze at low water . . . found Pardoo Station's cutter up on the reef, broken in half; there were two gins dead in the mangroves; there were two white men and about seven binghis about before the boat struck the reef; one of the binghis that was saved said that the skipper had the jib and mainsail, as well as the engines, going, but the sea was too big for them to go about, and consequently they were washed about 50ft. up on the rocks; we had a look around the wreck and found three life buoys in the cabin, so we came to the conclusion that they did not have time to put them on.[31]

On the second day of the inquiry William Moxon, the company's manager for Western Australia, entered the witness box. Under oath he declared that the storm had struck without warning on Wednesday, March 20th, after *Koombana* had left port. He told the court that the well-respected

Nor'-West pearler Captain Challenor, near Bedout Island on Tuesday evening, had dropped anchor in "a dead calm sea and glorious sunshine." This assertion rewards investigation. On the day the *Broome Chronicle* published "Luggers in the Gale," *The Hedland Advocate* offered sage advice to mariners.

> THE COSSACK WILLY-WILLY.
> (By Capt. Challenor.)
> There is an old copy book maxim that "Fortune favors the brave," but in this Nor'-West of Australia it should be altered to "Fortune favors the pearler who keeps a watchful eye on the barometer."
> Working about 12 miles north of Bezout Island we had during the week experienced almost unnatural heat, and for four days a falling barometer, nothing much to worry about but the fall was very evident and not to be disregarded. Having to meet the Paroo on the 18th I went into Cossack, and was there for two days with the same conditions—very great heat and the steady decline, most noticeable. On the 19th I anchored about 6 miles to the east of Bezout with 10 other luggers in sight, a dead calm and a glorious sunset. About midnight a sudden gust of wind woke me up and heavy clouds were rolling up from the east. From then the wind began to increase, and by 5 a.m. there was a very big sea running . . .[32]

The *Advocate* article quickly identifies itself as the source of William Moxon's evidence, but two inconsistencies leap from the page and beg for attention. Firstly, it was not Bedout Island that had enjoyed the glorious sunshine, but Bezout Island, more than a hundred miles to the west. It was a mistake easily made and easily forgiven; indeed, a cynic might see that as its greatest attraction. Secondly, Moxon drew from the article to assert that the storm had struck without warning, but that was not John Challenor's message to his readers. The storm had arrived without the *usual* indications, but by attention to the barometer and its "steady decline, most noticeable," danger had been recognised and avoided.

Paradoxically, although Captain Challenor's article shows the extent of William Moxon's misrepresentation, it also suggests that to casual observers at Port Hedland on the day of *Koombana*'s departure, there was no clear indication of a blow.

On Monday, April 29th, the Reverend William Patrick placed his existence beyond doubt by appearing at the inquiry and giving evidence.[33] He testified that on the Port Hedland jetty before *Koombana* and *Bullarra* departed, he had spoken with *Koombana* passenger and Derby wharfinger, Captain William Pearson. The wharfinger had expressed no concern about the weather; indeed, the possibility of a storm did not arise in their conversation. This also favours the view that only the barometer told the story.

In this context, we return briefly to the confusion between two islands of similar name. Bezout Island is only five miles from Point Samson, where *Koombana* spent most of Monday, March 18th. If Captain Challenor at Bezout Island saw the glass steadily falling, *Koombana*'s cautious master must have seen it also. This delivers the most plausible explanation for Tom Allen's reported disinclination to leave port: having noted the fall in the glass, he read the weather differently to those who had not.

On the question of *Koombana*'s draft and trim, the court accepted the Adelaide Steamship Company's testimony. Its finding declared:

> She sailed from Port Hedland on March 20, 1912, at about 10.20 o'clock a.m., drawing 19 ft. aft and about 12 ft. forward in excellent trim.[34]

The Hedland Advocate disputed these numbers.

> Several can be found to prove the ship drew no more than 16ft 6in aft and 11ft for'ard as she lay at anchor at the Hedland jetty.[35]

By a small piece of good fortune, this contest may be confidently adjudicated. When *Koombana* disappeared, her log book disappeared with her. But that log was a new one, commenced a few weeks before the disaster. The old log, in accord with usual practice, had been forwarded to the office of the chief harbourmaster. The surviving log contains the record of Tom Allen's first visits to Port Hedland; it records *Koombana*'s draft, for'ard and aft, for each departure. Here, in support of an abstract concept called truth, are those entries:

> 22/09/11 09.30: 14′ 8″ frd 18′ 6″ aft
> 05/10/11 08.40: 13′ 0″ frd 17′ 8″ aft
> 25/10/11 11.25: 14′ 3″ frd 18′ 0″ aft
> 01/11/11 14.10: 12′ 2″ frd 18′ 8″ aft
> 10/12/11 12.50: 15′ 3″ frd 17′ 9″ aft
> 25/12/11 00.50: 13′ 6″ frd 16′ 9″ aft[36]

Examined carefully in conjunction with tide records,[37] the numbers suggest that *Koombana*'s draft for her last departure would have been about 18 feet aft and 13 feet for'ard. It would certainly have been less than the 19 feet claimed by the company, and almost certainly more than Barker's 16 feet 6 inches. The most reasonable supposition is about halfway between the conflicting accounts. Formal log entries confirm that *Koombana*, while entering or leaving Port Hedland, took ground three times in four months.[38] For Tom Allen, the Hedland bar was a perpetual annoyance; over time, it became his practice to empty more ballast tanks. The inquiry made assumptions about the state of *Koombana*'s tanks on the morning of March 20th. Those assumptions were almost certainly wrong.

The question of whether *Koombana*'s propeller thrashed the surface is also easily settled. The top of her propeller was at the 18ft. 3in. mark.[39]

Thus, if she drew less than 18 feet 3 inches, the blades of her propeller would be visible above the surface of the water as they turned; if she drew more than 18 feet 3 inches her propeller would, at rest, be submerged. But when those great iron blades turned, a few inches either way made little difference. *Koombana*, as the townsfolk of Port Hedland knew, threw water from her propeller on every departure from their port. Tom Allen's draft notes are unequivocal: they affirm the local account and contradict Captain Upjohn. On no recent occasion had Captain Allen left with more than four inches of water over his propeller, and on Christmas Day, 1911, the tips of the blades were fully eighteen inches clear of the surface.

If *Koombana*'s propeller thrashed the calm water of the harbour, what must it have done in wind and swell at the entrance? It is difficult to accept the company's assertion that the ship barely twitched when she met a moderate swell and a stiff crosswind at the harbour entrance.[40] Her propeller must at times have been exposed, and exposed more than a few inches. This is not to say that it was "flogging the air" or that *Koombana* was "lifting her stern way out of the water."[41] Memory is both frail and creative.

Finally, there remains the issue of the alleged conversation between Tom Allen of *Koombana* and Harry Upjohn of *Bullarra*. As part of his regular news gathering, *Hedland Advocate* editor Walter Barker came to the jetty on the morning of departure, to speak to passengers and crew, and to watch the two steamers depart. He later wrote:

> Scores of people discussed the weather outlook with Capt. Allen, who gave everyone, including the writer, the impression that he did not want to leave port. "Twenty-four hours here," he declared to the writer, "will not hurt; I might bump the outer bar going out on a sea like this." Capt. Allen's attitude changed immediately Capt. Upjohn had a conversation with him, after which he said, "I am going out; the Broome passengers, who think they will get to Broome to-morrow, will be lucky if they get there on Saturday—I'm going straight out to sea, and will fill my tanks when I get outside."[42]

A few weeks later, Barker told *The Sunday Times* that after the decision had been made, Captain Allen seemed "palpably uneasy and disinclined to go."[43] He noticed some luggers blocking the channel and asked the Port Hedland harbourmaster to move them on. And when one still remained, he said that he would not go out unless it was removed.

At the inquiry, an attempt was made to dismiss as fiction any late conversation between captains. In the witness box, under oath, Captain Upjohn denied that any such conversation had taken place.[44] By this stage of proceedings, however, *Bullarra*'s master had a credibility problem.[45] With similar conviction he had made statements about *Koombana*'s draft and trim that were so implausible as to cast doubt on everything else he said.

In this respect, Walter Barker stood apart from Harry Upjohn. The people of Port Hedland knew that the editor of the local paper was vehement to a fault and prone to exaggeration, but none could recall any occasion on which he had printed a statement he knew to be false. In his three years as newspaper proprietor he had angered some and exasperated many, but none would assert that he had ever lied to his readers.

What words were exchanged by Allen and Upjohn may never be known,[46] but it is probably safe to assume that the conversation took place and that it played a significant part in Tom Allen's decision to put to sea.

SOMEHOW, TRAGEDY SHARPENS the public fascination for symmetry and coincidence. In 1912, how strange it seemed that two ships, of similar size, from the same company, had been lost in cyclones on opposite sides of the country, at the same latitude and a year apart, almost to the day.[47]

These parallels between *Koombana* and *Yongala* are certainly interesting, but hardly illuminating. Yet between these disasters exists one further parallel, both interesting and illuminating. That the *Koombana* inquiry was brought to a close with scarcely a mention of *Yongala* was, in a sense, a personal triumph for Matthew Moss. On behalf of the Adelaide Steamship Company he sought an open finding and got it, but the wording of that finding carried a black irony that cannot have escaped his notice. For the sake of direct comparison, the *Koombana* finding must here be restated:

> In conclusion, the Court simply finds, without indulging in useless speculation, that the stability and seaworthiness of the S.S. "Koombana" were unassailable, and the competency and carefulness of master, Captain Allen, beyond question, and after being lost sight of at sea on the 20th March 1912, her fate passes beyond human knowledge and remains a mystery of the sea.

Thirteen months earlier, an inquiry similarly convened had delivered its verdict regarding *Yongala*:

> While it is both gratifying and reassuring that the vessel's stability and seaworthiness remain unassailable, and the competency and carefulness of Captain Knight unimpeachable, the Board, with no desire to indulge in idle speculation, simply finds that after becoming lost to view by the lightkeeper at Dent Island, the fate of the Yongala passes beyond human ken into the realms of conjecture to add one more to the long roll of mysteries of the sea.[48]

It appears that not one of the *Koombana* inquiry's critics noticed this extraordinary antecedent. Awareness of it could only have sharpened the suspicion that the outcome owed little to evidence or testimony. Indeed, had Walter Barker discovered this plagiarism, he must surely have declared the "handling of the whitewash brush" not merely capable, but experienced!

CHIEF HARBOURMASTER CHARLES IRVINE retired to an orchard in 1917, but poor health cut short his enjoyment of it. He died in 1922. Obituaries spoke of a young man who had captained the Adelaide Steamship Company's *Rob Roy*, and of an older man who had left his mark upon the port of Fremantle.[49]

Only much later would an important family recollection come to light. In 1911, when Irvine heard that the pastoralist David Forrest was looking to hire a manager for his Minderoo Station on the Ashburton River, he recommended his brother Claude for the position. Claude, who had been managing a merino stud in South Australia, was duly appointed. In February 1912 he brought his family to Western Australia and stayed with his brother at the harbourmaster's residence in Fremantle.

Claude's children would recall that when Uncle Charlie learned that they were to travel north by *Koombana*, he vehemently opposed it, declaring that the ship was top-heavy, and a very bad sea boat.[50] Reluctantly, their father accepted his brother's advice, and glamourous *Koombana* was forsaken for old, rusty *Bullarra*, departing a few days earlier. As it happened, the Irvines would have been safe aboard either ship. They disembarked in Ashburton Roads on March 15th, five days before the disaster unfolded further north.

THE KOOMBANA INQUIRY placed Charles Irvine in a difficult position. As chief harbourmaster, he was its sponsor. Its finding, at least officially, was his own. He probably believed that in the absence of survivors, the inquiry was unlikely to reach any conclusion that would help the families of the lost to win compensation. He understood also that the Adelaide Steamship Company would be severely punished, but not by his finding or through his agency. There would be an immediate financial loss through the under-insurance of the ship,[51] and an irrecoverable loss of business. Moreover, it seemed likely that the Nor'-West mail contract, which the company had held for several years and which underpinned the profitability of the run, would soon be handed to the new State Steamship Service. This, then, was the de facto verdict: the company exonerated by the inquiry would be banished by broader circumstance.

In the wake of several disasters, there was growing unease about the direction of ship design and the terrible price that might be paid for high cabins and a comfortable ride. Just two days after *Koombana* was declared lost, that sentiment was voiced in a gentle but persuasive letter to the editor of *The West Australian*.

> Sir,—It seems only a few months since we were mourning the loss of the Waratah, and even less than that of the Yongala, and now of the Koombana right on our own shores. The ships mentioned above were as fine a trio as ever sailed out of a port, the very latest in marine architecture—the last word in comfort and beauty combined. What

is the reason for these disasters? The aggregate loss of life is simply appalling. Not one single word from either, not one survivor from among all those hundreds. The writer has seen and admired each of these fine ships. There is no doubt of their great beauty. They were almost like things of life, and yet there has been a feeling (even while admiring) that the height from the water line seemed to a lay mind abnormal, and the thought has come, "What would happen in a Nor'-West willy willy?" What has happened? Alas, a fine ship, with its precious burthen, vanished. I have no doubt that the foremost architects have proved, theoretically, that this latest type of ship is equally as seaworthy as, say, the Albany and Bullarra (both of which have come successfully through strenuous times). With a wind blowing at such a rate, and with such force as in this recent blow, the great resistance offered by the height of the Koombana from the water line to her bridge must, in my opinion, have had a great deal to do with her undoing . . . I have come to the conclusion that in the architecture of these floating palaces we have sacrificed something and brought the margin between danger and safety to a very narrow limit when storm conditions prevail.
Yours, etc. KIANU.[52]

THE COURT OF MARINE INQUIRY could never establish *Koombana*'s fate. To do that was beyond its mandate and beyond its human capability. Over the years, many theories have been advanced. Few bear close scrutiny. Ironically, it is Walter Barker's summation from *The Hedland Advocate* of April 6th, 1912 that survives the unhindered reappraisal that the passing of time permits. Here now, in the court of careful reassessment, under different rules and before the greater jury, the "journalistic busybody" will have the last word.

> The following theories as to the Koombana's fate have been hazarded:
> 1. Mountainous seas flooded the ship by means of her cattle decks and she sank.
> 2. Bedout light being extinguished, Capt. Allen misjudged his position in the dark, the ship struck and turned over, or her bottom being torn she subsequently sank in deep water.
> 3. Machinery became disabled, and the vessel, left to the fearful wind and seas, foundered.
> 4. That when the vessel attempted to alter her northward course, to face the hurricane, she heeled over, the wind drove the water from her bottom, and the next big sea turned her completely over.
> Nos. 2 and 4 are held by seamen most competent to judge. The opinion generally held by Nor'-West residents was that the Koombana would meet her fate in the first willy willy she struck, and we have a sad fulfilment of that prophecy.[53]

15

FORTUNE'S CROOKED SMILE

ON WEDNESDAY, NOVEMBER 15TH, 1911, the simmering trouble at the Whim Well copper mine boiled over. About eighty men called a strike and downed tools, citing the company's failure to pay a living wage, its poor record compared to other mines in the Nor'-West, and its new requirement that shovellers work ten-hour shifts underground.[1]

A thousand miles away in the capital, the company found new men and signed them up, but when it became known that it was neglecting to tell its new recruits that a dispute was already in progress, the trouble at the mine rapidly escalated. On arrival at Whim Creek the newcomers received a briefing from the union; most decided to join the strike. For that show of solidarity, the accidental activists were brought before the local magistrate and convicted of breach of contract. Each was ordered to repay the steamer fare of £5, or face a month's imprisonment.[2]

The Whim Creek strike was never likely to be a simple two-cornered contest. The dispute divided the ragtag workforce along national and cultural lines. Almost to a man, the Britishers were staunch unionists; by contrast, many of the Europeans had no experience of collective bargaining, had experienced conditions far worse, and had lower expectations. Those who elected to keep working became targets of abuse and intimidation and the unsegregated miners' camp quickly became unmanageable. To protect its few remaining workers, and to give the district's only police officer some respite, the company created a new camp on the mining lease itself.[3] But rather than ease tensions, the new compound increased antipathy toward the strike-breakers, who were now seen as enjoying the protection and patronage of the bosses.

On December 7th, to the surprise of many, the dispute ended. After three weeks of lost production, the company capitulated. The union's success was widely reported, and Adelaide newspaper *The Advertiser* included details of an interim agreement.

Whim Well copper mine, 1910.

A TROUBLE SETTLED.
Perth, December 8.
The labor trouble at the Whim Creek Copper Mine has been ended, the employers agreeing to concede the following rates for six months:—Miners in shafts, 15/–; winzes and rises, 14/2; elsewhere, 13/4; timbermen, 13/–; truckers, mullockers & shovellers, surface hands, 13/4, with extra 1/8 extra for wet ground; 47 hours a week, inclusive of crib time; rockbreakers, 10/–; orebreakers, 10/–; dressing plant 6/4; surface hands, 47 hours, exclusive of crib time.[4]

Constable Fred Growden welcomed the agreement, but if he thought that things would settle now that the men were back at work on better pay, he was quickly disabused. The resumption of work brought the antagonists together. As the union men saw it, the 'scabs' were now enjoying benefits they had been unwilling to fight for. The unionists warned the strike-breakers to keep to themselves and to avoid any encounter beyond the perimeter of the mine.

A week or so after the end of the strike, Italian mineworker Joseph Seleno came to see the constable. He said that he was thinking of returning to his old camp near the hall, but was worried that some of the men might "knock him about." To Growden, Seleno seemed a decent chap; he told the Italian that if he called in again before making the move, he would ensure that he was not interfered with.[5]

Whim Well copper mine plant and rail siding, 1910.

Perhaps Joseph Seleno had second thoughts about moving camp, or perhaps he decided to test the water in a different way. On the evening of Saturday, December 23rd, he and his compatriot Frank Cattellini went to the pub for the first time in three weeks. In the side bar of the Federal Hotel the barman greeted the men, served their drinks and, in a matter-of-fact way, advised them not to stay long. With a nod of thanks for the drinks, they ignored the advice.[6]

As the front bar steadily filled, the two Italians kept to themselves. It was a little before 10 p.m. when a yell of "Where are the scabs?" came from beyond the partition. The two Italians looked at each other, stood up, and went to investigate. In the front bar they met a group of six or seven men just arrived from the Whim Creek Hotel down the road. Among the new arrivals were mine labourers George Connelly, Jim Aylward and Tom Darlington; all had been drinking for hours.

Seleno and Cattellini were both sober but handled the situation very differently. Cattellini was agitated, jittery, pacing back and forth with one hand inside his coat; Seleno walked slowly, trying to appraise the situation. Realising that his assailants were working to some sort of plan, he took a couple of steps backward, rested his elbows on the bar and kept his hands close and high. With only the barman behind him, he watched and waited.

He did not wait long. Jim Aylward stepped up to Cattellini and demanded to know what he had under his coat. But almost before the

Italian could reply, Aylward landed two heavy punches to his head. Over Seleno's shoulder, publican Tom Hill yelled at the two men to get out. To his surprise they complied, but as all eyes followed the fight out of the door, Seleno, on his blind side, took a punch to the side of the head. The blow knocked his hat off and left a cut over his left eye.

After replying to something that Cattellini yelled in Italian from the verandah, Seleno stooped down, picked up his hat and placed it on the bar. And then, as if wishing to wind back the clock by a few seconds, he picked up his hat and put it back on his head. Neither Seleno nor the publican had seen who threw the punch, but Seleno figured it was Aylward's mate Thomas Darlington; he shaped up to Darlington and yelled to the room: "How many you want to fight me?"

Fearing a free-for-all, the publican vaulted the bar and shepherded the whole crowd out through the double doors. Apart from a single patch of light, the verandah was dark. It was impossible for anyone to make out precisely what was happening; indeed, it was too dark for Seleno and Darlington to land punches. A few feet from the door, the two men ended up in a clinch, wrestling on their feet.[7]

At the Federal Hotel, fistfights were a common occurrence. Tom Hill, pleased to have cleared the room and spared the furniture, only stood by the door for a minute or so, deciding whether this latest stoush could work itself out. There was no sign of Cattellini; he had run off, apparently. And since no one seemed inclined to interfere in the scuffle between Seleno and Darlington, he returned to the bar. After a couple of minutes he heard Jim Aylward yell "The bastard's got a knife!" but before he could ascertain exactly who had a knife, the front doors burst open. Thomas Darlington, bleeding badly, staggered in, supported by George Connelly. At the bar Darlington said nothing; he simply leant forward and appeared to rest his head.[8]

Connelly asked Hill to keep an eye on the injured man while he fetched the doctor. He then rushed away, declaring, "Give me a gun and I'll shoot the bastards!" A moment later, Darlington's legs gave way. He slumped awkwardly but was caught by the nearest drinker and guided to the floor. His head now unsupported, a four-inch gash across the right side of his neck was plainly visible. The man who had broken his fall placed his hand over the wound in a vain effort to stop the flow of blood.[9]

Constable Growden had expected a busy night. It was Saturday and it was payday, the first on the new deal and the last before Christmas. A little before ten o'clock, on his round, he called at the Whim Creek Hotel, where many of the mineworkers were drinking. At the bar he learned that a bunch of union men, angry and well fuelled, had just left for the Federal Hotel where two 'scabs' were reported to be drinking.

As he approached the Federal Hotel, P.C. Growden heard agitated voices and the sound of heavy feet on boards. As he picked up his pace, he met George Connelly running for the doctor. Told of the stabbing, the constable dashed the last hundred yards. On reaching the injured man, he was surprised to be pushed aside by mine labourer Herbert Hayman who declared, "I am a first-aid man." To the experienced police officer it was painfully clear that Thomas Darlington was beyond any aid, save perhaps of a spiritual kind. He turned to Tom Hill behind the bar and asked for a cork. He then knelt down, gave the cork to the "first-aid man" and instructed him to push it down behind the collarbone against the jaggedly torn artery.[10]

When Joseph Shelmerdine arrived a few minutes later, there was nothing for the doctor to do but to pronounce life extinct.

Constable Growden did not know if the two Italians would return to their camps or 'go bush.' In the bar he asked young mine labourer Matthew Murphy to help him, and outside on the street he commandeered Harry Haile with horse and cart to drive them to the mining lease. As he approached Joseph Seleno's camp, Growden saw a dim light burning. He called a halt. With his nervous citizen deputies hanging back, he walked the last hundred yards. The arrest of Joseph Seleno would turn out to be the simplest part of a long and difficult night. Twenty yards from the glowing tent, the constable called "Are you there, Seleno?"

Without hesitation came the reply. "Yes, who is that?"

"Police. Growden."

Without neither anguish nor gravitas Seleno said: "All right. I know you want me."

It was almost as if Seleno's mission was to put his visitors at ease. Emboldened by the very subject of their fears, Haile and Murphy now came alongside the constable; the three walked together into the camp. At a basin near his tent, Seleno stood stripped to the waist, washing his face and hands. Growden knew the rules of arrest and spoke clearly: "Is that you, Seleno?" But before the arresting officer could warn his prisoner or affirm any right to silence, Seleno turned, faced him and said: "Yes, I know you want me. I kill that man."[11]

As he spoke, Seleno walked into the light. His face was clean, but partly congealed blood matted his hair and covered his chest and arms. When Constable Growden asked about the knife used in the attack, Seleno said nothing. He simply walked to a table by his bed, retrieved the weapon and handed it over.

When Growden asked Seleno where his mate was, Seleno replied "Out the back." Cattellini had been hiding in darkness a little way off; he had apparently heard the conversation between Seleno and the constable. When Growden called "Are you there, Cattellini?" the Italian stepped from behind a hessian wall and allowed himself to be arrested. Once again, Cattellini's response to adversity was very different to that of his

Whim Creek police station, 1910.

compatriot. In response to the constable's questions he declared that he had no knife and had not left his camp all evening.

At the Whim Creek police station, Joseph Seleno wanted to explain the whole affair, but was advised to rest and gather his thoughts before saying much more. Growden had two good reasons for silencing his unusual prisoner. He was not sure that Seleno fully understood the gravity of his situation, or how his prospects might be harmed by what he said. He also knew that Seleno was the least of his worries, and that he was urgently needed elsewhere.[12]

Indeed, the benign composure of the accused was in sharp contrast to the wild mood that had developed outside the Federal Hotel. When Doctor Shelmerdine heard threats of lynching he addressed the men from the verandah but failed to pacify them. When Growden returned, the two men discussed the situation. They agreed that without support they could not guarantee the safety of the prisoners. A little before midnight, they woke the postmaster to telegraph for reinforcements from Roebourne, 25 miles away.[13]

The reinforcements were not needed. In the early hours of Christmas Eve, the lynch mob lost its cohesion as one by one its champions sobered up, and anger subsided into regret. After a few hours of sleep, aggrieved men prepared themselves as best they could for the funeral of a friend.

Thomas Darlington was 33 years of age and married, but his wife would not witness his burial. Few women accompanied their husbands to this unshaven outpost. At the graveside, in place of family, fellow workers and drinking mates paid respect deep or shallow. Jim Aylward did not attend.[14]

As the funeral party dispersed, Dr Shelmerdine advised the witnesses among the mourners that his coronial inquest would begin immediately. Over two days, he and Constable Growden took enthusiastic but inconsistent testimony from men who had been in one or both hotels on the Saturday night. To his surprise, Growden learned that Seleno was a former soldier; among personal effects retrieved from his camp were discharge papers from Légion étrangère—the French Foreign Legion. He also learned that "Frank Cattellini" was an invention; Lawrence Cappelli had been working under an assumed name to conceal a prior conviction.[15]

When the inquest concluded, the two Italians were transferred to Roebourne Gaol to await trial: Seleno for wilful murder, and Cappelli for his supposed part in it. Growden and Shelmerdine took great care to ensure that the information they released to the press was measured and unprejudiced, but their diligence had little effect upon *The Advertiser*, which squeezed every drop of drama from the facts it had been given.

STABBED TO DEATH BY AN ITALIAN.
AN HOTEL TRAGEDY.
Perth. December 27.
Thomas Darlington was killed during a quarrel with an Italian named Sileno, at Whim Creek on Saturday night. Sileno was getting the worse of a fight with Darlington, at the Federal Hotel, when, with a knife handed to him by Capelli, another Italian, Sileno stabbed Darlington first in the thigh and then in the neck. Darlington's jugular vein was severed, and he died in a few minutes. Both Italians are under arrest, and extra constables have been sent from Roebourne to Whim Creek to prevent the miners from carrying out an alleged threat to lynch the prisoners. The affray started as the result of someone calling the Italians scabs.[16]

ON THE AFTERNOON OF MONDAY, MARCH 18TH, 1912, Commissioner Norbert Keenan, K.C. arrived in Roebourne. He had come north by *Koombana* to hear the case of Rex v. Seleno & Cappelli.[17] A few hours after *Koombana* cast off and continued north, the first witnesses arrived from Whim Creek. The steamer *Paroo*, southbound from Singapore to Fremantle, had deviated from her usual track to call at Depuch Island and collect the men. Captain Richardson later told *The West Australian*:

When we were anchored in the passage there was a heavy swell coming in from the N.E., and I could tell there was some dirty weather about—in fact, it was apparently so near that I was seriously thinking of clearing round the Monte Bello Islands and leaving Onslow out of the itinerary altogether. However, I called in during the following morning, and got through without mishap. I have been lucky with several of these blows, in being either a day or so ahead or astern of some of them.[18]

The steamer *Bullarra*, which had arrived in Port Hedland as *Paroo* left, was also southbound. She too was under instructions to call at Depuch, to collect the witnesses for the second day of the trial. The appointment was not kept. Four hours out of Hedland, *Bullarra* encountered horrendous sea conditions; her master discarded any thought of weaving among reefs and islands in fading light. Without hesitation, he chose the dark simplicity of the open sea.[19]

In sultry, unpredictable weather the trial began. The first day proceeded to plan but the second certainly did not. When the prosecution witnesses failed to appear, Commissioner Keenan fell back upon evidence gathered at the coronial inquest. In the statements handwritten by Fred Growden and Joseph Shelmerdine, the union men clearly emerged as the aggressors. Moreover, the statements of Aylward, Kay and Connelly were guarded and evasive, especially when seen beside the astonishing forthrightness of the accused murderer. With the witness stand empty and with time to spare, Keenan gave Joseph Seleno an unusual opportunity to speak in broken English on his own behalf.

The men who had come to the Federal Hotel with Thomas Darlington were united in their belief that Seleno had used Cappelli's knife to stab their friend. They claimed that Cappelli had concealed a knife under his coat and had passed it to Seleno during the fight on the verandah. That summation was almost certainly correct,[20] but ultimately it was supposition regarding the knife that brought the prosecution case undone. In the gloom of the hotel verandah, none had seen any more than the glint of a blade, and none could say precisely how or when the knife had passed from one man to the other.

If the prosecution witnesses thought that any guilt lifted from Cappelli would naturally settle upon Seleno, they were to be disappointed. The odd mix of the known and the unknown worked to the advantage of both defendants. Cappelli could not be convicted upon the mere fact of his owning the knife, but that same fact remained powerful and influential in Seleno's defence. The commissioner was inclined to accept that Seleno had come to the Federal Hotel without any weapon at all, and once there had remained sober, had not invited trouble, and had only taken and wielded a knife in a moment of fear or madness.

On the afternoon of Thursday, March 21st, 1912, as Roebourne residents barricaded windows and prepared for the arrival of the dread visitor, Commissioner Keenan delivered his verdict. Seleno was found guilty of the lesser charge of manslaughter and sentenced to three years' imprisonment with hard labour. Cappelli was acquitted.[21]

For Seleno, the verdict was a huge relief. At day end, he was back on the same straw mattress on the floor of the lock-up, but the cell to which he returned in the evening was not the cell he had left in the morning. It was as if the wind, in his absence, had swept away the fear of death and laced the air with salt and sweet salvation.

THE PRISONER, AWAITING TRANSFER TO FREMANTLE, was told that he would not leave from Point Samson, as the jetty had been badly damaged by the storm. He would be taken to Cossack by tram and transferred to a steamer in the roads. Although there was no further official communication, news of life outside reached him in snippets both sympathetic and mischievous. Whim Creek, he learned, had been hit hard by the storm. The mine had all but ceased production. Two big ships, partly loaded, had been caught in the anchorage. The larger of the two had gone to pieces, and the dead had been buried on Depuch Island. The trial witnesses had been caught, too. Tom Hill had drowned, but the others had survived. After three days at sea, *Bullarra* had limped into Cossack without her funnel. No rest for her crew, though; they had built a funnel of corrugated iron and gone back to sea to search for *Koombana*.

IN 1912, FREMANTLE PRISON WAS CHANGING. A new wing had opened, and a commission of inquiry had recommended that the cells of the old main block be doubled in size by knocking down every second internal wall. There were new workshops too, reflecting the prevailing view that prisoners—or at least a better class of prisoner—should be gainfully employed within the precinct. Whether Joseph Seleno was impressed or amused by the modern principles of incarceration is not known. What is clear is that, for delivery of hard labour, this government agency could not match either the French Foreign Legion or the Whim Well Copper Mining Company.

Seleno adjusted well to the rhythm of life in the temperate south. Like all inmates, he watched, listened and took a keen interest in the pattern of arrivals and departures. By the end of his first year, he had reason to think that freedom of a kind might soon be offered.

On July 9th, 1913 a little piece appeared deep on page six of *The West Australian*:

A Prohibited Immigrant.—The latest undesirable who is to be deported by order of the Minister for Customs is Joseph Seleno, of Italian birth, a native of Turin, Italy. In December, 1911, Seleno, figuring in an affray at a hotel at Whim Creek, stabbed another European named Darlington in the neck. Darlington succumbed, and

Seleno was sentenced to imprisonment for three years on a charge of manslaughter. He began to serve the sentence in March, 1912, and on June 23 last he was released from prison. The dictation test was applied to him, and he failed. The order authorising his deportation has been received by the Collector of Customs at Fremantle, and Seleno is being detained at the Fremantle Gaol until the departure of the Singapore boat which is to take him from the Commonwealth.[22]

Three days later, Joseph Seleno was escorted to his temporary accommodation: a demountable lock-up on the 'tween deck of the S.S. *Minderoo*. His future was entirely uncertain—but then, he had never railed against the past or the present. When Lady Luck smiled, he simply smiled back, accepting her wry munificence with characteristic candour.

16

THE SHADOW OF MISFORTUNE

TWO WEEKS after the discovery of wreckage erased all doubt that *Koombana* had foundered, the Adelaide Steamship Company received a cable from its agents in London. They had been contacted by Alexander Stephen & Sons, the ship's builders, who wanted to know if the company had any objection to their engaging in discussion with the Government of Western Australia regarding the cost of replacing the ship. It was a strange request. At their regular weekly meeting, the Adelaide Steamship Company's directors decided that nothing was served by withholding consent. They advised accordingly.[1]

Although it may seem strange that one of the hardest players in a hard game should offer a helping hand to a new competitor, the company did not give its blessing with magnanimity. It recognised that times had changed and that the case for building a vessel like *Koombana* could no longer be made.

IT IS NEVER EASY to pinpoint the beginning of a long drought. At Carnarvon, in March and April of 1911, no rains fell. But then, none were expected. The winter rains were about half of what the wool growers considered reasonable, and the showers of spring scarcely moistened the soil. Here, at the southern limit of the tropical monsoon, it was reasonable to hope for summer rain, but none came. And the great storm of March 1912, which might have delivered relief in the wake of destruction, brought only the news of disaster.

It is difficult to know when the locals began speaking plainly of drought. When the state government's Commissioner for Tropical Agriculture, Mr A. Dispeissis, visited Carnarvon in the first week of November 1911, there was lamentation of the dry season but no despondency; indeed, the visiting expert had much to say that the residents were delighted to hear. He declared that the alluvial land on the banks of the Gascoyne, for fifty miles from the river's mouth, were perfectly suited to intensive irrigation farming.[2] Local bank manager Edwin Angelo accepted that assessment at face value; with the help of an irrigation specialist from the agriculture department, he established an experimental ten-acre plot.[3] With water from four shallow wells, the irrigation farm on his property "Leura" was an immediate success, and when Minister for Public Works Bill Johnson[4] visited the town in May 1912, the Angelo brothers were able to show a fine crop of tomatoes, vegetables, Japanese millet and lucerne.[5] It is not surprising that the little farm was chosen as the showpiece for the minister's visit. It was almost the only good news the town had to offer.

1911 would turn out to be the first of three punishing seasons. At the end of 1912, the pioneers declared they had seen nothing like it. The 21-month drought of 1891 and 1892 was drier, but on that occasion the preceding seasons had been splendid, and the grass cover so heavy that stock never ran short of dry feed. This was different: in many places all pasture disappeared, and cartage costs doubled as the roads along the Gascoyne and Lyons rivers were reduced to furrows of windblown sand.[6] The 1912 Crop and Live Stock Return, compiled by the police officers of the various districts, made sobering reading:

> The Minilya, Lower Gascoyne, and Wooramel portions of the Gascoyne district, and also the town of Carnarvon, experienced an exceptionally dry season, in places the squatters having had little or no rain. The country throughout is looking very dry and bare, the stock having had nothing but scrub to subsist on for the past 12 months. The losses of stock have been very heavy throughout the district, and unless a good fall of rain is registered within the next few months, the future will be disastrous. The losses of stock in and around Carnarvon have also been very heavy, practically all the stock on the Carnarvon Commonage have perished, many of them through the scarcity of water, which has proved a great drawback in Carnarvon for some time past.[7]

At 2 a.m. on Tuesday, May 27th, 1913, one Carnarvon resident woke to what he later described as a weird crackling sound. In half-sleep, he thought the rain had come. It had not. Flames had engulfed the Carnarvon Hotel and the town had come out to watch.[8] "The sight was magnificent," said one enthusiastic spectator, "the various colors thrown out by the burning iron and matchwood creating a beautiful effect." For a town suffering both drought and a rat plague, there was another aspect to the entertainment. The same gentleman would recall:

> An enormous quantity of rats was destroyed in the two large trees in the courtyard. These could be seen working their way out on the branches until, overcome by the heat, they fell into the flames. This must have gladdened the hearts of our local health board as they certainly saved the bonus which is now being offered. A couple of

dogs enjoyed themselves catching the strays which endeavored to escape, greatly to the amusement of the large crowd that had collected by this time.[9]

Although the night was mild and the breeze soft, there was never any possibility that the fire could be suppressed. The local council had baulked at the cost of providing a dedicated water main for fire fighting, and a local volunteer brigade, after early enthusiasm, had lost cohesion. Antiquated hoses and reels, rented from a government department, had recently been packed up and shipped back to Fremantle.[10]

In the days after the fire, the town was rife with rumour. Perhaps the gossip was symptomatic of hard times, but two unusual circumstances should be noted. The hotel was about to be sold; in fact, the final pre-sale inspection was completed just a few hours before the fire broke out. And in the ashes of the hotel office, the safe was found to be open.[11] Retiring manager John Murphy explained that after discovering the fire he rushed to retrieve the takings from the safe, only to be driven back by the heat before he had time to close it. With his hair singed and the soles of his feet scorched, he had been taken to the local hospital. Resident Magistrate Charles Foss conducted an inquiry into the blaze but found no evidence of arson and remonstrated with his fellow citizens for rumour-mongering.[12]

Six weeks after the fire, the rains came. On July 13th and 23rd, 1913, good falls were registered everywhere: in the town, and at almost every station from Yaringa in the south to Yalobia in the north. "The country has been quite transformed," declared *The Northern Times*. "Feed is springing up everywhere, and all the pools are full. The Wooramel River ran twice and the Gascoyne again flowed into the Doorawarrah country. The drought is now completely broken."[13]

To imagine that a drought may be broken in a day or a week is greatly appealing. More often, relief is neither dramatic nor definitive, and the end of a drought may be as difficult to fix as its onset. Unfortunately, dry conditions returned; only after a cyclonic inundation in February 1914[14] did the squatters decide that their long ordeal was over. And for many, the drought's ill effects did not end with the greening of the land. Heavy debts were carried into better years.[15]

ONSLOW HAD LONG LAMENTED its lack of shipping facilities, but when the drought came, the town's campaign for a new deep-water jetty and stock race assumed new intensity. The Ashburton River pastoralists found themselves unable to respond to the dry conditions; they could not reduce their stock numbers by selling what the land would no longer support. By the spring of 1911, even the 'overlanding' of wool had become difficult. There was so little feed and water along the tracks to Carnarvon and Point Samson that only camel teams could make the journey without distress. Some of the growers simply withheld their clip at a time when wool prices were high and their need for cash greater than ever.[16]

As drought took hold in the north, the Labor government of John Scaddan came to power in the capital.[17] To the residents of Onslow, Scaddan's new Minister for Public Works, Bill Johnson, seemed the right kind of target for a deputation. Within weeks of his elevation Johnson had condemned the previous government's neglect of the Nor'-West. Things would be different now, he promised.[18]

In the first week of February 1912, Onslow's advocates travelled south by steamer to plead for a new jetty. They left empty-handed. Johnson advised that the government simply could not afford to do what they asked. Part of the problem was that their preferred jetty site was west of the town, on the other side of the Ashburton River. The combined cost of jetty, tramway and bridge was estimated to be £70,000, which by coincidence was the amount included in the forward estimates for all Nor'-West projects. Clearly, a cheaper solution had to be found.[19]

There was some room for optimism. A few weeks later the new government honoured one of its pledges: it appointed Edward Tindale as the first Resident Engineer for the North-West.[20] The townsfolk decided that at the first opportunity they would work with—and work upon—the man sent to Nor'-West service. The Onslow correspondent for *The Sunday Times* welcomed the news that Mr Tindale would soon visit their town. "The people of this district are asking for a jetty," he wrote, "they care not where, as long as it is a suitable place, to enable them to ship their stock."[21]

Engineer Tindale arrived at Onslow by the little government steamer *Una* on December 8th, 1912. Immediately, the residents felt that progress was being made. An extension of the existing jetty was quickly ruled out. Tindale estimated that to reach water deep enough for the steamers, an extension of more than a mile would be required. An alternative site, however, drew his attention. Twelve miles to the east of Onslow, at Beadon Point, there was deep water less than 500 yards from shore, and a reliable supply of fresh water. Tindale was so impressed by the possibilities that he set *Una* to work on a preliminary survey of the seabed.[22]

The locals imagined that the lower cost of the short jetty would more than compensate for the additional length of tramway, but Tindale travelled the route with them and shook his head. He told the locals that the difficulties of running the tramway over marsh and mangrove outweighed the advantages of the new jetty site. The engineer may have thought that the matter would end there, but Onslow had one more card to play. The townsfolk declared plainly that if the town and the new jetty could not be connected, the town would pick itself up and move. A report published by *The Northern Times* on December 21st, 1912 marks an important moment in the history of the town. The Onslow correspondent wrote:

> Mr. Tindale has not given us much hope of getting a tramline from the point to the town, as the country is too rough and it would cost a large sum of money. A road has been found through the marsh to the main road, and if a jetty is built at the point, it will mean that the teams and traffic will go that way, which will consequently be the shifting of the town of Onslow.[23]

Onslow could not have demonstrated its commitment more forcibly. Engineer Tindale was enthusiastic about the jetty plan and greatly impressed by the town's determination to see it realised. He told the grateful citizens that a survey party would arrive in about the middle of March.

In February 1913, summer storms delivered uneven rainfall across the district and set the Ashburton River flowing again, but the relief was short-lived. In the autumn the sky cleared and drought conditions returned. March came and went, but the promised survey party never arrived. Edward Tindale, it appears, was overruled.

Although the residents of Onslow could not have known it, their campaign had some way to run.[24] Nine years later, on July 29th, 1922, *The Northern Times* reported:

> Onslow News.
> (From our own correspondent)
> Onslow, July 25.
> Beadon at last! In five minutes after the receipt of a wire from Mr. Teesdale, M.L.A., stating that the contractor's tender for the building of the Beadon jetty had been accepted, all Onslow was talking and drinking in excited groups, and vainly trying to realise the good news.[25]

THE RESIDENTS OF COSSACK had long predicted that the Point Samson jetty, projecting boldly into open water, would fall to the first willy-willy that struck it. They were almost right. The cyclone that crossed the coast about thirty miles to the east in the early hours of Friday, March 22nd, 1912, delivered a glancing blow. The first inspection revealed serious damage to the 'T-head' and the loss of about fifty piles, although the water was left so opaque that it was impossible to say if the piles were gone altogether or merely knocked over. The Roebourne wharfinger, responsible for shipping facilities at both Point Samson and Cossack, telegraphed the chief harbourmaster at Fremantle, describing the damage done and outlining options for keeping some port facilities open. While the jetty remained out of commission, he said, the steamers would have no alternative but to anchor in the roads and deliver cargo by lighter to the wharf at Cossack. Both the main tramline from Point Samson and the spur line from Cossack had been damaged. Because Cossack would for a time be the only working port, he recommended that highest priority be given to the repair of that section of line.[26]

On April 21st, 1912, the Minister for Public Works embarked on an extended tour of the Nor'-West. It was never intended as an inspection of the storm-ravaged centres; indeed, the minister's travel plans were already in place when the cyclone struck. He would, nonetheless, visit the affected communities to see for himself what needed to be done.[27]

When Bill Johnson stepped ashore at Cossack in the first week of May 1912, he was unimpressed. He could see no good reason why White Australia should tolerate an Asiatic enclave in which Japanese, Malays and Koepangers outnumbered whites by almost two to one. Of course, Johnson's ministerial portfolio related to civil rather than social engineering, and there were other matters to be attended to.

After inspecting the damage to the jetties and tramways, Johnson took a view strikingly different to that of the wharfinger. He decided that the line to Cossack should be left unrepaired, and that all efforts should be directed to restoring the connection between Point Samson and Roebourne.[28] He went further still, suggesting that if the tramway to Point Samson line were realigned, to place it beyond the reach of floodwaters, the line to Cossack could be done away with altogether. In Perth a few weeks later he reported on the progress of the tramway alignment.

> This work is now in hand, and when it is completed there will be little or no danger of further washaways, and the result will be that there will be practically no further use for the line to Cossack. In these circum-stances I have instructed that the Cossack portion of the line be lifted; portion of the rails used for the extra twenty chains required in the deviation, and the remainder stacked for transshipment to Onslow.[29]

In Cossack and Roebourne, most residents considered the minister's position absurd, and they petitioned the government to have the decision reversed. But Johnson, unmoved, saw that his instructions were carried out.[30] Three years later, in May 1915, the Adelaide Steamship Company's marine superintendent James Crossley prepared for his directors a confidential report on the risks and challenges of the Nor'-West trade. Of Point Samson he wrote:

> During the 1912 cyclone, this jetty was damaged and for several months vessels could not use it. The cargo was then lightered by the "Wester" to Cossack and thence to Roebourne by steam tram, but since then the Laborites and partisans of the White Australia policy persuaded the Minister for Works (when there on a visit), to have the tramway torn up. This was done and the rails thrown on one side. It would be interesting to see what happens if another cyclone visits this district, as if one does, it is sure to damage the Jetty again, and failing the Jetty, Cossack Creek wharf is the only landing place for cargo, and there is some distance (9 or 10 miles I believe) with bad roads between

Cossack and Roebourne. The objection to the two places being connected by rail was due to the fact that there are so many colored people in Cossack (pearlers).[31]

THE LOSS OF KOOMBANA HIT PORT HEDLAND HARD. It was not that many from the town were among the missing; rather, it was the loss of a friendship that had grown between a town and a ship. In a sense, it was an accidental intimacy. Twice each month for three years, *Koombana* had tied to a jetty in the middle of the town, and by the combined mischief of tide and sandbar had usually stayed overnight. It had become the habit of crew and townsfolk to socialise, either in the ship's saloon and smoke room, or in homes and hotels on shore. And the town's welcome was extended to *Koombana*'s passengers, especially those of the far north who passed through the port regularly on their seasonal migrations.

When *Bullarra* and *Koombana* left Port Hedland on Wednesday March 20th, 1912, almost the whole town turned out to watch.[32] It was a light, bright distraction from what was shaping as a very bad year. Thirteen days later, when the Blue Funnel liner *Gorgon* brought undeniable evidence of *Koombana*'s loss, the news swept through the town like a chill wind, leaving behind a yearning for answers that no court of marine inquiry could relieve.

By the middle of 1912, the lamentation of two dry seasons had given way to the direct confrontation of drought. Although the port was unusually busy with large stock shipments, the bustle did not speak of prosperity. Pastoralists were reducing their stock numbers and garnering cash for whatever lay ahead. More than any other town on the coast, Port Hedland had nailed its colours to the mast of progress. That mindset could be traced to 1906, when the town was selected as the starting point for the Pilbara railway. For six years—three of anticipation and three of construction—the residents had believed that upon completion of the line their town would become a thoroughfare for miners and prospectors making their way to the interior.[33] Port Hedland, they predicted, would become the unofficial capital of the Nor'-West—if it was not already.

Perhaps the townsfolk were unrealistic, or perhaps the tide of fortune turned. When the railway reached Marble Bar in July 1911, the boost to Port Hedland was noticeable but not dramatic, and the bloom did not last. By the winter of 1912 the mining centres of Marble Bar and Nullagine were surviving rather than thriving, and the lack of water was proving as great a problem for the miner as it was for the pastoralist. In March 1913, station owner Tom Anderson wrote in his diary:

> The outlook in this State is not too good owing to the Banks & all business people pressing those who owe them money. . . . Our Premier (Scaddan) is away in England trying to borrow £5,000,000. The State

debt is already £90 per head. Our population being 300,000. If he fails to get it which is likely then pressure all round will continue. If he does get it; then greater pressure later on. 300,000 people cannot pay interest on unlimited millions badly spent. Still on we go![34]

Not everyone in the Nor'-West laid blame for the downturn at the feet of John "Happy Jack" Scaddan; indeed, Port Hedland with its miners, shearers and railway workers was broadly sympathetic to the Labor government. That is not to say that Port Hedland's dealings with the Public Works Department were any more satisfying than those of Onslow or Cossack. In March 1914, the town had its own little stoush with Minister Johnson and his staff. The department had built a new school for this, the hottest of all coastal towns, but the design included neither windows nor ventilation on the ocean side. A few days into the school year, the classroom proved so suffocatingly hot that the parents, united, withdrew their children.[35]

In more amiable times the problem might have been solved quickly and quietly. On this occasion, however, the official channels were tested. Having declared their objections, the parents proposed a solution: for less than £5, a competent local carpenter would install floor-level ventilation on the sea-breeze side. For reasons that may never be known or understood, the Public Works Department declined the offer, insisting that its own man would attend to the matter when he called by in two or three months. As if to add insult to injury, the department then suggested that the problem had arisen because the parents had fallen under the spell of an activist headmaster.

A few weeks later, when the Singapore-bound steamer *Charon* arrived, passenger A. T. Saunders (a first cousin of *Koombana*'s late master Tom Allen) observed that a broad malaise seemed to have gripped the community. He wrote:

This is clearly a decaying town. Many shops and houses are empty, and there are announcements in some windows of departures from the town. It is hard to say what keeps the place alive, except the shipment of stock and wool and the forwarding of stores to the inland stations. . . . I understand that there is only one train a week, and that sometimes, though the steamer may arrive a couple of hours after the train is timed to depart, the departure is not delayed, and consequently the mails for the interior are left to lie at Hedland for a week or so. I can hardly believe that this is true, but I am assured that it is a fact.[36]

As the water situation became worse, the town became very quiet indeed. Even the shipping of stock became difficult, there being nothing at all for animals to drink after their arrival at the yards. The late arrival of a steamer, by as little as a day, could mean high mortality. It was a risk few stock owners were willing to take.[37] Intermittently, the town well began running dry. Thereafter, drinking water was brought twenty miles by rail from Poondina. The locals had no alternative but to buy what they could not do without, at five shillings per hundred gallons.[38]

Perhaps the lowest ebb was reached in the early hours of June 15th, 1914, when Dalgety's Building caught fire. It was the first serious fire in the town's short history. With no water for firefighting, the townsfolk simply stood and watched as the warehouse and its contents were destroyed. At least there was no suspicion of arson. To the building's owner, it was "just one of those things." He shrugged his shoulders and wondered if the rats had got into the matches.[39]

By October 1914 the Hedland-based pearling boats had begun mixing fresh and brackish water, to remain at sea a little longer. The recent take of shell had been excellent, and not even the outbreak of war could suppress the stubborn optimism of one pearler. The market for his product had all but vanished, and yet he declared: "If this war does not last long, there will be a large number of pearlers making Port Hedland their headquarters next year."[40]

IN BROOME, the tragedy of *Koombana* fell upon a deep, pre-existing pessimism. The great source of consternation was the Australian Government's edict that after 1913, the use of indentured coloured labour would no longer be permitted.[41] Nor'-West newsman Walter Barker wrote:

> The unrest occasioned by the cloud which threatens the pearling industry has resulted in a poor display of interest in local public matters. The impression conveyed to visitors is that there exists a feeling which says "Oh, let it slide until we are sure that they are not going to close down the industry!" The splendid streets of three years ago have been allowed to fall into such a state of disrepair that it will now tax the resources of the municipality to bring them up to their erstwhile state of perfection.[42]

Much had occurred in the space of a few months. On October 26th, 1911, in the federal parliament, Queensland member Fred Bamford formally moved for the appointment of a royal commission to inquire into the conduct of the pearling industry. Among those who rose to speak was John Forrest, formerly Premier of Western Australia. Forrest supported the motion but recommended that commissioners be chosen from outside the parliament. He argued that the work of the commission would require extensive travel to remote places, including Broome. It would be impossible, he said, for any member to meet the demands of the commission and still fulfil his obligations to the parliament. Although Forrest's argument was reasonable, his ulterior motive was to have the commission chaired by someone other than Bamford, whose uncompromising White Australia views were well known. Indeed, Bamford had been elected to the parliament in 1901, after campaigning for the elimination of Kanak labour from the Queensland sugar industry.[43]

Fred Bamford prevailed. On February 29th, 1912, he was chosen to lead the Royal Commission on the Pearl-shelling Industry, with six parliamentary colleagues comprising his panel. Although the make-up of the commission did not augur well for the future of Broome, some in the town remained optimistic. If the commissioners were to visit Broome, and see at first hand how the industry was run, dispensation would surely be granted. An early concession seemed to support that view. The commission recognised that it could not complete its work before the pearlers made their labour arrangements for the 1914 season. The deadline for the use of coloured labour was extended by a year, to the end of 1914.[44]

February 1912 also marks the beginning of the so-called "white experiment," sponsored by prominent members of the Broome Pearlers' Association. On February 4th, Perth's *Sunday Times* both explained and hailed the initiative.

WHITE DIVERS FOR THE PEARLING INDUSTRY
An Interesting Experiment
An important step in the direction of settling the vexed question of white divers versus Asiatics was taken on Feb. 1 with the arrival of 12 experienced divers from England with their necessary tenders.

It will be remembered that the Pearlers' Association of Broome, in order to thoroughly test the question whether white divers are capable of performing the arduous work of finding pearl shell in deep water, arranged to set apart a certain number of luggers, to be manned by white divers and tenders, these men to be employed for a sufficient time to decide the point beyond the shadow of a doubt.

In order that none but the best and most experienced men should be obtained, the matter was placed in the hands of Messrs. Siebe, Gorman and Co., the celebrated manufacturers of diving gear, in conjunction with a committee of Broome pearlers now resident in London, and the 24 men now arrived are those chosen by the selectors.

The whole of these interesting immigrants are ex-naval divers, that is, men who have not only a practical experience of the work under all conditions, but who also have a thorough knowledge of its scientific aspect. They are, in addition, imbued with all the traditions of a service which imposes so high a standard of duty that the idea of shirking or evading either danger or responsibility is an impossibility. Under such conditions as these, the experienced body of men may be relied upon to give the Pearlers' Association loyal and active support in their attempt to solve the problem that lies before them, and it only remains for the association, on the other hand, to see that the test is carried out under absolutely fair working conditions, and that no unconscious bias in favor of the Asiatic diver is allowed to interfere.[45]

The experiment did not begin well. When Minister for Public Works Bill Johnson visited Broome on May 17th, as part of his Nor'-West tour, the pearlers made the mistake of admitting that they did not expect the white divers to succeed. Johnson's conclusion, shared with an enthusiastic audience in Carnarvon three weeks later, was that the pearlers did not want the experiment to work and were actively undermining it. The pearlers of Broome, he said, needed to understand that the day for coloured labour had gone. The crowd cheered.[46]

Johnson's speech was reported in *The Northern Times*, the circulation of which extended to Broome and beyond. The master pearlers were not impressed. They knew how much the experiment was costing. Not only were the English divers paid at several times the going rate; they demanded better equipment, took more time to set up, and insisted upon longer breaks. All of the sponsors understood that no first-time pearl diver would match an experienced hand in his first year, but none had anticipated how great the associated loss would be. The London market had never been stronger, and with each jump in the price of shell came greater frustration at the white divers' failure to deliver.[47]

Without doubt, the divers were under extreme pressure. There was pride at stake also, especially for those among them who had confidently predicted their own success.[48] After a few weeks at sea, some were pushing the limits of diving safety. It is perhaps not surprising that the first casualty was William Webber, the spokesman and unofficial leader of the group. On June 7th, off Cape Latouche Treville, Webber remained on the seabed too long and returned to the surface without any of the recommended intermediate stops. Aboard the lugger *Eurus* he lit a cigarette, sat quietly for a few minutes and then collapsed backward onto the deck. After being undressed and carried to a bunk, he sank into a coma.[49]

Marine engineer Jim Low had been responsible for installing new engine-driven compressors on the white divers' luggers. After going out with the boats to ensure that the equipment ran smoothly, he returned to Broome convinced that the white experiment was pure folly. To his sister Jane he wrote:

> One of the white divers one of Siebe Gorman's crack men died of paralysis last week, he wouldn't work to the scientific method and refused to be recompressed after the attack. He was of the old school who had made a name for himself in the diving world, recovering treasure from wrecks, went with the McMillan expedition through Central Africa bringing up specimens out of the deep potholes somewhere or other and now has finished up here. He wouldn't let

them save his life because he didn't believe in the method. They could have forced him down but couldn't keep him down, or so he told them.

Tomorrow I go out again with another engine and air compressor to start two more of the white men, but I am going to keep them near Broome this time . . . I know a place where shell is mighty scarce but every one has got something in it, baroque or pearl; we'll practise there. I have never seen or heard of the last crowd I was out with since I left them, nor has anyone else. They are off quite on their own somewhere or other. Their engine must be going all right or the Malay child has killed them all, one or the other.[50]

A few weeks later, a Broome pearler noticed an odd coincidence. In a short, sharp letter to the editor of *The West Australian*, he declared:

The irony of fate! At Carnarvon on June 7 the Minister for Works (Mr. W. D. Johnson), with the confident assertiveness begotten of utter lack of power to grip the complexity of the subject, let himself go on the pearling industry. He assured his audience that "white men were able to escape the dreaded paralysis and would prove more capable than colored divers. The difficulty facing white divers at present was that they were not being shown where and how to find shell. That would be soon overcome and the experiment would prove wholly successful." Throughout the same day, on board a lugger between La Perouse and Broome, the tide of life of William Webber, a white diver, was slowly ebbing away under the influence of the diver's dread disease—paralysis. What a terrible answer to the irresponsible vapourings of a mere mortal![51]

On July 4th, 1912, Jim Low wrote again to his sister. Now he railed against the dogged stupidity of it all.

Two of the white divers have got "fed up" and shook the sand of Broome from their feet; there is now only five left. I am afraid "white diving" is doomed. Meg says that "Diving" was to be included in the Ordinary School curriculum or that there was a rumour to that effect, owing to the actions of the Australian Government. I call that planting unhealthy seeds of false romance in defenceless youngsters' brains, their imaginations fired with visions of monstrous jewels of fabulous value waiting to be picked up off the ground floor of Fairyland. And the rotten tucker and the roaring sou-easter and the little craft with the contemptible dog kennel misnamed a cabin where you get gyrated and bumped like a spud in a patent rotary peeler in the unstilly watches of the night[52] and pray for daylight on the arrival of which you crawl thence with contorted anatomy and a feeling in your inside as if somebody had been mixing you up with a porridge spurtle, and the snarling cockeye and the raving typhoon that catches you and dessicates. 'Tis the true romance when you're ten thousand miles away but it isn't known by that name here.[53]

The master pearlers allowed another month to pass before answering the criticism of Minister Johnson. When the time came, the facts spoke for themselves.

> The result after five months' work is that Mr. Piggott has lost £500 over the experiment, besides his outlay in plant, etc. One of the divers is doing odd jobs round Broome; two of them have left for Fremantle, calling it a "dog's life"; the fourth is in the Broome Hospital suffering from divers' paralysis. Mr. Stanley Piggott's two divers are still at it; they have up to the present got 5 cwt. of shell. Mr. Piggott is £400 out of pocket so far, and both of his men have expressed their determination not to stop at it when their agreement is up—they call it "scavengers' work." Messrs. Robison and Norman's men have up to the present got 5cwt., and R. and N, are out £400. Both their men have also expressed their determination not to stop any longer at it than the year. Messrs. Moss and Richardson's diver lost his life whilst working in 19 fathoms off Wallal . . . The statement of Mr. Johnson that the men have not been shown where to get the shell is untrue in every particular, as in all cases the white divers have been sent out with the rest of the boats belonging to their respective masters, except in the case of Mr Sydney Piggott, who sent an old Manila diver out with his boat. They have worked the grounds with the Asiatic divers all round them picking up shell, and we cannot do any more. We have put them where the shell is, and if they cannot learn to pick it up themselves we cannot teach them. As far as Broome is concerned, the whole experiment up to the present has been a howling failure.[54]

After eighteen months the royal commission had taken evidence at Cairns, Thursday Island and Melbourne, but had still not travelled west to the undisputed headquarters of the Australian pearl-shelling industry. Recognising that they had little to show and much yet to do, the commissioners proposed a further extension of the existing arrangements. The end date for the use of indentured coloured labour was set back a further two years, to the end of 1916.[55]

In the first week of August 1914, the news of war in Europe passed through Broome like a shock wave. Suddenly, the three great centres of the pearling industry in Europe—Paris, Berlin and Vienna—were fully enveloped by conflict. It seemed that the industry, if not killed off altogether, would remain suspended for the duration of the war. For a few weeks the shipping of shell continued, but in October the London distributors announced that they could accept no more. They were holding a thousand tons: sufficient, they said, to supply all of Europe for a few months after the end of hostilities.[56]

Most of the crews saw out the 1914 season, with the knowledge that the next lay-up would be like no other. When the fleet came in, boats were stored, lent, given away, and in some cases simply handed over to creditors. Indentured workers were sent home and their erstwhile masters went south to enlist.[57]

In May 1916, more than four years after its proclamation, the royal commission arrived in Broome. It found the town's remaining pearlers united in their conviction that white diving would never be reconsidered. The commissioners faced a stark choice. In their final report to the governor-general,[58] in September 1916, they admitted to a great deal of soul-searching and ultimately to a change of heart.

> Since presenting the progress report the opinion of your Commissioners has undergone a change of considerable importance, particularly in regard to the labour question. Having carefully weighed the evidence and having no reason to doubt the credibility of those who were examined on this point, and further having visited the principal centres of the pearl-shelling industry in Australia, and noted the conditions under which it is conducted, your Commissioners have decided that diving for shell is not an occupation which our workers should be encouraged to undertake. It may be urged that Europeans have successfully undertaken the work of diving for shell, which is true of the past, but the European diver is non-existent at the moment, and boat owners who have dived in shallow or comparatively shallow water dive no longer, but employ the Asiatic, who cheerfully takes the risks and puts up with the consequences.[59]

Derby and Wyndham, at opposite ends of a vast, rich beef province, proudly declared themselves the capitals of West and East Kimberley respectively. They had much in common, but by the tragedy of *Koombana* the two towns could not have been treated more differently. Because *Koombana*'s run only extended to Wyndham on alternate months, the last outpost was spared all casualties, although many of the lost were well known there.

At Derby, by contrast, the loss was intense and personal. From a white population of about ninety, a dozen close friends and relatives were stolen: Louise Sack, Dean Spark, Captain Pearson, Frank Buttle, Fred Clinch, Rob Jenkins and his daughter Edith, George and Ally Piper, the Gilhams, and Jim Ronan's nephew Will Smith. Years later, Tom Ronan would write:

> It is one of the most complete sea tragedies in history. It was when word came through that the search for the Koombana had been abandoned that I first saw my mother in tears. Will Smith was no blood kin of

hers, but he was the sort of lad who won the hearts of everyone, from children like Trix and me to toughened old bush battlers of the sort who worked with him on Napier. I can remember him as being tall and dark-eyed, with the assurance of a man and the gusto of a boy. Seldom as we saw him, our little world seemed smaller when we knew he had gone from it forever.[60]

For three years Derby, like Port Hedland, had enjoyed great rapport with the ship and her crew. It was an unusually equal relationship, the town and ship having similar populations. And the two populations were never entirely distinct; rarely did the two come together without some exchange of faces. Here, the loss of *Koombana* was both tangible and intangible: an overwhelming sadness and an inexplicable vacancy, as if a constellation had vanished from the night sky.

The two Kimberley 'capitals'—one in mourning, the other in sympathy—continued to prosper through 1912. The far north was largely unaffected by the drought proving so debilitating further south. A few weeks before Christmas, a Fitzroy River squatter delivered a cheerful end-of-year report to *The Northern Times*.

> The wet season has opened auspiciously: good early thunderstorms and heavy rains, with every appearance of a splendid season. Already it seems that there will be a record wool clip next year, and the fat oxen that delighteth the heart and other parts of Perth people and the dark men of Java and Singapore most probably will go away next year in greater numbers than ever before, thereby making Derby a flourishing seaport, which is a consideration for the capital city of—not Australia, but the new State of North-West Australia (though I believe Port Hedland sees herself in that light). The quiet season is now with us; all teams except Gogo are painted and put away for next year, all droving is finished, and, incidentally, all the surplus men are sacked to save a few bob, though when the 1913 season starts there will be the same cry as in 1912, for more labor. If Premier Scaddan passes his Bill for the abolition of aboriginal labor, things will be turned upside down. The Kimberley landowner loves black bruther because he is cheap, and at present he doesn't see how he can possibly get on without him. The price of wool has caused these owners to smile this year, and some splendid prices have been realised; also the price of fat stock—both sheep and cattle—has been good, so everything in the garden is lovely.[61]

The summer rains did not quite match the cattleman's expectation—but then, they did not need to. Even in a dry year, the land bred more cattle than could be shipped. Indeed, it could be argued that the region had been drought-proofed by government inactivity. Without the promised freezing and canning facilities, demand would never match supply, even in a dry year.

The need for beef processing at Wyndham or Derby had been recognised for a dozen years,[62] but planning had been interrupted by several changes of government. The pastoralists were optimistic that the new Labor ministry, seeing the possibility of a profitable state-run enterprise, would move quickly. After all, the new Minister for Public Works, Bill Johnson, had been a member of the royal commission that had specifically recommended the establishment of freezing works at Wyndham.[63]

It was not to be. When Johnson visited the town in May 1912, he changed his mind. He decided that the people of Perth could have their meat from the Murchison and Ashburton districts, which had hitherto been shut out of the trade by big players who chartered steamers to carry their stock to Fremantle direct. The magnates of the far north, Johnson decided, could make their money by shipping live cattle into Asia. "The people of Java and the Philippines," he declared, "even the coloured races—who have previously subsisted on rice—are now looking for a supply of beef."[64]

Upon his return to Perth, Johnson reported the outcomes of his Nor'-West tour. When he declared that the construction of a freezing facility at Wyndham could not be justified, the Kimberley cattle-breeders were incensed. Frank Connor, whose company held six million acres of prime Kimberley land, shared his thoughts with the readers of *The West Australian*.

> It is generally estimated that works can be erected in Wyndham for £100,000. Now, for the sake of argument, let us double this cost and make it, say, £200,000. At 4 per cent the interest will be £8,000. Now at least 20,000 cattle can be put through these works at a saving of, say, £2 per head, or, to give Mr. Johnson plenty of margin, say £1 per head, £20,000, plus the canning and marketing of another 20,000 head that are rotting on the plains of Kimberley every year because they would not pay to freight here or elsewhere. Why, the whole position is too absurd for words. . . . If Mr. Johnson is right the whole of America and New Zealand are fools, the commercial world is an ass, and Mr. Johnson is the commercial Messiah who will lead the people to the land of promise and cheap meat.[65]

There was never likely to be agreement between Connor and Johnson. The magnate and the minister were glaring at each other across a great ideological divide. The cattle king saw a profitable venture going begging; the minister, with an aversion to doing anything that would increase the wealth of the already wealthy, saw an opportunity to level the playing field and supply the workers of the capital with cheaper meat.

The Kimberley cattle kings were not averse to expanding their live exports into Asia; indeed, it was they who had established the trade, and with very little assistance from government. Already, 1200 head per month were leaving Wyndham for Manila, and shipments to other destinations were being negotiated. And it was Connor who in October 1912 sealed the largest-ever single contract for the supply of live cattle: 23,000 animals to be shipped progressively to Manila.[66] To the press, Connor declared proudly that there were now 13,000 American troops in the Philippines "all fed on Australian beef."

While accepting congratulations, Connor warned that change was inevitable and that the state government needed to be wary. He knew for a fact that Dr John Gilruth,[67] the administrator of the Northern Territory, was negotiating to increase the live cattle trade out of Port Darwin, even offering to establish processing facilities there if a demand of 10,000 head per annum could be guaranteed.[68] If the Territory plan went ahead, Connor hinted, Wyndham could kiss its future good-bye.

Events did not play out exactly as Connor had predicted, but his warning was timely nonetheless. Toward the end of 1913, rumours circulated that British and American interests were seeking to acquire Kimberley cattle runs. January 1914 brought the news that a British firm, the Union Cold Storage Company, had purchased the entire station portfolio of Copley Brothers and Patterson, one of the largest Kimberley landholders. In a single transaction, seven million acres and 140,000 head of cattle changed hands.[69]

It was immediately obvious that business in the far north was to be conducted in new ways and on a different scale. The Union Cold Storage Company, established in 1897 by brothers William and Edmund Vestey, was a pastoral, processing and shipping conglomerate with interests spanning four continents. There were refrigeration and meat processing works in China, Russia and Argentina; agencies and offices in Britain, Europe and Russia; and the Blue Star line of steamships. The purchase of Copley's Kimberley assets was little more than the opening gambit of the company's Australian game. In a few months, it secured further properties and extracted federal government concessions for the establishment of its own processing works at Port Darwin.[70]

When word of a meat works in the adjacent territory reached Perth, *The Sunday Times* launched a blistering attack on the Scaddan government. Under the banner "Good-bye to the Kimberleys" it declared:

> Are we at this moment losing the Kimberleys? According to the very best information the whole of that immense and rich province which forms the northernmost portion of this State is already gone. . . . Port Darwin will become a great tropic port, because the centralisation of the cattle trade will give it the required stimulus to progress. Wyndham, on the other hand, will be suppressed, annihilated. . . . If the State had installed freezing and chilling works at Wyndham two

years ago instead of wasting the money on a State steamer that they are now anxious to sell, the Union Cold Storage Company, which is master of the situation, would probably have fallen in with the channel thus created. If the Government had provided a good supply of water at Wyndham instead of specking in marine derelicts, the chances are that Wyndham would have been saved.[71]

One of the strangest elements of this story is that the Scaddan government did eventually commit to the building of a freezing and canning works at Wyndham. Of course, with an aggressive competitor over the border to the east, the business case was not as strong as it once was, but most believed that a beef-canning business would never fail while the troops of the empire remained at war.

Construction of the Wyndham facility proceeded neither smoothly nor quickly. After a much-publicised falling-out with the firm engaged to build the plant, the government undertook to complete the project itself, using a day-labour workforce.[72] Four years and £600,000 later, the plant commenced full production. The year was 1919 and the armistice had already been signed.

WHEN THE SUNDAY TIMES attacked the Scaddan government for "specking in marine derelicts" rather than providing for the future of Wyndham, it was firing two arrows from the one bow. The newspaper's opinion of the government's entry into the shipping business was well known to its readers, but there was paradox in its choice of illustration. It was the Kimberley pastoralists, in partnership with the residents of Broome, Derby and Wyndham, who in December 1911 had petitioned the government for a state-owned steamship to be placed on the Nor'-West run.

In the beginning, the petition had nothing to do with beef cattle. It related only to the extreme isolation of Derby and Wyndham, and the treatment that residents had from the commercial shipping lines. The petition began:

> We, the undersigned residents of East and West Kimberley, and the North-West, do humbly petition the Government to put into commission a State boat between Fremantle and Wyndham.
> The reasons for making the petition are:—
> (1) That the services as carried out by the steamship companies are not run in the interests of the North-West nor of the State;
> (2) That twice during the past twelve months the residents of Derby and Wyndham have been reduced almost to a state of famine, both as regards supplies for human consumption and fodder for stock, not to mention the inconvenience occasioned by the irregularity of the mails.[73]

The first instance of serious neglect had occurred in December 1910, when a northbound steamer bypassed both Derby and Wyndham and overcarried all pre-Christmas supplies to Singapore. Four months passed before the ship returned. Needless to say, no perishable cargo survived, and little of any value was delivered.

The second instance, in November 1911, related specifically to *Koombana*. The protracted firemen's strike, which delayed the ship's departure from Fremantle by twenty days, affected all towns from Shark Bay to Wyndham. In the tropical heat of the far north, where perishables could only be ordered in small quantities, the situation quickly became serious. Derby and Wyndham ran short of flour, tinned milk, butter, potatoes, and onions. Also long overdue were supplies for the general stores and much-needed fodder.

According to local newspaper reports, the petition was signed by "practically everyone in Derby" and by "every adult person in Broome, with the exception of about six."[74] When the Broome and Derby copies were sent south to the capital, Wyndham's petition was still doing the rounds of the backblocks. By the time it reached the premier's desk in June 1912, the State Steamship Service was already open for business. The government had purchased the 2,900-ton steamer *Darius* and immediately renamed it "Kwinana". To experienced observers, the 24-year-old ship was not the ideal platform for a leap into the competitive world of commercial shipping, but at least a start had been made. Five months later a second vessel, faster and somewhat younger, was purchased. The 2,800-ton *Mongolia*, built in 1901, was renamed "Western Australia."

To manage the steamship service, Colonial Secretary John Drew hired a thirty-year-old former Adelaide Steamship Company accountant, Walter Sudholz. At the outset the new business had neither structure nor procedures; to place it on a secure footing was a daunting assignment. And daunted the new manager would be. By the end of 1912, rumours of bungling and inefficiency were rife. Four months later, the management of the service became a full-blown public embarrassment.

On April 22nd, 1913, *The West Australian* published a long article by a journalist who identified himself only as "Observer".[75] After failing to secure an interview with either the colonial secretary or Walter Sudholz, "Observer" speculated that the true financial position of the steamship service was being concealed, and that losses for the 1912–13 year would far exceed the figure of £6,500 being touted as a reasonable first-year result. After detailing breaches of contracts, instances of undercharging, and damage to lights and jetties for which the service would ultimately be held liable, he predicted that the real working loss for the year would be at least £20,000. In what amounted to a direct challenge, he suggested that the colonial secretary either did not know the financial position or was reluctant to reveal it.

The article brought an immediate and angry response. For a few days, "Observer" and John Drew exchanged claim and counterclaim in letters to *The West Australian*.[76] Significantly, while "Observer" remained detached, Drew became insulting and dismissive, but left the charge of financial mismanagement largely unanswered. The brief exchange generated great public interest, and set the stage for an even more pivotal contribution. In the first week of May 1913, former state parliamentarian Joseph J. Holmes entered the fray, also through the agency of *The West Australian*. Holmes did not attempt any overview of the State Steamship Service; rather, he confined his comments to a single voyage of the *Kwinana* in which he, as shipper of livestock, had a particular interest. He began by making a frank admission.

> Naturally when these steamers were purchased I made it my business to watch their movements very closely, and I found there was useful space available the value of which the Government did not seem to appreciate, and I frankly admit that I stepped into the breach with two objects in view, namely:
> (1) To utilise this space at a profit.
> (2) To show that those who were endeavouring to control these steamers were absolutely incompetent.
> When I relate the following facts I think it will be admitted that I have succeeded on both points.[77]

With precision and panache, Holmes recounted a comedy of errors. His credibility was greatly enhanced by the fact that he was in no way a conscientious objector to the state's entry into the shipping business. He was a moderate supporter who limited his remarks to his own recent dealings with the steamship service, and with manager Walter Sudholz in particular. For John Drew, the Holmes letter was a turning point. He must have realised that the information he had been receiving from his manager was neither complete nor accurate. He acted swiftly and made no effort to conceal the fact that his hand had been forced. He announced the appointment of a royal commission, "to inquire into the allegations made by Mr. J. J. Holmes and published in the 'West Australian' of May 6, and generally into the management of the service." It was possibly the first time ever that a royal commission had been established, declaredly, on the strength of a single letter to the editor of a newspaper.[78]

The royal commission, which commenced in the Fremantle Local Court on June 4th, 1913, was a fiasco. The experienced Joseph Holmes presented his evidence systematically and well, but Walter Sudholz was in difficulty from the start. After struggling through two sessions of cross-examination, Sudholz was warned by Commissioner Alcock that the allegations made against him were serious and that he needed to get his facts together. Next morning, a correspondence clerk from the shipping office came to the court to advise that his manager was too ill to attend. The commission was adjourned. After ten days, Sudholz returned to the witness stand but fared no better. After a request to be excused was denied, he broke down and left the court. A medical certificate, tendered later, indicated that he had suffered a nervous breakdown.[79]

In the course of the next six weeks, Colonial Secretary Drew made three controversial decisions. Sudholz's resignation was expected; the surprising postscript was that the government had agreed to his request to remain in the service as chief accountant. Next came the announcement that the royal commission had been abandoned, and would not be required to submit any report. Drew argued that the manager's resignation had made the inquiry unnecessary. Few agreed; the popular, cynical view was that the colonial secretary, having shed all blame to Sudholz, wanted the matter closed.[80]

Had the government appointed a new manager with sound industry credentials, criticism of its other decisions might have been blunted. It did not; it announced that responsibility for the running of the steamship service would be assumed by the head of the Fremantle Harbour Trust, and not as a full-time commitment but as an additional duty. For the usually respectful *Western Mail*, this was the final insult to intelligence. On Friday, August 29th, 1913, its searing editorial began:

> From first to last the history of the State steamships almost suggests that the Government is bent on a demonstration of how a public enterprise should not be conducted. However this may be, it is certainly a fact that the steamships venture has been characterised by a series of blunders so egregious as to be calculated to wreck any project no matter how intrinsically sound in itself. Every step taken so far has been demonstrably the wrong step, and each act of policy more fatal than its predecessor.[81]

The first full-year financial statements of the State Steamship Service were tabled in parliament on December 16th, 1913. The declared loss for the 1912–13 year was £19,365, very close to the figure that "Observer" had arrived at eight months earlier. Some commentators noted that even this poor result had only been achieved by placing an unrealistically high value on a decrepit fleet, and by underestimating depreciation and outstanding liabilities. One commentator put the true figure at closer to £50,000.[82]

Heavy losses notwithstanding, John Drew never wavered in his defence of the State Steamships initiative. After things had settled a little, he told a reporter from *The West Australian*:

> The Kwinana and the Western Australia were purchased with a two-fold object—first, to assist the producers in the north west of the State; and, second, to reduce the price of meat to the consumers in the metropolitan area. Both objects have been attained. . . . One certain

effect must be the advancement of the pastoral industry, and the utilisation in the near future of vast areas of grazing land not now taken up. The consumer has also benefited materially. The Government opened cash meat stalls at Perth, Fremantle, and Subiaco, reducing the price of meat on the average 3d. per pound. These stalls have been extensively patronised, and have shown a good profit. They have had a wonderful effect in steadying and regulating the price of meat. More than this it is not the desire of the Government to do.[83]

While many admired the Scaddan government's perseverance, lampooning the State Steamship Service remained a popular diversion. In February 1914, one Shark Bay squatter shared his *Kwinana* experience with readers of *The Sunday Times*.

I took the Kwinana for a very good reason—she was the only boat I could take. I booked first saloon and was told nothing about berth accommodation. When I boarded the boat they quietly told me that the berths were full, but after a bit of trouble an official very obligingly arranged a stretcher shake-down for me in the best part of the ship. At least I think it is the best part on ordinary ships, but if it is the best on the Kwinana I should like to see the worst. On the same deck and next door were a mob of sheep being brought down; on the other side was a prisoner condemned to death for murder. So you may judge that pleasant surroundings did not make up for my failure to get a proper berth. That wasn't all. There must have been somewhere in the region of 40 people in the saloon, and in the dining room there were only 16 seats. As there were some seven officers who used to roll down regularly to meals you can judge for yourself how a man would feel who didn't get in the first sitting. The food? It was good and plain food, particularly the latter. During the time I was on the vessel I could never locate the simplest conveniences, so I presume there were none.[84]

Perhaps surprisingly, the institution would have the last laugh. The State Steamship Service would survive war, depression, and many changes of government. It would outlive all of its early advocates and critics. It would win begrudging respect, later loyalty, and even a little affection along the road to an honoured place in the coastal life of Western Australia.

ON APRIL 9TH, 1912, seven days after the fate of *Koombana* was placed beyond doubt, the Adelaide Steamship Company instructed its London agents to arrange for the collection of insurance.[85] *Koombana* had a nominal replacement value of £100,000 and was insured for 75 per cent of that amount.[86] Had replacement been contemplated, the company would certainly have lamented the £25,000 shortfall. But in a climate of pessimism, the loss of the ship was not a financial disaster; indeed, there is a sense in which the disappearance of the ship relieved the company of an intractable problem. Allowing for depreciation, *Koombana*'s insured value and 'book' value were similar. The company was almost certainly satisfied by its insurance settlement; indeed, had an offer of £75,000 been made for the ship in the weeks before her loss, her owners might seriously have considered it.

How quickly conditions had changed. Through 1910, *Koombana* had dominated the Nor'-West trade, with heavy passenger demand in both directions, consistent southbound loadings of wool, cattle and pearl shell, and an invaluable, year-round backload of rails and sleepers for the Pilbara railway. By February 1912, however, all revenue was under threat. The rail work had all but ceased. With drought gripping the wool districts, the company recognised that even its share of the wool trade was at risk. Pastoral conglomerate Dalgety's represented all of the opposition ships, and the word was about that its local agents were demanding shipping loyalty from all those to whom credit had been extended.[87] Cattle-industry prospects were not much better; in a trend unlikely to be reversed, the magnates were chartering their own vessels. And who could say if Broome, the prosperous showpiece of the Nor'-West, was about to be flattened by the White Australia juggernaut?

The greatest uncertainty attached to the state government's entry into the shipping business. At first the commercial operators did not take the move seriously. The popular view was that the government would learn, at great expense to the taxpayer, that the industry was "not all beer and skittles."[88] The expectation was that the venture would fail and that the Nor'-West trade would revert to the familiar two-cornered contest between the Adelaide company and the Singapore line. Only after two state ships had been placed on the run did the commercial operators recognise that their loss of business would not depend to any great extent on whether the government managed its ships well or badly. The coast simply did not provide sufficient revenue to support a third competitor, especially one willing to run its ships at a loss.

For the Adelaide Steamship Company there was an added impost. Its contract for the carriage of Nor'-West mail was due to expire on the last day of February 1913. It seemed inevitable that the next three-year contract would be handed to the State Steamship Service. With a view that can only be described as fatalistic, the company scouted for a vessel well matched to its diminishing prospects, and available for a year of service in the west. It was soon announced that the S.S. *Allinga* would take up *Koombana*'s Nor'-West running.[89]

Allinga, built in 1897, was slow, stuffy and hot, and had a habit of discharging discoloured water from her rusty pipes, but she was perfectly capable of delivering the mail and handling what remained of the company's Nor'-West business. State manager William Moxon did his best to present the replacement in a positive light, but his praise of *Allinga* as "a fine serviceable steamer" was difficult to sustain. Indeed, company secretary P. D. Haggart was probably more amused than troubled by a report he received from marine superintendent James Crossley.

> "Allinga". This steamer I regret to say is not making a good name for herself as far as passengers are concerned. This is due to her speed. The Nor'westers refer to her as the "Lingerer", although the people who do travel by her (and who are not pressed for time) speak well of her.[90]

In a matter of months, the Adelaide Steamship Company saw its market share carved up between competitors. Although *Koombana* had set new standards of luxury and comfort, there was no loyalty that could reasonably be transferred to *Allinga*. Almost overnight, the West Australian Steam Navigation Company's *Minderoo* and the Blue Funnel liner *Gorgon* became the vessels of choice for Nor'-West passengers. Anticipating further decline, the Adelaide Steamship Company brought the smaller, cheaper *Bullarra* home to Port Adelaide for refurbishment.

As anticipated, the Nor'-West mail contract was lost. In the first week of March 1913, the Adelaide Steamship Company announced that *Allinga* would be withdrawn from Nor'-West service. In an interview for *The Western Mail*, William Moxon insisted that the decision should not be put down to 'sour grapes' but to simple commercial reality. The state's vessels, he conceded, had taken a large slice of the trade, and while he felt no rancour, there were unfortunate consequences. None of the commercial operators was doing well enough to offer a better class of ship. There was now no possibility, he said, that "boats of the Koombana type" would be placed on the run.[91]

IT WAS IN THESE HARDER TIMES, in the shadow of misfortune, that the mystique of *Koombana* began to take root. There was a feeling that when *Koombana* vanished, the good times vanished with her. A year after the disaster there were more ships on the Nor'-West run than ever before, but none could compare. All struggling to turn a profit, they seemed unrefined and unkempt. After the outbreak of war, *Koombana* stood yet further apart. She belonged to another time, perhaps to a world that no longer existed. In April 1909, when *Koombana* entered Port Hedland for the first time, Walter Barker had written: "The wildest dreams of residents in this climate, who contemplate a comfortable sea trip, are here realised."[92] That was five years ago. It seemed like ten.

In popular imagination, a paradox became *Koombana*'s pedestal. Considered unlucky and accident-prone in her working life, and unquestionably ill-fated at the last, she would ever after be associated with a brief period of optimism. Conceived in prosperity, she was the product of a business opportunity astutely recognised and firmly grasped: a vision, a challenge, a response, a reward. "The beautiful ill-fated Koombana," Harriet Lenehan called her.[93]

FOR A COUPLE OF YEARS the Adelaide Steamship Company found enough Nor'-West work to keep *Bullarra* busy, but in January 1915 a Japanese firm made an offer for the vessel and a deal was quickly done. After twenty years of coastal service, 'the old Bull' steamed away.[94]

To fill the vacancy, *Allinga* came west again, but she did not linger. War made her attractive; in December 1915 she too was sold away.[95] There was no scramble for a replacement this time, and no announcement to the press. The Adelaide Steamship Company, accepting the inevitability of its Nor'-West demise, quietly withdrew.

17

The Man Behind the Ghost

The dim figure stepped from the shadow into the light which came through the open windows. It was a man, dressed not in the white or khaki of the tropics, but in the flowing robes of a Jewish rabbi, with the traditional small round hat on his head. He stood there in the light for a moment and then, before the bishop could do or say more, disappeared. The apparition did not leave by the door or disappear through the open windows but vanished into thin air there, in the light, under the eyes of Bishop Trower. And so the story of the Bishop's ghost began under the unimpeachable guarantee of a bishop of the Church of England.

"Life and Letters", *The West Australian*, November 26th, 1938.

THIS SINUOUS TALE begins with a death, but not that of Abraham Davis, whose beautiful Broome home Bishop Trower would come to occupy. It begins with the death, on December 12th, 1586, of Stefan Báthory, Grand Duke of Lithuania and elected King of Poland.

Long-serving Stefan had no natural or immediate successor. Custom required that the nobles of the land convene on a prescribed day to choose, from among their ranks, the new king. The election was set down for August 18th, 1587. All knew that this conference would be difficult; support was sharply divided between rival factions and between the principal aspirants: Sigismund III Vasa, son of King John of Sweden, and Maximilian III, Archduke of Austria. On the appointed day negotiations continued late into the evening but, as midnight approached, consensus seemed as far off as ever. Rather than fail to meet their obligations under the law, the nobles accepted a novel proposal: that a much-admired civil servant might fill the regal void. "Saul the Jew," who had long advised the late king and who now assisted the parties in their deliberations, enjoyed such broad respect that the opposing camps voted unanimously to make him *Rex Pro Tempore*, to reign until the political impasse could be broken. According to folklore, the evening ended with toasts of "Long Live our Lord, the King!" in the several languages of the Polish-Lithuanian Commonwealth.[1]

On the following day, the nobles reconvened. Differences were resolved or put aside to reach a verdict: Sigismund would be the next King of Poland. And Saul Katzenellenbogen, whose elevation to royalty had captured the public imagination, became Saul Wahl—"wahl" meaning "chosen" or "anointed" in common parlance.

His unusual duty done, the one-day King of Poland gave back the throne and became a common citizen once again. His rule was brief, but to his children and to their children, his exaltation was permanent and inalienable. Three centuries and a dozen generations later, Woolf Davis, orthodox Jew and president of the East Melbourne Hebrew congregation, determined that his offspring would not break the chain. His son would carry the name "de Vahl" and in his turn claim descent from the Saul of blessed memory.

Abraham de Vahl Davis was born on December 16th, 1863, the sixth of eleven children.[2] The first-born boy, Moses de Vahl, had died in infancy; by that common tragedy, Abraham became the eldest son. At age ten he was sent to the newly established Melbourne Hebrew School. With the support of a successful and tight-knit community, the little school flourished. It opened in 1874 with ninety pupils; by its fourth year it had two hundred. Standards were high. Although the school was formally dissevered from the new state school system, it willingly received the visits of the government inspectors who reported well on its discipline and academic performance. Despite its extended Hebrew curriculum, the school was among the best in the colony in all regular subjects. Indeed, the school's chairman took delight in telling the large gathering at the third annual prize-giving that, in public English examinations, the school had achieved a pass rate of 90 per cent, compared to averages of 58 per cent in Victoria and 70 per cent in England herself![3]

Support from the Melbourne business community extended to having the names of all prize recipients published in *The Argus*. Woolf and Rachel Davis must have been pleased to see their bright children listed and lauded, especially young Abraham who consistently took prizes for Hebrew and Hebrew translation. For the most part, the prizes consisted of "handsome books, the gifts . . . of gentlemen who take a deep interest in the institution,"[4] but there were also cash incentives that spoke clearly of this community's commitment to education. In 1877, the first student to matriculate received a purse of ten guineas—a huge sum, equivalent to several weeks of adult wages.[5]

If Woolf Davis had hoped that Abraham would follow in his footsteps and affirm both faith and lineage, he could not have been disappointed. In 1894 Abraham married Cecily Altson and a year later the couple produced a son. Like his father, Abraham named his first-born boy Moses de Vahl but the child, like his namesake, succumbed in the first year of life. As was the case for Woolf and Rachel, Abraham and Cecily suffered the loss of an infant only once. Their later children enjoyed good health and the next-born boy, Gerald de Vahl, became the eldest son exactly as his father had done. By 1899, Abraham had further emulated his father by becoming president of the East Melbourne Hebrew congregation.

The title was the same but the world had changed since his father had accepted the position. In Melbourne, the Jewish community was well established and respected, but its members were keenly aware of rising anti-Semitism in Europe. Perhaps more than any other segment of the Australian community, Australian Jews maintained a keen and careful interest in world affairs. They read, listened and watched for any change of demeanour toward their race.

In the last years of the nineteenth century, one event more than any other sharpened that particular consciousness. When French Army counter-intelligence became aware that artillery information was being passed to the Germans, suspicion fell on Captain Albert Dreyfus, a rich Alsatian Jew; he was arrested for treason in October 1894. Three months later, largely upon the evidence of a handwriting expert, Dreyfus was convicted in closed court martial and sentenced to life imprisonment on Devil's Island in French Guiana.[6]

Before his departure, Dreyfus was paraded before his former comrades and formally stripped of all rank. In an almost theatrical display, buttons and epaulettes were torn from his uniform and his sword broken in two. Both had been specially prepared for the occasion: the buttons and epaulettes had been removed and lightly resewn, and the ceremonial sword cut in two and rejoined with solder.[7]

At the time of his formal *dégradation*, the officers responsible for Dreyfus's conviction genuinely believed that he was guilty, but by the end of 1896 they must have suspected his innocence. When Dreyfus's former commanding officer Lieutenant Colonel Picquart became the new Director of Espionage, he uncovered evidence that the crime had been perpetrated not by Dreyfus but by one Ferdinand Esterhazy. Picquart's revelations were not welcomed by his superiors; for his audacity, he was transferred to a desert post in southern Tunisia.[8]

Rather than disgrace themselves and the French Army, senior officers closed ranks. Over three years they committed perjury, forged documents and silenced opposition. And in a desperate bid to mollify a deeply suspicious public, they placed Esterhazy on trial—and engineered his acquittal.[9]

If the *faux* trial of Esterhazy was contrived to bring closure, it failed; indeed, its effect was precisely the opposite of that intended. It now seemed beyond doubt that officers of the highest rank were protecting a man whom they knew to be guilty of espionage. Two days after the acquittal, French magazine *L'Aurore* (*The Dawn*) published an article that must rank among the most influential of all time. "*J'Accuse…!*" was an open letter from acclaimed novelist Émile Zola to the president of the republic; it accused no less than five generals of complicity in a gross miscarriage of justice.[10] Zola concluded:

> In making these accusations I am aware that I am making myself liable to articles 30 and 31 of the law of 29/7/1881 regarding the press, which makes libel a punishable offence. I expose myself to that risk voluntarily.
>
> As for the people I am accusing, I do not know them, I have never seen them, and I bear them neither ill will nor hatred. To me they are mere entities, agents of harm to society. The action I am taking is no more than a radical measure to hasten the explosion of truth and justice.
>
> I have but one passion: to enlighten those who have been kept in the dark, in the name of humanity which has suffered so much and is entitled to happiness. My fiery protest is simply the cry of my very soul. Let them dare, then, to bring me before a court of law and let the inquiry take place in broad daylight! I am waiting.
> With my deepest respect, Sir.
> Émile Zola, 13th January 1898[11]

The reaction to *J'Accuse...!* was instant and electric. France had never been so suddenly or sharply polarised. When Zola was arrested and charged with criminal libel, supporters and detractors clashed outside the court. But the tide had turned; neither condemnation nor conviction could undo the work of the pen. Zola had bluntly declared that the persecution

"J'Accuse...!" published in L'Aurore, *January 13th, 1898.*

of Albert Dreyfus was, at its heart, anti-Semitic. Dreyfus, he insisted, had fallen not to common or accidental misfortune but to *la chasse aux «sales juifs», qui déshonore notre époque*: the 'dirty Jew' obsession that is the scourge of our time.

Zola's letter became a rallying cry for Jewish communities around the world and the East Melbourne congregation was no exception. When a retrial was granted in late 1899, Abraham Davis sent a formal letter of support to Dreyfus.

> Dear Sir,—I desire, on behalf of the members of the East Melbourne congregation, to extend to you the assurance of our deepest sympathy with you in the unexampled distress which you have undergone, and of our sincere admiration of the fortitude which you have displayed throughout the agonizing experience of the past five years. I would couple with these expressions toward you the further assurance that the members of this congregation, in common with the vast majority of the people in Australia, have been thrilled with admiration at the heroism and devotion of your wife, to whose fearless championship, no doubt, the granting of a re-trial is due . . .[12]

When the new court martial commenced on August 7th, 1899, most Dreyfus supporters believed that acquittal was a foregone conclusion. It was not. To a new chorus of astonishment and outrage, he was reconvicted. But Dreyfus would not long remain in prison. Hundreds of French and foreign correspondents had come to Rennes in Brittany for the trial. They had followed this story for five years, from Paris to French Guiana and back; they understood that it was no longer about the martyrdom of one man. In their despatches, they openly canvassed the greater danger: that France, deeply divided, risked descent into chaos if it could not break the obduracy of its military elite. With all eyes upon it, the French government overturned the conviction and released the prisoner.[13]

Another five years would pass before the grace of the state extended to exoneration. In July 1906, in the space of a few weeks, Albert Dreyfus was declared innocent, readmitted to the army with high rank, given new command and made *Chevalier de la Légion d'honneur*. Justice was seen to be done.

A YEAR AFTER ABRAHAM MARRIED CECILY ALTSON, his younger sister Rebecca married a determined young businessman named Mark Rubin. The young husbands could scarcely have been more different, but Rebecca's choice of partner would have a life-changing impact upon Abraham also.

Rubin was a Lithuanian immigrant who arrived in Australia in 1886, with very little English and even less money. In Melbourne, he found what work he could. After a stint as a wharf labourer, he started a small business; for a time, he hawked haberdashery from a barrow. His round soon extended into country Victoria, but his restless pursuit of success would take him further still: to the opal fields at White Cliffs in the far north-western corner of New South Wales. For a few years Rubin mined and traded the raw stone, but increasingly he turned his hand and mind to the polishing and presentation of the unique gem. By the time he became engaged to Rebecca, he could fairly call himself a jeweller.[14]

But Mark Rubin was not destined to make his fortune from opal; that would come from an opportunity yet more distant. According to folklore, Rubin discovered Broome and its mother-of-pearl by paying close attention to the seasonal travels of a competitor. The story may be fanciful[15] but the profitability of his new calling was not; in the early days, the pearl-shellers of the remote Nor'-West often returned from their forays with shell and pearls worth far more than the boat.

Rubin's rise to prominence in Western Australia was truly spectacular. By 1902 he needed a business partner to buy in Broome what he now knew that he could sell in London. A close, confidential relationship was imperative, and his articulate brother-in-law emerged as the logical choice.

In the early years of the Rubin–Davis partnership, the demarcation of roles was not so clear. Both were learning the business, and both spent time in England and in the warehouses and gem-houses of Europe. When Abraham departed for London in 1904, his wife accompanied him, but she did not make the journey merely to support her husband. Cecily, it seems, had business of her own to attend to and, like Abraham, was building a reputation for unusual expertise.

Cheapside House,
Chiltern, August 10th, 1904.
Dear Madame,

We desire to intimate that Madame Cecily E. Davis, the accredited representative of Weingarten Bros., of New York, makers of the celebrated "W.B." Erect Form Corsets, will give a demonstration of the great utility and suitability of the various models of these Corsets for the different figures.

Madame Davis, the great corset expert, will be in attendance at our establishment from August 15th to 20th (both dates inclusive), with the object of fitting the celebrated American "W.B." La Vida Corsets. We suggest that it is desirable to give us a call during Madame's visit, even if not wanting corsets at present, so that the number or design suitable for your figure may be registered in our books for future reference.

No charge for fitting.

The celebrated "W.B." Corsets are 7s 11d, 10s 6d, 12s 6d, 20s, up to 50s. Do not miss this opportunity of a life time, as Madame's visit cannot possibly be extended beyond the above mentioned dates.

Requesting the favor of a visit.
I am, Yours respectfully,
H. DENNY.[16]

Cecily's choice of business did not sit well with Abraham, especially when, after their return to Australia, she announced that she would not return immediately to Broome. Instead, she would continue selling corsets as a travelling saleswoman. Reluctantly, Abraham accepted the seasonal separation and returned to his own pressing work.

Winter months in Broome were busy. Rubin rarely visited now; he was fully engaged in London and Europe and left his partner to do the buying and to manage boats and men. The latter was no small task: Rubin's fleet grew to thirty luggers and five schooners, and Abraham bought into other operations on his own account, becoming part-owner of *Moa*, *Mozel*, *Princess Mary* and *Experience*.[17]

The routine was hard, but Abraham enjoyed the life that pearls made possible. A little south of the town centre he built a graceful, wide-verandahed bungalow overlooking Roebuck Bay. The house, which he named "De Vahl," welcomed many visitors. At different times it was a place of business and a retreat from business. For Broome's little Jewish community it became their Saturday synagogue, with Davis as part-time rabbi. And when Abraham's sixteen-year-old daughter Dorothy came to stay, the house was thrown open for a party favourably reviewed by the *Broome Chronicle*:

> Cards of invitation were issued by Mr. and Miss Davis for an At Home at their residence "De Vahl," on the 24th June, and proved quite a social success. Guests were received by Mr. and Miss Davis from 8 to 8.30 at the main entrance of their beautiful home, and dancing was soon in full swing. The card tables were also well attended. An innovation was two Limericks, and a guessing competition, for which prizes were given, and these were all won by visitors from south. In the programme of twelve dances were included two leap year dances and a slipper dance, which proved quite successful. Dancing was kept up until about 1.30, and the wide verandah around the house which made an excellent ballroom, was taxed to the utmost by the numerous visitors, who voted it a very smart affair.[18]

Cecily Davis returned to Broome in the winter of 1907, but not even the most beautiful home in the town would keep her there. The climate, she insisted, was affecting her health. At the end of the pearling season, Abraham accompanied his wife to Melbourne, where the advice of several doctors was sought. Once again he returned to Broome alone. A few weeks later, he received a letter from Cecily. She had, "for the sake of her health," departed for South Africa with her brother.

"De Vahl" in the good times.

The year 1908 was the most profitable ever, but Rubin and Davis were keenly aware of two potential threats to their business. They understood that growing unrest in Europe could change the commercial landscape, and change it quickly. They also recognised that their industry, so dependent upon indentured coloured labour, could be destroyed by new legislation enacted to keep Australia white. As support for the elimination of coloured labour grew, Davis became increasingly exasperated by what he saw as ill-informed, xenophobic commentary, especially from the neighbouring town to the south. In its editorial of January 16th, 1909, *The Hedland Advocate* had declared:

> It is becoming plainly apparent that the Chinese and Japanese are now entering the northern ports of Australia in hordes . . . White men cannot compete with them in business and they are driving the workers out from every avenue of employment. At the present time there are fully 50 colored men walking about Broome emaculately dressed, each man displaying six sovereigns on his coat as buttons, while numbers of white men are reduced to begging for a feed. And this in a "White Australia"![19]

Under the rules governing indentured foreign labour, men were engaged for the business of pearling only. Although they spent time ashore, they were not permitted to work ashore except in the handling of shell and the maintenance of boats and equipment. The *Advocate*'s editor Walter Barker now alleged that the regulations were being openly flouted and that the coloured men were working as carpenters and waiters, taking work from whites. "It is here," Barker wrote, "where the shoe pinches for the true Australian."[20]

These indignant outpourings might have withered on a provincial vine, had they not been picked up and reprinted by a Sunday magazine in the capital. To Abraham, travelling south to catch a steamer for Melbourne, it was particularly galling that unsupported allegations of corruption in Broome were, through the agency of Perth's *Truth*, now reaching a wider audience. After arriving in Fremantle, he called at the newspaper's office and declared that he would like an opportunity to present an alternative view. *Truth* agreed to his request for an interview and, a few days later, gave space and prominence to his comments.[21]

Davis began with an explanation of the indenture system.

> The process of engaging and deporting men is of interest to you, as you have committed yourself to the adoption of the article in the Port Hedland paper, and I will tell you just what we have needed to do to get men—and to get rid of them.
>
> When we want a man or a number of men we have to apply to the collector for a permit to engage him or them in Singapore. We have to say why we want the men, and what have become of those they are intended to replace. I have a man die—they do, a big percentage of the divers, from paralysis—and I must get another. I report to the collector, who wires the department in Melbourne detailing the circumstances and asking that I have permission to obtain the help I require. He recommends the application, and in the course of a few days the reply comes that it is granted. Then I instruct our agents in Singapore to give me the class of man I want.
>
> The cost of getting a man is about £14. There are a good many charges; first the medical certificate, then the fare, then, probably in advance, the agent's fees, and incidentals. Perhaps the man, after he is engaged and passed by the doctor, goes on a final razzle the night before he ships to come to us, and when he arrives is found to be unfit for work as a consequence of the night out with the boys—and girls. Then we have to send him back at our cost; first, because he is no use to us; and next, because the collector will not allow him to land. These men are indentured for three years, and with each application we have to put up a bond of £100 that we will keep to our contract, hold the man while he is in our employ, and when the term of his engagement is up either renew it or deport him. It was also said that it is the practice of masters to send time-expired men out on a lugger a little way, bring them back at night when the collector is in bed, and put them to work again. This is incorrect, and nonsense anyhow.
>
> It is as serious and formal a business to get rid of a man as to get him. The collector has a complete list of all on the boats, with their

photographs, descriptions, and finger prints, and, more than that, he knows most of them. When the time is up we have to get his ticket and inform the shipping-master of his desire to leave for his home. The first question asked is as to his ticket. Then the man is interrogated, and it must be made quite clear to the officials that he is satisfied and willing to go. Everything being in order, the collector takes the tickets and, the day the steamer is to call, has all the boys lined up and marched aboard. They are tallied off in the presence of the captain and the purser and handed over, then, to the ship. The collector sees them aboard, and does not leave till the gang-plank is hauled in.

Having argued that the rules were well understood and usually complied with, Davis added:

The idea that the colored labor of the port is of the cheap kind is another mistake. We cannot indent men for domestic service, and have not got them. There are none of the comforts of tropical India in the Nor'-West—no cheap nigger with a fan to brush the flies off his master, no punkah-wallah to keep the air moving when he wants to rest. No, nothing of that kind, of which you may have read in books.

Uncharacteristically, *Truth* stepped aside from sensationalism to present a wide-ranging commentary. Davis continued:

There appears to be an idea in the public mind, and the newspapers do not do anything in the way of removing it, that the Nor'-West—and Broome particularly—is one of the God-forgotten corners of the Commonwealth; that the pearlers are a kind of slave-driving Legrees, and the divers and deck hands on the boats are treated as the slaves were in the days prior to the abolition. Which is all just so much plain bunkum. The white men, to the number of a couple of hundred, engaged in the industry are the equal in every way of a similar body of white men in any part of the world. There are in the waters of the coast some 2000 men employed, and the fact that the place is regarded as the paradise of the policeman may be mentioned against repeated stories of riot or revolt and running amok and raising hell generally. Now and again there is trouble, in the case, perhaps of a diver going ashore, getting too much drink and into a row in the Japanese quarter. There are a number of Japs and Chinese there; but they are mostly citizens of long standing, who claim to be Englishmen and hold the colored men in a good deal of contempt. There are Japanese women there, just as there are on the goldfields of the State; and I do not know that it is not a good thing that for the few white women in the country they are there. But all the places are under the supervision of the police and the authorities, and the town is quite as law-and-order-loving in its general arrangements as any place in the State.

Like most of the Broome pearlers, Davis was adamant that his industry would not survive any indiscriminate prohibition of coloured labor. He did not waste the opportunity to make his point, although he may have regretted his choice of words.

> As to working the trade with white labor, it is impossible. In the first place you would not get white men to do the work and live the life under the only conditions in which there would be a possibility of carrying on at a profit. If we were to advertise for white men to take the places of the colored men on the luggers we would not get a hundred. We lose a large number from diver's paralysis, and I suppose it is no harm to say, in such a "white" office as that of "Truth", that it is preferable for black men to be sent to this deadly work than for the white man to be offered up on the altar of Mammon.

The following year, Broome's pearlers received clear indication that their opinions would not prevail. The federal government declared that after 1913, the use of indentured coloured labour would not be tolerated. Reactions to the edict varied greatly.[22] Some shrugged their shoulders and declared that they would "go for their lives for three years and then chuck it." Others gambled that a white diving regime would prove so difficult to implement that the deadline would inevitably be pushed back. Larger operations had the most to lose. Among the master pearlers, Hugh Richardson, Hugh Norman and Sydney Pigott began to consider seriously the possibility of training white divers. Mark Rubin and Abraham Davis did not; they began diversifying, swapping pearling investments for pastoral land in a well-informed shift from luxuries to necessities.

BY THE BEGINNING OF 1910, Abraham Davis was recognised as the pre-eminent pearl buyer on the Western Australian coast. Although well known and respected in both Broome and Melbourne, he was increasingly troubled by the rigour and dislocation of his divided life. Letters of remonstration to Cecily in South Africa remained unanswered, and since her departure, their son Gerald had gone to live in Sydney with Abraham's sister and her husband, Reverend Phillip Phillipstein. For two years, he had seen his boy only briefly, during summer holidays. From *Koombana* on April 4th, with Gerald's thirteenth birthday only a few days away, he wrote:

My darling son,
    I am writing these lines to reach you on your Bar Mitzvah. I am unable unfortunately, to be with you on the happy occasion, and I think you will understand how deeply I regret this. But my sincerest prayers will be offered to God, on that day, that He may crown you with His choicest gifts: a good heart, and a good name. To achieve

these, you have but to follow humbly the Law which God gave to our ancestors in the olden days. Love and fear Him : fear and love Him. Commit all your thoughts to Him who alone is a true guide : meet all your troubles and pain with courage and contentment : for none can escape these, and only those can endure them who recognize that our Father in Heaven tries us, and in the end will reward our trust and faith. Be brave and true, my dear lad, in all your actions : do not soil your thoughts with aught unclean, nor your hands with any base acts. Be true & loyal to the faith of our fathers : to the race to which we belong. Do all your work with goodwill, earnestness, and sincerity; be gentle to all : kind and helpful to the aged, poor or suffering. Do not let selfishness or self indulgence claim you, but let justice be your watchword in all you do.

And I pray that the Grace of our Heavenly Father be with you; and that you may grow, from strength to strength in works of goodness, charity and truth. God be with you, my darling boy, and bless you throughout all your days! Amen and Amen!

Your loving father,
Abraham Davis.[23]

Read in isolation, this letter may seem austere and impersonal, but two weeks later Abraham wrote to Gerald again, delivering a fond embrace to complement the firm, fatherly handshake.

My darling old laddie,

I suppose you are in a state of joyful excitement on account of your approaching Bar Mitzvah which, P.G., you are to celebrate in a few days. I only wish I could have been with you, and shared in your happiness, but of course we must all do our duty first of all, even if we personally suffer by it. Well, dear, I am quite sure that you will acquit yourself worthily: and I am proud and thankful that God has blessed me with a good and faithful sonnie, who will do his level best to do all that becomes a Jew.

I hope you have settled down to good steady work at school & now that your barmitzvah is practically accomplished I want you to go in for music, carpentry, physical exercise, drawing (also chocolate eating). I need not tell you once again to be watchful to help Aunty & Uncle in every way & not to make their labour of love in looking after you any greater by want of consideration. I hope Auntie Min is a stringent Comptroller of your Exchequer, and that when I come next year (P.G.) to Sydney, you will have a huge accumulation of gelt to add to your deposit of £20/–/– in Melbourne Savings Bank. . . .

I trust your military ardour is as hot as ever, & that you will lead your gallant men with frantic signals right into the very jaws of the tuckshop!

Abraham Davis with his son Gerald, c. 1911.

Write and let me know all you have been doing since I left. Don't send me such tiny scraps of letters, or I shall be compelled to double your income.

I am very busy this week, dear old boy, so will now conclude.

Praying God's blessing on you, now and for ever more.

Your loving father.[24]

Pressure of work did not normally permit any departure from Broome during the winter, but in the last week of May 1911, just a few weeks into the new pearling season, Davis boarded the *Paroo* for Fremantle and after spending a few days in Perth, continued to Melbourne by the *Kanowna*. It appears that the principal purpose of this trip was to initiate divorce proceedings against Cecily. By July, Davis was back in Broome, but his mind was elsewhere. Private investigator Leonard McCallum had traced Cecily and a man named Jack Hattrick to a boarding house in Sydney, and court proceedings were set down to commence in November.[25] On October 21st, the following advertisement appeared in the *Broome Chronicle*:

> For Private Sale.
> In lots to suit purchasers.
> ON ACCOUNT OF MR. A DAVIS.
> The whole of his FURNITURE, PICTURES, GLASSWARE, &c.,
> now at his residence "De Vahl."
> Intending purchasers can make appointments with the undersigned
> to inspect at convenient time.
> J. J. Taylor, Commission Agent, etc.
> Dampier Terrace.
> Telephone 73.[26]

A week later, the same newspaper delivered a discreet message of support to a well-liked and respected member of the Broome community.

> Bon Voyage.—Among the passengers on the Charon is Mr. A. Davis (of M. Rubin) who is taking a trip to the Old Country, on a health restoring cruise. We join with his many friends in wishing Mr. Davis a pleasant and beneficial trip and that he will return in his usual buoyant spirit.[27]

It was not simple recuperation that led Abraham to leave for London. He had determined to be far away when his private affairs went on public display. To gain a divorce on the grounds of misconduct, Cecily's misdemeanours would be presented in court; he had little doubt that they would also be served up to a salacious public. When the case commenced a few weeks later, daily newspapers across the country offered a running commentary. In Melbourne, *The Argus* was particularly attentive.

> Mr. Woolf said that in 1901, after prior disagreements, the husband and wife became reconciled. The petitioner went to England on business, and returned in 1903. There were further disagreements and reconciliations. In 1905 or 1906, the parties went to live in lodgings in Western Australia, where petitioner found certain letters secreted, and taxed his wife with the question, "Do you swear before our child's grave and your living parents that you are innocent?" Respondent said she was innocent, and petitioner gave her the benefit of the doubt. Marital relations were resumed. Petitioner submitted the letters to a lawyer and was informed that, while they showed indiscretion, they did not establish proof of misconduct. In 1908, petitioner brought his wife to Melbourne for medical advice, and afterwards himself returned to Western Australia. A little later respondent wrote and told petitioner that she was advised to take a trip to South Africa for her health's sake. Respondent, in spite of her husband's protests, left for South Africa with her brother, who was on a trip to Australia. On

March 3 petitioner wrote to his wife to Africa, remonstrating with her for her disobedience. Respondent remained away for two years, until 1910, and, except for two letters, never communicated with her husband or children. In the meantime petitioner took other advice, and was told that references in the letters to "torrid kisses," double beds, the communication of the respondent's bedroom number to the co-respondent could only mean one thing.

Petitioner allowed his wife £6 a week, with an extra allowance for the children. When respondent arrived in Melbourne in 1910, a letter was handed her from her husband, asking who "Sandy" was and other pertinent questions relating to the man, the author of the compromising letters to the respondent. The daughter had gone away to her mother, but the boy had remained with his father. Respondent went to live with her daughter at Pott's Point, Sydney, and passed herself off as a widow and her daughter as her niece, and also accounted for Hattrick's presence by saying he was her business manager. On finding out about the real state of affairs, Mrs. Fuller, who kept the boarding house at Pott's Point, asked them to leave. From there they went to the Wentworth Hotel, and afterwards to North Sydney, where the pair were now living under the same roof. In 1911 it had been ascertained that Hattrick paid a number of cheques into Cecilie E. Davis's banking account. In 1905 the respondent, against her husband's wishes, went travelling with corsets for Sargood's, and the co-respondent first saw respondent in a train, and fell in love with her at first sight "in spite of the powder on her face," and not long after there was a question in a letter from co-respondent, asking respondent if she got the note he left for her in the toe of her shoe the morning she left Ararat.[28]

Public interest might have faded rapidly, had Cecily and her long-time lover not refused to answer some delicate questions. Their reticence did not alter the outcome, but the referral of legal questions to a higher court delayed the decision and kept newspaper hounds on the scent. In December 1911, a decree nisi was granted on the grounds of both desertion and misconduct. Jack Hattrick was ordered to pay costs.[29]

ON MARCH 8TH, 1912, Abraham Davis boarded *Koombana* at Fremantle for the run north to Broome. While the ship offered ten days of relaxation and indulgence to other Broome-bound passengers, Abraham and his newly hired assistant John Evans had appointments to keep. At Shark Bay, Cossack and Port Hedland, there were pearls to be viewed and possibly purchased in a series of rapid-fire meetings with sellers and agents.[30] After an overnight stay in Port Hedland, the whistle-stop trading was done. At 10.30 a.m. on Wednesday, March 20th, 1912, *Koombana* slid over the bar on the morning high tide and continued north.

Of the great storm that claimed *Koombana*, much has been written. When *Gorgon*, southbound from Singapore, made the discovery that ended all hope, Broome was cast into a limbo between sadness and disbelief. Hugo and Gilbert Harper had lost their brother George; Syd Pigott his wife and two stepdaughters. Captain Stuart, Abe Davis and George Simpson were gone, as were Mr Milne and all of the Public Works men bound for Derby. Many were shocked to learn that James Davis, who had travelled to Fremantle to welcome the English divers, was also among the missing. He had arrived home safely by *Paroo*, but had found it necessary to return to Port Hedland on business.[31]

For Jim Low and Jock McDonald, ex-*Koombana* engineers now established in Broome, the loss was cause for the broadest lament: for Broome acquaintances lost, for a fine ship in which they had sailed together from Glasgow, and for fellow officers and crewmen who had remained with her to the end. In a letter to his sister Jane back home, Jim wondered:

> Did the London papers not get mixed up in the two men of the name of Davis that went down with the "Koombana", Siebe Gorman's representative and Abe Davis the great pearl buyer and expert of the firm Rubin Davis of London & Broome, the finest speaker I think I ever heard, witty and to the point. A very strict Jew he was, so strict that his wife and daughter jibbed and cleared . . .[32]

After the divorce proceedings, Abraham had prepared a new will, naming his business partner and brother-in-law Mark Rubin as his executor. But when Abraham was lost at sea with *Koombana*, the signed, witnessed copy of his new will was lost with him. Fortunately, a Melbourne solicitor held a draft of the document and was in a position to swear both to its authenticity and to its recent execution. In a brief Supreme Court hearing, probate was granted.[33] That should have cleared the way for the estate to be settled in a dignified way, but the chronicle of Davis v. Davis was not quite done. There was a late surprise for the court and a final twist for avid readers of the divorce columns. Cecily, who had for years pursued her separate life with Jack Hattrick, applied to the court to have the decree dissolving her marriage to Abraham set aside, on the grounds that he had died before the date on which the decree was to become absolute.

If the return to court was remarkable for its apparent cynicism, it was also enlivened by the unresolved mystery of *Koombana*. The *Sydney Morning Herald* revived the story under the banner: "A Melbourne Divorce. Remarkable Position. Is the Petitioner Alive?"

> The matter came before Mr. Justice Cussen in the Practice Court when Mr. McFarlane appeared to support the application, and Mr. Hogan to oppose . . .
> Mr. Hogan: I appear for the petitioner.
> Mr. Macfarlane: We say there is no petitioner.

Mr. Hogan: I appear for the representatives of the petitioner, and ask for an adjournment. We do not know where he is. He may not be dead. If so, I appear for his executors.

Mr. Justice Cussen held that Hogan appeared for the executors of Davis, and adjourned the matter till Thursday.[34]

It is not known what communication passed between the parties over the next few days, or what pressure was brought to bear. When the matter returned to court, solicitor Hogan requested that the summons be dismissed without costs. The executors, he said, had gained the consent of the applicant. Cecily Davis did not appear.[35]

THE ESTATE OF ABRAHAM DE VAHL DAVIS took many years to settle. There were formal partnerships to be dissolved and informal arrangements to be understood. Abraham had entered into partnerships not only with his brother-in-law, but also with friend Maurice Aarons, who lost his life in battle at Gallipoli in August 1915.[36] Matters were further complicated by the fact that Abraham's will granted unusual discretion to the executor, Mark Rubin, who conducted business using funds from the unfinalised estate for several years after Abraham's death.[37] Finally, in February 1922, newspaper advertisements declared a final date for the registration of any outstanding claim against the estate.

By then, Broome was a very different place. The town had lost its prosperity to a decade of global tumult, and much of its cosmopolitan vibrancy to the politics of a young, headstrong nation. The beautiful bungalow overlooking Roebuck Bay remained, but it was no longer "De Vahl"; it had become the residence of Gerard Trower, the first Anglican Bishop of the North-West. And when the bishop reported waking to see a white figure in a pool of light, his experience was embraced by long-time townsfolk who willingly cast back to better days. The visitor, they surmised, was the ghost of Abraham Davis, the great pearl buyer lost with *Koombana*, roaming his former home in rabbinical robes, searching for a lost fortune in pearls.[38]

How perverse!—that an articulate man, of culture and conviction, should be remembered not for his accomplishment but for a much-publicised divorce, an untimely death, and for bizarre, stereotypical appearances in the afterlife.

But all is not lost. From life and letters, by careful assemblage, the man may be remade. Lest we *imagine*.

18

Mythical Beauty

IF WE ARE TO BELIEVE Australian writer Ion "Jack" Idriess, the pearl buyer Abraham de Vahl Davis, visiting Port Hedland on Tuesday, March 19th, 1912, purchased a pearl like no other. Placed before him by a pearler recently arrived from Cossack was a 'perfect round' 65 grains in weight, of soft rosae tint and deep oriental lustre. It was not the largest pearl ever found in the Nor'-West, but perhaps the most exquisite. Idriess insists that Davis acted in good faith, unaware that the pearl had been seven years from the sea, that it had been an object of obsession, and that several men had met their deaths because of it.

Jack Idriess was a traveller. He moved among his readers and never tired of matching his subjects to their interests. His stories—Australian tales of adventure for the most part—read easily and sold extremely well. But for determined disentanglers of fact and fiction, his work poses many problems. Idriess was both a collector and manufacturer of folklore: a careful weaver who judged well what his readers would accept and embrace. His personal paragon was that special, seductive tale, capable of sliding mistress-like into the minds of men, to be coveted, possessed, adorned and ultimately taken for granted.

The tale of the roseate pearl is just such a temptress. The present challenge is to inquire after the truth, leaving as much of the mystique as may survive the interrogation.

JACK IDRIESS first stepped onto the Broome jetty on December 23rd, 1933. He remained in the town for the summer lay-up, gathering material for what he called his "pearl book."[1] It has always been imagined that the tale of the roseate pearl, which became the backbone of *Forty Fathoms Deep*, was stitched together during this time from the recollections of the town's long-time residents. Indeed, the tale was brought to light in just such a fashion, but not by Jack Idriess. Three years earlier, the Sydney-based journalist Ernestine Hill had found her way to the port of pearls and had done well to keep the locals talking. Of one prized informant she wrote:

> With a world of romance and adventure at his fingertips, it was his pet vanity to avoid writing and writers, determined that "what I know will die with me" but, typically Irish, by a cautious stratagem of contradiction, mild and polite, he could be made to talk.[2]

One product of Ernestine Hill's Nor'-West adventure was a titillation piece published by Sydney newspaper *The Sun* in 1932. Under the banner "Grim Tales Of The Pearl Game, Where Greed Laughs At Murder,"[3] Hill wrote:

> In 1904 there happened in Broome the Liebglid pearl murder, surely the strangest story ever told in a strange history, in which four men were sent to their deaths for a pearl that not one of them had seen.
>
> On the fishing-grounds out from the Eighty-Mile Beach a Swedish pearler of that time found a pearl in his first year out. In amateurish delight he made for the nearest white man to celebrate his prize, a lugger owned by one Lilley, in company with Victor Nabos, a shrewd Manila diver.
>
> Glass after glass of squareface was raised to the luck of the new beauty, and, when the Swede pulled off, practically incapable, in his dinghy, it was a bit of baroque that rattled reassuringly in his treasured tin matchbox. The pearl remained behind with Nabos who, for safe hiding, on his next night watch, wound it round and round in a strand of rope near the tiller. When Nabos returned to Broome the pearl had gone, but he was arrested and served a term of imprisonment for stealing it.
>
> It was then that Liebglid, a Jewish traveller in gimcrack jewellery, in reality a buyer of snides, heard of the missing pearl, offered £500 for it, and became the eager, credulous prey of Pablo, a Manilaman; Simeon, a Patagonian sailor of gorilla strength; and Charlie Hagen, a Scandinavian of sorts, barber, and saloon-keeper.
>
> Clandestine meetings on the sandhills and the dark jetty, in which the glass marble stopper of a lemonade bottle masqueraded as the pearl, and Liebglid was killed by a slingshot in a cabin of the derelict schooner Mist, lying opposite Broome, his mangled body left by the tide in the mangroves. Mystery surrounded the murder until, through the influences of a priest in the confessional who refused absolution till the crime was disclosed, the Manilaman turned King's evidence, and the three murderers were hanged.

Here in broad outline was the foundation upon which Jack Idriess would build *Forty Fathoms Deep*. Throughout his writing life Idriess travelled to remote places, ever determined to be more than a "main roads explorer." It now appears that he discovered this story without leaving his home in suburban Sydney. Other anecdotes from "Grim Tales" also found their way into Jack's pearl book; indeed, Hill's piece was full of little nuggets of the kind that Idriess travelled in search of, and built his career upon.[4]

THAT THE PEARL WAS STOLEN on the day of its discovery is beyond doubt. Indeed, the events surrounding the find are very much as Ernestine Hill recorded them. A beautiful round pearl was fished by the lugger *Cleopatra* in waters off Wallal on June 17th, 1905.[5] The shell was gathered by the boat's Swiss diver, Silber Gala, one of the few Europeans making a living in that dangerous game. It was Augustine, Gala's tender, who opened the shell and discovered the pearl. He immediately passed it to Gala, as if to acknowledge him as the natural custodian.

In a sense the find was a lucky one for *Cleopatra*'s part-owner and master, Gustav Ulbricht. The boat was new and this was Ulbricht's first season in Nor'-West waters. But it is not quite fair to assert that Ulbricht bubbled with naive excitement and rushed off to the nearest boat to show his prize. Ulbricht and Gala did, however, row across to the schooner *Alto*, to show the pearl to Captain Franck and to have it weighed.[6]

In Jack Idriess's version of events, the more experienced master was greatly impressed by what was handed to him.

> He examined the pearl with the love that pearlers lavish on these gems of the sea. He had never had the luck to win one like this himself. It was the most exquisite gem he had ever seen. Almost reverently he laid it upon its cotton-wool on the little cabin table. He sighed; this wondrous thing meant a fortune, for him who owned it. He weighed it under the fascinated eyes of the stranger.
>
> "Sixty-five grains!" he murmured. "You are lucky, mate. This stone will take very little cleaning, judging by the eye. There are several spots on it; a skin or two will remove them. Suppose it loses ten grains in the cleaning, its weight would be fifty-five grains—a beauty. I wish I had half your luck."
>
> "What should it be worth?" the man almost whispered.
>
> "Impossible to estimate until it is cleaned. Depends mostly on the depth and lustre. judging by looks, it will be rosae tint which is the most prized. Its shape is a perfect round. Should it clean as it promises, a big buyer would pay you anything from one hundred pounds per grain."
>
> "Phew! Five thousand five hundred pounds."
>
> "Yes, easily. Mind, if it was mine I would demand more. You could ask what you liked for a gem of this class."
>
> "Heavens! I wonder what the buyer will get for it?"
>
> The pearler laughed. "He will sell it as a gem of all the seas," he sighed. "He can approach the rich men of the world as buyers. He will make a fortune out of it, far more than you will."[7]

It is important to record that no one aboard the schooner *Alto* was connected with the theft of the pearl; that occurred later, aboard *Cleopatra*. Word of a great find spread from boat to boat; in the late afternoon Carl Lilly, skipper of the lugger *Toniko Toko*, came across with his diver Victor to see the pearl and celebrate in the usual way. It is not known exactly when or how the switch was made. At the beginning of a long drinking session, the special pearl and a smaller one were in a metal matchbox in Silber Gala's coat pocket, but when the bottles were empty and the visitors had left, so had the pearls. In their place lay two pieces of misshapen 'baroque', of comparable size and weight.[8]

At Broome the diver Victor was identified as the thief, not by discovery of the pearl in his possession but by the emergence of a written agreement in which he undertook to make a present to Augustine if he kept his mouth shut. Not only had the agreement been signed by Victor and Augustine, it had been witnessed by Sebastian, another *Cleopatra* crewman. By that remarkable triangular stupidity, the matter came to court.[9] Through all of this, the pearl made no appearance. Victor claimed that it had been stolen from him before he reached port, and a search warrant executed on *Toniko Toko* revealed nothing.[10]

As far as can be told, Broome extended little sympathy to Gustav Ulbricht or Silber Gala. Indeed, interest in the missing pearl might have quickly faded, had not a rumour spread through the billiard saloons and gambling houses that the commercial traveller Mark Liebglid had been flashing money and letting it be known that he was in a buying frame of mind. The figure of £500 was bandied about.

A few days later, Broome residents were shocked by news of a murder in their midst. The *Dampier Despatch* reported:

> A terrible tragedy was enacted in Broome on Wednesday night. At about 10.45 piteous cries for help were heard from the foreshore opposite Messrs Robison and Norman's. Some men in the vicinity reached the spot in time to see a dinghey being pulled from the shore towards the lugger "Rose", belonging to Yee Ah Chun. They hailed the boat, but it did not return. At 9.30 on Thursday morning a coloured seaman belonging to Captain Mills' lugger reported to Councillors Haste and Nick that the dead body of a white man was lying amongst the mangroves. These gentlemen found the body awash with the incoming tide and brought it ashore. The head was fearfully battered about but it was subsequently recognised as that of Mark Liebglid, the local representative of Messrs Falk & Coy and Messrs Friedman & Co. Later it was found that Mr Liebglid's premises were all open, and that his samples of jewellery were spread around his bedroom.[11]

It was all too clear that Mark Liebglid had played a dangerous game, and that the hunter had become the prey.

Suspicion quickly fell on 'Manilaman' Simeon Espada. A day or two before the murder, Simeon had been seen in his boarding house making a slingshot from a heavy iron rowlock.[12] And when Norwegian Charles Hagen was questioned, he identified Simeon as the man he had seen walking with Mark Liebglid in the sandhills late on Monday night. On September 1st, Simeon was arrested on suspicion of murder. Over the next few days, Hagen also came under scrutiny. He had difficulty explaining bloodstains on a pair of white trousers he had delivered to Soon Lee's laundry, and made contradictory statements of his whereabouts at the time of the murder. On September 9th, he too was arrested.[13]

With two men in custody but no clear picture of how Mark Liebglid had met his death, the police had a problem. Desperate for a new lead they lent heavily on Pablo Marquez, who seemed to know more than he had revealed. The breakthrough came on Saturday, September 16th, when Pablo declared that he wanted to make a full statement in the presence of Resident Magistrate Warton, Sergeant Byrne, and Father Russell, a Catholic priest. Byrne always insisted that Pablo came willingly and without inducement but Pablo, it seems, believed that he would gain immunity by turning "King's Evidence."[14]

Three days later *The West Australian* reported:

THE BROOME MURDER.
CONFESSION BY ONE OF ACCUSED.
STORY OF HORRIBLE BRUTALITY.
LIEBGLID BATTERED TO DEATH.
THREE MEN IMPLICATED.
Broome, September 18.
Pablo Marques, who on Saturday made an unfinished statement regarding events that immediately preceded the murder of Mark Liebglid, made a full confession of the whole affair before Fr. Russell, Mr. Warton, R.M., and, Sergeant Byrne to-day. The story told by Marques is one of horrible brutality, in which Marques, Simeon Espada, and Charles Hagen, who are all under arrest on suspicion are concerned. Marques states that on the night of the murder Liebglid accompanied him and Simeon Espada and Charles Hagen to the wreck of the schooner Mist, a short distance from the shore, Liebglid being assured that a valuable pearl was hidden in the wreck. The four got into a dinghy belonging to the lugger Tauriko Toko and rowed to the Mist. There Espada produced a glass marble—the stopper of a lemonade bottle—wrapped in paper, and presented this to Liebglid as the "valuable pearl." Liebglid, on viewing the valueless piece of glass, said, "Why make a fool of me?" Thereupon Espada struck him on the head with a sling-shot, and as the Mist's deck was canted Liebglid fell overboard into 8ft. of water. The unfortunate man was unable

to swim, and in consequence he clutched the side of the dinghy and screamed, "Help! Police! They are murdering me. I am done." Espada plunged into the sea and endeavoured to drown Liebglid, and as the latter clung to the boat, Hagen and Marques battered his head to force him to release his hold. Hagen struck Liebglid in the face with his bare fist, which became smeared with blood, and to get rid of the blood he wiped his hand on his trousers. Hagen next endeavoured to drag the almost lifeless body into the dinghey, with a view to plunder, and to loosen Liebglid's hold on the boat. Espada smashed the victim's hands. Liebglid's cries had attracted persons with lanterns to the beach, only a few yards away. Upon one of these persons calling out "What's going on there? What's wrong?" the party on the boat became scared and dropped Liebglid's body into the sea.

Marques concluded his confession by stating that he and his two companions then pulled in the dinghey through the mangroves to the foreshore below Carter's foundry. There they landed and made good their escape. It is stated that the police discovered on Hagen's trousers blood-stains, which appear to corroborate Marques's story concerning the action taken by Hagen to clean his hand after striking Liebglid in the face. The discovery of these stains first aroused suspicion against Hagen, Espada, and Marques, and led to their arrest. An inquest in connection with the murder will be resumed on Wednesday next.[15]

The derelict schooner Mist *as crime scene:*
an 'X' marks the spot where the body of Mark Liebglid was discovered.

It should immediately be recorded that in its rush to bring these gruesome details to the public, *The West Australian* grossly misrepresented Pablo Marquez's statement. In fact, Pablo had protested his innocence; he had confessed only to being present when the murder was committed. Somehow, beneath his sensational story, that life-and-death distinction was buried.

At the coronial inquest Pablo insisted that Mark Liebglid had asked him to come with him for the purchase of a pearl, and had promised that there would be some money for him if the deal went through. The pearlers of Broome, and the coroner's white jury in particular, never accepted that part of his testimony. Why, they wondered, would an educated Jew want the assistance of a coloured man, and a coloured man too small to be of any use in a fight. They never budged from a simple, race-based assumption that two 'Manilamen' had conspired.

Careful reading of the testimony of Simeon Espada (translated) and of Pablo Marquez (given in English) opens a possibility as chilling as it is simple: that Pablo was only present at the murder because Mark Liebglid, having arranged a meeting with Simeon, decided that he needed an interpreter.[16] Simeon spoke no English. His native tongue was Tagalog, the dominant regional dialect of the Philippines and the dialect spoken in the capital. To the pearlers of Broome, Tagalog speakers were 'Manilamen' and their language simply 'Manila'. By Broome's reckoning, Simeon and Pablo were both Manilamen. In fact, they were of different race and could scarcely have looked more different. Simeon was tall and thick-set. His facial features were Japanese but his skin was dark. Pablo was short and of slim build, but also of mixed race. It was difficult to tell his homeland by his appearance. The two men were acqaintances but had never been friends and, contrary to all supposition, had never worked on the same boat.

In *Forty Fathoms Deep*, Jack Idriess wrote:

> The case excited keen attention. The attempt to sell as a huge pearl a lemonade stopper wrapped in a handkerchief was unique. But among the twenty-eight witnesses called there were many who evidently were afraid of saying too much. Never throughout the inquiry did the existence of the true pearl come out publicly.[17]

Nothing could have been further from the truth. Few in Broome doubted that the missing pearl and the murder of Mark Liebglid were linked. Two nights before his death, Liebglid had been seen walking along the beach at midnight with a big coloured man. When his friends cautioned him, he said he knew the man was dangerous, but if he got the pearl described to him, his fortune was made.[18] After Simeon's arrest on September 1st, there was a second bloom of speculation. A few days before the murder, Simeon had signed on to *Toniko Toko* as cook. No one was quite sure if he had found the stolen pearl aboard the boat, or if he had signed on merely to make his claim of finding it more plausible.[19] And on September 6th Pablo Marquez, under suspicion but not yet under arrest, testified that he had spoken to Mark Liebglid about a pearl Simeon claimed to have. Here in Pablo's broken English is part of his sworn statement:

> The Jew said, "I want speak you." He said, "Did you see anything tonight?" I said, "No." He said he was waiting for a "big thing" now. I said "Good luck to you." Hagen was waiting. He and I went to Billiard Room verandah. Asked me for money I owed. I said to-morrow. Then went macaroni house, was eating when Jew came. I said "How you got on?" He said "He take me long way and show me only piece of barroque, he reckon he got big thing which he bring to-morrow." Told him I'd seen the barroque too. I know that man. He said it's a big Jap man with a Jap cap on. I went home, he too. This was about 11.30 p.m. Monday. I told him that man no Japanese.[20]

Jack Idriess shared Broome's view that Pablo was as guilty as sin.[21] The Pablo Marquez of *Forty Fathoms Deep* is a shifty-eyed crewman who spies upon the pearl thief to see where he will hide his ill-gotten prize. From below deck, he watches intently as the pearl is concealed in a length of hemp rope, its position marked with a tiny thread of coloured cotton. Later, in darkness, Pablo makes his move.

Ashore in Broome, the fictional Marquez realises that he can have his pearl and sell it too. With Simeon Espada and Charlie Hagen, he conspires to lure Mark Liebglid to the derelict schooner *Mist*. But as the conspiracy unravels and the police close in, he entrusts the pearl to an old Manilaman named Sulu, who under threat of death is left to choose an undiscoverable hiding place.

Broome folklore throws up a multitude of possibilities; Jack Idriess, it appears, simply chose the most inventive. After watching a hornet come and go from its nest under the corrugated-iron roof of his shack, old Sulu smiles to himself. He soaks a little piece of black silk in insecticide and wraps the pearl in it. Later, in darkness, he scrapes away dried mud to make a neat hole in the side of the nest. He presses the pearl into the hole, knowing that the hornet upon its return will not rest until the damage is daubed over.

Perhaps, while the three accused languish in the Broome Gaol awaiting transfer to Fremantle, we may pause to consider where the roseate pearl sits among the greatest of pearls.

The question was often asked: how large do pearls grow? And where are the greatest pearls ever found? A paragraph from *The Western Mail* of February 12th, 1910 helps to answer both questions.

The World's Largest Pearl.—Bombay advices which reached Perth by the G.M.S. Bremen last week state that when the mail left that city there was on view what is described as the finest pearl that has ever been fished from the bottom of the seas. Its weight is 34 carats, and it is nearly three-quarters of an inch in diameter. There is, it is stated, only one other pearl of equal beauty, the Pellegrina, now in the Museum of Zosima in Moscow. This pearl has hitherto been considered a priceless gem, owing to its globular shape with a flawless skin of Oriental lustre, but the weight of the Pellegrina is only 28 carats. Those connected with the pearl industry of this State will be interested in this magnificent jewel now in Bombay.[22]

The language of the jeweller will not be familiar to all. The common measures of a pearl's size and weight are derived not from the inch and ounce of the British, but from the gram and millimetre of the French. A *carat* is one fifth of a gram, and a *grain* is one quarter of a carat.[23] Lest heads begin to spin, let what is needed be confined to a table, to permit conversion between two different measures of a pearl's diameter and two different measures of its weight.

DIAMETER		WEIGHT	
INCHES	MILLIMETRES	CARATS	GRAINS
1/4	6	1.8	7
5/16	8	3.6	14
3/8	10	6	25
7/16	11	10	40
1/2	13	15	60
9/16	14	21	85
5/8	16	29	115
11/16	17	38	150

The relationship between diameter and weight for a natural round pearl.

A keen observer may notice that the two great pearls of Moscow and Bombay, at 28 and 34 carats respectively, differed in diameter by a single French millimetre. And that the roseate pearl of *Forty Fathoms Deep*, at 65 grains, was a little more than half an inch in diameter.

Although the size of a pearl was never the sole determinant of its value, the influence of size upon value was very striking. All else being equal, a doubling of weight delivered far more than a doubling of price. There also existed a hierarchy of desirability based on shape, but the appraisal of size and shape in combination was the business of experts. Ernestine Hill offered her readers a neat summation:

From the personal photograph album of
Cossack pearler and publican Tom Rogers,
an unidentified and over-exposed image
of a 65-grain perfect round pearl.
Inset: actual size.

Seed-pearl, flat button, high button, double button, "pear" or "drop,"
and perfect round—so run the values ascending, and the usual worth
of a perfect round is the square of its grains in pounds. A 20-grain
pearl of fair quality might be expected to bring £400. But a jewel of
distinction is a pearl without price.[24]

What delivered that distinction could be unusual symmetry or colour
or brilliance. It could also be good fortune. In 1918, a superb round pearl
of 47½ grains, of perfect size and colour to become the centrepiece of a
special necklet, fetched in London the extraordinary price of £14,000.[25]

A pearl of great brilliance always commanded a higher price, but lustre
and colour were inextricably bound. They could only be judged together
and holistically because a fine pearl had not only a basic hue but also a
palette of deep secondary colours known as "orient".[26] For fine pearls, as
for fine wine, a premium was placed upon complexity.

The influence of colour upon value was further complicated by culture
and complexion, as Perth's *Sunday Times* explained:

London jewellers, for England's fair beauties, buy mostly the white
pearl; vivacious Parisiennes, the most avid buyers, prefer the roseate
Oriental stone, while the harems and courts of the Indies and the East
seek the straw-colored jewels that harmonise with dark complexions.[27]

If the appraisal of pearls was complex and subjective, the fickleness of
the market added yet another layer of uncertainty. In November 1907,
The West Australian reported:

A well-known Hatton Garden dealer states that pearls have gone up 75 per cent in the past five years, and really fine stones of this kind will fetch almost any price. A fine Orient pearl, which twenty years ago could have been bought for £20, will now sell for as much as £160. With sapphires and diamonds it is much the same—the former having trebled their value in five years, rubies alone having fallen back.

There is a tremendous demand for high-class gems and jewels in America, three-fifths of the total output from De Beers diamond mines, in South Africa, having been secured by American buyers. Of course, Broome is only interested in pearls, but as they are to some extent in sympathy with other gems, the opinion quoted should be reassuring to those engaged in our great Nor'-West pearling industry.[28]

If changing times cast doubt upon the true value of pearls, there was no doubt whatever that fortunes had been made by trading them. Between 1905 and 1910, demand for the finest of the fine made Mark Rubin a millionaire, and a millionaire in pounds sterling. After 1907 the 'pearl king' was rarely seen in Broome; he left the local buying and the management of his fleet to his brother-in-law Abraham de Vahl Davis, who would earn fame in his own way and in his own right. In those years Broome buzzed with tales of fabulous pearls and the prices fetched for them in the gem houses of London and Paris. Davis, for reasons not difficult to discern, worked hard to contain the optimism of his prospective clients. In a 1909 interview with Perth's Sunday *Truth*, he declared:

You accept some extraordinary stories as to the value of pearls found. For instance, there was a yarn going the rounds of the press some time ago, as to the finding of a pearl worth from £10,000 to £12,000. No such gem has ever been found in the waters of this coast. That special pearl, for which a special value was claimed, went round all the purchasers of London, and came back to Broome unsold, and eventually I bought it for my firm at £750. All the stories of pearls of great price want a big discount off.[29]

Perhaps, between hard reality and wishful thinking, the truth of the roseate pearl may also be negotiated.

BY STEAMER, THE ACCUSED MURDERERS were conveyed to Fremantle to await trial in the Supreme Court of Western Australia. Also southbound were 26 witnesses: nineteen for the prosecution and seven for the defence.

In substance and sequence, the trial echoed the coronial inquest.[30] The statements taken in Broome were tendered to the court on the first day; they became the foundation of the prosecution case. Over five days, as witnesses repeated and defended their depositions, there seemed little likelihood that the jurors in the capital would contradict their peers in Broome. On Saturday, November 11th, the trial drew to a close. Justice

Burnside, in the course of a three-and-a-half-hour summing-up, declared what all in the court already knew: that the case had been made more complex and difficult by the discordant accounts of the three accused. "I hope," he said, "that some day the Legislature will alter the law which allows three men who are charged with a crime to be indicted together."[31]

Burnside then told the jurors that in assessing the guilt or innocence of each man, they should disregard entirely the depositions of the other two. That, he must have known, was an impossible request. Each man's prospects had been harmed, perhaps irrevocably, by the testimony of the other two. After deliberating for five hours, the jury found all three men guilty of wilful murder. Immediately, the three state-appointed defence attorneys applied to have the convictions referred to the Full Court, on the grounds that the evidence of conspiracy was too weak to support the convictions. In response, Justice Burnside declared: "I attach to the sentence of death perhaps a graver importance than it may deserve, and I do not feel inclined to pass a sentence that I am not certain will be carried out."[32] He agreed to the request, and remanded the prisoners.

THE CONVICTIONS WERE CONFIRMED, and on the day of sentencing, the public gallery was full. Indeed, *The Western Mail* described it as "unwholesomely crowded half an hour before the time appointed."[33] The public did not come to learn the fate of the three men; that was already known. They came to witness the passing of the death sentence. They came to be affronted. They came to be horrified.

Three men would be condemned at once, but it was not that fact alone that gave the circumstance its dark attraction. *The Western Mail* reported:

> Representing three different races, the adjudged partners in crime entered the dock apparently unmoved, the white man leading, the diminutive yellow man in the second place, and the black man last.[34]

What made this case so shocking was not the callousness and brutality of the crime, or even that three men had conspired to commit it. It was the notion that three men of different race—one white, one yellow, one black—had collaborated, and collaborated as equals.

There being no other business before the court, the moment came quickly. "The sentence," *The Western Mail* continued, "was delivered in absolute silence, except for a stifled cry uttered somewhere in the back of the court as his Honour produced the black cap emblematic of the dread extremity of human law."[35]

A correspondent for *The Sydney Morning Herald* noted the prisoners' reactions.

> Hagen received the dread pronouncement with the same unconcern that he exhibited throughout the trial. His face betrayed not the slightest emotion, and his step was firm as he descended from the dock

to the cells in the basement of the Court. Espada looked more solemn than usual, but otherwise wore a composed air. Pablo Marquez, who is in delicate health, betrayed some emotion as he accompanied his fellow prisoners to the cells, and gave vent to audible sobs as he disappeared from the view of the spectators.[36]

Some in the gallery observed that immediately upon the close of proceedings, Hagen tried to attract the attention of his counsel. Richard Haynes, K.C. either did not hear or else decided that his duty was done. He stood up, turned away, and walked out.

BY SEVERAL ACCOUNTS, Charles Hagen was broken by the verdict. In his cell on death row he rambled, railed and rationalised, telling one reporter that if he had not called the police a lot of asses for not arresting certain men, everything would have been different.[37] Almost daily came new explanations, strikingly misaligned. There was clear evidence of mental breakdown.

Pablo Marquez, too, was overwhelmed by his circumstances and in poor physical health, but he continued to enjoy the support of his state-assigned attorney William Purkiss who, in the course of the trial, had become convinced of his client's innocence. As the day of execution approached Purkiss kept working, within the gaol and without, to comfort his former client and to have the sentence overturned.[38]

Although the discretion of mercy belonged to the governor, the advice of the executive council was rarely disregarded. When the ministers of cabinet met on the morning of December 8th, they recommended that the sentences be carried out. The governor accepted their view. That evening, the governor of Fremantle Gaol visited each condemned man in his cell. He reported that Simeon Espada in particular seemed untroubled by the news; when he walked past Simeon's cell a few minutes later, he was asleep.

The problem for Pablo Marquez was that Simeon's account of the murder was almost the mirror image of his own. Each man accused the other. But three days before the planned execution, a breakthrough came. Simeon recanted; he confessed his own guilt and admitted that Pablo had been no more than a bystander. Suddenly, the two men's stories were fully aligned. The substance of Simeon's confession was conveyed to the colonial secretary, for consideration by the executive, and Purkiss made a powerful plea to the press.[39] Simeon's statement, he said, "was made in circumstances of the most solemn nature, in full knowledge of the serious-ness of its import, and in view of the fact that death to him was imminent."

The next morning, some newspapers went so far as to predict that the executions would be postponed.[40] It was not to be. The executive council stood true to its name and recommended that justice take its course.

THURSDAY, DECEMBER 14TH, 1905 was one of the most remarkable days in the long history of capital punishment. The authorities, for reasons that may never be known, had decided that the white man Hagen should be executed first, and that one hour later, the two coloured men should drop side-by-side and simultaneously.

At 8 a.m. Charles Hagen was led out; he conversed with the Reverend G. O'Halloran as he walked to the gallows. When the linen hood was drawn over his head, he was asked if he had anything to say. "Yes," he said, "let me see."[41]

So began Hagen's final, rambling declaration of innocence. He spoke calmly and with conviction, but whether he was still of sound mind is extremely doubtful. He took many short breaks to moisten his lips, only to resume with a new preoccupation. After a full twelve minutes, he seemed to bring his discourse toward a close, but struck out once more in a new direction. His final fixation was his Broome acquaintance Carpio, who by police and other accounts had gone mad on the night after the murder. "I am going to die," Hagen declared, "but Lucas and Carpio know more of the murder than I do. Carpio is a great friend of Pablo's—"

At this point, Mr O'Halloran stepped forward and whispered something. Hagen ignored him. "I am not going to say too much, but I am going to die, and I want to speak. Gentlemen. I have studied palmistry, and I have always feared something dreadful would happen to me. Carpio would kill or rob anybody for money. Let anyone look at his left hand, and the line of murder is clear. Anything for money: that is Carpio."

O'Halloran, apparently unwilling to let a condemned man spend his last minutes condemning another, intervened again. "Very well, sir," said Hagen, "I will not say much more."[42]

When the hood was fitted for the second time, Hagen kept the executioner in check. "Draw the rope tight," he said, "put it firmly round my neck. Steady! Not too tight." A moment before the lever was pulled, Hagen uttered his final words: "Gentlemen, I am going. I am away now."

AT 9 A.M. THE TWO 'MANILAMEN' were brought to the scaffold. Pablo was agitated and muttering, but was settled somewhat by a Roman Catholic priest. He accepted the hood quietly. Simeon, like Hagen, indicated that he wanted to speak. He attempted some pidgin English, but the only words clearly heard were never fully understood. "Me kill white man," he declared, "Pablo he give me schooner for £600."[43] All traces of English soon disappeared, but the animated statement continued. It was difficult to know what purpose it served, since the words were unintelligible to all but the man standing beside him.

Suddenly, Simeon said something that greatly offended Pablo. After a sharp retort, the two argued heatedly in Tagalog. All pleas to settle were ignored; for a few moments, the two men seemed utterly oblivious to their circumstances. The absurd theatre proved too much for the executioner, who broke down and cried. According to one newspaper man, he kept one hand on the lever while struggling to wipe tears from his face with the other.[44]

As the condemned men exchanged insults in a language no one understood, chief warder Webster noticed that Simeon had somehow managed to get one of his bound hands around the rope. Webster called for silence, stepped in, and broke Simeon's clasp. From that moment forward, the precise sequence of events is unclear. It seems that both the chief warder and the bleary-eyed executioner were equally determined that Simeon should not clutch the rope a second time. When Simeon did indeed move to save himself, two plans were enacted simultaneously: the chief warder stepped forward onto the trapdoor, and the executioner pulled the lever. Espada and Marquez went to their deaths, and the chief warder further still, to the stone floor twelve feet below.

After a communal gasp, the silence of the astonished was broken by the clatter of boots on metal stairs. Prison staff rushed to the aid of Webster who, semi-conscious and bleeding from the head, was rushed to the prison hospital.

FOR ERNESTINE HILL, the 'tellable' tale of the roseate pearl ended with the execution of Hagen, Espada and Marquez. She wrote:

> The pearl itself was never traced. Doubtless it was carried to Singapore in a cake of soap, the binding of a book, the elaborate construction of a Japanese woman's hair, or in the hollow of an Asiatic slipper, underneath the little toe—for all of these are time-honored hiding-places for stolen jewels of the sea.[45]

For Ion Idriess, however, the story does not end at the gallows. The reader of *Forty Fathoms Deep* is subjected to a stream of florid imaginings, each more ludicrous than the last. The pearl, we are told, remained in the wasp's nest for fully three years, because old Sulu could do nothing while two equally obsessed men knew that he had it. The jealous contenders, diver Castillo Toledo and man-about-town Gomez, are clearly fictional. Idriess claims that after Toledo was drowned in the great storm of December 1908,[46] Sulu was freed to sell the pearl to Gomez and to fulfil a long-held wish: to return to his homeland. The account of Sulu's arrival in Manila leaves little doubt that both Broome and non-fiction have been left far behind.

> When the steamer arrived, old Sulu could hardly walk down the gangway, his knees were trembling so, his heart was beating painfully—he could barely see. With a set smile on his lined old face he walked gropingly along the wharf. He stretched out his foot to step upon his native land and fell—dead.[47]

The carnage of the pen continues. New owner Gomez wakes to find that the pearl has been stolen from a pouch around his waist. His reaction to the discovery of his loss also warrants quotation, with similar imputation.

> Very late next morning, Gomez awoke. Dazedly. He lay for a time staring up at the roof, his senses gradually returning. Automatically, his hands felt for the tiny bag. With a cry he leapt from the bed. Trembling in every limb he stared down at his middle, his eyes glaring, his mouth opening pathetically. Slowly he turned towards the door. Then throwing his arms above his head, he ran screaming through the house. He ran amuck. Ten minutes later he committed suicide.[48]

By Jack Idriess's accounting, the roseate pearl had been the undoing of seven men. That four were real and three were invented seemed inconsequential. He wrote:

> I never learnt who actually stole the pearl from Gomez. Rumour spread, particularly after the drowning of Toledo, that there was a curse upon the pearl; that he who possessed it died; and that it would return to the sea. Maybe three coloured men living could connect the particulars; but they keep the secret, superstitiously awed by the fact that the curse worked out so truly. Perhaps it is as well that the history should simply fade away.[49]

That history has faded to fiction stands as the most reasonable conclusion. But there are questions to be answered and observations to be made before that verdict is delivered.

In pure fiction, one imagines, the pearl would emerge perfect from the sea. But the pearl of *Forty Fathoms Deep* does not. We are told that it came to light with tiny marks and spots, that it was cleaned January or February of 1909, and that by deft touch it came to perfection with the loss of three 'skins' and only a grain or two of weight. Jack Idriess could easily have written the cleaning of the pearl out of his story altogether, but he was clearly unwilling to do that. The most plausible explanation is that the source of that information was none other than the pearl cleaner Thomas Bastian "T.B." Ellies, who was still active in Broome when Idriess arrived there in 1933.

The citizens of Broome were wary of visiting writers; they had been burned before. But Jack Idriess was welcomed; many had read his early books, especially *Gold-Dust and Ashes*, *Lasseter's Last Ride*, and *The Desert Column*.[50] If Broome found Jack Idriess relaxed and personable, it was partly because the gathering of stories for a pearl book was not his primary reason for being there. He had been invited to join a police patrol to the remotest parts of the Kimberley;[51] it was that rare opportunity that had brought him to the far north. But until the end of the wet, that adventure—and the gathering of material for *Over The Range*—would have to wait.

Although lingering in Broome was not part of Idriess's plan, he quickly discovered that there was material for several books in the fact and folklore of this remarkable town. Research began well, but in the course of three months some of his most valued informants stopped talking. Some of the pearlers, it appears, became convinced that Jack was working for the government, gathering evidence of illicit pearl trading. By similar suspicion, he also lost the support of Japanese 'big gun' Nishioka, who apparently decided that he was a naval secret service officer sent to spy on the Japanese pearlers.[52]

As some sources dried up, the support of T. B. Ellies became ever more important, not only as an unrivalled primary source, but also as the arbiter and reconciler of conflicting stories. For this critical service, Ellies was well rewarded in *Forty Fathoms Deep*: he was hailed as a pearl cleaner of almost magical abilities, and as the very soul of discretion.

It now seems possible that T.B., in his conversations with Idriess, admitted to having cleaned the roseate pearl and, having made that admission, described in detail the pearl and the work he had done. Once that information was received, it could hardly be discarded or reworked, even if the cleaning of the pearl created problems elsewhere in the narrative.

Pearl cleaner Thomas Bastian Ellies, known to all in Broome as "T.B.".

It is also plausible that Ellies agreed to tell Idriess what he knew about the pearl, on the strict condition that he not be identified as the person who had cleaned it. A fair reason is not difficult to make out. When the pearl is supposed to have been cleaned, in January or February of 1909, Ellies was on the payroll of Rubin & Davis, who recognised his extraordinary talent and paid a handsome retainer to monopolise it.[53] If Ellies cleaned the pearl at that time, he was clearly in breach of the terms of his engagement. In short, he was 'moonlighting'.

The text of *Forty Fathoms Deep* contains circumstantial evidence that there was such a gentlemen's agreement between Ellies and the author. Idriess's account of the skinning of Bernard Bardwell's double-button pearl is a rich and evocative homage to T.B. and his marvellous hands.[54] In sharp contrast, the skinning of the roseate pearl—of far greater importance to the narrative—is glossed over in a few uncomfortable lines:

> Gomez had cleaned his pearl. In the heart of his ramshackle boarding-house, within four iron walls he had stood and gazed while a coloured expert skinned the gem. Taking only three skins from it, it had unfolded as a perfect round with a soft rosae glow; a magnificent thing, warm and beautiful; a pearl of perfect loveliness putting to utter shame the corrugated walls of the dingy room.[55]

It is reasonable to conclude that the "coloured expert" was T. B. Ellies, and that Jack Idriess's obfuscation was deliberate.

THE WORKS OF ION L. IDRIESS are careful composites of fact and fiction. It is a characteristic of his storytelling that real people and places, even photographs, are used to confer authenticity upon the whole. Although real people keep company with figments of the author's imagination, there are rules governing the interaction. For the most part, historical figures are portrayed faithfully and respectfully, as if in gratitude for what might be called "credibility services rendered." The guiding principle is that good reputations are not to be damaged by invention.

Readers of *Forty Fathoms Deep* may be surprised by the late appearance of the very real Abraham de Vahl Davis and the ill-fated steamship *Koombana*. Many will suspect that facts are once again being called in support of fiction: mere accessories to an elaborate contrivance by which a cursed pearl will be returned to the sea. But once again we are stopped short of outright dismissal by the observation that the author is neither enjoying nor exploiting the licence of fiction. Rather, he seems to be struggling with elements of a story he has been told. Paradoxically, it is Idriess's clumsy attempt to reconcile the irreconcilable that lends some late credibility.

The two elements that defy reconciliation are: firstly, that the roseate pearl had been cleaned; and secondly, that Abraham Davis bought it in good faith. Idriess knows that Davis, a great pearl expert, would have recognised that the pearl had been cleaned and therefore was not recently fished from the sea.

By his own unwritten rules, Jack Idriess's challenge was to tell the story without besmirching the character of Abraham Davis. The sale had to be presented as legitimate; there could be no insinuation that Davis bought the pearl knowing it to be 'snide'. Idriess's solution—if 'solution' be fair description—was to ignore the problem altogether.

> Then a man wished to see Mr Davis privately. He was a pearler, had just come in from outside and had a magnificent pearl. He had fished it himself south down the coast.
>
> Davis bought the pearl in all good faith; everything apparently was all clear and above board. This was a recognized pearler selling a pearl he had fished from the sea himself. But of all the gems that had passed through Davis's hands this alone was priceless. He congratulated himself that he had arrived at Port Hedland just when the pearler had sailed in.[56]

Once again, in a few awkward lines, an important element of *Forty Fathoms Deep* is dispensed with. It is as if Jack Idriess, accomplished storyteller, is mumbling into his chest.

A fresh look at the author's dilemma leads to a surprising conclusion: the reputation of Abraham de Vahl Davis was never threatened by the story that Jack Idriess had to tell. Rubin & Davis of London & Broome had a reputation for legitimacy and guarded it jealously, but the firm did occasionally receive stolen pearls.

On June 16th, 1909, at the Broome Quarter Sessions, pearler Simon K. Dean faced a charge of having "received one pearl, well knowing the said pearl to have been stolen." On the second sitting day, Abraham Davis took the stand as a prosecution witness.[57] He was first asked to describe the pearl to the court. "It was a high round button pearl of $64\frac{1}{16}$ grains," he said, "in its natural state." When asked to clarify what he meant by "in its natural state", Davis explained that an experienced buyer could tell if a pearl had been cleaned. "Pearl merchants call a cleaned pearl a 'made' pearl," he added.

Under cross-examination Davis explained that the pearl had been offered to his firm in September 1907. He and the accused had been unable to agree on a price, so it was agreed that the stone should be sent on consignment to London. An advance of £400 was paid to Dean, and Davis took possession of the pearl.

Davis, it appears, had procedures to cover circumstances such as these. When he told the court that he and Dean had been unable to agree on a purchase price, it was true, strictly speaking. But there is little doubt that the prices he offered reflected his confidence in the legitimacy of the seller. He probably had some doubts about Simon Dean and made sure that no outright purchase would be agreed to. The 'trick', if there was one, was to lead the seller toward a consignment arrangement without arousing any suspicion that his integrity was in question.

To accept a pearl on consignment involved a trade-off. If the stone fetched a high price in London or Paris, the owner would enjoy the greater windfall. But for the deal-maker, the initial outlay was a small fraction of the anticipated return and the risks were greatly reduced. Moreover, a year or more might pass before a European sale was finalised. There was plenty of time for inconsistency to surface, or for a new offer of outright purchase to be made.

We can now deal confidently with the question of whether Abraham Davis would have accepted this pearl of exquisite beauty but questionable provenance. The answer is an unequivocal "Yes!"

THAT ABRAHAM DE VAHL DAVIS was in Port Hedland on the night of Tuesday, March 19th, 1912, is nowhere disputed. He was returning to Broome for the start of the 1912 pearling season. He was travelling north by *Koombana*, viewing and buying pearls as he proceeded. It was later reported by several newspapers that he had carried £2,500 in cash for purchases along the way.[58] At times, *Koombana*'s purser Hedley Harris must have felt more like a bank teller, so frequent the requests for access to the safe.

At different ports, business was conducted in different ways. At Shark Bay there was no deep-water jetty. Clients came by lighter to the ship at anchor, for meetings in cabin or saloon. Port Hedland offered greater convenience. Firstly, there was always more time. Because *Koombana* could only enter or leave the harbour on the highest tide of the day, an overnight stay was unavoidable. Secondly, the jetty was a short walk from the town. Davis could come to a meeting empty-handed and, if a deal was struck, return to the ship to withdraw money.

All trading ended on the morning of Wednesday, March 20th, 1912, when Davis boarded *Koombana* for the last leg of a long journey.

THERE IS AN INTRIGUING ASPECT to the pearl cleaning issue that enriches our story at its very end. If Abraham Davis recognised that the pearl offered to him had been cleaned, he must have suspected that it was T. B. Ellies who had cleaned it. After all, who would entrust such a stone to anyone else? By eyeglass, he may even have recognised the master's deft touch. And if the skinning was so light as to leave no signature, that would lead to precisely the same conclusion.

Carrying the precious pearl and his expert's understanding of it, Davis would have boarded *Koombana* with a new lightness of step, eager to be back in Broome. Certainly, this was a gem he would enjoy holding, admiring, and unveiling to a small circle of friends, but one private showing must surely have preceded all others. Without doubt, he would soon have called upon T.B. in his tiny workshop.

What would Davis have said or asked? Quite possibly nothing at all. It is easy to imagine that he would have closed the door behind him, sat down, placed the pearl on felt between them, and left the soul of discretion to do the talking.

FROM THIS ANT-LIKE EXPLORATION, one certainty emerges. To the intrigue of Broome in its pearling heyday, new writers will come and new readers will follow. And yet it is here that the trail of the roseate pearl is lost. Through the foreshore camps and the laneways of Chinatown we are led onward in translucent optimism, forever enticed. Finally, we accept that the truth will not be lifted from the pages of *Forty Fathoms Deep*, or indeed from these pages.

If there be some consolation, it is that seawater may one day drain from a rusted safe raised from the seabed, and that by its opening the final acquisitions of Abraham Davis may be revealed. Until that day the truth, or part of it, will remain with *Koombana* at the bottom of the sea, tightly pressed for long silence in silt and folded iron.

Acknowledgments

Perhaps a hundred people have contributed to this project.

Firstly, I thank all those, in Western Australia and elsewhere, who have a family or community link to the *Koombana* tragedy and who have willingly shared letters, photographs and recollections. After each of their names, I will place in parentheses the name of the relative or community member lost with the ship. I thank Bethwyn Brandis (Fred Clinch); Jean Northover (James William Clarke); Ann Parker and Joan Kennedy (George Simpson); Shirley Brown (Tom Binning); Joy Rowe (Tom Forrest); Cathy Wallace and Sandra Hill (Harry Briden); Val Moir (the Quinlan brothers); Olwyn Parr and Jane Burke (Robert & Evan Davies); Ethel Hodgson, Beryl Hall and Kim Daymond (Louise Sack); Vila Liebich (Rob & Edith Jenkins); Jim McGowan (Frank McGowan); Gordon Innes (William Innes); Rae Clayton (John Mangan); Sue Stoecker (Anastasia Freer), Aly Loney (Florrie Price); Graham de Vahl Davis, Lyn Yelland and Deb Kerimi (Abraham de Vahl Davis); Declan Quaile (three crew members from Termonfeckin, Drogheda, Ireland); Jim Mayhew (Jane Pigott, Alice & Genevieve Skamp); and Liz Goode (Captain Tom Allen).

In particular, I note the contribution of Bethwyn Brandis who, on the ninetieth anniversary of *Koombana*'s disappearance, sought to make contact with other members of *Koombana*'s extended family. Bethwyn's "Can you help?" advertisement in *The West Australian* drew a surprising response, and her correspondence became the starting point for my study of *Koombana*'s passengers and crew.

My dealings with Graham de Vahl Davis also warrant special mention. Without Graham's information and advice, my essay on his grandfather ("The Man Behind the Ghost") would have been very extremely difficult to write; indeed, I may not have attempted it.

In parallel with my research and writing, the search for the wreck of the *Koombana* has continued. I have enjoyed the exchange of ideas with all of the following (many of whom have been chasing *Koombana* for much longer than I): the late Captain Roy Marsh; former MMA pilots Don Anderson, Reg Adkins and Tony Turner; the late Malcolm Barker; Koombana Search Group prime movers Kerry Thom and Ted Graham; 2007 search sponsor Mike Capelhorn and his skipper Kane Noack; also

John van Uden, Graeme Wignall, Brian Sorrell, Bob Kozyrski, and Tracy Kirk (on behalf of her father Adrian Martin). Scanning the seabed, I might add, is an expensive business; the recent support of Fugro Survey is greatly appreciated.

Among those who deserve recognition are several archivists, curators, librarians, and local history officers. I thank the staff of the State Records Office of Western Australia, and acknowledge the enthusiastic help I received from Jo Pritchard and Robyn Offer of the Karratha Local History Office, Pennie Pemberton of the Noel Butlin Archives Centre in Canberra, Trish Parker of the South Hedland Library, and Dr Michael McCarthy of the Western Australian Maritime Museum.

There are also those who, purely from interest in the *Koombana* story, volunteered their time. Particular thanks are due to Laurie and Veronica Parrett, who offered to trace items of interest in England and Scotland, and who returned with digitised ship plans and very striking photographs of the ship's interior. Thanks also to Doug and Coral Harrison, who made available the photo album of Cossack policeman and publican Tom Rogers, and to writer and publisher Bob Sheppard, always busy with his own research but never too busy to pass on information about *Koombana*.

For their positive influence on the *Koombana Days* manuscript, two individuals stand apart.

Jim Mayhew, former journalist and grandson of Broome pearler Stanley Pigott, took a keen interest in the project and slid naturally into a mentoring role. I have benefited greatly from Jim's careful commentary, and I value the friendship that has grown from our shared interest in the Nor'-West and its history.

Finally, as if to prove that the path to publication need not be tortuous, I offer sincere thanks to my Fremantle Press editor: the insightful, delightful Georgia Richter.

APPENDICES

APPENDIX I. KOOMBANA CHRONOLOGY

Abbreviations: dep = departed, arr = arrived.

Completion
S.S. *Koombana* was launched from the shipyard of Alexander Stephen & Sons, at Linthouse on the Clyde, on Wednesday, October 28th, 1908. Sea trials followed.

"Trip Out"
December 30th, 1908 – February 19th, 1909.
Glasgow to Melbourne via Cape Town, Durban, Fremantle, and Adelaide.
Master: John Rees
Progress: Dep Glasgow Dec 30th 1908, arr Cape Town Jan 23rd 1909, Durban Jan 27th, Fremantle Feb 11th; dep Fremantle Feb 12th, arr Adelaide 17th, Melbourne 19th; docked for inspections and adjustments Feb 22nd–24th.
Incidents: Two strange suicides: intending passenger Edwin Couch found shot dead, apparently by his own hand, before departure from Glasgow; and passenger J. H. Taylor, reported to be in some financial distress, went missing two days after departure from Durban.

Trip No. 1
February 27th – March 8th, 1909. Melbourne to Fremantle via Adelaide.
Master: John Rees
Progress: dep Melbourne Feb 27th, arr Adelaide March 1st; dep Adelaide 3rd, arr Fremantle 8th.
Notes: In *Koombana*'s log, this voyage from Melbourne to Fremantle was identified as "Trip No. 1", so the first Nor'-West voyage became "Trip No. 2".

Trip No. 2
March 12th, 1909 – April 15th, 1909. Fremantle to Derby and return, via ports.
Master: John Rees
Progress: Northbound: dep Fremantle March 12th, arr Geraldton 13th, aground at Shark Bay 15th–25th, reloading and bunkering 25th–29th, arr Carnarvon 30th, Samson April 1st, Hedland 3rd, Broome 5th, Derby 7th. Southbound: dep Derby April 8th, arr Samson 11th, Fremantle 15th.
Incidents: *Koombana* lay hard aground beside the Denham channel for 10 days, with transfer of cargo to and from S.S. *Winfield* extending the delay to 15 days.

Trip No. 3
April 20th – May 9th, 1909. Fremantle to Derby and return, via ports.
Master: John Rees
Progress: Northbound: dep Fremantle April 20th, arr Samson 25th, Broome 28th, Derby 30th. Southbound: dep Derby May 1st, arr Samson 4th, Fremantle 9th.
Incidents: *Koombana* holed in a reef strike near Gantheaume Point on the evening of April 28th.
Notes: Premier Newton Moore was aboard, for a tour of the Nor'-West.

Trip No. 4
May 12th – June 3rd, 1909. Fremantle to Derby and return, via ports.
Master: John Rees
Progress: Northbound: dep Fremantle May 12th, arr Geraldton 13th, Samson 18th, Broome 22nd, Derby 24th. Southbound: dep Derby May 26th, arr Geraldton June 2nd, Fremantle 3rd.
Incidents: At Geraldton (northbound) on April 13th, the ship ran aground on the eastern side of the jetty. At Geraldton (southbound) on June 2nd, there was further trouble: two steel hawsers were broken during a difficult crosswind docking.
Notes: After the reef strike on Trip No. 3, the hull was inspected at Broome on April 22nd, at low tide. Some damage was discovered.

Trip No. 5
June 5th–13th, 1909. Fremantle to Sydney, for repair.
Master: John Rees
Progress: Eastbound: dep Fremantle June 5th, arr Albany 6th, Sydney 13th.
Notes: In *Koombana*'s absence, the Huddart-Parker liner *Burrumbeet* took up the Nor'-West running.

Docking & Lay-up
June 14th – July 23rd, 1909. Sydney.
Notes: Dry-docking revealed a seventy-foot gouge in the bottom of the hull, and a split a few feet
    long by the keel. Thirteen plates were removed and replaced, and a six-foot steel strap was used
    to reinforce the keelson.

Trip No. 6
July 24th – August 5th, 1909. Sydney to Fremantle, via Melbourne and Adelaide.
Master: John Rees
Progress: Westbound: dep Sydney July 24th, arr Melbourne 26th, Adelaide 30th, Fremantle August 5th.
Incidents: As *Koombana* crossed the Great Australian Bight, saloon passenger Mr Proctor suffered a
    broken leg while walking the decks.

Trip No. 7
August 8th–28th, 1909. Fremantle to Derby and return, via ports.
Master: John Rees
Progress: Northbound: dep Fremantle Aug 8th, arr Carnarvon 11th, Derby 19th.
    Southbound: dep Derby August 21st, arr Samson 23rd, Carnarvon 25th, Fremantle 28th.

Trip No. 8
September 3rd–24th, 1909. Fremantle to Derby and return, via ports.
Master: John Rees
Progress: Northbound: dep Fremantle Sept 3rd, arr Hedland 12th, Broome 14th, Derby 16th.
    Southbound: dep Derby Sept 17th, arr Broome 18th, Cossack 19th, Fremantle 24th.

Trip No. 9
September 29th – October 25th, 1909. Fremantle to Wyndham and return, via ports.
Master: John Rees
Progress: Northbound: dep Fremantle Sept 29th, arr Samson Oct 4th, Hedland 5th, Broome 7th,
    Derby 9th, Wyndham 12th. Southbound: dep Wyndham Oct 14th, arr Fremantle 25th.
Incidents: Leaving Port Hedland southbound on the night of October 19th, the ship ran aground in
    the channel and was stuck for about twelve hours.
Notes: *Koombana*'s first visit to Wyndham.

Trip No. 10
November 2nd–29th, 1909. Fremantle to Wyndham and return, via ports.
Master: John Rees
Progress: Northbound: dep Fremantle Nov 2nd, arr Geraldton 3rd, Samson 9th, Hedland 10th,
    Wyndham 17th. Southbound: dep Wyndham Nov 18th, arr Samson 23rd, Fremantle 29th.
Incidents: At Geraldton (southbound) on November 3rd, *Koombana* scraped the bottom again.
Notes: The first locomotives for the Pilbara railway were delivered to Port Hedland.

Trip No. 11
December 1st, 1909 – January 2nd, 1910. Fremantle to Wyndham and return, via ports.
Master: John Rees
Progress: Northbound: dep Fremantle Dec 4th, arr Samson 10th, Broome 14th, Derby 16th,
    Wyndham 20th. Southbound: dep Wyndham Dec 21st, arr Samson 27th, Fremantle Jan 1st, 1910.
Notes: For a variety of reasons, the start and end dates of a voyage will not always coincide with
    the dates of departure and return. The dates recorded often reflect the early engagement or late
    discharge of the crew.

Trip No. 12

January 3rd–26th, 1910. Fremantle to Derby and return, via ports.

Master: John Rees

Progress: Northbound: dep Fremantle Jan 3rd, arr Samson 12th, Broome 15th, Derby 17th. Southbound: dep Derby Jan18th, arr Samson 21st, Fremantle 26th.

Trip No. 13

January 27th – March 1st, 1910. Fremantle – Bunbury – Fremantle – Wyndham – Fremantle, via ports.

Master: John Rees

Progress: dep Fremantle Jan 27th, arr Bunbury 27th; dep Bunbury 28th, arr Fremantle 28th. Northbound: dep Fremantle Feb 1st, arr Carnarvon 4th, Samson 7th, Hedland 8th, Broome 10th, Derby 12th, Wyndham 15th. Southbound: dep Wyndham Feb 16th, arr Samson 23rd, Fremantle March 1st.

Incidents: On February 8th, north-east of Depuch Island, *Koombana* struck by squall; heeled over and slowly came right.

Notes: 37 Aborigines, the first to be released from the island lock hospitals, boarded at Carnarvon for repatriation to their home districts.

Trip No. 14

March 5th–26th, 1910. Fremantle to Derby and return, via ports.

Master: John Rees

Progress: Northbound: dep Fremantle March 5th, arr Samson 12th, Derby 17th. Southbound: dep Derby March 17th, arr Samson 20th, Fremantle 26th.

Trip No. 15

March 27th – April 29th, 1910. Fremantle to Wyndham and return, via ports.

Master: John Rees

Progress: Northbound: dep Fremantle April 1st, arr Samson 7th, Wyndham 16th. Southbound: dep Wyndham April 17th, arr Samson 23rd, Fremantle 29th.

Trip No. 16

April 30th – May 30th, 1910. Fremantle to Derby and return, via ports.

Master: John Rees

Progress: Northbound: dep Fremantle May 1st, arr Hedland 12th, Broome 14th, Derby 21st. Southbound: dep Derby May 22nd, bypassed Hedland, arr Cossack 25th, Fremantle 30th.

Incidents: *Koombana* 'neaped' (trapped by the tide) at Broome for five days (May 15th–20th).

Notes: Running several days late, Captain Rees bypassed Port Hedland on the return trip, to the great annoyance of that town.

Trip No. 17

May 31st – June 22nd, 1910. Fremantle to Derby and return, via ports.

Master: John Rees

Progress: Northbound: dep Fremantle June 3rd, arr Samson 9th, Hedland 10th, Broome 12th, Derby 14th. Southbound: dep Derby June 15th, arr Samson 18th, Fremantle 22nd.

Notes: Colonial Secretary James Connolly and Chief Harbourmaster Charles Irvine aboard for a tour of the Nor'-West. First steam locomotive for the Roebourne–Samson tramway delivered.

Trip No. 18

June 23rd – July 21st, 1910. Fremantle – Bunbury – Fremantle – Derby – Fremantle, via ports.

Master: John Rees

Progress: Dep Fremantle June 23rd, arr Bunbury 23rd; dep Bunbury 24th, arr Fremantle 24th. Northbound: dep Fremantle July 1st, arr Samson 7th, Depuch Island 8th, Hedland 8th, Broome 10th, Derby 13th. Southbound: dep Derby July 14th, arr Broome 15th, Samson 16th, Fremantle 21st.

Trip No. 19

July 22nd – August 23rd, 1910. Fremantle to Sydney and return, for second annual overhaul.

Master: John Rees

Progress: Eastbound: dep Fremantle July 22nd, arr Sydney 30th. Dry-docked July 30th – Aug 6th.
    Westbound: dep Sydney August 9th, arr Melb. 11th, Adelaide 13th, Albany 21st, Fremantle 22nd.

Trip No. 20
August 24rd – September 25th, 1910. Fremantle – Bunbury – Fremantle – Wyndham – Fremantle.
Master: John Rees
Progress: dep Fremantle Aug 23rd, arr Bunbury 24th; dep Bunbury 25th, arr Fremantle 25th.
    Northbound: dep Fremantle Aug 28th, arr Samson Sept 2nd, Broome 5th, Derby 7th,
    Wyndham 12th. Southbound: dep Wyndham Sept 13th, arr Samson 19th, Fremantle 24th.

Trip No. 21
September 26th – October 29th, 1910. Fremantle to Wyndham and return, via ports.
Master: John Rees
Progress: Northbound: dep Fremantle Sept 29th, arr Samson Oct 5th, Wyndham 14th.
    Southbound: dep Wyndham Oct 15th, arr Hedland 21st, Fremantle 27th.
Incidents: Fire broke out in hold No. 1 on October 20th, when *Koombana* was southbound between
    Broome and Port Hedland. The fire, attributed to spontaneous combustion in damp wool, defied
    all attempts to extinguish it; it was suppressed for seven days until the ship reached Fremantle.
Notes: Among the passengers for the run north were members of a Swedish scientific expedition
    headed by Dr Eric Mjoberg.

Trip No. 22
October 30st – November 24th, 1910. Fremantle to Derby and return, via ports.
Master: John Rees
Progress: Northbound: dep Fremantle Oct 31st, arr Samson Nov 6th, Broome 9th, Derby 11th.
    Southbound: dep Derby Nov 13th, arr Broome 14th, Hedland 16th, Samson 18th, Fremantle 24th.

Trip No. 23
November 25th – December 24th, 1910. Fremantle to Wyndham and return, via ports.
Master: John Rees
Progress: Northbound: dep Fremantle Nov 27th, arr Samson Dec 2nd, Hedland 3rd, Broome 5th,
    Derby 7th, Wyndham 11th. Southbound: dep Wyndham Dec 12th, arr Samson 18th, Fremantle 24th.
Notes: *Koombana* arrived in Broome three weeks after the devastating cyclone of November 19th.

Trip No. 24
December 25th, 1910 – January 23rd, 1911. Fremantle to Derby and return, via ports.
Master: John Rees
Progress: Northbound: dep Fremantle Dec 29th 1910, arr Samson Jan 4th 1911, Hedland Jan 5th,
    Broome 7th, Derby 9th. Southbound: dep Derby 10th, arr Hedland 13th, Fremantle 19th.
Incidents: At Victoria Quay, Fremantle on the night of January 21st, fodder in the holds caught fire.
    Extinguished by the Fremantle fire brigade.

Trip No. 25
January 24th – February 21st, 1911. Fremantle to Wyndham and return, via ports.
Master: P. C. Hurrell
Progress: Northbound: dep Fremantle Jan 26th, arr Samson Feb 1st, Hedland 2nd, Broome 4th,
    Derby 6th, Wyndham 9th. Southbound: dep Wyndham Feb 10th, arr Fremantle 21st.
Incidents: At Wyndham jetty on February 10th, *Koombana* was struck by a 'cock-eyed bob';
    three of four mooring lines parted, but no damage was done to the ship.
Notes: John Rees on leave; *Koombana* was captained by P. C. Hurrell for this voyage only. The Russian
    barque *Glenbank* was destroyed by a cyclone at Legendre Island on February 6th, five days after
    Koombana had passed by.

Trip No. 26
February 22nd – March 17th, 1911. Fremantle to Derby and return, via ports.
Master: John Rees (back from leave)
Progress: Northbound: dep Fremantle Feb 23rd, arr Samson March 3rd, Derby 8th. Southbound: dep
    Derby March 9th, arr Samson 12th, Fremantle 17th.

Trip No. 27
March 18th – April 18th, 1911. Fremantle to Wyndham and return, via ports.
Master: John Rees
Progress: Northbound: dep Fremantle March 23rd, arr Carnarvon 26th, Samson 29th, Broome April 1st,
    Wyndham 6th. Southbound: dep Wyndham April 7th, arr Carnarvon 14th, Fremantle 17th.
Notes: Joining the ship at Carnarvon on March 27th were 37 convalescent Aborigines, part of the
    second repatriation from the island lock hospitals.

Trip No. 28
April 19th – May 20th, 1911. Route: Fremantle to Derby and return, via ports.
Master: John Rees
Progress: Northbound: dep Fremantle April 24th, arr Geraldton 25th, Carnarvon 28th, Onslow 30th,
    Samson May 1st, Hedland 2nd, Broome 4th, Derby 10th.
    Southbound: dep Derby May 11th, arr Broome 13th, Hedland 14th, Samson 15th, Fremantle 20th.
Incidents:
    1. At Fremantle before departure, *Koombana* was accidentally rammed by the S.S. *Pilbarra*.
    2. At sea between Geraldton and Shark Bay, fireman Rankin died of a heart attack.
    3. For the second time, *Koombana* was 'neaped' at Broome. Delayed four days on this occasion.
Notes: English anthropologist Radcliffe-Brown travelled north to Carnarvon with a new team,
    after falling out with Daisy Bates.

Trip No. 29
May 23rd – June 18th, 1911. Fremantle to Wyndham and return, via ports.
Master: John Rees
Progress: Northbound: dep Fremantle May 23rd, arr Samson 29th, Hedland 30th, Broome June 1st,
    Derby 3rd, Wyndham 6th. Southbound: dep Wyndham June 7th, arr Samson 13th, Fremantle 18th.

Trip No. 30
June 20st – July 12th, 1911. Fremantle to Derby and return, via ports.
Master: John Rees
Progress: Northbound: dep Fremantle June 21st, arr Samson 27th, Hedland 28th, Broome 30th,
    Derby July 2nd. Southbound: dep Derby July 4th, arr Samson 6th, Fremantle 11th.

Trip No. 31
July 13th – September 6th, 1911. Fremantle to Sydney and return, via Melbourne.
Masters: John Rees, Tom Allen
Progress: Eastbound: dep Fremantle July 13th, arr Sydney 21st.
    Dry-docked July 22nd – Aug 16th. Laid up Aug 16th–24th.
    Westbound: dep Sydney Aug 28th, arr Melbourne 30th, Fremantle Sept 6th.
Incidents: Before departure from Fremantle on May 13th, second cook William Jones was killed in a
    fall down the main companionway.
Notes: Marconi wireless telegraphy apparatus was installed as part of this third annual overhaul.
    John Rees relinquished his command on August 16th. The ship was then laid up for eight days,
    pending the arrival of her new master, Thomas Allen.

Trip No. 32
September 12th – October 12th, 1911. Fremantle to Wyndham and return, via ports.
Master: Tom Allen
Progress: Northbound: dep Fremantle Sept 12th, arr Samson 19th, Hedland 21st, Broome 23rd,
    Derby 25th, Wyndham 28th. Southbound: dep Wyndham 29th, arr Samson Oct 5th, Fremantle 11th.
Incidents: *Koombana* ran aground entering Port Hedland on September 21st.

Trip No. 33
October 13th – November 8th, 1911. Fremantle to Derby and return, via ports.
Master: Tom Allen
Progress: Northbound: dep Fremantle Oct 17th, arr Samson 23rd, Hedland 25th, Derby 28th.
    Southbound: dep Derby Oct 29th, arr Hedland 31st, Samson Nov 1st, Fremantle 8th.

Incidents: At Port Hedland on October 25th, ship got into shoal water and touched bottom again.
Notes: On return to Fremantle, baker Edwin Albrecht claimed to have been assaulted by chief steward
Frank Johnson. The resulting court case triggered the *Koombana* firemen's strike.

Trip No. 34

November 9th, 1911 – January 3rd, 1912. Fremantle to Wyndham and return, via ports.
Master: Tom Allen
Progress: Northbound: dep Fremantle Nov 30th, arr Shark Bay Dec 4th, Carnarvon 4th, Samson 7th,
Hedland 9th, Broome 11th, Derby 13th, Wyndham 17th. Southbound: dep Wyndham Dec 18th,
arr Derby 20th, Broome 22nd, Hedland 24th, Samson 25th, Onslow, 26th, Carnarvon 27th,
Shark Bay 28th, Geraldton 29th, Fremantle 30th.
Incidents: Three incidents, all related to *Koombana*'s delayed departure and the lunar cycle: she
touched bottom at Shark Bay on December 4th, took ground near the Carnarvon jetty later that
day, and struggled to escape Port Hedland in the early hours of Christmas Day.
Notes: The strike kept *Koombana* tied up at Fremantle for three weeks (November 8th–30th).

Trip No. 35

January 9th – February 6th, 1912. Fremantle to Wyndham and return, via ports.
Master: Tom Allen
Progress: Northbound: dep Fremantle Jan 9th, arr Shark Bay 12th, Carnarvon 12th, Onslow 15th,
Samson 16th, Depuch 17th, Hedland 18th, Broome 20th, Derby 22nd, Wyndham 26th. Southbound:
dep Wyndham Jan 27th, arr Fremantle Feb 6th.
Incidents: At Port Hedland (northbound) on January 18th, *Koombana* struck the sandbar again.

Trip No. 36

February 8th – March 7th, 1912
Route: Fremantle to Wyndham and return, via ports.
Master: Tom Allen
Progress: Northbound: dep Fremantle Feb 9th, Onslow 14th, Samson 15th, Hedland 17th, Broome 19th,
Derby 21st, Wyndham 25th. Southbound: dep Wyndham Feb 25th, arr Broome 29th,
Hedland March 1st, Carnarvon 3rd, Fremantle 6th.

Trip No. 37

March 12th–20th, 1912. Fremantle to Derby and return, via ports.
Master: Tom Allen
Progress: Northbound: dep Fremantle March 12th, arr Geraldton 13th, Shark Bay 15th, Carnarvon 15th,
Onslow 17th, Samson 18th, Port Hedland 19th; dep Port Hedland March 20th.
Koombana was last seen at about 12.30 p.m. on Wednesday, March 20th, heading north or north-east.

APPENDIX II. NAUTICAL GLOSSARY

This listing is selective: it includes only terms left unexplained in the narrative.

abeam
 alongside or abreast, at right-angles from the ship's centreline.

aft
 the after part of a vessel, towards the back or stern.

amidships
 in or toward the part of a ship midway between bow and stern.

astern
 at or toward the stern of a vessel, or behind the vessel.

awash
 approximately level with the sea surface, so that waves wash over.

barque
 a sailing ship square-rigged on all but the mizzen mast (aftermost mast),
 with the mizzen mast rigged with fore and aft sails.

(on) *beam ends*
 inclined so much on one side that the horizontal members supporting the deck
 approach a vertical position.

bow
 the forward part of the hull of a vessel.

port bow or *starboard bow*
 either to port or starboard, the hull surface that curves inward toward the bow.

bow line
 a mooring line from a ship's bow.

bowline
 a basic sailor's knot that forms a loop but does not slip,
 and remains easy to untie after being pulled tight.

chine
 the line of intersection, or area of transition, between the side and the bottom of a hull.

dead reckoning
 the determination of a ship's position by course steered and progress estimated,
 with allowance for drift, but without the aid of landmarks and without celestial observations.

forecastle (also *fo'c'sle*)
 the forward part of the upper deck of a ship, often reserved for crew accommodation.

graving dock
 a dry dock where the hulls of ships are repaired or maintained.

gunwale
 the upper edge of the side of a vessel.

hawser
 a cable or rope used for mooring or towing a ship.

hawsepipe
 an inclined pipe through which the anchor chain passes,
 and which holds the shank of the anchor when the anchor is raised.

heave to
 to place or configure a vessel so as to minimise its movement through the water,
 often by keeping the vessel's head to the wind.

heel
    to lean to one side as a result of the wind, waves or a turn.

helm
    the tiller or wheel used for steering a ship.

inshore
    (adjective) at sea but close to land, or (adverb) towards or closer to the shore.

keelson
    a longitudinal stiffening member above and attached to the keel of a ship.

ketch
    a two-masted, fore-and-aft rigged vessel in which the after (mizzen) mast is shorter
    than the forward (main) mast.

lee side
    the downwind or 'shelter' side of a vessel: the side that the wind touches last
    as it passes over.

lighter
    a boat or barge used for the transfer of cargo between ship and shore, or from ship to ship.

lugger
    The name derives from "lugsail", a four-sided sail hoisted on a yard oblique to the mainmast.
    Nor'-West pearling luggers were typically two-masted, lugsail-rigged vessels of 12–14 tons.

miss stays
    to fail in the attempt to 'come about', ie. to place a sailing vessel on the opposite tack.

mizzen mast
    the mast aft of the mainmast.

The lugger Essie *under full sail, c. 1916.*

neap tides (or '*neaps*')
: within the lunar cycle, the days on which the rise and fall of the tide are least.

neaped
: trapped by tide; a vessel is said to be 'neaped' when, having entered a port on a high tide, it has an insufficient depth of water to leave.

poop
: an enclosed superstructure at the stern of a ship, above the main deck, often extending from the mizzen mast to the stern.

port
: the side of a ship that is on the left when one is facing forward.

port quarter, *starboard quarter*
: either to port or starboard, the aft part of a ship's side.

quartermaster
: a seaman with particular responsibility for steering and signals.

rudder post
: on a ship with a single screw propeller, an additional sternpost, aft of the propeller, to which the rudder is attached.

sea and *swell*
: "sea" is the disturbance of the ocean surface directly attributable to local wind conditions; "swell" refers to the succession of long, crestless waves arriving at a location or passing beneath a vessel, but not directly attributable to local conditions.

schooner
: a vessel with at least two masts, having fore-and-aft sails on all masts.

to *slip* (anchor cable)
: to release an anchor cable entirely, thus sacrificing the anchor.

spring tides (or '*springs*')
: within the lunar cycle, the days on which the rise and fall of the tide are greatest.

to *stand on one's track*
: to maintain one's course.

starboard
: the side of a ship that is on the right when one is facing forward.

steerage
: the part of a ship offering the cheapest passenger accommodation.

step (of a mast)
: a block fixed to the keel of a boat, to carry and distribute the weight of a mast.

sternpost
: the principal vertical member at the stern of a ship, extending from keel to deck.

swell
: see "*sea* and *swell*"

T-head
: a T-shaped addition to a jetty, to facilitate the berthing of vessels, often built where prevailing winds blow parallel to the shore.

'tween deck or *'tween decks*
: typically, storage space between the main deck of a ship and the hold.

weather side
: the windward or 'upwind' side of a vessel: the side that the wind touches first as it passes over.

APPENDIX III. UNITS & CONVERSIONS

LATITUDE & LONGITUDE

Positions on the surface of the earth, on land or sea, may be expressed in degrees of latitude north or south of the Equator, and degrees of longitude east or west of Greenwich. Degrees are divided into sixty minutes, with each minute subdivided into sixty seconds. Latitude and longitude are usually given in that order.

Abbreviations:

    N, S, E, W = north, south, east, west
    deg. or ° = degrees
    min. or ′ = minutes
    sec. or ″ = seconds

For example, the location of the Bedout Island light is S 19° 35′ 17″ E 119° 06′ 04″.

LENGTH & DISTANCE

Under the Imperial system, there are 12 inches to the foot, 3 feet to the yard, 22 yards to the chain, and 80 chains to the mile.

Conversions:

    1 inch is about 25 millimetres.
    1 foot is about 300 millimetres.
    1 yard is a little less than a metre.
    1 mile is about 1,600 metres or 1.6 kilometres.

Note that a mile on land—the "statute mile"—is different to the "nautical mile" used at sea. The nautical mile, being exactly equal to one minute of latitude, has particular usefulness for mariners. One nautical mile is about 1,850 metres.

Examples:

    page 218: "At 5′ 0″ tall, butcher Charlie Walker . . ." 5′ 0″ is about 152 cm.
    page 58: "a seventy-foot gouge in the bottom of the hull" 70 feet is about 20 metres.
    page 18: "a hundred yards offshore" 100 yards is about 90 metres.
    page 52: "90 miles to the post office" 90 miles is about 145 kilometres.

DEPTH

1 fathom = 6 feet = 1.83 metres.
"Forty Fathoms Deep" is 240 feet or about 75 metres.

SPEED

1 knot = 1 nautical mile per hour = 1.15 (statute) miles per hour = 1.85 kilometres per hour.
Koombana's top speed was about 14½ knots or 27 kilometres per hour.

VOLUME

Under the Imperial system, there are eight pints to the gallon.
One pint is about 570 millilitres, and one gallon is about 4.5 litres.

Examples:

    page 100: "3 pints of tea" is about 1.7 litres.
    page 269: "five shillings per hundred gallons" 500 gallons is about 2,300 litres.

WEIGHT

Under the *avoirdupois* system, there are 16 ounces to the pound, 14 pounds to the stone, 8 stone to the hundredweight, and 20 hundredweight to the ton. One ton, therefore, is 2,240 pounds. This is very close to the metric tonne, at 1,000 kilograms or 2,205 pounds.

Other weight conversions:
>An ounce is about 28 grams.
>A pound is about 450 grams.
>A stone is a little over 6 kg.
>A hundredweight is a little over 50 kg.

Abbreviations: oz. = ounces, lb. = pounds, cwt. = hundredweight.

Examples:
>page 100: "1½ oz. sugar" is about 40 grams or 12 teaspoons.
>page 105: "Rosie, who tips the scales at 15 stone . . ." 15 stone = 95 kilograms.
>page 138: "iron tanks weighing 800 pounds apiece" 800 lb. is about 360 kg.
>page 244: "a basket containing 1½ cwt. of shell" 1½ cwt = 76 kilograms.

TEMPERATURE

There is no simple multiplier to convert from degrees Fahrenheit to degrees Celsius. 70° Fahrenheit = 21° Celsius; similarly, 80°F = 27°C, 90°F = 32°C, 100°F = 38°C.

There is one instance only in the narrative, on page 141: "the temperature may rise to 120 degrees Fahrenheit." 120°F = 49°C.

MONEY

There are twelve pence (pennies) to the shilling, and twenty shillings to the pound, with a guinea being 21 shillings.

Abbreviations:
>£ = pounds
>s = shillings
>d = pence (pennies).

An amount of three pounds, seven shillings and sixpence would be written as £3 7s. 6d. or £3/7/6. In common speech, seven shillings and sixpence was simply "seven and six."

The change in the value of the currency over 100 years is so great that no conversion to decimal currency is meaningful. However, in 1878, "a purse of ten guineas" (page 288) was equivalent to about three months' pay at a modest adult wage. And in 1904, Daisy Bates was hired on "a junior clerical wage of eight shillings a day"(page 94). That was a little more than the basic adult wage set in 1907 at seven shillings per day, or £2/2/– for a six-day working week (page 116).

NOTES

1 A TICKET TO THE FUTURE

1   a. "Local News", *Geraldton Guardian* (WA), Saturday 12 December 1908, p. 2.
     b. "New s.s. Koombana", *The Hedland Advocate* (Port Hedland, WA), Saturday 19 December 1908.
     c. "A Fine New Steamer", *Daily News* (Perth, WA), Monday 15 February 1909, p. 9.

2   a. "A Fine New Steamer", *Daily News*, Monday 15 February 1909, p. 9.
     b. "A New Steamer", *The Advertiser* (Adelaide, SA), Thursday 18 February 1909, p. 10.
     c. "Nor'-West Shipping Trade", *The Western Mail* (Perth, WA), Saturday 20 Feb. 1909, p. 14, 26.

3   "New Steamer Koombana", *Daily News*, Friday 12 February 1909, p. 3.

4–6 "S.s. Koombana", *The Hedland Advocate*, Saturday 13 March 1909, p. 8.

7   "The S.S. Koombana", *The Northern Times* (Carnarvon, WA), Saturday 13 March 1909, p. 4.

8   a. "The Wool Trade, 1903–4", *The Western Mail*, Saturday 02 April 1904, p. 8.
     b. "Australasian Wool Production, 1904–5", *The Western Mail*, Saturday 15 July 1905, p. 10.
     c. "Roebourne Pastoral Notes", *The Northern Times*, Saturday 24 November 1906, p. 2.
     d. "Notes", *The Western Mail*, Saturday 18 May 1907, p. 4.

9   a. "The Fisheries Department", *The Western Mail*, Saturday 18 July 1903, p. 11.
     b. "Pearling Industry", *Geraldton Guardian*, Friday 23 August 1907, p. 2.
     c. "Broome Pearlers", *The Northern Times*, Saturday 11 January 1913, p. 8.
     d. "Pearling", *The Western Mail*, Friday 21 December 1917, p. 39.

10   "The Wealth of Kimberley", *The West Australian*, Wednesday 18 September 1907, p. 6.

11   a. "Derby Notes", *The Western Mail*, Saturday 18 May 1907, p. 10.
     b. "Water Provision at West Kimberley", *The Western Mail*, Saturday 06 January 1912, p. 35.

12   "The Far North Cattle Industry", *The Western Mail*, Saturday 02 February 1907, p. 8.

13   The first Australian national census, conducted in April 1911, declared the population of Western Australia—"Exclusive of Full-blooded Aboriginals"—to be 282,114, with about 107,000 (38 per cent) residing in the Perth metropolis. Significantly, only about 5,600 individuals (2 per cent) lived north of the 26th parallel. The distribution of "Nor'-Westers" was approximately: Shark Bay, 220; Carnarvon, 730; Lower Gascoyne, 160; Upper Gascoyne, 300; Minilya, 300; Ashburton district, 430; Roebourne district, 830; Port Hedland, 610; Broome, 870; Derby and West Kimberley, 730; East Kimberley, 220; Wyndham, 150.

14   "Pilbarra Railway Route", *The West Australian*, Saturday 31 March 1906, p. 8.

15   a. "Nor'-West Coastal Mail", *The Northern Times*, Saturday 15 December 1906, p. 3.
     b. Adelaide Steamship Company, minutes of directors' meeting, Wednesday 12 December 1906. Noel Butlin Archives Centre, Australian National University, 0186/Z535 Box 12.

16   Adelaide Steamship Company, minutes of directors' meeting, Monday 25 March 1907.

17   Ship Plans, S.S. *Yongala* & *Grantala*, Armstrong Whitworth & Co., 1903. Noel Butlin Archives Centre, Australian National University, 0186/N46/1084.

18   Adelaide Steamship Company, minutes of directors' meeting, Wednesday 11 September 1907. Noel Butlin Archives Centre, Australian National University, 0186/Z535 Box 12.

19   a. Adelaide Steamship Company, minutes of directors' meeting, Wednesday 25 September 1907.
     b. Adelaide Steamship Company, minutes of directors' meeting, Wednesday 02 October 1907.
     c. Adelaide Steamship Company, minutes of directors' meeting, Wednesday 27 November 1907.

20   "A Fine New Steamer", *Daily News*, Monday 15 February 1909, p. 9.

21   Adelaide Steamship Company, minutes of directors' meeting, Wednesday 04 December 1907.

22   a. Editorial, *The Northern Times*, Saturday 07 September 1907, p. 2.
     b. "The Pilbarra Railway", *The Hedland Advocate*, Saturday 20 February 1909, p. 3.
     c. Editorial, *The Hedland Advocate*, Saturday 01 May 1909, p. 4.
     d. "The Railway", *The Hedland Advocate*, Saturday 16 October 1909, p. 3.

23   a. "Nor'-West Lights", *The West Australian*, Wednesday 29 June 1910, p. 2.
     b. "Lighthouses – N.W. Coast", Harbour & Light Department, WA, 1911. State Records Office of WA, Cons 1066 Item 1911/549.

24   General Arrangement, S.S. "Koombana", ship plans on linen, Alexander Stephen & Son, 1907. National Maritime Museum, Greenwich, London.

25   Adelaide Steamship Company, 1907, *No. 429: Specification for the Building of a Steel Screw Steamship with Triple Expansion Engines*. University of Glasgow Archives, UCS3/11/31.

26   a. "The Koombana Launched", *The Sydney Morning Herald*, Thursday 24 December 1908, p. 8.
     b. Adelaide Steamship Company, minutes of directors' meeting, Wednesday 03 June 1908. Noel Butlin Archives Centre, Australian National University, 0186/Z535 Box 12.
     c. Adelaide Steamship Company, minutes of directors' meeting, Wednesday 07 October 1908.
     d. Adelaide Steamship Company, minutes of directors' meeting, Wednesday 28 October 1908.
     e. Adelaide Steamship Company, minutes of directors' meeting, Tuesday 29 December 1908.
     f. Adelaide Steamship Company, minutes of directors' meeting, Wednesday 06 January 1909.

2   Narrow Seas

1   The modern spelling of Shark Bay has been adopted in the narrative, but all variants—"Shark's Bay," "Sharks' Bay", and "Sharks Bay"—will be encountered in quoted sources.

2   "S.S. Koombana", *Geraldton Guardian* (WA), Tuesday 16 March 1909, p. 2.

3   a. "The S.S. Koombana", *The Northern Times* (Carnarvon, WA), Saturday 20 March 1909, p. 3.
     b. "s.s. Koombana", *The Northern Times*, Saturday 12 June 1909, p. 2.

4   "Blue sky, red sunset." Science students may recall a classroom physics demonstration in which a beam of light is passed through water artificially clouded by the addition of sodium thiosulfate and a few drops of acid. As the reaction proceeds, the illuminated water acquires a blue hue while the emerging beam weakens to a rusty red.

5   a. "The Stranded Koombana", *The West Australian*, Thursday 18 March 1909, p. 5.
     b. "With The Koombana", *The Western Mail* (Perth, WA), Saturday 10 April 1909, pp. 14, 27.

6   "With The Koombana", *The Western Mail*, Saturday 10 April 1909, pp. 14, 27.

7   "Phases of the Moon: 1901 to 2000", http://eclipse.gsfc.nasa.gov/phase/phases1901.html.

8   "The Adjustment of General Average per 'Koombana' S.S., on a voyage to north west ports of Western Australia", insurance calculation and apportionment following grounding of *Koombana* at Shark Bay in March 1909, Holmes & Neill, Average Adjusters, Sydney, 18 July 1910. Battye Library Archives, 2216A. Includes extract of *Koombana*'s log.

9   Low, James Galloway, *Letters, 1904–91*, Battye Library, ACC 2612A (listing: MN 681). Letter from Jim to his friend Peggy, 09 May 1909.

10–14 "With The Koombana", *The Western Mail*, Saturday 10 April 1909, pp. 14, 27.

15   Low, James Galloway, letter to Peggy, 09 May 1909. See 9 above.

16   "The Adjustment of General Average" (insurance calculation). See 8 above.

17   a. "The S.S. Koombana", *Geraldton Guardian*, Thursday 18 March 1909, p. 2.
     b. "With The Koombana", *The Western Mail*, Saturday 10 April 1909, pp. 14, 27.

18   "The Adjustment of General Average" (insurance calculation). See 8 above.

19   "The Adjustment of General Average" (insurance calculation). Itemisation of cargo losses.

20–21 "With The Koombana", *The Western Mail*, Saturday 10 April 1909, pp. 14, 27.

22–23 "The Adjustment of General Average" (insurance calculation). Extract of *Koombana*'s log.

24   "With The Koombana", *The Western Mail*, Saturday 10 April 1909, pp. 14, 27.

25   a. "With The Koombana", *The Western Mail*, Saturday 10 April 1909, pp. 14, 27.
     b. "The Adjustment of General Average" (insurance calculation). Extract of *Koombana*'s log.

26   Low, James Galloway, letter to Peggy, 09 May 1909. See 9 above.

27   "The Adjustment of General Average" (insurance calculation). Extract of *Koombana*'s log.

28   a. "With The Koombana", *The Western Mail*, Saturday 10 April 1909, pp. 14, 27.
     b. "The Adjustment of General Average" (insurance calculation). Extract of *Koombana*'s log.

29–30 "The Adjustment of General Average" (insurance calculation). Extract of *Koombana*'s log.

31   "With The Koombana", *The Western Mail*, Saturday 10 April 1909, pp. 14, 27.

32   a. "With The Koombana", *The Western Mail*, Saturday 10 April 1909, pp. 14, 27.
      b. "The Adjustment of General Average" (insurance calculation). Extract of *Koombana*'s log.

33   "With The Koombana", *The Western Mail*, Saturday 10 April 1909, pp. 14, 27.

34   "The Adjustment of General Average" (insurance calculation). Extract of *Koombana*'s log.

3 GULLIVER'S TRAVELS

1   Arago, J. (Jacques), 1823, *Narrative of a Voyage Round the World (Promenade Autour du Monde)*, Reprint 1971, Da Capo Press, New York, p. 166.

2   "The Nor'-West Ports", *The West Australian*, Tuesday 28 June 1910, p. 5.

3   "Shark Bay's History", http://www.sharkbay.org/default.aspx?WebPageID=185.

4   a. "Shark's Bay", *Perth Gazette and West Australian Times*, Friday 05 December 1873, p. 3.
      b. "The Nor'-West Ports", *The West Australian*, Tuesday 28 June 1910, p. 5.

5   Low, James Galloway, *Letters, 1904–91*, Battye Library, ACC 2612A (listing: MN 681). Letter from Jim to his friend Peggy, 09 May 1909.

6   "Coloured Labor", *The West Australian*, Tuesday 10 February 1914, p. 4.

7   Low, James Galloway, letter to Peggy, 09 May 1909. See 5 above.

8–9   "The Nor'-West Ports", *The West Australian*, Tuesday 28 June 1910, p. 5.

10   a. "The River in Flood", *The Northern Times* (Carnarvon, WA), Saturday 23 January 1909, p. 2.
      b. "A Disastrous Flood", *The Northern Times*, Saturday 30 January 1909, p. 2.

11   Miller, Cecily Agnes, 1996–2000, *Photographical history of Carnarvon and the Gascoyne Region*, Shire of Carnarvon, WA.

12   "From Bernier to Wyndham", *The West Australian*, Thursday 28 April 1910, p. 2.

13   "The Nor'-West Ports", *The West Australian*, Tuesday 28 June 1910, p. 5.

14   "The Great Nor'-West", *The West Australian*, Thursday 02 September 1909, p. 6.

15   "The Nor'-West Ports", *The West Australian*, Tuesday 28 June 1910, p. 5.

16   "The Great Nor'-West", *The West Australian*, Thursday 02 September 1909, p. 6.

17   "The Nor'-West Ports", *The West Australian*, Tuesday 28 June 1910, p. 5.

18   "Storm at Onslow", *The West Australian*, Monday 12 April 1909, p. 4.

19   "The Tien Tsin's track to the Harding River", *Perth Gazette and West Australian Times*, Friday 05 June 1863, p. 2.

20   "Exploration and Settlement of the N.W. Coast", *Perth Gazette and West Australian Times*, Friday 25 September 1863, p. 2.

21–22 "The Pearl Shell Fisheries at Tien Tsin, North-West Australia", *The Sydney Morning Herald*, Thursday 26 May 1870, p. 5.

23   "Notes from the Nor'-West", *The West Australian*, Tuesday 28 March 1882, p. 3.

24–25 "The Nor'-West Ports", *The West Australian*, Tuesday 28 June 1910, p. 5.

26   "Nor'-West Ports" (letter to the editor), *The West Australian*, Tuesday 05 July 1910, p. 2.

27   "New Steamer for Nor'-West", *The Hedland Advocate* (Port Hedland, WA), 10 April 1909, p. 6.

28   "Government Attention Needed", *The Hedland Advocate*, Saturday 20 March 1909.

29   "The Nor'-West Ports", *The West Australian*, Tuesday 28 June 1910, p. 5.

30   "Passing Notes", *The Hedland Advocate*, Saturday 27 February 1909.

31   "Colored Invasion in the North of Australia" (editorial), *The Hedland Advocate*, Saturday 12 December 1908, p. 6.

32   "Challenge" (advertisement), *The Hedland Advocate*, Saturday 18 December 1909, p. 3.

33   "Passing Notes", *The Hedland Advocate*, Saturday 13 March 1909, p. 8.

35   "The Passing of Condon", *The Hedland Advocate*, Saturday 09 December 1911.

36   "The Nor'-West Ports", *The West Australian*, Tuesday 28 June 1910, p. 5.

37–38 Low, James Galloway, letter to Peggy, 09 May 1909. See 5 above.

39   "From Bernier to Wyndham", *The West Australian*, Thursday 28 April 1910, p. 2.

40   Tables of distances, W.A. ports, recommended tracks from port to port, Adelaide Steamship Company, c1907. Noel Butlin Archives Centre, Australian National University, 0186/N46/835/27.

41   "The Nor'-West Ports", *The West Australian*, Tuesday 28 June 1910, p. 5.

42   Ronan, Tom, 1964, *Packhorse and Pearling Boat*, Cassell Australia, Melbourne, Chapter 2.

43   Low, James Galloway, letter to Peggy, 09 May 1909. See 5 above.

44   "The Nor'-West Ports", *The West Australian*, Tuesday 28 June 1910, p. 5.

45   Low, James Galloway, letter to Peggy, 09 May 1909. See 5 above.

46   "From Bernier to Wyndham", *The West Australian*, Thursday 28 April 1910, p. 2.

47–48 "The Nor'-West Ports", *The West Australian*, Tuesday 28 June 1910, p. 5.

49–50 "From Bernier to Wyndham", *The West Australian*, Thursday 28 April 1910, p. 2.

51   Battye, J. S. (James Sykes)(ed.), 1915, *The History of the North West of Australia, embracing Kimberley, Gascoyne, and Murchison Districts*, V. K. Jones & Company, Perth.

52–53 Moore, Doug, *Papers*: extracts from his account of his life in the Kimberley 1904–1914, Battye Library, ACC 3829A (listing MN 1237).

54   "The Nor'-West Ports", *The West Australian*, Tuesday 28 June 1910, p. 5.

55   Durack, Mary, 1983, *Sons in the Saddle*, Constable, London, p. 269.

56   "From Bernier to Wyndham", *The West Australian*, Thursday 28 April 1910, p. 2.

4 OF FEAR AND FASCINATION

1   a. "The Koombana Mishap", *The West Australian*, Saturday 07 August 1909, p. 12.
     b. "Grounding of the Koombana", *Daily News* (Perth, WA), Saturday 07 August 1909, p. 7.

2   General Arrangement, S.S. "Koombana", ship plans on linen, Alexander Stephen & Son, 1907. National Maritime Museum, Greenwich, London.

3   a. "The New Steamer Koombana", *Daily News*, Tuesday 04 May 1909, p. 9.
     b. "Shipping", *The West Australian*, Wednesday 05 May 1909, p. 6.

4   Low, James Galloway, *Letters, 1904–91*, Battye Library, ACC 2612A (listing: MN 681). Letter from Jim to his friend Peggy, 09 May 1909.

5   a. "The Geraldton Harbour", *The West Australian*, Saturday 15 May 1909, p. 12.
     b. Adelaide Steamship Company, minutes of directors' meeting, Wednesday 19 May 1909. Noel Butlin Archives Centre, Australian National University, 0186/Z535 Box 12.

6   "Local News", *Geraldton Guardian* (WA), Thursday 03 June 1909, p. 2.

7   "The Nor'-West Mail Service", *Daily News*, Friday 04 June 1909, p. 5.

8   "S.S. Koombana", *The Northern Times* (Carnarvon, WA), Saturday 12 June 1909, p. 2.

9   a. "Damaged Koombana in Dock", *The Sydney Morning Herald*, Tuesday 15 June 1909, p. 8.
     b. "Grounding of the Koombana", *Daily News*, Saturday 07 August 1909, p. 7.
     c. Nutley, David, "The Koombana" (unpub.), Department of Maritime Archeology, WA Museum.

10   a. "The Koombana Mishap", *The West Australian*, Saturday 07 August 1909, p. 12.
     b. Adelaide Steamship Company, minutes of directors' meeting, Wednesday 23 June 1909.

11   a. "An Unlucky Steamer", *Kalgoorlie Miner* (WA), Saturday 05 June 1909, p. 11.
     b. "Local News", *Geraldton Guardian*, Tuesday 08 June 1909, p. 2.

12–13 "The Waratah", *The West Australian*, Thursday 09 December 1909, p. 7.

14   "Clydesite" (online magazine), http://www.clydesite.co.uk/articles/upperriver.asp.

15   a. "The New Steamer Waratah", *The Advertiser* (Adelaide, SA), Tuesday 29 September 1908, p. 10.
     b. "SS Waratah", *Wikipedia*, http://en.wikipedia.org/wiki/SS_Waratah.

16   "The New Steamer Waratah", *The Advertiser*, Tuesday 29 September 1908, p. 10.

17   "The Waratah", *The West Australian*, Saturday 14 August 1909, p. 11.

18   a. "Professor Bragg And The Waratah", *The Register* (Adelaide, SA), Tuesday 17 August 1909, p. 5.
     b. "The Waratah Enquiry", *The Register* (Adelaide, SA), Friday 20 January 1911, p. 5.

19   "SS Waratah", *Wikipedia*, http://en.wikipedia.org/wiki/SS_Waratah.

20   "Wireless and the Waratah", *The Sydney Morning Herald*, Tuesday 10 August 1909, p. 6.

21   a. "The Overdue Waratah", *The Sydney Morning Herald*, Wednesday 04 August 1909, p. 9.
     b. "Missing Vessels", *The Argus* (Melbourne), Thursday 05 August 1909, p. 7.
     c. "The Missing Waratah", *The Mercury* (Hobart, Tas.), Saturday 14 August 1909, p. 5.

22   "The Waratah", *The Sydney Morning Herald*, Wednesday 11 August 1909, p. 9.

23   "SS Waratah", *Wikipedia*, http://en.wikipedia.org/wiki/SS_Waratah.

24–25 "Is it the Waratah?", *The Argus*, Wednesday 11 August 1909, p. 7.

26–27 "The Waratah", *The Advertiser*, Monday 16 August 1909, p. 7.

28   a. "Missing Vessels", *The Argus*, Thursday 05 August 1909, p. 7.
   b. "The Missing Waratah", *The Mercury*, Saturday 14 August 1909, p. 5.

29   a. "The Waratah", *The West Australian*, Thursday 09 December 1909, p. 7.
   b. "The Missing Waratah", *The Mercury*, Monday 13 December 1909, p. 5.

30   "The Missing Waratah", *The Argus*, Thursday 23 December 1909, p. 7.

31   a. "Tenders Called For", *The Argus*, Wednesday 29 December 1909, p. 6.
   b. "The Waratah", *The Argus*, Friday 31 December 1909, p. 5.
   c. "Five Tenders Received", *The Argus*, Saturday 08 January 1910, p. 19.

32   "The Lost Waratah", *The Sydney Morning Herald*, Friday 04 March 1910, p. 7.

33–34 "The Waratah", *The Register*, Friday 11 March 1910, p. 9.

35   "The Lost Waratah", *The Advertiser*, Friday 11 March 1910, p. 9.

36   a. "Southern News", *The Northern Times*, Saturday 12 February 1910, p. 3.
   b. "Koombana Inquiry", *The Sunday Times* (Perth, WA), Sunday 26 May 1912, p. 5.
   c. Moore, Doug, *Papers*, extracts from his account of his life in the Kimberley 1904–1914, Battye Library, ACC 3829A (listing MN 1237).

37   a. "Busy Port", *The Hedland Advocate* (Port Hedland, WA), Saturday 18 December 1909, p. 6.
   b. "S.S. KOOMBANA", *The Hedland Advocate*, Saturday 18 December 1909, p. 6.
   c. "The Koombana", *The Hedland Advocate*, Saturday 14 May 1910, p. 6.

38   a. "General News", *The Hedland Advocate*, Saturday 26 June 1909, p. 3.
   b. "The Koombana", *The Hedland Advocate*, Saturday 19 February 1910, p. 4.

39   "The Waratah", *The Advertiser*, Saturday 08 October 1910, p. 14.

40   "A message from missing steamer 'Waratah'", police report, Fremantle, 08 November 1910. State Records Office of WA, AN16/5 Item 1909/821.

41   "The Waratah", *The Advertiser*, Monday 31 March 1913, p. 16.

42   a. "The Waratah", *The Advertiser*, Monday 16 February 1914, p. 7.
   b. "Mystery of the Waratah", *The Mercury* (Hobart, Tas.), Tuesday 26 May 1914, p. 3.

43   a. "Fire on the s.s. Koombana", *The Hedland Advocate*, Saturday 22 October 1910.
   b. "The Lost Waratah", *The Argus*, Monday 19 December 1910, p. 7.
   c. Official Log Book, S.S. *Koombana*, 13/8/1910 – 13/01/1911. State Records Office of WA, ACC 1056 AN 16/4 Item 116.

45   "The Waratah Enquiry", *The Register*, Friday 20 January 1911, p. 5.

46   a. "The Waratah", *The Register*, Thursday 12 January 1911, p. 5.
   b. "The Waratah", *The Hedland Advocate*, Saturday 21 January 1911.

47   "The Waratah", *The Hedland Advocate*, Saturday 21 January 1911.

48   a. Adelaide Steamship Company, minutes of directors' meeting, Wednesday 05 May 1909. Noel Butlin Archives Centre, 0186/Z535 Box 12.
   b. Adelaide Steamship Company, minutes of directors' meeting, Wednesday 19 May 1909.
   c. Adelaide Steamship Company, minutes of directors' meeting, Monday 09 August 1909.
   d. Adelaide Steamship Company, minutes of directors' meeting, Wednesday 01 February 1911.

49   "Peeps at People", *The Sunday Times* (Perth, WA), Sunday 28 March 1909, Third section, p. 1.

50   "Koombana Aground Again", *The Northern Times*, Saturday 24 December 1910, p. 5.

51   a. "News and Notes", *The West Australian*, Monday 23 January 1911, p. 6.
   b. "Telegrams", *The Hedland Advocate*, Saturday 28 January 1911, p. 4.

52   a. "Wreck of a Barque", *The Northern Times*, Saturday 11 February 1911, p. 2.
   b. "Wreck of the Glenbank", *The Sunday Times*, Sunday 12 February 1911, p. 7.

53   "Wreck of the Glenbank", *The Sunday Times*, Sunday 12 February 1911, p. 7.

54   "News & Notes", *The Northern Territory Times and Gazette* (Darwin, NT), Friday 17 February 1911, p. 3.

55   "News and Notes", *The West Australian*, Wednesday 22 February 1911, p. 6.

56   a. "The Loss of the Waratah", *The West Australian*, Saturday 25 February 1911, p. 11.
   b. "Cablegrams", *The Hedland Advocate*, Saturday 04 March 1911.

57   a. "The Yongala", *Queanbeyan Age* (NSW), Friday 31 March 1911, p. 2.
   b. "Yongala Wrecked", *The Northern Times*, Saturday 01 April 1911, p. 2.
   c. "The Missing Yongala", *The Hedland Advocate*, Saturday 08 April 1911.

58   Letter, Captain A. W. Newbery, master of S.S. *Pilbarra*, to Captain Winzar, Fremantle, 20 April 1911, in "Collision between 'Pilbarra' and 'Koombana' at Victoria Quay", Harbour & Light Department, WA, 1911. State Records Office of WA, Consignment 1066, Item 1911/333.

59   Trip books, April 1909 – May 1913, Adelaide Steamship Company. Noel Butlin Archives Centre, Australian National University, 0186/N46/808.

60   Official Log Book, S.S. *Koombana*, 28/8/1911 – 21/01/1912. State Records Office of WA, ACC 1056 AN 16/4 Item 117.

5 THIS LATEST MARVEL OF SCIENCE

1   "Inventor of the Week Archive", http://web.mit.edu/invent/iow/marconi.html.

2–4   "Marvellous Marconi and his Wireless Wonders" (editorial), *The Register* (Adelaide, SA), Saturday 11 March 1905, p. 4.

5   Hancock, Harry E., 1950, *Wireless at Sea, the First Fifty Years: a history*, Marconi International Marine Communication Company, London.

6   "Liner 'Republic' Rammed At Sea", *The New York Times*, Sunday 24 January 1909.

7   McEwen, Neil, "SOS, CQD and the History of Maritime Distress Calls", *The Telegraph Office* (online magazine), http://www.telegraph-office.com/pages/arc2-2.html.

8   Collins, Francis A., 1912, *The Wireless Man*, http://earlyradiohistory.us/1912wm2.htm.

9   "Liner 'Republic' Rammed At Sea", *The New York Times*, Sunday 24 January 1909.

10   Collins, 1912, *The Wireless Man*. See 8 above.

11   a. "Ethergraphs on Ocean Vessels", *The Sydney Morning Herald*, Monday 01 February 1909, p. 7.
        b. "Wireless Telegraphy", *The Barrier Miner* (Broken Hill, NSW), Monday 01 February 1909, p. 1.
        c. "RMS Republic (1903)", *Wikipedia*, http://en.wikipedia.org/wiki/RMS_Republic_(1903).

12   "Ethergraphs for Ocean Vessels", *Border Watch* (Mount Gambier, SA), 03 February 1909, p. 3.

13   a. "The Overdue S.S. Waratah", *The West Australian*, Monday 09 August 1909, p. 5.
        b. "'Wireless' Equipment", *The Argus* (Melbourne), Friday 10 September 1909, p. 5.

14   "Wireless Telegraphy At Sea", *The West Australian*, Wednesday 13 July 1910, p. 7.

15   Marconi International Marine Communication Company was a subsidiary of Marconi's Wireless Telegraph Company.

16   "Wireless Telegraphy At Sea", *The West Australian*, Wednesday 13 July 1910, p. 7.

17   a. "Shipping", *The West Australian*, Friday 04 December 1908, p. 6.
        b. "Shipping", *The West Australian*, Saturday 12 December 1908, p. 10.
        c. "Shipping", *The Register* (Adelaide, SA), Tuesday 22 December 1908, p. 6.
        d. General news, *The Argus*, Tuesday 22 December 1908, p. 6.
        e. "Shipping", *The Sydney Morning Herald*, Saturday 26 December 1908, p. 10.

18–19   Ronan, Tom, 1964, *Packhorse and Pearling Boat*, Cassell Australia, Melbourne, Chapter 1.

20   Cuneen, Chris, "McIntosh, Hugh Donald (1876–1942)", *Australian Dictionary of Biography* (online), http://adb.anu.edu.au/biography/mcintosh-hugh-donald-7373.

21   a. "Boxing", *The Western Mail* (Perth, WA), Saturday 02 January 1909, p. 37.
        b. "Boxing Classics – Jack Johnson v Tommy Burns – December 26 1908", http://www.saddoboxing.com/boxing-article/Jack-Johnson-v-Tommy-Burns.html.

22   "Burns–Johnson Fight Pictures", *The Sydney Morning Herald*, Monday 04 January 1909, p. 3.

23   a. Ward, Geoffrey C., 2006, *Unforgivable Blackness: The rise and fall of Jack Johnson*, Random House.
        b. Orbach, Barak, "The Johnson–Jeffries Fight and Censorship of Black Supremacy", *NYU Journal of Law & Liberty*, 2010, Vol. 8, pp. 270–346.

24   "Jeffries Will Meet Johnson", *Los Angeles Times*, Monday 01 March 1909, p. 12.

25   "Scenes in London", *The Sydney Morning Herald*, Wednesday 06 July 1910, p. 10.

26   "The Great Fight", *The West Australian*, Wednesday 6 July 1910, p. 7.

27–28   "Johnson Wins", *Daily News* (Perth, WA), Tuesday 05 July 1910, p. 8.

29   "Wireless Telegraphy At Sea", *The West Australian*, Wednesday 13 July 1910, p. 7.

30   "Johnson Wins", *Daily News*, Tuesday 05 July 1910, p. 8.

31   "The Booker T. Washington Era", *African American Odyssey* (online resource), http://memory.loc.gov/ammem/aaohtml/exhibit/aopart6.html.

32–33   "Hawley Harvey Crippen", *Wikipedia*, http://en.wikipedia.org/wiki/Hawley_Harvey_Crippen.

34   a. "The Crippen Murder", *The Brisbane Courier* (Qld), Wednesday 20 July 1910, p. 5.
        b. "Cablegrams", *The Hedland Advocate*, Saturday 06 August 1910, p. 4.

35   a. "Wireless on the Otranto", *The Brisbane Courier*, Tuesday 26 July 1910, p. 4.
        b. "Wireless Telegraphy in Australia", *The West Australian*, Monday 7 August 1911, p. 4.
        c. "Wireless on the s.s. Koombana", *The Hedland Advocate*, Saturday 12 August 1911.

36   "Wireless and the Waratah", *The Sydney Morning Herald*, Tuesday 10 August 1909, p. 6.

37   a. Adelaide Steamship Company, minutes of directors' meeting, Monday 31 October 1910. Noel Butlin Archives Centre, 0186/Z535 Box 12.
        b. Adelaide Steamship Company, minutes of directors' meeting, Wednesday 01 February 1911.

38   a. "Twenty One Years Old!", *The Argus*, Thursday 12 July 1934, p. 7.
        b. Goot, Murray, "Fisk, Sir Ernest Thomas (1886–1965)", *Australian Dictionary of Biography*, http://adb.anu.edu.au/biography/fisk-sir-ernest-thomas-6177.

39   a. "Wireless on the s.s. Koombana", *The Hedland Advocate*, Saturday 12 August 1911.
        b. "Marconi Wireless on the Koombana", *The West Australian*, Friday 08 September 1911, p. 6.

40   Hemans, Felicia, "The Graves of a Household" (poem), http://digital.library.upenn.edu/women/hemans/records/graves.html.

41   "Wireless Telegraphy in Australia", *The West Australian*, Monday 7 August 1911, p. 4.

42   "News and Notes", *The West Australian*, Wednesday 21 April 1909, p. 6.

43   "Rival Wireless Systems", *The Sydney Morning Herald*, Monday 04 December 1911, p. 10.

44   a. "Wireless Telegraphy", *The West Australian*, Thursday 29 June 1911, p. 7.
        b. "Marconi Patent", *The Register*, Thursday 13 July 1911, p. 6.

45   "The Marconi Judgment", *The Colonist* (Nelson, NZ), Friday 14 July 1911, p. 3.

46   a. "Commonwealth Wireless System", *The Advertiser* (Adelaide, SA), Monday 12 Feb. 1912, p. 15.
        b. "Wireless Telegraphy", *The Sydney Morning Herald*, Thursday 15 February 1912, p. 10.

47   a. "Trade and Finance", *The Mercury* (Hobart, Tas.), Monday 21 July 1913, p. 3.
        b. "Twenty One Years Old!", *The Argus*, Thursday 12 July 1934, p. 7.

48   "Speech in the Sky", *The Argus*, Wednesday 09 November 1910, p. 13.

6 The Great Divide

1   "The Native Question", *The Hedland Advocate* (Port Hedland, WA), Saturday 14 May 1910.

2   Salter, Elizabeth, 1971, *Daisy Bates: "The Great White Queen of the Never-Never"*, Angus & Robertson, Sydney, Chapter 10.

3   a. "St John's (Newfoundland) Relief Fund", *The West Australian*, Saturday 01 October 1892, p. 3.
        b. "Correspondence", *The West Australian*, Friday 07 October 1892, p. 6.
        c. "Correspondence", *The West Australian*, Thursday 20 October 1892, p. 6.
        d. "Bishop Gibney and the Nor'-West Settlers", *The West Australian*, Tuesday 25 Oct. 1892, p. 3.
        e. "Correspondence", *The West Australian*, Tuesday 01 November 1892, p. 6.
        f. "Interview with Bishop Gibney", *Daily News* (Perth, WA), Tuesday 28 November 1899, p. 4.

4   Salter, Elizabeth, 1971, *Daisy Bates: "The Great White Queen of the Never-Never"*, Angus & Robertson, Sydney, Chapter 8.

5   Salter, 1971, *Daisy Bates,* Chapter 10.

6   a. Salter, 1971, *Daisy Bates,* Chapter 8.
        b. Salter, 1971, *Daisy Bates,* Chapter 10.

7   "Gibney at Glenrowan", *The Argus* (Melbourne), Monday 19 July 1880, p. 7.

8   Trappists: Catholic missionaries and monastics of the Cistercian Order of the Strict Observance.

9   a. Salter, 1971, *Daisy Bates,* Chapter 10.
        b. Durack, Mary, 1969, *The Rock and the Sand*, Constable, London, Chapter 11.

10   a. "Notes", *The Western Mail* (Perth, WA), Saturday 25 August 1900, p. 22.
        b. "Shipping", *The West Australian*, Monday 27 August 1900, p. 4.

11   Bates, Daisy M., 1944, *The Passing of the Aborigines*, John Murray, London, Chapter 1.

12–13   Durack, 1969, *The Rock and the Sand,* Chapter 10.

14   a. Roth, Walter Edmund (Commissioner), Government of Western Australia, 1905, *Royal Commission on the Condition of the Natives* (report).
        b. Durack, 1969, *The Rock and the Sand,* Chapter 10.

15   Salter, 1971, *Daisy Bates,* Chapter 11.

16   Few terms pose more difficulty than "half-caste". In any modern context the term is offensive, but in the first decade of the twentieth century it carried specific meaning and significance. A view broadly held in the white community was that Aboriginal people would disappear within a generation or two, and that white responsibility extended only to palliative care. The phrase "to smoothe the dying pillow" is often attributed to Daisy Bates. Of course, white responsibility could only be so contained and time-limited if interbreeding were minimised. Increasingly, first-generation part-Aboriginal children were taken from their mothers, to be placed in the care of missionaries or (later) made wards of the state. Although white support for the missions was sincere, government policy reflected a perverse desire to see "half-caste" children quarantined.

17   a. Roth, 1905, royal commission report. See 14a above.
      b. Durack, 1969, *The Rock and the Sand,* Chapter 16.

18   Durack, 1969, *The Rock and the Sand,* Chapter 10.

19   Durack, 1969, *The Rock and the Sand,* Chapter 11.

20   Bates, Daisy M., 1944, *The Passing of the Aborigines*, John Murray, London, Chapter 1.

21   a. Salter, Elizabeth, 1971, *Daisy Bates, "The Great White Queen of the Never-Never"*, Angus & Robertson, Sydney, Chapter 11.
      b. Durack, 1969, *The Rock and the Sand*, Chapter 4.

22   Bates, 1944, *The Passing of the Aborigines*, Chapter 1.

23–24 Bates, 1944, *The Passing of the Aborigines,* Chapter 2.

25   "Roman Catholic", *The Western Mail* (Perth, WA), Saturday 02 February 1901, p. 57.

26   Salter, 1971, *Daisy Bates,* Chapter 11.

27   a. "Through The Murchisons", *The Western Mail* (Perth, WA), Saturday 02 July 1904, p. 20.
      b. "Mainly About People", *Daily News* (Perth, WA), Saturday 20 August 1904, p. 1.
      c. "Pictorial Post Cards", *The Sunday Times* (Perth, WA), Sunday 28 August 1904, p. 10.

28   a. "Western Australian Aborigines", *The Western Mail*, Saturday 24 August 1907, p. 44.
      b. Salter, 1971, *Daisy Bates,* Chapter 8.

29   Salter, 1971, *Daisy Bates,* Chapter 14.

30   a. Salter, 1971, *Daisy Bates,* Chapter 14.
      b. "R. H. Mathews", *Wikipedia*, http://en.wikipedia.org/wiki/R._H._Mathews.

31   Salter, 1971, *Daisy Bates,* Chapter 14.

32   "The Treatment of Aborigines", *The West Australian*, Saturday 16 April 1904, p. 7.

33   a. Roth, Walter Edmund, Government of Queensland, 1897, *Ethnological Studies Among the North-West-Central Queensland Aborigines.*
      b. Reynolds, Barry, "Roth, Walter Edmund (1861–1933)", *Australian Dictionary of Biography* (online), http://adbonline.anu.edu.au/biogs/A110471b.htm.

34   "The Australian Aboriginals", *The West Australian*, Monday 29 August 1904, p. 7.

35   "The Aborigines of this State", *Daily News*, Friday 02 September 1904 (3rd edition), p. 3.

36   a. "Dr. Roth's Photographs", *The Brisbane Courier* (Qld), Friday 10 June 1904, p. 4.
      b. "Yokohama Hamilton as a Guardian of Morality", *The Worker* (Brisbane, Qld), Saturday 25 June 1904, p. 3.
      c. Editorial, *Dampier Despatch* (Broome, WA), Saturday 16 September 1905, Issue No. 228, p. 338.

37   "The Aborigines Question", *The West Australian*, Wednesday 15 February 1905, pp. 2–3.

38   "Blacks Brutally Treated", *The Sydney Morning Herald*, Wednesday 01 February 1905, p. 6.

39   "Treatment of the Aborigines", *The Sydney Morning Herald*, Friday 03 February 1905, p. 6.

40   "The Aborigines", *The Western Mail*, 07 August 1909, p. 38.

41   Low, James Galloway, *Letters, 1904–91*, Battye Library, ACC 2612A (listing: MN 681), Letter from Jim to his friend Peggy, 09 May 1909.

42   a. "A Page from the Past of the Wild North-West", *The Sunday Times*, Sunday 14 January 1923, p. 1.
      b. "A Page from the Past", *The Sunday Times*, Sunday 21 January 1923, p. 1.

43   a. "West Australian Prisons", *The West Australian*, Tuesday 24 December 1907, p. 8.
      b. "The State Prisons", *The West Australian*, Saturday 04 September 1909, p. 5.
      c. "Prisons of the State", *The West Australian*, Thursday 20 October 1910, p. 4.

44–45 "Our Black Brother", *The West Australian*, Friday 01 July 1910, p. 3.

46   "Cattle Killing in the North", *The West Australian*, Monday 15 January 1912, p. 8.

47   "The Penguin's Cruise", *The Western Mail*, Saturday 06 March 1909, p. 17.

48   a. "The Aborigines of the State", *The West Australian*, Friday 29 November 1907, p. 3.

    b. Higgins, Henry B. (President), Commonwealth Court of Conciliation and Arbitration, *Ex parte HV McKay (Harvester Case)(1907) 2 CAR 1*, Court decision (the "Harvester Judgement"), published by Law Internet Resources, Parliament of Australia, http://www.aph.gov.au/binaries/library/intguide/law/harvester.pdf.

8   a. "Rerum Novarum", *New Advent* (online), http://www.newadvent.org/cathen/12783a.htm.
    b. Leo XIII, Pope, Catholic Church, 1893, *Rerum novarum*, English translation of Pope Leo XIII's encyclical, http://www.vatican.va/holy_father/leo_xiii/encyclicals/documents/hf_l-xiii_enc_15051891_rerum-novarum_en.html.

9   a. "Good Wages Court", *The Independent* (Footscray, Vic.), Saturday 09 November 1907, p. 2.
    b. "The Harvester Judgment", http://www.abc.net.au/federation/fedstory/ep3/ep3_events.htm.

10   a. "Good Wages Court", *The Independent* (Footscray, Vic.), Saturday 09 November 1907, p. 2.
    b. "Ex parte H.V. McKay", *Wikipedia*, http://en.wikipedia.org/wiki/Harvester_Judgment.
    c. "The Harvester Judgment", http://www.abc.net.au/federation/fedstory/ep3/ep3_events.htm.

11   Adelaide Steamship Company, minutes of directors' meeting, Monday 13 November 1911. Noel Butlin Archives Centre, Australian National University, 0186/Z535 Box 12.

12   "Koombana Still At Fremantle", *The Hedland Advocate*, Saturday 18 November 1911.

13   "Strike on the Koombana", *The Hedland Advocate*, Saturday 18 November 1911.

14   a. "The Koombana's Firemen", *The West Australian*, Tuesday 21 November 1911, p. 7.
    b. "S.S. Koombana's Firemen", *The Argus* (Melbourne), Wednesday 22 November 1911, p. 14.

15   "Koombana Strike", *The Hedland Advocate*, Saturday 02 December 1911.

16   a. "The Koombana Firemen", *The West Australian*, Saturday 25 November 1911, p. 11.
    b. "Koombana Strike", *The Northern Times* (Carnarvon, WA), Saturday 25 November 1911, p. 3.
    c. Adelaide Steamship Company, minutes of directors' meeting, Monday 20 November 1911.

17   a. "The Koombana Firemen", *The West Australian*, Saturday 25 November 1911, p. 11.
    b. "Koombana Strike", *The Hedland Advocate*, Saturday 02 December 1911.

18   a. "Better Conditions for Seamen", *The Sydney Morning Herald*, Monday 27 November 1911, p. 8.
    b. "Federal Arbitration Court", *The Worker* (Brisbane, Qld), Saturday 02 December 1911, p. 14.

19   "Federal Arbitration Court", *The Worker*, Saturday 02 December 1911, p. 14.

20   Fitzpatrick, Brian and Cahill, Rohan J., 1981, *The Seamen's Union of Australia 1872–1972: A History*, Seaman's Union of Australia, Sydney, Chapter 5.

21   a. "Federal Arbitration Court", *The Worker*, Saturday 02 December 1911, p. 14.
    b. Fitzpatrick et al, 1981, *The Seamen's Union of Australia 1872–1972*, Chapter 5.

22   a. "The Koombana Firemen", *The West Australian*, Saturday 25 November 1911, p. 11.
    b. "Successful Seamen", *The Sydney Morning Herald*, Saturday 25 November 1911, p. 21.

23–24   "The Koombana Firemen", *The West Australian*, Saturday 25 November 1911, p. 11.

25   Adelaide Steamship Company, minutes of directors' meeting, Monday 27 November 1911.

26   a. "The Koombana", *The Hedland Advocate*, Saturday 02 December 1911.
    b. Adelaide Steamship Company, minutes of directors' meeting, Monday 04 December 1911.

8 The Dread Visitor

1   "A Catechism of Cyclones", *The Sunday Times* (Perth, WA), Sunday 31 March 1912, p. 1.

2   "Tropical Cyclones Affecting Carnarvon", Australian Government Bureau of Meteorology, http://www.bom.gov.au/cyclone/history/wa/carnarvon.shtml.

3   Henderson, Graeme & Kandy-Jane, 1988, *Unfinished Voyages: Western Australian shipwrecks 1851–1880*, University of Western Australia Press, Nedlands, WA, pp. 67–71.

4   "Orissa famine of 1866", *Wikipedia*, http://en.wikipedia.org/wiki/Orissa_famine_of_1866.

5   "Taiping Rebellion", *Wikipedia*, http://en.wikipedia.org/wiki/Taiping_Rebellion.

6–7   "Disastrous Hurricane at the North-West Settlement", *Perth Gazette and West Australian Times*, Friday 24 May 1872, Supplement p. 1.

8   Henderson, Graeme & Kandy-Jane, 1988, *Unfinished Voyages*, pp. 185–188. See 3 above.

9   a. Morris, Edward E., 1898, *Austral English: A Dictionary of Australasian Words, Phrases, and Usages*, Macmillan, London.
    b. *Macquarie Dictionary* (online), http://www.macquariedictionary.com.au.

10   "The Pearling Fleet, North West", *The West Australian*, Tuesday 17 February 1880, p. 3.

11   "Cossack and Roebourne", *The West Australian*, Monday 11 May 1885, p. 3.

12–14 "Disaster At The North West", *The West Australian*, Tuesday 8 February 1881, p. 3.

15 a. "Disaster At The North West", *The West Australian*, Tuesday 8 February 1881, p. 3.
b. "Western Australia", *The Argus* (Melbourne), Tuesday 29 March 1881, p. 6.

16 "Notes from the Nor'-West", *The West Australian*, Tuesday 28 March 1882, p. 3.

17 a. "Our Pearl Shell Fisheries", *The Western Mail* (Perth, WA), Saturday 10 July 1886, p. 18.
b. Edwards, Hugh, 1983, *Port of Pearls*, Rigby, Adelaide, Chapter 6.

18 "Terrible Disaster on the Pearling Grounds", *The West Australian*, Friday 29 April 1887, p. 3.

19 Coppin, Christopher W., "A North-West tragedy: the big blow of 1887", *Early Days* (Western Australian Historical Society), December 1947, Vol. 3, pp. 37–40.

20 a. "Terrible Disaster on the Pearling Grounds", *The West Australian*, Friday 29 April 1887, p. 3.
b. "Roebourne Notes", *The West Australian*, Friday 13 May 1887, p. 3.

21 Cairns, Lynne and Henderson, Graeme, 1995, *Unfinished Voyages: Western Australian shipwrecks 1881–1900*, University of Western Australia Press, Nedlands, WA, pp. 89–95.

22 a. "The Recent Gale on the North-West Coast", *The West Australian*, Friday 03 March 1893, p. 6.
b. "The Storm at Exmouth Gulf", *The West Australian*, Saturday 04 March 1893, p. 3.

23 "Storm at Carnarvon and Sharks Bay", *The West Australian*, Monday 27 February 1893, p. 6.

24–26 "Western Australia", *The Sydney Morning Herald*, Wednesday 01 March 1893, p. 8.

27 "Storm at Bunbury", *The West Australian*, Wednesday 01 March 1893, p. 2.

28 "Cyclone at the North West", *The West Australian*, Saturday 28 March 1896, p. 3.

29 a. "The Recent 'Willy Willy At Condon", *The West Australian*, Monday 06 April 1896, p. 3.
b. "Willy-Willy at Condon", *The Daily News* (Perth, WA), Saturday 18 April 1896, p. 5.

30 a. "The Hurricane in the Nor'-West", *The West Australian*, Tuesday 05 April 1898, p. 5.
b. "Cossack Hurricane", *The Inquirer & Commercial News* (Perth, WA), Friday 08 April 1898, p. 9.
c. Untitled, *Northern Public Opinion and Mining and Pastoral News* (Roebourne, WA), 09 April 1898.

31 "The Hurricane in the Nor'-West", *The West Australian*, Tuesday 05 April 1898, p. 5.

32 "Another Pearling Disaster", *The West Australian*, Monday 14 December 1908, p. 7.

33 "The Broome Cyclone", *The Mercury* (Hobart, Tas.), Wednesday 30 December 1908, p. 5.

34 Edwards, Hugh, 1983, *Port of Pearls*, Rigby, Adelaide, Chapter 10.

35 a. "The Broome Cyclone", *The Advertiser* (Adelaide, SA), Thursday 24 November 1910, p. 9.
b. "Broome Cyclone", *The Advertiser*, Friday 25 November 1910, p. 9.

36 Knight, Rupert Leonard Tower, interviewed by Chris Jeffery, 1977. Transcript: State Library of WA OH202.

37 Low, James Galloway, *Letters, 1904–91*, Battye Library, ACC 2612A (listing: MN 681). Letter from Jim to his sister Jane, 21 June 1912.

9 The Lore of Storms

1 Tables of distances, W.A. ports: recommended tracks from port to port, Adelaide Steamship Company, c. 1907. Noel Butlin Archives Centre, Australian National University, 0186/N46/835/27.

2 "The Nor'-West Ports", *The West Australian*, Tuesday 28 June 1910, p. 5.

3 a. "Cyclone at Onslow", *The West Australian*, Thursday 30 December 1897, p. 5.
b. "Rough Weather During the Christmas Holidays", *Northern Public Opinion and Mining and Pastoral News* (Roebourne, WA), Saturday 01 January 1898, p. 2.

4–5 "The Hurricane of '97", *The West Australian*, Thursday 28 March 1912, p. 7.

6 Macnab, John, 1897, *Catechism of the Laws of Storms*, 3rd edition, George Philip & Son, London.

7 Conrad, Joseph, 1902, *Typhoon*, Putnam, New York, Chapter 5.

8–9 "Reid's Law of Storms", *The Sydney Morning Herald*, Thursday 02 May 1850, p. 3.

10–11 "The Hurricane of '97", *The West Australian*, Thursday 28 March 1912, p. 7.

12 Conrad, 1902, *Typhoon*, Chapter 3.

13 "The Company and the North West Coast", *Newsletter*, 30 June 1971, found in *Records, 1875–1994*, Adelaide Steamship Company. Noel Butlin Archives Centre, ANU, 0186/N46/634.

14 "The Hurricane of '97", *The West Australian*, Thursday 28 March 1912, p. 7.

15 *Northern Public Opinion and Mining and Pastoral News*, Saturday 09 April 1898.

16 a. "The Hurricane in the Nor'-West", *The West Australian*, Tuesday 05 April 1898, p. 5.
b. "Cossack Hurricane", *The Inquirer & Commercial News* (Perth, WA), Friday 08 April 1898, p. 9.

17   "Koombana Still Missing", *Geraldton Guardian* (WA), Thursday 28 March 1912, p. 2.

18   "The Nor'-West Gale", *The West Australian*, Thursday 23 March 1899, p. 5.

19   Langford, Captain, "Captain Langford's Observations of his Own Experience upon Hurricanes, and their Prognosticks", *Philosophical Transactions*, 1698, Vol. 20, pp. 407–16.

20   Youmans, William Jay (ed.), "Sketch of William C. Redfield", *Appleton's Popular Science Monthly*, Vol. L, November 1896 – April 1897, p. 112.

21   Redfield, William Charles, "Various papers on meteorology", *American Journal of Science and Arts*, 1838, Vols XX, XXV, XXVIII, XXXI, XXXIII.

22   "Representation of the Colonies", *Hobart Town Courier* (Tas.), Saturday 18 February 1832, p. 4.

23   a. "Metereology No. VII", *The Sydney Herald*, Friday 11 March 1842, p. 2.
       b. Reid, William, 1838, *An Attempt to Develop the Law of Storms by Means of Facts*, J. Weale, London.

24   Reid, William, 1849, *The Progress and Development of the Law of Storms; and of the Variable Winds, with the Practical Application of the subject to Navigation*, J. Weale, London.

25   a. "Reid's Law of Storms", *The Sydney Morning Herald*, Thursday 02 May 1850, p. 3.
       b. Reid, 1849, *The Progress and Development of the Law of Storms*.

26   "Reid's Law of Storms", *The Sydney Morning Herald*, Thursday 02 May 1850, p. 3.

27   a. Dove, Heinrich William, 1862, *The Law of Storms,* Longman, Green, Longman, Roberts & Green, London.
       b. Birt, William Radcliff, 1879, *Handbook of the Law of Storms,* George Philip & Son, London.
       c. Meldrum, Charles, 1874, *Notes sur la Forme des Cyclones dans l'Ocean Indien*, Challamel aîné, Paris.
       d. Ley, William Clement, 1880, *Aids to the Study and Forecast of Weather*, Great Britain Meteorological Office, London.

28   Piddington, Henry, 1848, *Sailor's Horn-book for the Law of Storms*, John Wiley, New York.

29   Macnab, John, 1897, *Catechism of the Laws of Storms*, 3rd edition, George Philip & Son, London.

30   Meyers, Jeffrey, University of Colorado, "Conrad's Examinations for the British Merchant Service", *Conradiana*, 1991, Vol. 23, No. 2, pp. 123–132.

31   Conrad, Joseph, 1902, *Typhoon*, Putnam, New York, Chapter 2.

32   "The Nor'-West Trade", *The West Australian*, Monday 19 March 1900, p. 6.

33   Conrad, 1902, *Typhoon*, Chapter 1.

10   THE KOOMBANA BLOW

1   The British colony of Natal, having Pietermaritzburg as its administrative centre and Durban (Port Natal) as its principal port, became a province of the Union of South Africa in May 1910.

2   a. "A Nor'-West Cyclone", *The West Australian*, Monday 25 March 1912, p. 7.
       b. "Six Days Out", *The West Australian*, Wednesday 27 March 1912, p. 7.
       c. *Crown of England*, among ships mentioned by Captain J. L. Vivian Millett, available online, http://freepages.family.rootsweb.ancestry.com/~treevecwll/milletts2.htm.

3   a. Editorial, *The Northern Times* (Carnarvon, WA), Tuesday 26 March 1912, p. 2.
       b. Loney, Jack, 1987, *Australian Shipwrecks. Volume 4, 1901–1986*, Marine History Publications, Portarlington, Victoria.

4   The killing of Thomas Darlington, and the subsequent trial of Italian mine workers Joseph Seleno and Lawrence Cappelli, are the subject of Chapter 15: "Fortune's Crooked Smile".

5   "Six Days Out", *The West Australian*, Wednesday 27 March 1912, p. 7.

6   "Cheating The Cyclone", *The West Australian*, Wednesday 10 April 1912, p. 7.

7–8   "Six Days Out", *The West Australian*, Wednesday 27 March 1912, p. 7.

9   "Cheating The Cyclone", *The West Australian*, Wednesday 10 April 1912, p. 7.

10   "Six Days Out", *The West Australian*, Wednesday 27 March 1912, p. 7.

11   a. "No Tidings", *The West Australian*, Monday 01 April 1912, p. 7.
       b. "The Shipping Disaster at Depuch Island", police report, Constable F. H. Growden, Whim Creek, 04 April 1912, found with "Storm on N.W. Coast – Ships 'Crown of England' and 'Concordia' wrecked", State Records Office of WA. Cons 430 Item 1912/1727.

12   "Cheating The Cyclone", *The West Australian*, Wednesday 10 April 1912, p. 7.

13   "Six Days Out", *The West Australian*, Wednesday 27 March 1912, p. 7.

14   "The Shipping Disaster at Depuch Island" (police report). See 11b above.

15   "No Tidings", *The West Australian*, Monday 01 April 1912, p. 7.

       b. "The Native Questions", *The West Australian*, Tuesday 10 December 1907, p. 6.

       c. "Disease Amongst Natives", *The West Australian*, Friday 29 May 1908, p. 3.

49   a. "Disease Amongst Natives", *The West Australian*, Friday 29 May 1908, p. 3.

       b. "The Penguin's Cruise", *The Western Mail*, Saturday 06 March 1909, p. 17.

50   "The Aboriginal Hospitals", *The West Australian*, Thursday 04 March 1909, p. 2.

51–52 "The Lock Hospital", *The Northern Times* (Carnarvon, WA), Saturday 20 November 1909, p. 2.

53   a. "Native Lock Hospitals", *The West Australian*, Saturday 02 July 1910, p. 9.

       b. "Study of Native Races", *The West Australian*, Friday 14 April 1911, p. 5.

54   "Native Lock Hospitals", *The West Australian*, Saturday 02 July 1910, p. 9.

55   a. "The North-West", *The West Australian*, Monday 27 June 1910, p. 5.

       b. "Native Lock Hospitals", *The West Australian*, Saturday 02 July 1910, p. 9.

       c. "The Lock Hospitals", *The Western Mail*, Saturday 08 April 1911, p. 43.

56   "The North-West", *The West Australian*, Monday 27 June 1910, p. 5.

57   a. "Western Australian Aborigines", *The Western Mail*, Saturday 24 August 1907, p. 44.

       b. "The Aborigines", *The Daily News* (Perth, WA), Wednesday 06 October 1909, p. 11.

       c. Salter, 1971, *Daisy Bates,* Chapter 15.

58   "Exploration in Western Australia", *The West Australian*, Wednesday 18 May 1910, p. 8.

59   "Notes of the Week", *The Western Mail*, Saturday 12 February 1910, p. 34.

60   a. "Aborigines Amelioration", *The Hedland Advocate*, Saturday 02 July 1910, p. 5.

       b. "News and Notes", *The West Australian*, Saturday 01 October 1910, p. 10.

       c. "Primitive Man in Western Australia", *The West Australian*, Monday 03 October 1910, p. 2.

       d. "News and Notes", *The West Australian*, Tuesday 04 October 1910, p. 6.

       e. Salter, 1971, *Daisy Bates,* Chapter 17.

61   "Tribal Fight", *The Northern Times*, Saturday 17 September 1910, p. 2.

62   "My Natives and I", *The West Australian*, Wednesday 04 March 1936, p. 21.

63–64 Grant Watson, E. L. (Elliot Lovegood), 1946, *But To What Purpose: the autobiography of a contemporary*, The Cresset Press, London, Chapter 14.

65   a. Grant Watson, 1946, *But To What Purpose*, Chapter 14.

       b. Salter, 1971, *Daisy Bates,* Chapter 17.

66   Grant Watson, 1946, *But To What Purpose*, Chapter 14.

67   Grant Watson, 1946, *But To What Purpose*, Chapter 15.

68   Grant Watson, 1946, *But To What Purpose*, Chapter 14.

69–71 "Study of Native Races", *The West Australian*, Friday 14 April 1911, p. 5.

72   a. "Our Interviews", *The Northern Times*, Saturday 21 January 1911, p. 5.

       b. "The Aborigines", *The West Australian*, Friday 05 April 1912, p. 6.

73   a. "The Aboriginal Hospitals", *The West Australian*, Thursday 04 March 1909, p. 2.

       b. "The Lock Hospital", *The Northern Times*, Saturday 20 November 1909, p. 2.

       c. "News and Notes", *The West Australian*, Tuesday 8 February 1910, pp. 4–5.

       d. "Western Australian Aborigines" (letter to the editor), *The West Australian*, Sat 29 July 1911, p. 8.

74   a. "News and Notes", *The West Australian*, Tuesday 8 February 1910, pp. 4–5.

       b. "From Bernier to Wyndham", *The West Australian*, Thursday 28 April 1910, p. 2.

7 A Sea Change For Sailors

1   "News and Notes", *The West Australian*, Saturday 11 November 1911, pp. 10–11.

2   "Steward Must Leave", *The Sydney Morning Herald*, Monday 13 November 1911, p. 10.

3   a. "The Koombana Firemen", *The West Australian*, Saturday 25 November 1911, p. 11.

       b. "The Koombana Strike", *The Hedland Advocate* (Port Hedland, WA), Saturday 25 November 1911.

4   a. "Steward Must Leave", *The Sydney Morning Herald*, Monday 13 November 1911, p. 10.

       b. "Strike on the Koombana", *The Hedland Advocate*, Saturday 18 November 1911.

       c. Adelaide Steamship Company, minutes of directors' meeting, Monday 13 November 1911. Noel Butlin Archives Centre, Australian National University, 0186/Z535 Box 12.

5   Fitzpatrick, Brian and Cahill, Rohan J., 1981, *The Seamen's Union of Australia 1872–1972: A History*, Seaman's Union of Australia, Sydney, Chapter 5.

6   "The Harvester Judgment", http://www.abc.net.au/federation/fedstory/ep3/ep3_events.htm.

7   a. "Harvester Case", Sir Richard Kirby Archives (online),
         http://www.e-airc.gov.au/kirbyarchives/harvest.

16   "Cheating The Cyclone", *The West Australian*, Wednesday 10 April 1912, p. 7.

17   a. "Six Days Out", *The West Australian*, Wednesday 27 March 1912, p. 7.
     b. "No Tidings", *The West Australian*, Monday 01 April 1912, p. 7.
     c. *Storm on N.W. Coast* , police report, 4th April 1912.

18   "Cheating The Cyclone", *The West Australian*, Wednesday 10 April 1912, p. 7.

19   "Tinned dog": slang for any cheap, tinned meat.

20   "Cheating The Cyclone", *The West Australian*, Wednesday 10 April 1912, p. 7.

21   "Six Days Out", *The West Australian*, Wednesday 27 March 1912, p. 7.

22   "Cheating The Cyclone", *The West Australian*, Wednesday 10 April 1912, p. 7.

23   a. Editorial, *The Northern Times* (Carnarvon, WA), Tuesday 26 March 1912, p. 2.
     b. "No News of the Koombana", *The Sunday Times* (Perth, WA), Sunday 31 March 1912, p. 1.
     c. "Maginnis, Edward Peter", handwritten summary card, Karratha Local History Office.

24   a. "A Nor'-West Cyclone", *The West Australian*, Monday 25 March 1912, p. 7.
     b. Telegram, Gerrans, postmaster Whim Creek, to Chief Harbourmaster, Fremantle, Sunday 24 March 1912, in "Depuch Island Anchorage Gale", Harbour & Light Department, WA. State Records Office of WA, Cons 1066 Item 1912/0432.
     c. Telegram, Sub-Inspector Houlahan, Roebourne, to Commissioner of Police, Perth, Monday 25 March 1912, in "Storm on N.W. Coast – Ships 'Crown of England' and 'Concordia' wrecked", WA Police Department. State Records Office of WA. Cons 430 Item 1912/1727.

25   "Six Days Out", *The West Australian*, Wednesday 27 March 1912, p. 7.

26   a. "The Cyclone", *The West Australian*, Tuesday 26 March 1912, p. 5.
     b. "The Shipping Disaster at Depuch Island" (police report). See 11b above.

27   Telegram, Gerrans, Postmaster, Whim Creek, to Chief Harbourmaster, Fremantle, Monday 25 March 1912, in "Depuch Island Anchorage Gale", Harbour & Light Dept, WA. See 24b above.

28   "A Nor'-West Cyclone", *The West Australian*, Monday 25 March 1912, p. 7.

29–30 Testimony of Harry Upjohn, master of S.S. *Bullarra*, in "Extracts, Court of Marine Inquiry, loss of S.S. 'Koombana'", Harbour & Light Dept, WA, 25 April – 6 May 1912. Author's private collection.

31   "Through The Cyclone", *The Western Mail* (Perth, WA), Saturday 20 April 1912, p. 35.

32–33 "Knew No Hymns", *The Northern Times* (Carnarvon, WA), Saturday 01 June 1912, p. 4.

34   a. Telegram, Gerrans, Postmaster, Whim Creek, to Chief Harbourmaster, Fremantle, Monday 25 March 1912, in "Depuch Island Anchorage Gale", Harbour & Light Dept, WA. See 24b above.
     b. Telegram, Sub-Inspector Houlahan, Roebourne, to Commissioner of Police, Monday 25 March 1912, in "Depuch Island Anchorage Gale", Harbour & Light Department, WA. See 24b above.
     c. Telegram, Sub-Inspector Houlahan, Roebourne, to Commissioner of Police, Tuesday 26 March 1912, in "Depuch Island Anchorage Gale", Harbour & Light Department, WA. See 24b above.

35   a. "Coastal Gales", *Broome Chronicle* (WA), Saturday 30 March 1912, p. 2.
     b. "The Nor'-West Cyclone", *The Western Argus* (Kalgoorlie, WA), Tuesday 02 April 1912, p. 34.

36   a. "Nor'-West Hurricane", *The Northern Times*, Tuesday 26 March 1912, p. 7.
     b. Telegram, Sub-Inspector Houlahan, Roebourne, to Commissioner of Police, Saturday 23 March 1912, in "Depuch Island Anchorage Gale", Harbour & Light Department, WA. See 24b above.

37   "The Cyclone", *The West Australian*, Tuesday 26 March 1912, p. 5.

38   a. "Six Days Out", *The West Australian*, Wednesday 27 March 1912, p. 7.
     b. "The Shipping Disaster at Depuch Island" (police report). See 26b above.

11 TOM ALLEN'S DILEMMA

1   a. "The Mail News", *The South Australian Register* (Adelaide, SA), Friday 26 June 1874, p. 5.
     b. "Story of the Koombana", *The Sunday Times* (Perth, WA), Sunday 31 March 1912, p. 12.

2   a. "The Late Captain Thomas Allen", *The South Australian Register*, Tuesday 15 Sept. 1885, p. 5.
     b. "The Late Captain Allen", *The South Australian Register*, Monday 12 October 1885, p. 3.

3   a. "Story of the Koombana", *The Sunday Times*, Sunday 31 March 1912, p. 12.
     b. "Old Memories", *The Mail* (Adelaide, SA), Saturday 12 July 1913, p. 9.

4   a. "Story of the Koombana", *The Sunday Times*, Sunday 31 March 1912, p. 12.
     b. "Old Memories", *The Mail,* Saturday 12 July 1913, p. 9.

5   A brief history of Fremantle's Commercial Hotel, later renamed The Emerald Isle Hotel: http://register.heritage.wa.gov.au/PDF_Files/O%20-%20A-D/Orient%20Hotel%20(I-AD).PDF.

6   "Story of the Koombana", *The Sunday Times*, Sunday 31 March 1912, p. 12.

7   a. "Shipping Intelligence", *The Register* (Adelaide, SA), Tuesday 13 June 1876, p. 4.
    b. "Story of the Koombana", *The Sunday Times*, Sunday 31 March 1912, p. 12.
    c. Summary of ship's articles, *Northern Monarch*, 1886–7, posted at
       http://archiver.rootsweb.ancestry.com/th/read/AUS-SAGEN/2009-06/1246155467.
8   a. "The Cuzco", *The South Australian Register*, Monday 10 June 1878, p. 5.
    b. "The Accident to the Steamship Cuzco", *The Sydney Morning Herald*, Saturday 15 June 1878, p. 5.
    c. "The Cuzco at Portland", *The Argus* (Melbourne), Monday 17 June 1878, p. 7.
    d. "The Mishap To The Cuzco", *The Australasian Sketcher with Pen and Pencil* (Melbourne),
       Saturday 06 July 1878, p. 62.
    e. "A Daring Act", *The Argus*, Tuesday 16 July 1878, p. 6.
    f. "Story of the Koombana", *The Sunday Times*, Sunday 31 March 1912, p. 12.
    g. "Captain of the Koombana", *The Mercury* (Hobart, Tas.), Wednesday 03 April 1912, p. 5.
9   "The Accident to the Steamship Cuzco", *The Sydney Morning Herald*, Saturday 15 June 1878, p. 5.
10–11 "The Cuzco", *The Argus*, Monday 08 July 1878, p. 6.
12 "Story of the Koombana", *The Sunday Times*, Sunday 31 March 1912, p. 12.
13 a. "Shipping", *The Sydney Morning Herald*, Tuesday 15 January 1884, p. 6.
    b. "Steam to Shoalhaven" (advertisement), *The Sydney Morning Herald*, Friday 29 Feb. 1884, p. 1.
    c. "Story of the Koombana", *The Sunday Times*, Sunday 31 March 1912, p. 12.
    d. "R. W. Miller & Company", *Flotilla Australia*, http://www.flotilla-australia.com/rwmiller.htm.
14 a. "Accident at Wallaroo", *The South Australian Register*, Monday 25 August 1884, p. 6.
    b. "Story of the Koombana", *The Sunday Times*, Sunday 31 March 1912, p. 12.
15 a. "Mining", *The South Australian Register*, Monday 18 October 1886, Supplement, p. 2.
    b. "Story of the Koombana", *The Sunday Times*, Sunday 31 March 1912, p. 12.
16 a. "Shipping", *The Inquirer & Commercial News* (Perth, WA), Friday 13 April 1894, p. 18.
    b. "Story of the Koombana", *The Sunday Times*, Sunday 31 March 1912, p. 12.
    c. "Captain of the Koombana", *The Mercury*, Wednesday 03 April 1912, p. 5.
17 "Shipping Notes", *The Western Mail* (Perth, WA), Friday 18 October 1895, p. 25.
18 a. "Shocking Accident At Fremantle", *The West Australian*, Monday 14 December 1896, p. 5.
    b. "The Marloo Fatality", *The West Australian*, Friday 08 January 1897, p. 2.
19 a. "The Marloo Fatality", *The West Australian*, Saturday 09 January 1897, p. 2.
    b. "Western Australia", *The Sydney Morning Herald*, Monday 11 January 1897, p. 5.
20–22 "The Marloo Fatality", *The West Australian*, Saturday 09 January 1897, p. 2.
23 a. "Story of the Koombana", *The Sunday Times*, Sunday 31 March 1912, p. 12.
    b. "Captain of the Koombana", *The Mercury*, Wednesday 03 April 1912, p. 5.
24 a. "Port Wallaroo", *The South Australian Register*, Thursday 05 June 1862, p. 4.
    b. "The Schah Jehan", *The South Australian Advertiser* (Adelaide, SA), Wednesday 02 July 1862, p. 2.
    c. "The Schah Jehan" (letter to the editor), *The South Australian Register*, Sat 12 July 1862, p. 2.
    d. "The Loss of the Schah Jehan", *The South Australian Register*, Thursday 07 August 1862, p. 2.
    e. "The Hansard", *The South Australian Register*, Wednesday 10 September 1862, p. 2.
25 "The Late Boat Accident in the Gulf", *The South Australian Register*, Wednesday 19 Sept. 1866, p. 3.
26 "Pilot for the Ophir", *The Advertiser* (Adelaide, SA), Thursday 04 July 1901, p. 6.
27 "History of the Visit", *The West Australian*, Monday 22 July 1901, p. 3.
28 "Arrival of the Duke", *The Register* (Adelaide, SA), Tuesday 09 July 1901, p. 5.
29 "Story of the Koombana", *The Sunday Times*, Sunday 31 March 1912, p. 12.
30 a. "Arrival of the Junee", *The Register*, Tuesday 30 April 1907, p. 8.
    b. "Captain of the Koombana", *The Mercury*, Wednesday 03 April 1912, p. 5.
31 a. "New Interstate Steamers", *Examiner* (Launceston, Tas.), Thursday 11 July 1907, p. 4.
    b. "New Steamers", *The Sydney Morning Herald*, Friday 15 November 1907, p. 10.
    c. "A Remarkable Vessel", *The Sydney Morning Herald*, Saturday 08 February 1908, p. 13.
32 a. "Adelaide Steamship Company", *The Advertiser*, Thursday 17 September 1908, p. 11.
    b. "Advertising", *The Argus*, Wednesday 23 December 1908, p. 1.
33 "Personal", *The Advertiser*, Saturday 1 May 1909, p. 9.
34 "The Koombana", *The Kalgoorlie Western Argus* (WA), Tuesday 12 September 1911, p. 27.
35–39 Official Log Book S.S. "Koombana", 28/8/1911 – 21/01/1912. State Records Office of WA. ACC 1056
       AN 16/4 Item 117.
40 "The Koombana", *The West Australian*, Thursday 11 April 1912, p. 5.
41 "Nor'-West Shipping", *The Hedland Advocate* (Port Hedland, WA), Saturday 17 February 1912.

42   a. "A Blow at Port Hedland", *The Hedland Advocate*, Saturday 23 March 1912, p. 5.
      b. Letter, W. Gardiner, Adelaide Steamship Company agent in Port Hedland, to W. E. Moxon, Manager for WA, 17 April 1912, included in "Extracts, Court of Marine Inquiry, loss of S.S. 'Koombana'", Harbour & Light Dept, WA, 25 April – 6 May, 1912. Author's private collection.

43–44 "The Koombana Inquiry", *The Hedland Advocate*, Saturday 25 May 1912, p. 10.

45   a. "Wreck of the Koombana", *The Sunday Times* (Perth, WA), Sunday 19 May 1912, p. 9.
      b. Letter, W. Gardiner, 17 April 1912. See 42b above.

46   Hardie, Jennie, 1978, "Bert Clark revisits Port Hedland" (unpub.), Port Hedland Library, LH335.

47   Clarke, Bert, interviewed by Jennie Hardie, 1977–78. Transcript: Port Hedland Library, PAM B/CLA.

48   Testimony of Harry Upjohn, master of S.S. *Bullarra*, in "Extracts, Court of Marine Inquiry, loss of S.S. 'Koombana'", Harbour & Light Dept, WA, 25 April – 6 May, 1912. Author's private collection.

49   Lourensz, R. S., Department of Science Bureau of Meteorology, 1977, *Tropical Cyclones in the Australian Region July 1909 to June 1975*. The track of the March 1912 storm as shown by Lourensz (see his Figure 2: Tropical cyclone tracks July 1911 – June 1913) is not accepted. The track shown here ("The early progress of the storm", page 187) reflects a new analysis of about 250 formal and informal observations of wind speed and direction.

12 The Stubborn, Silent Sea

1   Collins, W. E. (Algy), speech (untitled), recollections of *Koombana* search, and discovery of wreckage in particular. Transcript (undated) provided to the author by the late Malcolm Barker.

2   Dickson, Rod (transcribed & compiled), 1996, *Ships Registered in Western Australia from 1856 to 1969*, Maritime Heritage Association (Western Australia), http://www.maritimeheritage.org.au/documents/Shipping%20Register.pdf.

3   "The Cyclone", *The West Australian*, Tuesday 26 March 1912, p. 5.

4   Report from Dalziel, Broome wharfinger, to Irvine, Chief Harbourmaster, Fremantle, Friday 12 April 1912, in "Wreck of the 'Koombana' – photocopy of material relating to", Harbour & Light Department, WA, 1912. State Records Office of WA. WAS1618 Consignment 5055 Item 001.

5   Bennie, B. J., "Abstract of Log, Searching for R.M.S. Koombana", in "Wreck of the 'Koombana' – photocopy of material relating to". See 4 above.

6   a. "Copy, log of lugger McLhennan on a cruise in search of R.M.S. Koombana", found in "Wreck of the 'Koombana' – photocopy of material relating to". See 4 above.
     b. Dickson, Rod, *Ships Registered in Western Australia*. See 2 above.

7   "Search Party from Broome", *Broome Chronicle* (WA), Saturday 30 March 1912.

8   a. "S.S. Koombana", *The West Australian*, Monday 25 March 1912, p. 7.
     b. "The Cyclone", *The West Australian*, Tuesday 26 March 1912, p. 5.

9   "The Cyclone", *The West Australian*, Tuesday 26 March 1912, p. 5.

10   "The Singapore line" was a nickname for the ships, represented in Western Australia by Dalgety & Company, which shipped produce north via Singapore, rather than west via Durban and/or Cape Town. These ships belonged to two companies: the West Australian Steam Navigation Company and the Ocean Steamship Company, also known as the Blue Funnel Line.

11   "The Cyclone", *The West Australian*, Tuesday 26 March 1912, p. 5.

12   "Six Days Out", *The West Australian*, Wednesday 27 March 1912, p. 7.

13   a. "Arrival of the Bullarra", *Broome Chronicle* (WA), Saturday 30 March 1912.
     b. Collins, W. E. (Algy), speech (untitled), recollections of *Koombana* search, and discovery of wreckage in particular. Transcript (undated) provided to the author by the late Malcolm Barker.

14   "The Cyclone", *The West Australian*, Tuesday 26 March 1912, p. 5.

15   a. "Search Arrangements", *The West Australian*, Thursday 28 March 1912, p. 7.
     b. "At Fremantle", *The West Australian*, Thursday 28 March 1912, p. 7.

16   "The Company and the North West Coast", *Newsletter*, 30 June 1971, in Records 1875–1994, Adelaide Steamship Company, Noel Butlin Archives Centre, ANU, 0186/N46/634.

17   a. "Six Days Out", *The West Australian*, Wednesday 27 March 1912, p. 7.
     b. "No Tidings", *The West Australian*, Monday 01 April 1912, p. 7.

18   Collins, W. E. (Algy), speech (untitled), recollections of *Koombana* search, and discovery of wreckage in particular. Transcript (undated) provided to the author by the late Malcolm Barker.

19   a. "The Cyclone", *The West Australian*, Tuesday 26 March 1912, p. 5.
     b. "Nor'-West Hurricane", *The Northern Times* (Carnarvon, WA), Tuesday 26 March 1912, p. 7.
     c. "Not Sighted", *The West Australian*, Thursday 28 March 1912, p. 7.

20   "The Cyclone", *The West Australian*, Tuesday 26 March 1912, p. 5.

21   "The S.S. Koombana", *Broome Chronicle*, Saturday 30 March 1912.

22   "Nor'-West Cyclone", *Geraldton Guardian* (WA), Thursday 28 March 1912, p. 2.

23   a. "Six Days Out", *The West Australian*, Wednesday 27 March 1912, p. 7.
      b. "Not Sighted", *The West Australian*, Thursday 28 March 1912, p. 7.

24   Vessels Singapore-bound from Derby or Wyndham would, of necessity, navigate several narrow straits as they worked north-eastward along the Indonesian archipelago, from Surabaya to Batavia (Jakarta) to Singapore.

25–26 "A Skipper's Observations", *The West Australian*, Thursday 28 March 1912, p. 7.

27   "No News of the Koombana", *The Sunday Times* (Perth, WA), Sunday 31 March 1912, p. 1.

28   a. "The Cyclone", *The West Australian*, Tuesday 26 March 1912, p. 5.
      b. "S.S. Moira In The Gale", *Broome Chronicle*, Saturday 30 March 1912.
      c. "No Tidings", *The West Australian*, Monday 01 April 1912, p. 7.
      d. Telegram, Wood, R.M., Broome to Premier Scaddan for Capt. Mills, S.S. *Minderoo*, Tuesday 26 March 1912, in "Wreck of the 'Koombana' – photocopy of material relating to". See 4 above.

29–30 "The Koombana", *The West Australian*, Friday 29 March 1912, p. 7.

31   a. "Mr. Hugo Harper", *Broome Chronicle*, Saturday 13 April 1912.
      b. Bennie, B. J., "Abstract of Log, Searching for R.M.S. Koombana", in "Wreck of the 'Koombana' – photocopy of material relating to". See 4 above.

32   a. "Interview with Captain Mills", *Broome Chronicle* (WA), Saturday 06 April 1912.
      b. "The Ill-Fated Koombana", *The West Australian*, Saturday 13 April 1912, p. 12.

33   "No Tidings", *The West Australian*, Monday 01 April 1912, p. 7.

34   a. "No Tidings", *The West Australian*, Monday 01 April 1912, p. 7.
      b. Telegram, Joseph Gardiner, at Cossack, to Premier Scaddan, Perth, Saturday 30 March 1912, in "Wreck of the 'Koombana' – photocopy of material relating to". See 4 above.

36   Selection of sites of new Nor'-West lighthouses, in "Lighthouses – N.W. Coast", Harbour & Light Department, WA, 1911. State Records Office of WA, Cons 1066 Item 1911/549.

37   a. "Light for Bedout Island", *The Hedland Advocate*, Saturday 30 January 1909, p. 5.
      b. "Nor'-West Lights", *The West Australian*, Wednesday 29 June 1910, p. 2.
      c. "Loss of the Koombana", *The Northern Times*, Saturday 13 April 1912, p. 2.

38   Postcard, written by a crew member of S.S. *Bullarra*, 01 April 1912. Adelaide Steamship Company records, Noel Butlin Archives Centre, Australian National University, 0186/N46/595.

39   Collins, W. E. (Algy), speech. See 18 above.

40   "Loss of the Koombana", *The Northern Times*, Saturday 13 April 1912, p. 2.

41–42 "The Loss of the Koombana", *The Sunday Times*, Sunday 07 April 1912, p. 10.

43   "Loss of the Koombana", *The Northern Times*, Saturday 13 April 1912, p. 2.

44   "Koombana Foundered", *The Hedland Advocate*, Saturday 06 April 1912, p. 5.

45   Telegram from Captain Mills, upon arrival at Port Hedland, to Irvine, Chief Harbourmaster, Fremantle, Wednesday 03 April 1912, in "Wreck of the 'Koombana' – photocopy of material relating to". See 4 above.

46   "Interview with Captain Mills", *Broome Chronicle*, Saturday 06 April 1912.

47   Report from Dalziel, Broome wharfinger, to Irvine, Chief Harbourmaster, Fremantle, Friday 12 April 1912, in "Wreck of the 'Koombana' – photocopy of material relating to". See 4 above.

48   a. "The Koombana", *The West Australian*, Saturday 06 April 1912, p. 7.
      b. Telegram, Dalziel, Broome Harbourmaster to Irvine, Chief Harbourmaster, Fremantle, Friday 05 April 1912, in "Wreck of the 'Koombana' – photocopy of material relating to." See 4 above.
      c. Testimony of Harry Upjohn, master of S.S. *Bullarra*, in "Extracts, Court of Marine Inquiry, loss of S.S. 'Koombana'", Harbour & Light Department, WA, 25 April – 6 May, 1912. Author's private collection.

49   "Loss of the s.s. Koombana", *Geraldton Express* (WA), Saturday 06 April 1912, p. 3.

50–51 "The Koombana" (editorial), *The Northern Times* (Carnarvon, WA), Saturday 06 April 1912, p. 2.

52   Telegram from Irvine, Chief Harbourmaster, Fremantle, to Rantzau, master of *Una*, Tuesday 03 April 1912, in "Total loss of 'Koombana'. Charter of search ship 'Una'.", Harbour & Light Department, WA. State Records Office of WA, Series 2357 Cons 1066 Item 1912/0438.

53   Telegram from Gordon, Hedland wharfinger to Irvine, Chief Harbourmaster, Fremantle, Friday 06 April 1912, in "Total loss of 'Koombana'. Charter of search ship 'Una'." See 52 above.

54   Report from Rantzau, master of Una to Irvine, Chief Harbourmaster, Fremantle, Tuesday 16 April 1912, in "Total loss of 'Koombana'. Charter of search ship 'Una'." See 52 above.

55   a. "The Wrecked Koombana", *Broome Chronicle*, Saturday 13 April 1912.
      b. Telegram, Wood, Resident Magistrate Broome to Premier Scaddan, Perth, Friday 29 March 1912, in "Wreck of the 'Koombana' – photocopy of material relating to." See 4 above.
      c. Report, William Moxon, Adelaide Steamship Company, to Charles Irvine, chief harbourmaster, Fremantle, Saturday 30 March 1912, in "Wreck of the 'Koombana' – photocopy of material relating to." See 4 above.

56   Report, Dalziel, Broome wharfinger to Irvine, Chief Harbourmaster, Fremantle, Friday 12 April 1912, in "Wreck of the 'Koombana' – photocopy of material relating to." See 4 above.

13 THE ILL-FATED COMPLEMENT

1   There is insufficient space here to list all of the sources that relate to *Koombana*'s lost passengers and crew. Interested readers are directed to the *Koombana Days* online resource, which includes a dossier on each person known to have been aboard. http://www.koombanadays.com.

2   "The Steamer Koombana", *The Advertiser* (Adelaide, SA), Friday 12 April 1912, p. 8.

3   "The Koombana Firemen", *Geraldton Guardian* (WA), Saturday 06 January 1912, p. 1.

4   "A Disabled Steamer", *The West Australian*, Monday 10 August 1908, p. 5.

5   Quaile, Declan, "The Koombana Tragedy", *Termonfeckin Historical Society Review*, 2006, No. 6, pp. 27–29.

6   Research file, S.S. *Koombana*, 1973–, Department of Maritime Archeology, WA Museum, 189/73/4.

7   "Low Tide At Broome – Propeller of the S.S. Koombana" (photograph), *The Western Mail*, Saturday 05 August 1911.

8   Barker, Malcolm, 2001, *The Truth Is So Precious*, Success Print, Perth, WA, p. 48.

9   "News and Notes", *The West Australian*, Saturday 11 November 1911, pp. 10–11.

10   "News and Notes", *The Western Mail*, Saturday 22 July 1911, p. 33.

11   "Relatives On The Goldfields", *The Kalgoorlie Western Argus* (WA), Tuesday 02 April 1912, p. 32.

12   "Local and General", *Geraldton Guardian*, Thursday 8 February 1912, p. 2.

13   Clinch, Fred, letter to his wife Eliza, Sunday 17 March 1912, written aboard *Koombana* and posted at Onslow. Original held by family.

14   "Action by Australian Workers' Union", *The West Australian*, Thursday 30 May 1912, p. 8.

15   Price, Florrie, postcard sent to her friend Mrs Lambert, March 1912. Original held by family.

16   a. "The Presbyterian Mission", *The Western Mail*, Saturday 18 May 1912, p. 21–22.
      b. "The Broome Murder", *The Western Mail*, Saturday 11 May 1912, p. 22.

17   "World of Sport", *The Sunday Times* (Perth, WA), Sunday 05 March 1911, p. 14.

18   Briden, Mollie, 1983, *My Life in Port Hedland* (unpublished), handwritten memoir written by Mollie at age 77, two years before her death. Original held by family.

19   a. "The Hedland Bookings", *Broome Chronicle*, Saturday 06 April 1912, p. 2.
      b. "Koombana Foundered", *The Hedland Advocate*, Saturday 06 April 1912, pp. 5, 6, 8.
      c. "The Hedland Bookings", *Broome Chronicle*, Saturday 06 April 1912, p. 2.

14 BEYOND HUMAN KNOWLEDGE

1   "The Koombana Disaster", *Broome Chronicle* (WA), Saturday 13 April 1912.

2   "The Koombana", *The West Australian*, Tuesday 23 April 1912, p. 9.

3   "Extracts, Court of Marine Inquiry, loss of S.S. 'Koombana'", Harbour & Light Department, WA, 25 April – 6 May, 1912. Author's private collection.

4   a. "Loss of the Yongala", *The Sydney Morning Herald*, Wednesday 21 June 1911, p. 15.
      b. "Extracts, Court of Marine Inquiry, loss of S.S. 'Koombana'." See 3 above.

5   "The Koombana", *The West Australian*, Friday 26 April 1912, p. 8.

6–7   "Extracts, Court of Marine Inquiry, loss of S.S. 'Koombana'." See 3 above.

8   a. "Telephone Progress", *The Northern Times* (Carnarvon, WA), Saturday 05 August 1911, p. 2.
      b. Telegram from Moore, Chairman West Pilbara Roads Board, to Premier Scaddan, Perth, 25 April 1912, in "Wreck of the 'Koombana' – photocopy of material relating to", Harbour & Light Department, WA, 1912. State Records Office of WA, WAS1618 Cons. 5055 Item 001.

    c. Telegram from Coleman, Chairman West Kimberley Roads Board, to Premier Scaddan, Perth, 25 April 1912, in "Wreck of the 'Koombana' – photocopy of material relating to". See 8b above.

    d. Telegram from Broome Mayor Hugh D. Norman, on behalf of Council, to Premier Scaddan, 26 April 1912, in "Wreck of the 'Koombana' – photocopy of material relating to". See 8b above.

9   a. "The Koombana", *The Western Mail* (Perth, WA), Saturday 04 May 1912, p. 37.

    b. "Extracts, Court of Marine Inquiry, loss of S.S. 'Koombana'." See 3 above.

10   "Metacentric Height", *Wikipedia*, http://en.wikipedia.org/wiki/Metacentric_height.

11   "The Koombana", *The West Australian*, Friday 26 April 1912, p. 8.

12   "The Koombana", *The Western Mail*, Saturday 04 May 1912, p. 37.

13   Moore, Doug, *Papers*, Extracts from his account of his life in the Kimberley 1904–1914, Battye Library, ACC 3829A (listing MN 1237).

14   "Koombana Inquiry", *The Sunday Times* (Perth, WA), Sunday 26 May 1912, p. 5.

15   a. "Crew lists of ships arriving at Fremantle: 'Koombana' – 1/3/1910", Collector of Customs, WA. National Archives of Australia, K271 KOOMBANA 1 MAR 1910.

    b. "Crew lists of ships arriving at Fremantle: 'Koombana' – 29/4/1910", Collector of Customs, WA. National Archives of Australia, K271 KOOMBANA 29 APR 1910.

16   "Loss of the Yongala", *The Sydney Morning Herald*, Wednesday 21 June 1911, p. 15.

17   "Extracts, Court of Marine Inquiry, loss of S.S. 'Koombana'." See 3 above.

18   "The Koombana", *The Western Mail*, Saturday 04 May 1912, p. 37.

19   a. Telegram from Moore, Chairman West Pilbara Roads Board, to Premier Scaddan, Perth, Monday 25 April 1912, in "Wreck of the 'Koombana' – photocopy of material relating to". See 8b above.

    b. Telegram, Coleman, Chairman West Kimberley Roads Board, to Premier Scaddan, Perth, 25 April 1912, in "Wreck of the 'Koombana' – photocopy of material relating to". See 8b above.

    c. Telegram, Broome Mayor Hugh D. Norman, on behalf of council, to Premier Scaddan, Tuesday 26 April 1912, in "Wreck of the 'Koombana' – photocopy of material relating to". See 8b above.

20–21 "The Koombana", *The Western Mail* (Perth, WA), Saturday 04 May 1912, p. 37.

22   a. "Loss of the Koombana", *Broome Chronicle* (WA), Saturday 11 May 1912.

    b. Memo, Colonial Secretary's Office to Premier's department, Wednesday 27 April 1912, proposing response to requests for gathering of *Koombana* evidence in the Nor'-West, in "Wreck of the 'Koombana' – photocopy of material relating to". See 8b above.

23   "Koombana Inquiry", *The West Australian*, Saturday 04 May 1912, p. 12.

24   "The Koombana", *The Northern Times*, Saturday 11 May 1912, p. 5.

25   "Extracts, Court of Marine Inquiry, loss of S.S. 'Koombana'." See 3 above.

26   "Wreck of the Koombana", *The Sunday Times*, Sunday 19 May 1912, p. 9.

27   "The Koombana Inquiry", *The Hedland Advocate*, Saturday 25 May 1912, p. 10.

28   "A Blow at Port Hedland", *The Hedland Advocate*, Saturday 23 March 1912, p. 5.

29   "Extracts, Court of Marine Inquiry, loss of S.S. 'Koombana'." See 3 above.

30   "Koombana Foundered", *The Hedland Advocate*, Saturday 06 April 1912, p. 5.

31   "Luggers in the Gale", *Broome Chronicle*, Saturday 30 March 1912.

32   "The Cossack Willy Willy", *The Hedland Advocate*, Saturday 30 March 1912, pp. 5, 6.

33   "The Koombana", *The Western Mail*, Saturday 04 May 1912, p. 37.

34   "Extracts, Court of Marine Inquiry, loss of S.S. 'Koombana'." See 3 above.

35   a. "Wreck of the Koombana", *The Sunday Times*, Sunday 19 May 1912, p. 9.

    b. "The Koombana Inquiry", *The Hedland Advocate*, Saturday 25 May 1912, p. 10.

36   Official Log Book S.S. "Koombana", 28/8/1911 – 21/01/1912. State Records Office of WA, ACC 1056 AN 16/4 Item 117. Includes record of ship's draft, for'd and aft, for each departure from port.

37   "Phases of the Moon: 1901 to 2000", http://eclipse.gsfc.nasa.gov/phase/phases1901.html.

38   Official Log Book S.S. "Koombana", 28/8/1911 – 21/01/1912. State Records Office of WA, ACC 1056 AN 16/4 Item 117.

39   General Arrangement, S.S. "Koombana", ship plans on linen, Alexander Stephen & Son, 1907. National Maritime Museum, Greenwich, London.

40   "Extracts, Court of Marine Inquiry, loss of S.S. 'Koombana'", Harbour & Light Department, WA, 25 April – 6 May, 1912. Author's private collection.

41   a. "The Koombana", *The Western Mail*, Saturday 04 May 1912, p. 37.

    b. "The Koombana Inquiry", *The Hedland Advocate*, Saturday 25 May 1912, p. 10.

c. Knight, Rupert Leonard Tower, interviewed by Chris Jeffery, 1977. Transcript: State Library of WA, OH202.

42   "The Koombana Inquiry", *The Hedland Advocate*, Saturday 25 May 1912, p. 10.

43   "Wreck of the Koombana", *The Sunday Times*, Sunday 19 May 1912, p. 9.

44   "Extracts, Court of Marine Inquiry, loss of S.S. Koombana". See 40 above.

45   Barker, Malcolm, "The search for S.S. Koombana", a seminar hosted by the Maritime Archeological Association of Western Australia, Fremantle, 1983. Transcript: State Library of WA, OH1241. Includes discussion of Captain Upjohn's testimony at the *Koombana* inquiry.

46   "A Story of the Koombana", *Geraldton Guardian* (WA), Tuesday 06 March 1923, p. 4.

47   a. "Not Sighted", *The West Australian*, Thursday 28 March 1912, p. 7.
b. "Three Marine Mysteries", *The Sunday Times*, Sunday 31 March 1912, p. 1.
c. "Story of the Koombana", *The Sunday Times*, Sunday 31 March 1912, p. 12.
d. "Wreck of the Koombana", *Geraldton Express* (WA), Friday 26 April 1912.

48   "Loss of the Yongala", *The Sydney Morning Herald*, Wednesday 21 June 1911, p. 15.

49   "Death of Captain Irvine", *The Daily News* (Perth, WA), Wednesday 12 July 1922, p. 8.

50   Gordon, Doug, letter to Bethwyn Brandis, Mukinbudin, WA, 23 March 2002, in response to a notice in *The West Australian*, in which Mrs Brandis sought to make contact with descendants of those lost with *Koombana*. Copy provided to the author.

51   *Koombana* was insured for 75% of a nominal replacement value of £100,000.

52   Letters to the Editor, *The West Australian*, Tuesday 16 April 1912, p. 6.

53   "Koombana Foundered", *The Hedland Advocate*, Saturday 06 April 1912, p. 5.

15 FORTUNE'S CROOKED SMILE

1   "News and Notes", *The West Australian*, Thursday 16 November 1911, p. 6.

2   a. "Situations Vacant", *The West Australian*, Tuesday 14 November 1911, p. 10.
b. "News and Notes", *The West Australian*, Monday 04 December 1911, p. 6.
c. "Strikers Fined", *The Sydney Morning Herald*, Monday 04 December 1911, p. 7.

3   Testimony of James Lachlan Oborn, Coronial Inquest (Thomas Darlington), Whim Creek, December 1911. State Records Office of WA, Cons. 3631, Bundle 12: "Case 1 Rex v Seleno".

4   "A Trouble Settled", *The Advertiser* (Adelaide, SA), Saturday 09 December 1911, p. 21.

5   Testimony of Constable F. H. Growden, Coronial Inquest (Thomas Darlington). See 3 above.

6   a. Testimony of Thomas James Hill, Coronial Inquest (Thomas Darlington).
b. Testimony of Alexander Patrick Kay, Coronial Inquest (Thomas Darlington).

7   a. Testimony of Thomas William Hill, Coronial Inquest (Thomas Darlington).
b. Testimony of Rupert Love, Coronial Inquest (Thomas Darlington).
c. Testimony of George Westley Tozer, Coronial Inquest (Thomas Darlington).
d. Testimony of James Thomas Aylward, Coronial Inquest (Thomas Darlington).

8   Testimony of John Anderson, Coronial Inquest (Thomas Darlington).

9   Testimony of Thomas James Hill, Coronial Inquest (Thomas Darlington).

10   Testimony of Constable F. H. Growden, Coronial Inquest (Thomas Darlington).

11   a. Testimony of Constable F. H. Growden, Coronial Inquest (Thomas Darlington).
b. Testimony of Matthew Murphy, Coronial Inquest (Thomas Darlington).

12   Testimony of Constable F. H. Growden, Coronial Inquest (Thomas Darlington).

13   a. Testimony of George Westley Tozer, Coronial Inquest (Thomas Darlington).
b. "A Fatal Quarrel", *The Mercury* (Hobart, Tas.), Thursday 28 December 1911, p. 5.

14   Testimony of James Thomas Aylward, Coronial Inquest (Thomas Darlington).

15   a. Testimony of Constable F. H. Growden, Coronial Inquest (Thomas Darlington).
b. "Whim Creek Tragedy", *The Western Mail* (Perth, WA), Saturday 30 March 1912, p. 35.

16   "Stabbed to Death by an Italian", *The Advertiser* (Adelaide, SA), Thursday 28 December 1911, p. 9.

17   "Whim Creek Tragedy", *The Western Mail*, Saturday 30 March 1912, p. 35.

18   "A Skipper's Observations", *The West Australian*, Thursday 28 March 1912, p. 7.

19   "Extracts, Court of Marine Inquiry, loss of S.S. Koombana", Harbour & Light Department, WA, 25 April – 6 May, 1912. Author's private collection.

20   Testimony of James Lachlan Oborn, Coronial Inquest (Thomas Darlington).

21   "Whim Creek Tragedy", *The Western Mail*, Saturday 30 March 1912, p. 35.

22   "News and Notes", *The West Australian*, Wednesday 09 July 1913, p. 6.

23   Register of prisoners, Fremantle Prison, arranged by prisoner number, 1888–1959. State Records Office of WA, Series WAS-672 Cons 4173/9, Volume 9, p. 506.

16 THE SHADOW OF MISFORTUNE

1   Adelaide Steamship Company, minutes of directors' meeting, Monday 22 April 1912. Noel Butlin Archives Centre, Australian National University, 0186/Z535 Box 12.

2   a. "Our Interviews", *The Northern Times* (Carnarvon, WA), Saturday 18 November 1911, p. 2.
      b. "Irrigation at Carnarvon", *The Western Mail* (Perth, WA), Friday 29 August 1913, p. 16.

3   "Our Interviews", *The Northern Times*, Saturday 18 November 1911, p. 2.

4   "Notes and Comments", *The Sunday Times* (Perth, WA), Sunday 20 May 1906, p. 4.

5   "The Nor'-West", *The Western Mail*, Saturday 04 May 1912, p. 20.

6   a. "Drought Prospects", *The Northern Times*, Saturday 04 January 1913, p. 2.
      b. "North-West Pastoral News", *The Northern Times*, Saturday 30 August 1913, p. 2.

7   "North-West Pastoral News", *The Northern Times*, Saturday 30 August 1913, p. 2.

8–11 "Carnarvon Hotel", *The Northern Times*, Saturday 31 May 1913, p. 4.

12   "A Carnarvon Fire", *The Western Mail*, Friday 20 June 1913, p. 20.

13   "Downpour at Carnarvon", *The Western Mail*, Friday 08 August 1913, p. 37.

14   a. "Munda to Port Hedland in the Rain", *The Northern Times*, Saturday 21 February 1914, p. 5.
      b. "Monthly rainfall, Carnarvon Post Office", climate data online, Bureau of Meteorology, http://www.bom.gov.au/climate/data/index.shtml.

15   Crossley, James, Adelaide Steamship Company, 1915, "Observations on the North West Coast of Australia" (report). Noel Butlin Archives Centre, Australian National University, 0186/N46/1113.

16   a. "Onslow News", *The Northern Times*, Saturday 11 July 1908, p. 3.
      b. "Onslow's Claim To Attention", *The Northern Times*, Saturday 04 September 1909, p. 2.
      c. "Wool Sales", *The Northern Times*, Saturday 05 August 1911, p. 4.
      d. "Nor'-West Necessities", *The Sunday Times*, Sunday 24 November 1912, First Section p. 3.

18   "The North-West", *Daily News* (Perth, WA), Thursday 15 February 1912, p. 6.

19   a. "Onslow News", *The Northern Times*, Saturday 11 July 1908, p. 3.
      b. "The North-West", *Daily News*, Thursday 15 February 1912, p. 6.
      c. "Minister for Works", *The Northern Times*, Saturday 04 May 1912, p. 4.

20   a. "Public Works in the North-West", *The West Australian*, Saturday 17 February 1912, p. 11.
      b. "Off to the Cyclone Zone", *The Sunday Times*, Sunday 21 April 1912, p. 9.
      c. "Minister for Works", *The Northern Times*, Saturday 04 May 1912, p. 4.

21   "Nor'-West Necessities", *The Sunday Times*, Sunday 24 November 1912, First Section p. 3.

22   a. "Nor'-West Necessities", *The Sunday Times*, Sunday 24 November 1912, First Section p. 3.
      b. "Shifting Onslow", *The Northern Times*, Saturday 21 December 1912, p. 3.

23   "Shifting Onslow", *The Northern Times*, Saturday 21 December 1912, p. 3.

24   a. "Legislative Assembly", *The West Australian*, Thursday 18 September 1913, p. 8.
      b. "On the Ashburton", *The West Australian*, Saturday 15 May 1920, p. 7.

25   "Onslow News", *The Northern Times* (Carnarvon, WA), Saturday 29 July 1922, p. 2.

26   a. "Fremantle Telegrams", *The West Australian*, Tuesday 26 March 1912, p. 5.
      b. "Nor'-West Hurricane", *The Northern Times*, Saturday 30 March 1912, p. 3.
      c. Telegrams, Thomson, Cossack wharfinger, to Irvine, chief harbourmaster, Fremantle, 20–22 March 1912, in "Roebourne–Cossack–Port Samson tramline: washaway and gale of March 1912", Harbour & Light Dept, WA. State Records Office of WA, Acc 1066, AN16/5, 1912/431.

27   a. "Minister for Works", *The Northern Times*, Saturday 17 February 1912, p. 3.
      b. "Off to the Cyclone Zone", *The Sunday Times*, Sunday 21 April 1912, p. 9.

28–29 "The North-West", *The West Australian*, Monday 22 July 1912, p. 8.

30   a. "Cossack Tramway", *The Northern Times*, Saturday 31 August 1912, p. 4.
      b. "Mining & Pearling", *The Northern Times*, Saturday 15 March 1913, p. 2.
      c. "The North-West", *The West Australian*, Tuesday 29 September 1914, p. 3.

31   Crossley, James, Adelaide Steamship Company, 1915, "Observations on the North West Coast of Australia" (report), Noel Butlin Archives Centre, Australian National University, 0186/N46/1113.

32   "Loss of the Koombana", *The Northern Times*, Saturday 13 April 1912, p. 2.

33   a. "Pilbarra Railway Route", *The West Australian*, Saturday 31 March 1906, p. 8.
       b. "The Pilbarra Railway", *The Hedland Advocate* (Port Hedland, WA), Saturday 20 Feb. 1909, p. 3.
       c. Editorial, *The Hedland Advocate*, Saturday 01 May 1909, p. 4.
       d. "The Railway", *The Hedland Advocate*, Saturday 16 October 1909, p. 3.
       e. "Hedland–Marble Bar Railway", *The Hedland Advocate*, Saturday 22 July 1911.

34   Anderson, Thomas, personal diary 1885–1924. Battye Library, ACC 2808A (listing MN 720).

35   a. "Demand for Fresh Air", *The West Australian*, Wednesday 18 March 1914, p. 7.
       b. "A Trip Up the Nor'-West Coast", *The Sunday Times*, Sunday 10 May 1914, p. 23.

36   "A Trip Up the Nor'-West Coast", *The Sunday Times*, Sunday 10 May 1914, p. 23.

37   "The Pearling Industry", *The West Australian*, Tuesday 06 October 1914, p. 8.

38   a. "Port Hedland Water Supply", *The West Australian*, Wednesday 23 September 1914, p. 6.
       b. Clarke, Bert, interviewed by Jennie Hardie, 1977–78. Transcript: Port Hedland Library.
       c. Briden, Mollie, 1983, "My Life in Port Hedland", handwritten memoir. Original held by family.

39   "Fire at Port Hedland", *The Western Mail*, Friday 19 June 1914, p. 22.

40   "The Pearling Industry", *The West Australian*, Tuesday 06 October 1914, p. 8.

42   "Briefs for Broome", *The Hedland Advocate*, Saturday 27 January 1912, p. 10.

43   a. "The Pearling Industry", *The West Australian*, Friday 27 October 1911, p. 6.
       b. Hunt, D. W., "Bamford, Frederick William (1849–1934)", *Australian Dictionary of Biography*
         (online), http://adb.anu.edu.au/biography/bamford-frederick-william-5118.

44   "Pearling Industry", *The Register* (Adelaide, SA), Friday 01 March 1912, p. 5.

45   "White Divers For The Pearling Industry", *The Sunday Times*, Sunday 04 February 1912, p. 9.

46   "Minister for Works", *The Northern Times*, Saturday 08 June 1912, p. 4.

47   a. "Broome Pearlers", *The Northern Times*, Saturday 11 January 1913, p. 8.
       b. Bailey, John, 2001, *The White Divers of Broome*, Pan Macmillan, Sydney, pp. 223, 248.

48   "White Divers – A Sturdy Body of Men", *The Sunday Times*, Sunday 11 February 1912, p. 13.

49   a. "White Diver Dies", *The Sunday Times*, Sunday 16 June 1912, p. 12.
       b. "The Pearling Industry", *The West Australian*, Monday 29 July 1912, p. 4.
       c. Bailey, John, 2001, *The White Divers of Broome*, Pan Macmillan, Sydney, pp. 220–221.

50   Low, James Galloway, *Letters, 1904–91*, Battye Library, ACC 2612A (listing: MN 681). Letter from Jim to his sister Jane, 21 June 1912.

51   "The Pearling Industry", *The West Australian*, Monday 29 July 1912, p. 4.

52   When Jim Low refers to "the unstilly watches of the night", he is making an oblique, ironic reference to a poem by Thomas Moore which begins "Oft in the stilly night, Ere Slumber's chain has bound me, Fond Memory brings the light Of other days around me." Set to music by Sir John Stevenson in about 1818, "Oft in the Stilly Night" was still popular in Ireland when Jim Low left for Australia. It is also mentioned in James Joyce's *Portrait of the Artist as a Young Man* (1916).

53   Low, James Galloway, letter to sister Jane, 04 July 1912. See 50 above.

54   "White Divers", *The Northern Times*, Saturday 17 August 1912, p. 4.

55   "News and Notes", *The West Australian*, Wednesday 08 October 1913, p. 10.

56–57 "The Pearling Industry", *The Western Mail*, Friday 02 October 1914, p. 19.

58   a. "Pearling Commission Report", *The Western Mail*, Friday 08 September 1916, p. 31.
       b. Bamford, Frederick W. (Commissioner), Australian Federal Government, *Pearl-shelling Industry: report and recommendations of Royal Commission*, 1916, Government Printer, Melbourne.

59   "Pearling Industry", *The Western Mail*, Friday 08 September 1916, p. 49.

60   Ronan, Tom, 1964, *Packhorse and Pearling Boat*, Cassell Australia, Melbourne, Chapter 2.

61   "Fitzroy News", *The Northern Times*, Saturday 30 November 1912, p. 2.

62   "The Tick Question", *The West Australian*, Friday 14 November 1902, p. 4.

63   "Royal commissions held in Western Australia", Parliamentary Library, WA, http://www.parliament.wa.gov.au/.

64   "Government as Wholesale Butcher", *The Western Mail*, Saturday 31 August 1912, p. 12.

65   "The Meat Supply", *The West Australian*, Wednesday 28 August 1912, p. 10.

66   "A Cattle King", *The Cairns Post* (Qld), Thursday 14 November 1912, p. 2.

67   "Federal Affairs", *The West Australian*, Thursday 15 February 1912, p. 8.

68   "A Cattle King", *The Cairns Post* (Qld), Thursday 14 November 1912, p. 2.

69   "The Pastoral Industry", *The West Australian*, Monday 12 January 1914, p. 7.

70–71 "Good-bye to the Kimberley", *The Sunday Times*, Sunday 18 January 1914, First Section p. 4.

72   a. "Speech by Mr. Scaddan", *The Kalgoorlie Western Argus*, Tuesday 15 February 1916, p. 18.
        b. "Derby Meat Works", *The Sunday Times*, Sunday 05 March 1916, p. 2.

73   "Nor'-West Steamers", *Daily News*, Wednesday 05 June 1912, p. 5.

74   "Telegrams", *The Hedland Advocate*, Saturday 17 February 1912, p. 6.

75   "State Steamers", *The West Australian*, Tuesday 22 April 1913, p. 7.

76   a. "State Steamers", *The West Australian*, Wednesday 23 April 1913, p. 7.
        b. "State Steamers", *The West Australian*, Friday 25 April 1913, p. 7.
        c. "State Steamers", *The West Australian*, Monday 28 April 1913, p. 7.

77   "State Steamers", *The West Australian*, Tuesday 06 May 1913, p. 6.

78   "State Steamship Service", *The West Australian*, Thursday 22 May 1913, p. 6.

79   a. "State Steamship Service", *The Western Mail*, Friday 06 June 1913, p. 17.
        b. "State Steamships", *The West Australian*, Tuesday 17 June 1913, p. 7.
        c. "The State Steamers", *Daily News*, Tuesday 17 June 1913, p. 7.
        d. "State Steamships", *The West Australian*, Saturday 28 June 1913, p. 11.

81   "The State Steamships" (editorial), *The Western Mail*, Friday 29 August 1913, p. 35.

82   a. "State Steamers", *The West Australian*, Wednesday 17 December 1913, p. 7.
        b. "State Steamers", *The Western Mail*, Friday 26 December 1913, p. 12.

83   "State Steamship Service", *The West Australian*, Friday 27 February 1914, p. 4.

84   "The 'Comforts' Of The Kwinana", *The Sunday Times*, Sunday 08 February 1914, First section, p. 5.

85   Adelaide Steamship Company, minutes of directors' meeting, *Wednesday 10 April 1912*. Noel Butlin Archives Centre, Australian National University, 0186/Z535 Box 12.

86   "The Adjustment of General Average per 'Koombana' S.S., on a voyage to north west ports of Western Australia", insurance calculation and apportionment following grounding of *Koombana* at Shark Bay in March 1909, Holmes & Neill, Average Adjusters, Sydney, 18 July 1910. Battye Library Archives, 2216A.

87   Crossley, James, Adelaide Steamship Company, 1915, "Observations on the North West Coast of Australia" (report). Noel Butlin Archives Centre, Australian National University, 0186/N46/1113.

88   "Interview with Mr. Moxon", *Daily News*, Monday 20 May 1912, p. 6.

89   a. "Loss of the s.s. Koombana", *Geraldton Express* (WA), Saturday 06 April 1912, p. 3.
        b. Adelaide Steamship Company, minutes of directors' meeting, Monday 01 April 1912.

90   Crossley, James, Adelaide Steamship Company, 1915, "Observations on the North West Coast of Australia" (report), Noel Butlin Archives Centre, Australian National University, 0186/N46/1113.

91   "State Steamers", *The Western Mail*, Friday 09 May 1913, p. 13.

92   "New Steamer for Nor'-West", *The Hedland Advocate*, Saturday 10 April 1909, p. 6.

93   "Fremantle to Port Darwin", *The West Australian*, Thursday 24 July 1913, p. 9.

94   a. "Shipping", *The Register* (Adelaide, SA), Monday 11 January 1915, p. 6.
        b. "Shipping", *Daily News* (Perth, WA), Tuesday 19 January 1915, p. 3.

95   a. "Nor'-West Trade", *Daily News*, Wednesday 01 December 1915, p. 8.
        b. "Shipping", *Daily News*, Thursday 02 March 1916, p. 3.

17 THE MAN BEHIND THE GHOST

1   a. Rosenstein, Neil, 1990, *The Unbroken Chain: Biographical Sketches and the Genealogy of Illustrious Jewish Families from the 15th–20th Century,* revised edition, CIS Publishers, New York, pp. 5–9.
        b. Personal communication, Graham de Vahl Davis, grandson of Abraham de Vahl Davis, Nov. 2011.

2   Personal communication, Paul Mishura, archivist, Scotch College, Melbourne, 2011.

3–4   "Melbourne Jewish School", *The Argus* (Melbourne), Monday 13 March 1876, p. 7.

5   a. "Melbourne Hebrew School", *The Argus*, Monday 01 February 1875, p. 6.
        b. "Melbourne Jewish School", *The Argus*, Monday 13 March 1876, p. 7.
        c. "The Melbourne Hebrew School", *The Argus*, Monday 19 March 1877, p. 7.

6   a. "The Sale of French Military Plans", *The Argus*, Monday 24 December 1894, p. 5.
        b. Editorial, *The Argus*, Wednesday 23 March 1898, p. 4.
        c. "Dreyfus", *The Kalgoorlie Western Argus* (WA), Thursday 03 August 1899, p. 13.

7   "French Traitor Dreyfus", *Launceston Examiner* (Tas.), Saturday 16 February 1895, p. 7.

8   "The Dreyfus Case", *The Argus*, Saturday 11 August 1945, p. 27.

9–10   Wilkes, Donald E. Jr., 1998, *J'accuse ...! Emile Zola, Alfred Dreyfus, and the Greatest Newspaper Article in History*, Digital Commons @ Georgia Law, http://digitalcommons.law.uga.edu/fac_pm/34.

11   Zola, Émile (translated by David Short), "J'Accuse...!", *L'Aurore (The Dawn)*, Number 87, Thursday 13 January 1898, pp. 1–2.

12   "Alfred Dreyfus, the Martyred Soldier, Sends his Thanks for Hebrew Sympathy", unidentified newspaper clipping, 1899.

13   "Captain Dreyfus", *The Argus*, Wednesday 09 August 1899, p. 5.

14   a. "Socialites at Broome", *The Sunday Times* (Perth, WA), Sunday 07 August 1910, 3rd Section p. 1.
        b. Low, James Galloway, *Letters, 1904–91*, Battye Library, ACC 2612A (listing: MN 681). Letter from Jim to his sister Jane, 20 September 1912.
        c. Playford, John, "Rubin, Mark (1867–1919)", *Australian Dictionary of Biography* (online), http://adbonline.anu.edu.au/biogs/A110483b.htm.

15   a. Idriess, Ion L., 1937, *Forty Fathoms Deep*, Angus & Robertson, Sydney, Chapter 2.
        b. Playford, John, "Rubin, Mark (1867–1919)". See 14c above.

16   Advertising brochure, corsetry, London, 1904. Original held by Graham de Vahl Davis, grandson of Abraham & Cecily Davis.

17   Dickson, Rod (transcribed & compiled), 1996, *Ships Registered in Western Australia from 1856 to 1969*, Maritime Heritage Association (Western Australia), http://www.maritimeheritage.org.au/documents/Shipping%20Register.pdf.

18   "Social Notes", *Broome Chronicle*, Saturday 04 July 1908.

19   "Asiatic Influx", *The Hedland Advocate* (Port Hedland, WA), Saturday 16 January 1909, p. 4.

20   "Asiatic Influx", *The Hedland Advocate*, Saturday 30 January 1909.

21   a. "The Pearling Industry", *Truth* (Perth, WA), Saturday 20 February 1909.
        b. "The Pearling Industry", *Broome Chronicle*, Saturday 13 March 1909.

22   a. "General News", *The Hedland Advocate*, Saturday 08 April 1911, p. 10.
        b. "White Divers", *The Hedland Advocate*, Saturday 18 November 1911.
        c. Idriess, Ion L., 1937, *Forty Fathoms Deep*, Angus & Robertson, Sydney, Chapter 14.
        d. Playford, John, "Rubin, Mark (1867–1919)". See 14c above.

23   Letter from Abraham Davis to his son Gerald, written aboard *Koombana* 04 April 1910, to mark the occasion of the boy's bar mitzvah. Original held by Abraham's grandson, Graham de Vahl Davis.

24   A second letter, less formal, from Abraham Davis to his son Gerald, written Broome 20 April 1910, also to mark the boy's bar mitzvah. Original held by Abraham's grandson, Graham de Vahl Davis.

25   "Petition For Divorce", *The West Australian*, Tuesday 12 December 1911, p. 7.

26   "For Private Sale" (advertisement), *Broome Chronicle*, Saturday 21 October 1911.

27   "Bon Voyage", *Broome Chronicle*, Saturday 28 October 1911.

28   "Divorce Court. Davis v Davis", *The Argus*, Friday 01 December 1911, p. 5.

29   a. "A Divorce Case", *The Advertiser* (Adelaide, SA), Friday 24 November 1911, p. 10.
        b. "Davis v. Davis", *The Argus*, Tuesday 19 December 1911, p. 8.

30   a. "No News of the Koombana", *The Sunday Times*, Sunday 31 March 1912, p. 1.
        b. "A Monied Passenger", *The Murchison Times and Day Dawn Gazette* (Cue, WA), 02 Apr 1912, p. 3.
        c. "The Steamer Koombana", *The Advertiser* (Adelaide, SA), Friday 12 April 1912, p. 8.
        d. "State", *Geraldton Express* (WA), Monday 15 April 1912.

31   "The Koombana", *The West Australian*, Saturday 30 March 1912, p. 11.

32   Low, James Galloway, *Letters, 1904–91*, Battye Library, ACC 2612A (listing: MN 681). Letter from Jim to his sister Jane, 21 June 1912.

33   "Koombana Victim's Will", *The Sydney Morning Herald*, Wednesday 25 September 1912, p. 7.

34   "A Melbourne Divorce", *The Sydney Morning Herald*, Friday 22 November 1912, p. 10.

35   "A Koombana Echo", *The Register* (Adelaide, SA), Saturday 30 November 1912, p. 17.

36   a. Public Notice, *The Nor'-West Echo* (Broome, WA), c. 1915.
        b. Public Notice, *The Nor'-West Echo*, Saturday 11 August 1917.
        c. Advertiscment, *The Nor'-West Echo*, c. 1916.

37   a. "News and Notes", *The West Australian*, Friday 10 December 1915, p. 6.
        b. "News and Notes", *The West Australian*, Saturday 29 October 1921, p. 8.

38   "Life and Letters", *The West Australian*, Saturday 26 November 1938, p. 5.

18 MYTHICAL BEAUTY

1   a. Eley, Barbara, 1995, *Ion Idriess*, ETT Imprint, Sydney, Chapter 18.
     b. Eley, 1995, *Ion Idriess,* Chapter 19.

2–3 "Grim Tales of the Pearl Game", *The Northern Standard* (Darwin, NT), Friday 27 May 1932, p. 3.

4   a. "Grim Tales of the Pearl Game", *The Northern Standard*, Friday 27 May 1932, p. 3.
     b. Eley, 1995, *Ion Idriess,* Chapter 17.
     c. Eley, 1995, *Ion Idriess,* Chapter 18.

5   Untitled report, *Dampier Despatch* (Broome, WA), Saturday 30 Sept. 1905, Issue 231, pp. 353–354.

6   a. Untitled report, *Dampier Despatch*, Saturday 30 September 1905, Issue 231, pp. 353–354.
     b. Dickson, Rod (transcribed & compiled), 1996, *Ships Registered in Western Australia from 1856 to 1969*, Maritime Heritage Association (Western Australia), http://www.maritimeheritage.org.au/documents/Shipping%20Register.pdf.

7   Idriess, Ion L., 1937, *Forty Fathoms Deep*, Angus & Robertson, Sydney, Chapter 3.

8–9 Untitled report, *Dampier Despatch*, Saturday 30 September 1905, Issue 231, pp. 353–354.

10   a. Handwritten record of testimony, Police Sergeant John Byrne, Coronial Inquest (M. Liebglid), Broome, WA, 30 August 1905 – 26 September 1905, found bundled with *Case 3747: Rex v Hagen & Others*, Supreme Court of Western Australia, 1905. State Records Office of WA, Consignment 3473 Bundle 293.
     b. Typed transcript of testimony, Police Sergeant John Byrne, Coronial Inquest (M. Liebglid). See 10a above.

11   Untitled report, *Dampier Despatch*, Saturday 02 September 1905, Issue 219, pp. 308–309.

12   a. Handwritten record of testimony of Antony Pedro, Coronial Inquest (M. Liebglid). See 10a above.
     b. "The Broome Murder", *The Western Mail* (Perth, WA), Saturday 18 November 1905, p. 17.

13   a. Typed transcript of testimony, Charles Hagen, Coronial Inquest (M. Liebglid). See 10a above.
     b. Untitled report, *Dampier Despatch*, Saturday 16 September 1905, Issue 225, pp. 327–328.

14   a. Typed transcript of testimony, Pablo Marquez (recalled 25 Sept.), Coronial Inquest (M. Liebglid).
     b. Typed transcript of testimony, Pablo Marquez (continued 26 Sept.), Coronial Inquest (M. Liebglid).
     c. "The Broome Murder", *The West Australian*, Monday 18 September 1905, p. 5.

15   "The Broome Murder", *The West Australian*, Tuesday 19 September 1905, p. 5.

16   Typed transcript of testimony, Pablo Marquez (recalled 25 Sept.), Coronial Inquest (M. Liebglid).

17   Idriess, 1937, *Forty Fathoms Deep*, Chapter 8.

18   "The Broome Murder", *The West Australian*, Saturday 02 September 1905, p. 7.

19   a. Handwritten record of testimony, Police Sergeant John Byrne, Coronial Inquest (M. Liebglid).
     b. Typed transcript of testimony, Pablo Marquez (recalled 25 Sept.), Coronial Inquest (M. Liebglid).

20   Typed transcript of testimony, Pablo Marquez, Coronial Inquest (M. Liebglid).

22   "Notes of the Week", *The Western Mail*, Saturday 12 February 1910, p. 34.

23   a. "Pearl", http://www.geo.utexas.edu/courses/347k/redesign/gem_notes/pearl/pearl_main.htm.
     b. These conversion factors apply to the traditional "jeweller's grain" or "pearl grain", which is exactly 50 milligrams. Under the modern international system of units (SI), a grain is a little less than 65 milligrams.

24   "Famous Pearls of Broome", *The Sydney Morning Herald*, Saturday 07 May 1938, p. 21.

25   "The Star of the West", *The Western Mail*, Friday 08 March 1918, p. 26.

26   "Pearl", http://www.geo.utexas.edu/courses/347k/redesign/gem_notes/pearl/pearl_main.htm.

27   "Strange Story of Man Who Holds Key to Our Most Secret Industry", *The Sunday Times*, Sunday 26 October 1930, p. 9.

28   "In The Nor'-West", *The West Australian*, Monday 4 November 1907, p. 4.

29   "The Pearling Industry", *Broome Chronicle* (WA), Saturday 13 March 1909.

30   "The Broome Murder", *The Western Mail*, Saturday 18 November 1905, p. 17.

31–32 "The Broome Murder", *The West Australian*, Monday 13 November 1905, p. 3.

33–35 "The Broome Murder", *The Western Mail*, Saturday 25 November 1905, p. 37.

36   "The Broome Tragedy", *The Sydney Morning Herald*, Wednesday 22 November 1905, p. 10.

37   "The Broome Murder", *The Advertiser* (Adelaide, SA), Thursday 14 December 1905, p. 6.

38   a. "The Broome Murder", *The West Australian*, Wednesday 13 December 1905, p. 7.

b. "The Broome Murder", *The West Australian*, Thursday 14 December 1905, p. 5.

c. "William Purkiss", *Wikipedia*, http://en.wikipedia.org/wiki/William_Purkiss.

39   "The Broome Murder", *The West Australian*, Wednesday 13 December 1905, p. 7.

40   a. "News and Notes", *The West Australian*, Tuesday 12 December 1905, pp. 4–5.

b. "The Broome Murder", *The Advertiser*, Thursday 14 December 1905, p. 6.

41   "The Broome Murder", *The Kalgoorlie Western Argus* (WA), Tuesday 19 December 1905, p. 34.

42   a. "The Broome Murder", *The West Australian*, Friday 15 December 1905, p. 8.

b. "The Broome Murder", *The Kalgoorlie Western Argus*, Tuesday 19 December 1905, p. 34.

43   "The Broome Murder", *The Kalgoorlie Western Argus*, Tuesday 19 December 1905, p. 34.

44   a. "The Broome Murder", *The West Australian*, Friday 15 December 1905, p. 8.

b. "Three Men Hanged", *The Advertiser*, Friday 15 December 1905, p. 7.

45   "Grim Tales of the Pearl Game", *The Northern Standard* (Darwin, NT), Friday 27 May 1932, p. 3.

46   a. "The Broome Hurricane", *The Advertiser*, Thursday 17 December 1908, p. 7.

b. "The Broome Cyclone", *The Sydney Morning Herald*, Friday 18 December 1908, p. 10.

47   Idriess, Ion L., 1937, *Forty Fathoms Deep*, Angus & Robertson, Sydney, Chapter 13.

48   Idriess, 1937, *Forty Fathoms Deep,* Chapter 14.

49   Idriess, 1937, *Forty Fathoms Deep*, Chapter 17.

50   Eley, Barbara, 1995, *Ion Idriess*, ETT Imprint, Sydney, Chapter 19.

51   Eley, 1995, *Ion Idriess,* Chapter 18.

52   Eley, 1995, *Ion Idriess*, Chapter 19.

53   Idriess, 1937, *Forty Fathoms Deep*, Chapter 14.

54   Idriess, 1937, *Forty Fathoms Deep*, Chapter 23.

55   Idriess, 1937, *Forty Fathoms Deep*, Chapter 14.

56   Idriess, 1937, *Forty Fathoms Deep*, Chapter 17.

57   a. "Quarter Sessions", *Broome Chronicle*, Saturday 19 June 1909.

b. "Quarter Sessions", *Broome Chronicle*, Saturday 26 June 1909.

58   a. "No News of the Koombana", *The Sunday Times*, Sunday 31 March 1912, p. 1.

b. "A Monied Passenger", *The Murchison Times and Day Dawn Gazette* (Cue, WA), Tuesday 02 April 1912, p. 3.

c. "State", *Geraldton Express* (WA), Monday 15 April 1912.

Image Sources

INDEX